DETROIT FUTURE CITY

2012 DETROIT STRATEGIC FRAMEWORK PLAN

DETROIT FUTURE CITY
2012 Detroit Strategic Framework Plan

2nd Printing: May 2013

Printed by:

Inland Press
2001 W. Lafayette Blvd.
Detroit, MI 48216
(313) 961-6000
www.inlandpress.com

ISBN 978-0-9894038-0-1

CONTENTS

INTERNATIONAL

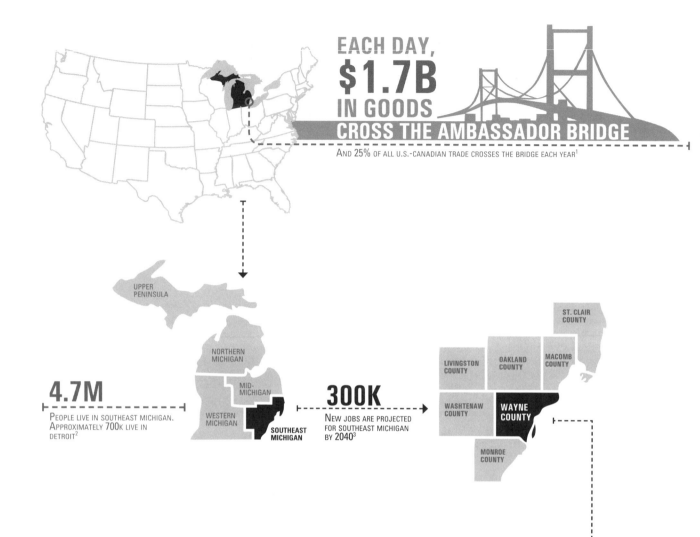

EACH DAY,
$1.7B
IN GOODS
CROSS THE AMBASSADOR BRIDGE

AND 25% OF ALL U.S.-CANADIAN TRADE CROSSES THE BRIDGE EACH YEAR[1]

REGIONAL

UPPER PENINSULA

NORTHERN MICHIGAN

MID-MICHIGAN

WESTERN MICHIGAN

SOUTHEAST MICHIGAN

ST. CLAIR COUNTY

LIVINGSTON COUNTY

OAKLAND COUNTY

MACOMB COUNTY

WASHTENAW COUNTY

WAYNE COUNTY

MONROE COUNTY

4.7M
PEOPLE LIVE IN SOUTHEAST MICHIGAN. APPROXIMATELY 700K LIVE IN DETROIT[2]

300K
NEW JOBS ARE PROJECTED FOR SOUTHEAST MICHIGAN BY 2040[3]

CITY

$422M
10 FOUNDATIONS HAVE INVESTED NEARLY $422M IN DETROIT FROM 2008-SUMMER 2011[4]

19M
AN AVERAGE OF 19 MILLION ANNUAL VISITORS AND TOURISTS COME TO DOWNTOWN DETROIT EACH YEAR[5]

18TH LARGEST
DETROIT WAS THE 18TH LARGEST U.S. CITY IN 2010[6]

4TH
LARGEST CITY IN 1940
IN 1940, DETROIT WAS THE 4TH LARGEST CITY IN THE UNITED STATES BY POPULATION[7]

1) Detroit Regional Chamber; 2) US Census 2010; 3) Southeast Michigan Council of Governments (SEMCOG); 4) DWPLTP Civic Engagement Audit; 5) Detroit Economic Growth Corporation; 6) US Census 2010; 7) US Census 1940

DETROIT IS...

...in the **TOP 20 LARGEST AMERICAN CITIES.**

...HOME TO 714,000 RESIDENTS who are resilient and already working to change the course of the city's prospects.

...a city of **GLOBAL ECONOMIC ASSETS,** including intermodal border crossings and industrial infrastructure that cannot be replicated anywhere else in the region.

...known globally for **A BRAND OF INNOVATION** in "making things" and growing in reputation for small-scale models of ingenuity.

...home to a civic network of **COMMITTED, PROACTIVE COMMUNITY-BASED AND PHILANTHROPIC ORGANIZATIONS.**

...A LAND-RICH ENVIRONMENT that can accommodate growth and innovation without displacement.

...poised to reposition itself as **MICHIGAN'S LEADING URBAN CENTER** once again, if there is a coordinated regional urban agenda that enables more mutually beneficial relationships with the region, state, and nation.

DETROIT IS CLOSER TO ITS FUTURE THAN WE IMAGINE.

A BROAD ENGAGEMENT OF LEADERSHIP

CITY OF DETROIT

MAYOR'S ADVISORY TASK FORCE

DETROIT ECONOMIC GROWTH CORPORATION

STEERING COMMITTEE

LONG TERM STRATEGY TEAM

PLANNING TEAM

CIVIC ENGAGEMENT

SHORT TERM STRATEGY TEAM

INTER-AGENCY WORK GROUP

PROCESS LEADERS

ROUND TABLES

WORKING GROUPS

COMMUNITY

RESIDENT, GOVERNMENT, NONPROFIT, BUSINESS, INSTITUTIONAL, CIVIC, PHILANTHROPIC, FAITH-BASED

FORWARD
LEADING DETROIT TOWARD ITS FUTURE

In 2010, an ambitious effort to re-imagine a better future for one of the world's most important and storied cities was launched. The project has been both an exciting and, at times, challenging journey. It has also been a collective journey, inviting diverse input from technical experts within Detroit and around the world and, most importantly, the community experts and everyday citizens who would be most affected by its recommendations. Each has played a critical role in forming what we hope will become a living framework for change and development in Detroit.

Now—after hundreds of meetings, 30,000 conversations, connecting with people over 163,000 times, over 70,000 survey responses and comments from participants, and countless hours spent dissecting and examining critical data about our city—we are proud to present Detroit Future City. We believe that within this document lies a path forward toward realizing the aspirations of an entire city. Within it lies a guide for decision making that is not exclusively for one entity or one mayor or one generation, but for each of us—and those who come after us—in our roles as citizens, philanthropists, developers, business people, neighborhood champions, parents, and beyond.

Ambitious but attainable, Detroit Future City begins to align our assets with opportunity, mapping a framework that best coordinates investment of our resources—people, time, money, brainpower, and more—in ways that can move us forward collectively. This framework explores how to best use our abundance of land (particularly publicly owned land), create job growth and economic prosperity, ensure vibrant neighborhoods, build an infrastructure that serves citizens at a reasonable cost, and maintain a high level of community engagement that is integral to success. And each is addressed with the understanding that in many ways, they are all interlinked.

Perhaps most importantly, we understand that this is not the end, but the end of the beginning. We realize that this document is a large body of work that represents over 2 years of conversations and thinking, and it needs to be understood by the various audiences that will use it. We are committed to turning paper and possibilities into action and accomplishment, and have already begun to construct the mechanisms for doing so.

As we move toward implementation of Detroit Future City, Detroit stakeholders will be able to continue to meet with technical experts so they can dive into the portions of the plan that will best amplify work already being done, while aligning it with a broader vision for the city. The creation of a formal organization that can be a champion for Detroit Future City, evolve it as a living document, act as a service provider for anyone that wants to understand and access the plan, and coordinate targeted projects and the partnerships needed to make them happen, is underway. In addition, we are working to identify on-the-ground pilot projects that can happen quickly and spur bigger things to come.

We are pleased to present and celebrate what's been accomplished so far, thank the thousands of you who have helped get us here, and look to a brighter future that reestablishes Detroit as the center of a vibrant region.

We look forward not only to the great things that will happen, but to the remarkable outcomes of our continued work together.

Sincerely,

**THE DETROIT WORKS PROJECT LONG TERM PLANNING
STEERING COMMITTEE**

"There were times when I thought I couldn't
last for long, but now I think I'm able to carry on
It's been a long, a long time coming
but I know a change is gonna come, oh yes it will"

"A Change is Gonna Come" Lyrics by Sam Cooke, 1963

BLUEPRINT FOR DETROIT'S FUTURE
EXECUTIVE SUMMARY

This document, the Detroit Strategic Framework, articulates a shared vision for Detroit's future, and recommends specific actions for reaching that future. The vision resulted from a 24-month-long public process that drew upon interactions among Detroit residents and civic leaders from both the nonprofit and for-profit sectors, who together formed a broad-based group of community experts. From the results of this citywide public engagement effort, a team of technical experts crafted and refined the vision, rendered specific strategies for reaching it, shared their work publicly at key points, and shaped it in response to evolving information and community feedback throughout the process.

The work of the Detroit Strategic Framework was guided by a talented Steering Committee of individuals from within Detroit, whose knowledge of civic engagement, nonprofit community work, and key areas such as land use, economic development, and the city itself were of deep value. Building a blueprint for a city as complex and rich in promise and challenges as Detroit required the integration of local expertise with leading thinkers and practitioners from around the globe. A list of the Planning and Civic Engagement Teams, along with the committees that guided the work and the Process Leaders who helped create the vision, is provided in the Acknowledgements appendix of this document.

A FRAMEWORK THAT BUILDS ON ASSETS. Detroit is no stranger to plans and proposed solutions to its need for urban revitalization. Twice in the past 15 years, Detroit has prepared a full citywide plan for its future: The 1998 Community Reinvestment Strategy Plan (which was never formally adopted), and the state-mandated Master Plan of Policies governing land use, created in 2004 and adopted by the City Council in 2009. The Detroit Strategic Framework marks the first time in decades that Detroit has considered its future not only from a standpoint of land use or economic growth, but in the context of city systems, neighborhood vision, the critical question of vacant land and buildings, and the need for greater civic capacity to address the systemic change necessary for Detroit's success. This plan is also the first to accept and address Detroit's future as a city that will not regain its peak population of nearly 2 million people.

Every city has its challenges and Detroit most certainly has urgent and long-standing ones. But not every city has the assets of Detroit. As Michigan's largest urban center, Detroit is home to the largest concentration of workers, health, education, cultural, and entertainment institutions; the busiest international border crossing in North America for international trade; host to 19 million annual tourists and visitors; a city of beautiful historic neighborhoods and commercial areas, including 245 sites or districts on the National Register of Historic Places and 8 National Historic Landmarks; and the second largest theater district in the country, second only to New York City. These assets make up the city's physical and economic capital.

Detroit's assets also include the resiliency, creativity, and ingenuity of its people and organizations—the city's human and social capital. Detroit's impressive talent base includes

- business leaders who forever changed the culture of industrial production and music;

- pioneers in new forms of transportation, infrastructure, and community food production;

- civic leaders who have organized and empowered community residents to exercise their voices and actively participate in the fate of their futures; and

- faith leaders who have held up Detroit communities by tending to their spiritual and human needs.

HOW WE ARRIVED AT THIS VISION

A PROCESS ROOTED IN BUILDING TRUST AND AUTHENTIC ENGAGEMENT.
The history of civic engagement in Detroit includes many examples of commitment and vision, but also includes planning fatigue and lack of trust, which have left residents to feel a sense of hopelessness, confusion, and skepticism about the intentions and outcomes of public conversations. There is a real perception that after years of promises and plans, there has been no visible change in the city. This, coupled with the severity of the City's current fiscal crisis, has prompted residents to focus on what can be done in the immediate future to meet their critical community needs, making it hard to focus on planning for five, ten, or twenty years out.

Any proposal to lift and transform Detroit must first acknowledge this critical reality, not as a barrier to progress but as a vital reminder that public engagement around the city's future must be authentic, transparent, interactive, and aligned with neighborhood goals for the well-being of all residents. In addition, the Detroit Strategic Framework was created with an understanding that no single sector—government, business, nonprofit, resident and neighborhood groups, or philanthropy—can achieve the city's brighter future alone. A broad range of community sectors and leadership will need to act collectively to implement the actions of the Strategic Framework, and to put Detroit on the path to stability, sustainability, and ultimate transformation into a model 21st century American city.

At the present time, many people and organizations remain living and/or working in silos, either by issue (education, housing, environmental justice); sector (public, private, nonprofit); geography (neighborhood, city, region, state); or more destructive divides such as racial and economic disparities, with only a few existing examples where diverse groups sit at the same table for collective dialogue and action. There is no time to lose: Detroit's future rests on the ability and willingness of these strong, but sometimes separated, groups to come together and help activate the change necessary to enable Detroit's recovery and resurgence.

The Detroit Strategic Framework emerged from the Detroit Works Project (DWP), launched in 2010. DWP included a track for Short Term Actions and a Long Term Planning initiative. The Long Term Planning initiative was a 24-month planning and civic engagement process that resulted in the vision and strategies described in this document, a comprehensive and action-oriented blueprint for near and long range decision making.

The Strategic Framework is **aspirational** toward a physical and social vision for the city; **actionable**, with strategies for new policies and implementation; and **accountable**, with assignment of implementation responsibilities.

Four core values were put in place at the beginning of the process, to create a shared vision and plan of action:

- **Aspirational** where it should be and practical where it must be
- **Respectful** of the city's history, community efforts, and new ideas
- **Just and equitable** in seeking to create benefits for all
- **Transparent and inclusive** of all voices participating to improve our community

HOW WE ARRIVED AT THIS VISION. The Long Term Planning initiative was led by a Mayor-appointed Steering Committee of 14 civic leaders representing business, philanthropy, community, faith-based institutions, and government. The Detroit Economic Growth Corporation (DEGC) managed the initiative, overseeing the work of the Planning Team of local, national, and international consultants representing the disciplines of urban planning and design, economics, engineering, landscape architecture, and real estate development. A Civic Engagement Team was also created to interact with many community groups, business leaders, and residents. The local partners led the Civic Engagement process along with a host of community and advocacy organizations and Process Leaders, who aided in gaining citywide input into the initiative as the Framework took shape.

The work of this diverse collaboration has created a process and a guide for decision making for Detroit's future—the Detroit Strategic Framework—with innovative strategies to move toward a more efficient and sustainable city and improve the quality of life and business in Detroit.

INFORMATION-DRIVEN KNOWLEDGE OF THE CITY'S ASSETS AND CHALLENGES. It is no news that Detroit faces serious challenges, including fiscal constraints, unemployment, housing foreclosures, crime, education issues, service delivery challenges, healthy food access, and environmental pollution. Yet these conditions can sometimes change rapidly from year to year. The planning process was based on a careful examination of the best available information about the city's current conditions and trends.

The recommendations and actions proposed in this Strategic Framework are informed by a wide range of reliable source materials that provide a comprehensive snapshot of the city's current conditions, policies, and trends. Eight audits were compiled to help shape the Framework recommendations:

1. Public Land Disposition Policies and Procedures
2. Urban and Regional Economy
3. Urban Agriculture and Food Security
4. Neighborhoods, Community Development, and Housing
5. Landscape, Ecology, and Open Space
6. Land Use and Urban Form
7. Environmental Remediation and Health
8. City Systems, Infrastructure, Transportation, and Sustainability

Through the early phases of the Strategic Framework planning initiative, this evidence was shared with the residents and stakeholders of Detroit, and combined with their "on-the-ground" experience of living with these issues in everyday life. It became clear that if we did nothing, the quality of life and businesses in Detroit would continue to decline.

The scope of the planning effort focused on priorities for change and clearly defined goals for improving human health, family and business wealth, safety, and the physical condition of the city. The ultimate objective of the Framework is to uplift the people, businesses, and places of Detroit by improving quality of life and business in the city. A strategic approach to advancing these quality of life and business goals involves a strategic focus on the "things we must do" to bring about change. This focus has been captured in the 12 Imperatives on the following pages.

A BLEND OF TECHNICAL AND COMMUNITY EXPERTISE. The Long Term Planning initiative was also designed to balance technical expertise with community expertise that draws on personal and organizational experiences and observations. The leaders of the process developed and implemented a careful methodology for gathering, integrating, and synthesizing anecdotal as well as data-driven inputs to inform the Framework's final recommendations.

The Community Experts, along with the Planning Team and Civic Engagement Team, collaborated to diversify engagement opportunities beyond traditional meetings, reaching out to people in many different ways, not only to give them information but also to ask them to share information. From the Detroit Stories oral history film project (detroitstoriesproject.com) and the Detroit 24/7 online game to the drop-in HomeBase in Eastern Market, telephone Town Halls, and "Roaming Table" that made the rounds to Detroiters in their own neighborhoods, the Detroit Works civic engagement activities deepened and broadened the available information for the process, adding to the research and data with valuable first-hand experiences and suggestions rooted in daily realities. Such ideas are not usually captured in planning efforts of this scale and comprehensiveness.

12 IMPERATIVE ACTIONS

1. We must re-energize Detroit's economy to increase job opportunities for Detroiters within the city and strengthen the tax base.

2. We must support our current residents and attract new residents.

3. We must use innovative approaches to transform our vacant land in ways that increase the value and productivity and promote long-term sustainability.

4. We must use our open space to improve the health of all Detroit's residents.

5. We must promote a range of sustainable residential densities.

6. We must focus on sizing the networks for a smaller population, making them more efficient, more affordable, and better performing.

7. We must realign city systems in ways that promote areas of economic potential, encourage thriving communities, and improve environmental and human health conditions.

8. We must be strategic and coordinated in our use of land.

9. We must promote stewardship for all areas of the city by implementing short- and long-term strategies.

10. We must provide residents with meaningful ways to make change in their communities and the city at large.

11. We must pursue a collaborative regional agenda that recognizes Detroit's strengths and our region's shared destiny.

12. We must dedicate ourselves to implementing this framework for our future.

THE THINGS WE MUST DO
QUALITY-OF-LIFE/QUALITY-OF-BUSINESS IMPERATIVES

The Detroit community and planning experts worked together to identify the important core values, project goals, quality-of-life, and quality-of-business elements that have driven the recommendations in this Framework. Early engagement efforts revealed that issues of access to jobs, safety, education, human health, and neighborhood appearance were universally critical to address. These sentiments were uniformly raised regardless of neighborhood population, ethnicity, income, or geography. Residents and businesses alike wanted an improved city and a better quality of life and business environment.

Through these public conversations, the Long Term Planning initiative focused its work on defining what an improved quality of life and business would require, and created a set of "mandates" that must be established if Detroit is to achieve visible and sustainable change. These 12 Imperatives are drawn from the quality-of-life and quality-of-business elements identified in the collaborative dialogue between technical and community experts.

Looking carefully at the data revealed by the policy audits described earlier, it became clear that "if we did nothing," the quality of life and businesses in Detroit would continue to decline. The scope of the planning effort focused on priorities for change as defined by the 12 imperatives.

KEY   QUALITY-OF-LIFE AND -BUSINESS DEFINITIONS   QUALITY-OF-LIFE ELEMENT  QUALITY-OF-BUSINESS ELEMENT

QUALITY-OF-LIFE ELEMENTS

DEFINITIONS
QUALITY-OF-LIFE AND -BUSINESS DEFINITIONS THAT HAVE BEEN DEFINED THROUGH THE CIVIC ENGAGEMENT PROCESS

SAFETY
The sense of physical and emotional security, primarily focused on the individual or family, but also extending to surroundings

HEALTH
Mental and physical well-being for all Detroiters

EDUCATION
The opportunity to gain a quality education for all ages, incomes, and abilities

PROSPERITY AND INCOME
The opportunity for long-term, fulfilling employment that allows for personal growth, self-sufficiency, and wealth creation

COMMUNITY
The inherent sense of belonging with neighbors, sharing common interests and working together to achieve common goals

PHYSICAL CONDITION
The state of constructed and natural surroundings

HOUSING
Quality dwelling options that provide shelter and safety for all residents

PUBLIC SERVICES
Core services provided by the city government and allied providers, ranging from utilities to maintenance and sanitation

MOBILITY
The ability to effectively and efficiently access employment, housing and services

QUALITY-OF-BUSINESS ELEMENTS

ENVIRONMENT
The physical, chemical and biotic factors that affect the surroundings and conditions in which a person, animal or plant lives

RECREATION
Places to accommodate physical activity and social interaction

CULTURE
Numerous events and cultural activities that define the social composition of daily life

RETAIL SERVICES AND AMENITIES
Places to facilitate material, service and entertainment needs

REGULATIONS
Permitting, zoning and other codes that need to be aligned to support job growth

ACCESS
Strategic improvements that are necessary to ensure efficient access via highways, rail, ports, and local streets

NETWORK
Proximity to related businesses, suppliers, and business services

COST
The operating cost environment for businesses compared to regional and peer cities

SERVICES
Effective and reliable government services that are necessary to support private investment

INFORMATION
Access to necessary knowledge and data for aligning businesses with workforce, incentives and public assistance

DETROIT TODAY
MAKING THE CASE FOR CHANGE: WHY BUSINESS AS USUAL WILL NOT WORK

It is often difficult to enter into a planning process that talks about the future city when community stakeholders believe that their basic needs are not being sufficiently met. Detroiters have long been anxious about the future of the city—concerned about the safety of their children and property, their increasing taxes and expectations for quality city services, their access to jobs and the cost of driving to work, the value of their homes, the ability to keep up with a mortgage, and the growing vacancy and abandonment surrounding them. Residents and businesses alike have been concerned about whether utilities would be shut off in the more vacant parts of the city, whether families might be forced to move from their homes (as in the days of urban renewal), or whether some city departments or community facilities would be shut down completely.

While there has been much speculation and fear around such unfair, unjust, unacceptable (and unnecessary) actions, one thing has become very clear—the way things are and "business as usual" are no longer acceptable. Detroiters demand and deserve reliable city services, safe streets, healthy environments, access to food, jobs, public transit, and places to play, learn, and engage with one another. Civic leaders in the public, private, nonprofit, grassroots, institutional, and philanthropic sectors understand that the city's economic drivers, cost to provide service, sources of funding, and service delivery mechanisms must be realigned to achieve a better quality of life for residents, businesses, and visitors.

RENEWING THE CIVIC CONVERSATION. The nature of civic interactions, actions, and conversations *about* Detroit's future also needs to change—both within and beyond the city limits. One of the most important findings from the Strategic Framework process was that although Detroit has many talented people and committed organizations, they are too disconnected from one another for collective dialogue and action on behalf of the city.

Just as there is no shortage of talented leaders in and for Detroit, there has been no shortage of discussion about Detroit. Reclaiming this conversation and reframing it demands that everyone who cares about Detroit set aside what they *think* they know about the city, and cultivate a deep, mutual understanding of what the city really is right now. Then, instead of "What to do about Detroit," the question becomes, "What can be done *in* Detroit, by Detroit, and *with* Detroiters?" To gain momentum and credibility for this new discussion, Detroit must be ready to show what it *is already doing*, speaking in many voices of a shared vision and specific recommendations that suit Detroit as it is today, and as it could be in ten or twenty years. Fortunately, part of the answer—despite very real barriers and challenges, from under-performing municipal services and constrained resources to decades-old racial and economic tensions—is that Detroit not only can do quite a lot, *Detroit is already doing it.*

New industries. Tech start-ups. Fresh, local food production. Collaborative work spaces. Downtown living. Neighborhood collaborations. Innovative and door-to-door approaches to social and human services. World class health care institutions and universities. Large-scale public art projects. Youth training and development, infant mortality prevention, and senior housing and other critical residential development by CDOs and churches. All of it happening right now.

"People do live here," said Wayne Ramocan, a participant in the Detroit Stories project. "People talk about the city like people don't actually live here… They just talk about the city as maybe an investment, or 'it's only land here,' or, 'it's only blight and vacant houses,' but it's more to it than that….Detroit is not barren."

The challenge is that Detroiters' important strides forward have gotten lost in the shuffle because they are often responses to crisis or solely issue- or neighborhood-focused. Yet the emergent or engaged civic institutions and residents who have taken on the city's toughest challenges at this level of detail have the ability and the vision to do more: They just need the capacity, in the form of information and resources. If these leaders for change cannot engage broadly and permanently to speak to the promising reality, real problems, and ambitious vision for Detroit, there will continue to be a flow of "solutions" that don't fit Detroit's real needs and aspirations, or a "business as usual" and crisis-driven approach to problem solving for the city. Five key trend areas help to drive this point home and make the case for change:

SAFETY, EDUCATION, HEALTH, AND PROSPERITY. Everyone in Detroit unanimously agrees that the key to Detroit's recovery and long-term prosperity requires the city to be safe, have better-educated youth and adults, provide healthier living environments, and offer access to jobs that pay at or above a living wage. A recent survey of Detroit residents revealed that nearly one-third of the respondents would leave the city within five years, citing safety as the top reason. Two years ago, attempts to take on wholesale reform of the educational systems failed. Almost one-third of Detroit children suffer from asthma, a rate three times the national average. Two-thirds of the total population suffers from obesity. Poverty increased 40% over the last decade, now affecting 36% of households.

The community's common response to these conditions is to request more police on the street, lower student-teacher ratios, faster clean-up of land contamination, and more job training. Many people feel that Detroit does not have the luxury to endure a long-term transformation: they need change to happen now.

Effective land use planning can create more densely populated communities that are more affordable to serve and can be safer with more "eyes on the street." Innovative landscape treatments can treat contaminated lands while providing recreational amenities at the same time. Surplus vacant land can become new opportunities to produce in-town jobs and put young people and those in alternative economies to work. And the network of educational institutions (K-12 and higher education) can create campuses and programming that prepare the next generation for the jobs of the future.

DETROIT'S POPULATION. Just over 700,000 people live in a city originally designed for 2 million people. Detroit's population has been in decline for decades and this trend is expected to continue. The Southeast Michigan Council of Government's (SEMCOG) forecasts for the city predict that the population will fall from the 2010 Census figure of 714,000 to 610,000 by 2030—a long way from the city's peak population of over 1.8 million in the early 1950s, but still keeping Detroit in the top 20 largest cities in the U.S. The composition of the city's population is also undergoing gradual changes. Today, the city has 6% more single-female headed households, 7% fewer children, and a senior population that is expected to grow from 11% to 17% over the next 20 years.   On average, Detroit families make only $28,000 per year compared to families in the region making $52,000 annually, and one-third of Detroit families make less than that.

These factors, together with the demographics of the current population, suggest that the total number of people in the city may not be as important as the diversity of its residents and the robustness of its job base. Detroit can be a vibrant city of 700,000 people or less if deliberate actions are taken to increase family wealth and the earning power of people who are now in poverty, retain young people in the city, attract recent graduates as new workers, welcome foreign-born families, and ensure the city's oldest residents can choose and afford to age in their homes.

DETROIT'S EMPLOYMENT. There is only 1 private sector job for every 4 Detroit residents. The fall in Detroit's population has been accompanied by a loss of jobs both in Detroit and the region in the last decade. There are approximately 275,000[1] jobs in Detroit today, with 70% at private sector employers and the remaining found in self-employment and local, state or federal government employment.

SEMCOG's baseline forecasts for Detroit over the next 20 years project a meager annual growth of 0.1%. This is well below the growth that Detroit could achieve with targeted strategies to attract, retain, and grow firms in the city's traditional and emerging clusters, which span industrial, digital, creative, education, healthcare, and local businesses service clusters. These clusters have helped grow the city's employment base after years of decline. Continued growth in these clusters will go a long way toward signaling that Detroit is no longer a "one-company" automobile town.

Much discussion and debate has focused on the availability of jobs and the readiness of Detroit's workforce to take those potential jobs. That discussion should be framed not as an "either/or" but as a "both/and." Too few jobs, high unemployment, poverty rates, the challenges of K-12 educational reform, and reduced workforce development funding all have an impact, not only on household incomes, but on the taxes and fees the city takes in to run and maintain essential services. Addressing this "chicken and egg" problem requires a strategy that addresses job creation in Detroit and the reform of K-12 and adult education as equally urgent priorities.

[1]Estimated by project team based on QWI, LEHD—On the Map, NETS, and Census Bureau Nonemployer Statistics, and project team analysis. Employment estimates can vary based on sources and methods. SEMCOG (2012) estimates that total employment in Detroit in 2010 was about 350,000.

DETROIT'S LAND VACANCY AND LAND USE. The city's 20 square miles of total vacant land is roughly equal to the size of Manhattan. This characterization of Detroit is supported by the housing statistics of rising foreclosure rates, falling home and property values, and an excess of vacant land and homes for which there is not enough demand to fill before property deterioration sets in. Many homeowners in particular have been unable to balance their checkbooks as they see housing and transportation expenses account for over 50% of their monthly income, while the value of their investments continues to decrease.

With nearly 150,000 vacant and abandoned parcels scattered throughout the city, every area of the city is vulnerable to some level of disinvestment. Despite a common perception, the majority of residents in the city live in areas that have only low or moderate levels of vacancy—less than 30%. This is not ideal, however, when more stable neighborhood options exist elsewhere in the region. This also leaves nearly 100,000 residents in areas of the city that are sparsely populated and unlikely to return to their previous traditional residential neighborhood character.

Detroit must transform its image of vacancy into an image informed by the new possibilities for 21st century land uses. This means creating new opportunities for vacant land to become assets that contribute tax dollars, produce jobs, or become a public amenity. It does not mean that the people who might remain in higher- vacancy areas should not receive essential city services. Becoming a more affordable city for families and government means that land uses, regulations, and investments must be strategically coordinated to create more efficiency and sustainability now and over the long term.

DETROIT'S CITY SERVICE DELIVERY SYSTEMS. The high taxes and costs of city services do not produce enough to improve service delivery or make the city more affordable. Detroit has large, centralized infrastructure systems that were designed to support a population of at least 2 million, with large areas of heavy industry. As a result, today's Detroit has systems that are oversized for the current population and are no longer aligned with where people and businesses now reside or will likely be in the future. The current systems of water, energy, roads, and telecommunications are not sufficiently oriented to a new economy that focuses on less resource-intensive manufacturing and new service sectors.

The systems are also aging. Many have reached the end of their effective design lives, and many more will do so during the next twenty years. Typically, this means that they are less reliable and use more energy and water than necessary to serve people, while contributing to both local and global pollution. Lower demand (fewer users) in many areas means low usage levels (sometimes as low as 30-40% of designed capacity), which results in inefficient operations and more system breakdowns. Crucially, it also means significantly reduced revenues from user charges and taxes. In spite of this situation, agencies are required to maintain uniform high service levels across the city and reinvest in maintaining the network as a whole. If we maintain "business-as-usual" standards, the gap will continue to widen between the availability of revenues and the cost to provide services, undermining the ability to maintain and upgrade systems, and having unacceptably negative consequences for the city's people, economy, and environment.

DETROIT FUTURE CITY
CLEAR VISION AND APPROACH FOR DETROIT'S FUTURE

The future Detroit can be envisioned through a series of time horizons, showing how the experiences of current and future residents, businesses, and visitors could change over the next 5, 10, 20 years and beyond. Details and time horizons for this vision shown on pages 30-31.

BY 2030, DETROIT WILL HAVE A STABILIZED POPULATION

BY 2030, THE CITY WILL NEARLY DOUBLE THE NUMBER OF JOBS AVAILABLE FOR EACH PERSON LIVING IN THE CITY

By 2030, Detroit will have a stabilized population between 600,000 – 800,000 residents, and will remain one of the largest top 20 cities in the United States. More importantly, the composition of Detroit's residents will be diverse and welcoming to all, including

- residents with deep generational roots in the city;

- the children of today's families deciding to stay in the city for higher education, finding work, and starting a business and a family;

- families and individuals who have transitioned from poverty because of access to new job opportunities and housing choices;

- college graduates from Michigan and around the country relocating to Detroit as a place to live and work as new professionals and young entrepreneurs;

- senior citizens who want to stay in the city and have the convenience of walkable neighborhoods, access to health care, and cultural amenities; and

- families from other countries seeking new opportunities for themselves and their children.

Instead of 27 private sector jobs for every 100 Detroiters, by 2030 the city will have close to 50 jobs for every 100 city residents. Seven districts of employment located through all quadrants of the city provide jobs, business start-ups, and business growth opportunities in modern industry, information technology, creative production, healthcare, education, and local entrepreneurship. City residents, as well as people from the region, find opportunities to link their specific levels of education with job prospects, as each growth industry will need workers with a wide a range of skills and education to fill jobs.

The current and new residents of the city will also have a range of choices for where to live in the city. Detroit has traditionally been dominated by single-family detached housing. However, with the changing demographics of the city, a more diverse range of housing options will be available by 2030 to support different lifestyle needs and choices. Residents will have the ability to choose from among several options for residential living in the city:

- Traditional neighborhoods with single-family houses, front yards, and garages;

- Neighborhoods that are more dense with townhouses, mid-rise and high-rise apartments, and condominiums that have improved access to public transit;

- Neighborhoods where housing is integrated into an open-space environment with recreation opportunities and a connection to nature;

- Neighborhoods that integrate housing with land stewardship and food production; and

- Neighborhoods that allow for the combination of living and production (Live+Make), whether clean manufacturing, processing, or creative arts.

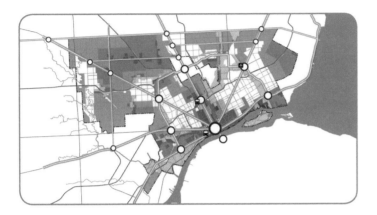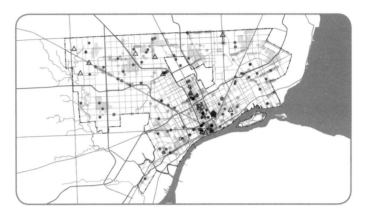

BY 2030, THE DETROIT METROPOLITAN REGION WILL HAVE AN INTEGRATED REGIONAL PUBLIC TRANSPORTATION SYSTEM

By 2030, the Detroit metropolitan region will have an integrated regional public transportation system that efficiently serves the region's 21 dispersed, yet interconnected employment centers. A new regional transportation authority aids the region in creating better transit connections, while public transit within Detroit will create better connections among neighborhoods and Detroit's seven primary employment districts. A new public transit loop creates a ring through the middle of the city, intersecting each of the key radial boulevards to provide more efficient intermodal connection points and different vehicle modes of rapid transit, from light rail to bus rapid transit, to mini-buses. The boulevards themselves are the right size to accommodate bicyclists, pedestrians, transit, and motor vehicles and landscaping that helps siphon off stormwater, buffer residents and workers from pollution, and aid in the overall image of a green, sustainable city.

This system will complement a multimodal freight and commercial system that upholds Detroit's role as the nation's busiest border crossing. This system builds on Detroit's emerging role as a global hub for transportation, distribution, and logistics (TDL) to contribute to a healthy economy and prosperous households.

In the spirit of innovation that has made the city great, Detroit will lead the world in developing landscape as 21st century infrastructure to transform vacant land areas into community assets that remediate contaminated land, manage stormwater and highway runoff, and create passive recreational amenities to improve human health and elevate adjacent land values—all without residential displacement, a big change from the urban renewal efforts of the 1960s and 1970s. The iconic boulevards and freeway corridors of the city are transformed to reinforce a new civic identity through the creation of linear carbon forests that clean air, and stormwater management landscapes that collect, treat and recycle water.

BY 2030, DETROIT WILL BECOME A CITY FOR ALL

By 2030, Detroit will be enhanced and sustained by a broad-based and ongoing civic stewardship framework of leadership drawn from among philanthropists, businesses, residents, faith institutions, major civic and cultural institutions, and a range of regional and national supporters.

The Framework recognizes that achieving the future vision for Detroit will not happen overnight, but will require a phased approach, with clearly defined implementation "horizons" or targets with metrics for evaluating the success of change. Along the path toward this goal, stakeholders can review progress and refocus priorities and strategies for the next phase of development.

By 2030, Detroit will become a city for all, with an enhanced range of choices for all residents, especially those who have stayed through the hardest times. By 2030, Detroit is a city of enhanced, varied, and active neighborhoods with strong civic support and a range of approaches to what it means to be "home." By 2030, the city has developed a strong, collaborative, community-based approach to the most difficult question it faced in 2010: how best to serve the approximately 10% of Detroiters who then lived in areas of highest vacancy, while also making decisions that would support and grow neighborhoods with more population. Residents who choose to stay in the highest-vacancy areas of the city will continue to receive services, while residents who formerly had no choices will have opportunities to move to different neighborhoods if they wish, with new incentives such as "house swap" programs and progressive efforts that help increase family wealth and access to affordable homes throughout Detroit. By 2030, neighborhoods that were once on the verge of such vacancy are saved through strategic investment, while areas that had relatively stable populations in 2010, or that grew since then, will continue along a sustainable path. Because the Strategic Framework also provides the flexibility for neighborhoods to vary their approaches due to special assets or community objectives, no neighborhood will be forced into a "one-type-fits-all" strategy.

LANDSCAPES AS INFRASTRUCTURE: RETHINKING APPROACHES TO 20TH CENTURY INFRASTRUCTURES

Much of Detroit's 19th and 20th infrastructure is nearing the end of its productive life. Although replacing and maintaining conventional infrastructure will remain important to Detroit's future, landscapes can also function in similar ways, yet are less expensive to construct and maintain than conventional systems. Landscape can be adapted to serve stormwater/wastewater, energy, roads/transportation, and waste infrastructure systems.

Blue infrastructures are water-based landscapes like retention ponds, and lakes that capture and clean stormwater, reducing the quantity and improving the quality of water that enters the combined stormwater/ sewage system.

Green infrastructures are forest landscapes that improve air quality by capturing air-borne pollutants from industry, vehicular exhaust along interstates, and infrastructure facilities like the Greater Resource Recovery Facility, which incinerates household waste. Green infrastructure also includes greenways, paths, and dedicated lanes for bicycling, walking, and running.

Landscape infrastructure can act as multiple kinds of infrastructure at once. For example, a combination blue (water) and green (plants and trees) corridor can capture stormwater along drainage swales alongside a major road, while integrating a greenway for bicycling and walking to support connections among home, work, and services.

Landscape systems have benefits that carry far beyond the inherent function they serve:

- **Environmental benefits:** cleaner air, soil, and water; captured stormwater; habitat for local wildlife and migrating birds.

- **Fiscal and economic benefits:** reduced maintenance and utility costs, fulfilling some roles of traditional systems; job creation, production of fresh food and other tangible products; an attractive, unique environment that can draw new businesses to Detroit.

- **Social benefits:** recreation and social life opportunities; neighborhood stabilization by acting as an amenity that helps to increase property values; improvement of resident health and comfort; new uses for and management of currently vacant land; renewal of the physical image of the city

Landscapes can address environmental justice by cleaning contaminated soil, improving air quality, buffering impacts of industry/infrastructure on residents, and reducing the cost of service (by reducing construction and operating costs). In short, landscape can help ensure that environmental burdens are not born disproportionately by Detroit's lower-income families and children.

By 2030, an enhanced and multi-functional open space system will provide a new and strong identity for the city, picking up where efforts like the Detroit RiverWalk have set a successful precedent.

A network of parks, plazas, wetlands, ponds and lakes, recreation centers, forests and orchards, community gardens, and remediation fields that clean the air and water through "blue" (water) and "green" (plants and trees) landscapes will populate the city, all connected by a multi-modal greenway system for pedestrians, bicycles, automobiles and transit.

THE TIME IS NOW. We have known for some time that doing business as usual is no longer an option for Detroit. The financial recession and foreclosure crisis in 2007—which undermined the city's progress in diversifying its economy and bringing back residents—drove home this reality and provided a distinct moment in time for strategic action. It created a heightened sense of urgency and opportunity among Detroiters, and has resulted in this initial work to solidify a public consensus for systematic reform and innovation.

To transform Detroit into a new, healthier, safer, more prosperous, and socially just city requires a new understanding of the city as it is right now, an imperative to share information and decision-making power, and a willingness to abandon fixed ideas and old approaches, in favor of fresh, clear-eyed understanding.

The 714,000 Detroiters who have stood their ground or chosen to come here are people who do not shy away from a challenge. That's good, because many more challenges lie ahead. Many of the recommendations of this plan can create successes in the very short term, perhaps as soon as two years from now. Yet the major and most sweeping innovations will take 20 or more years to realize. The ambition and aspiration embodied in this plan will be needed to continually inspire and replenish action, while its pragmatic approach to building on existing progress and conversations is intended to ground it in realistic possibilities for action.

To reach the goal of a Detroit Future City will call forth and try every one of the traits that have made Detroit great in the past and helped it survive to the present: ingenuity, innovation, civic commitment, and an unflinching, steel-spined ability to stand tall while facing the worst of the city's daily realities, while also embracing its possibilities.

Detroit will never be "fixed" because no city is ever "fixed." Cities are living places that require ongoing awareness and firm approaches to decision making which acknowledge changing realities and multiple voices, leading to pragmatic and agreed-on solutions. The Planning Elements in the Strategic Framework illustrate specific strategies that can be put in place now to create permanent change and transform Detroit.

THE TIME IS NOW

16

WHO USES THE PLAN?

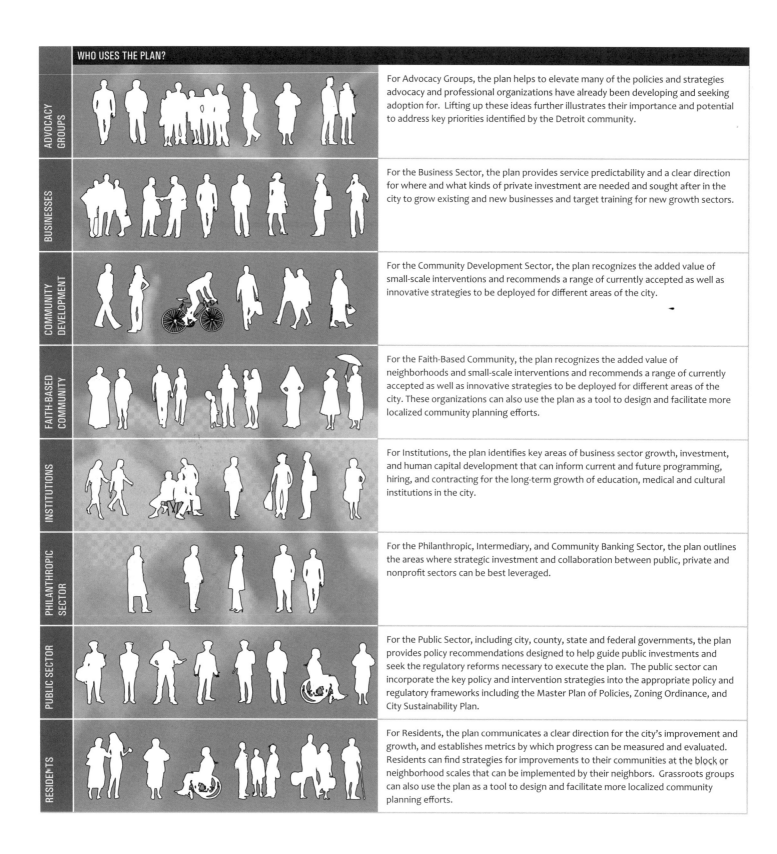

ADVOCACY GROUPS

For Advocacy Groups, the plan helps to elevate many of the policies and strategies advocacy and professional organizations have already been developing and seeking adoption for. Lifting up these ideas further illustrates their importance and potential to address key priorities identified by the Detroit community.

BUSINESSES

For the Business Sector, the plan provides service predictability and a clear direction for where and what kinds of private investment are needed and sought after in the city to grow existing and new businesses and target training for new growth sectors.

COMMUNITY DEVELOPMENT

For the Community Development Sector, the plan recognizes the added value of small-scale interventions and recommends a range of currently accepted as well as innovative strategies to be deployed for different areas of the city.

FAITH-BASED COMMUNITY

For the Faith-Based Community, the plan recognizes the added value of neighborhoods and small-scale interventions and recommends a range of currently accepted as well as innovative strategies to be deployed for different areas of the city. These organizations can also use the plan as a tool to design and facilitate more localized community planning efforts.

INSTITUTIONS

For Institutions, the plan identifies key areas of business sector growth, investment, and human capital development that can inform current and future programming, hiring, and contracting for the long-term growth of education, medical and cultural institutions in the city.

PHILANTHROPIC SECTOR

For the Philanthropic, Intermediary, and Community Banking Sector, the plan outlines the areas where strategic investment and collaboration between public, private and nonprofit sectors can be best leveraged.

PUBLIC SECTOR

For the Public Sector, including city, county, state and federal governments, the plan provides policy recommendations designed to help guide public investments and seek the regulatory reforms necessary to execute the plan. The public sector can incorporate the key policy and intervention strategies into the appropriate policy and regulatory frameworks including the Master Plan of Policies, Zoning Ordinance, and City Sustainability Plan.

RESIDENTS

For Residents, the plan communicates a clear direction for the city's improvement and growth, and establishes metrics by which progress can be measured and evaluated. Residents can find strategies for improvements to their communities at the block or neighborhood scales that can be implemented by their neighbors. Grassroots groups can also use the plan as a tool to design and facilitate more localized community planning efforts.

GUIDE TO THE STRATEGIC FRAMEWORK
HOW IT IS USED

The Detroit Strategic Framework establishes a set of policy directions and actions designed to achieve a more desirable and sustainable Detroit in the near term and for future generations. The Strategic Framework is organized into Five Planning Elements and a civic engagement chapter. These Five Elements include:

- The Economic Growth Element: The Equitable City
- The Land Use Element: The Image of the City
- The City Systems and Environment Element: The Sustainable City
- The Neighborhoods Element: The City of Distinct and Regionally Competitive Neighborhoods
- The Land and Buildings Assets Element: A Strategic Approach to Public Land

These Elements outline a detailed approach to addressing the realities and imperatives that will enable Detroit to move toward a more prosperous future.

PRAGMATIC, ADAPTABLE BLUEPRINT. The Framework represents the specifics of a vision that can remain flexible and be refined and enriched over time. It is not a master plan, but a shared framework that guides decision making among individuals, institutions, businesses, organizations, and neighborhoods toward a future city, which is culturally rich and offers opportunities for all of Detroit's residents, institutions, businesses, and neighborhoods.

The Strategic Framework is an inclusive shared vision that uses engagement to look beyond the city's historic barriers of geography, race, and economic differences. Equally important, it focuses on the assets of all areas to illustrate that all communities can be unique and be a part of the bigger image of Detroit, where a variety of neighborhood types is encouraged.

WHAT THE STRATEGIC FRAMEWORK IS AND ISN'T. As the Detroit Works process went forward, many people asked, "How is this plan different from any other?" and "How will it improve the quality of life in my community or for my business?" The answer is that, while the Strategic Framework addresses issues and presents recommendations in a similar format to other planning documents, it also is not intended to be a conventional "Vision Plan." That type of plan is usually highly aspirational and often presents static illustrative projection for what the future of a region, city, or community will look like, with little detail on how to achieve the vision.

The Strategic Framework is also not the Master Plan of Policies, the legally mandated, long-range document of land development policies that support the social, economic, and physical development and conservation of the city, proposed by the Mayor and approved by City Council in 2009. There are specific statutory procedures and formats required for that type of document, and it is typically executed by the municipality's planning agency.

The aim of the Strategic Framework is to recognize and adapt to an unpredictable future. The Strategic Framework is designed for flexibility and choices that will enable different sectors in Detroit to act both collaboratively and independently, and over different periods of time, but in a coordinated way. As a comprehensive and action-oriented blueprint for near- and long-range decision making, the Strategic Framework Plan is 1) **aspirational** toward a physical and social vision for the city; and 2) **actionable,** with strategies for new policies and implementation; and 3) **accountable,** with assignment of implementation responsibilities.

WHO THE FRAMEWORK IS FOR, AND WHO SHOULD MAKE IT HAPPEN. The Detroit Strategic Framework is one shared vision designed to guide the decisions of a wide range of implementers, investors, and regulators participating in the revitalization of Detroit. Every sector of Detroit will play an important and critical role in executing the vision, both independently and in collaboration with one another. Each sector can use the plan to guide its own decisions about investments, localize planning, align with public funding programs, conduct or encourage interim and permanent development, inform decisions about buying and selling land and businesses, and create partnerships across sectors.

HORIZONS FOR CHANGE. Just as the Strategic Framework is intended to offer recommendations and approaches that can adapt to changing realities in Detroit, so also the 10-, 20-, and 50-year Horizons adopted for the Framework are intended not as literal forecasts, but as aspirational possibilities and an aid to imagining the city's changes over time. These Horizons also offer four useful ways to look at progress and change in Detroit: Stabilization, Improvement, Sustainability, and Transformation.

THE PLANNING ELEMENTS
AN INTEGRATED APPROACH TO TRANSFORMING THE CITY AND ITS NEIGHBORHOODS

THE ECONOMIC GROWTH ELEMENT

The Economic Growth Element proposes five strategies to grow Detroit's economy in a way that is equitable for all Detroiters, supports Detroit's economic sectors, and can attract new residents and businesses:

- Support the Four Key Economic Growth Pillars that have already demonstrated promising job growth: education and medical employment ("Eds and Meds"), digital and creative jobs, industrial employment (both traditional and new technologies, large-scale and artisanal, manufacture and processes), and local entrepreneurship.

- Use place-based strategies to create core investment and employment centers, focusing on seven employment districts where job growth is already occurring.

- Encourage local entrepreneurship and minority-owned businesses.

- Improve education and skills development.

- Transform the city's land into an economic asset.

THE LAND USE ELEMENT

The Land Use Element offers land use strategies that are situated between the city's existing conditions and a range of preferred futures. The Detroit Strategic Framework organizes a wide variety of potential land use types within three levels of scale and purpose:

- FRAMEWORK ZONES that guide citywide and investment decisions in terms of the best ways to make positive change in areas with a range of physical and market characteristics. The most influential characteristic is vacancy, because of its infectious effect on physical and market conditions of an area.

- LAND USE TYPOLOGIES that provide the future vision for land use within the city. They are divided into three primary categories: neighborhood, industrial, and landscape.

- DEVELOPMENT TYPES that visualize how the physical development of buildings and landscape may occur within a particular land use typology. They are divided into four major categories: residential, commercial, landscape, and industrial.

In addition, the Detroit Strategic Framework recommends the following supportive strategies for land use:

- Create a new and diverse open space system for the city,

- Redefine corridors and complete streets, and

- Develop innovative regulatory reform.

THE CITY SYSTEMS ELEMENT

This City Systems Element describes the imperative of moving toward a more affordable, efficient, and environmentally sustainable city through reforms to service delivery throughout the city, and through transformation of the systems and networks that carry the city's water, waste, energy, and transportation. This chapter proposes six strategies:

- Reform system delivery to adapt to the current population and to better coordinate public and private service provision for more efficient and reliable services that will adapt to future needs.

- Create innovative landscapes (green and blue infrastructure) that actively clean the air and water to provide better environmental quality and public health for Detroit and its communities.

- Reshape transportation to establish Detroit within a regional, multimodal network that better serves commercial and personal transportation needs, especially in terms of connecting neighborhoods and employment districts, as well as better serving Detroit's freight industry.

- Improve lighting efficiency throughout the city.

- Enhance communications access in Detroit.

- Actively manage change, by continuing discussions that have already begun removing regulatory barriers, creating interagency cooperation at the city and regional levels, and establishing an interagency platform for coordinated decision making about city services.

THE NEIGHBORHOOD ELEMENT

The Neighborhood Element proposes six specific strategies to create a diverse range of neighborhood styles and choices that will appeal to a wide variety of people, while strengthening all neighborhoods across the city:

- Address quality-of-life issues that affect all Detroiters with a set of citywide strategies that work in all Detroit neighborhoods.

- Create dense, walkable, mixed-use neighborhoods in some parts of Detroit.

- Fuse art and industry in "Live+Make" neighborhoods in functionally obsolete industrial areas of Detroit.

- Repurpose vacant land to make Urban Green neighborhoods that use landscape as a predominant transformative element;

- Renew amenities in traditional, usually historic neighborhoods of single-family housing;

- Use productive landscape as the basis for a sustainable city by tapping innovative, broad-scale alternative uses of green and blue infrastructure and other productive landscapes, while upholding the quality of life for residents already in these areas of increasing vacancy.

THE LAND AND BUILDINGS ASSETS ELEMENT

To transform the vacant land of Detroit into a potential asset for the city's future, the Land and Building Assets Element calls for all the different public agencies that hold land to align their missions around a single, shared vision. This collaborative effort must reflect the aspirations for the city as a whole, as expressed in its land use and environmental plans, economic growth strategies, and neighborhood revitalization efforts. Such a transformative strategy must provide an integrated approach to land and buildings across the entire city, whether publicly or privately owned. Specifically, the Land and Buildings Assets Element proposes six strategies:

- Target vacant public land and buildings in employment districts for growth.

- Use vacant public land in neighborhoods as a tool for neighborhood stabilization.

- Transform largely vacant areas through blue and green infrastructure.

- Link public facility and property decisions to larger strategies.

- Make landscape interventions central to Detroit's revival.

- Use aggressive regulatory tools to reinforce land development, reuse, and management strategies.

CRITICAL FOUNDATION FOR THE CITY'S FUTURE

The Civic Engagement initiative resulted in five specific recommendations to create civic support for the Strategic Framework and calls for three central strategies to establish long-term civic capacity for the City of Detroit.

The five implementation recommendations related to the Strategic Framework are:

- Establish a Detroit Strategic Framework Consortium, charged with stewarding the implementation and civic engagement of the Strategic Framework into the future.

- Enlist additional champions for implementation and policy reform in addition to the Consortium membership.

- Inform, educate, and equip key stakeholders to continue to "take the plan to the city."

- Strengthen and complement the public sector with a regional agenda that recognizes Detroit's strength and the region's shared destiny, and that extends and shares ownership of civic engagement in recognition of Detroit's role in the nation and the world.

- Report back for transparent and ongoing progress.

The three engagement strategies for a sustainable civic capacity on behalf of Detroit over the long term are

- Extend capacity by building on four key components of long-term civic capacity: city government; philanthropy; Detroit institutions (including the nonprofit and business sectors); and Detroit residents.

- Develop and share knowledge and information inclusively, continually, and with transparency, and demonstrate that the input has value and is being used.

- Engage people with a mosaic of tactics that have varied and broad appeals and possibilities, and that are woven together to have combined effectiveness.

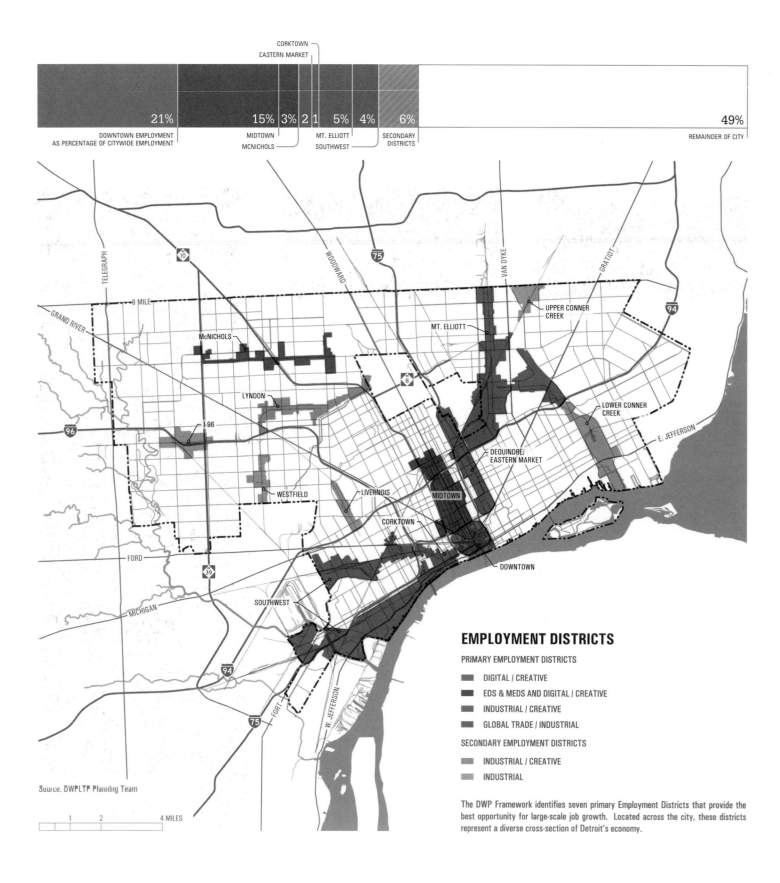

| 21% | 15% | 3% | 2 | 1 | 5% | 4% | 6% | 49% |

DOWNTOWN EMPLOYMENT
AS PERCENTAGE OF CITYWIDE EMPLOYMENT

CORKTOWN
EASTERN MARKET

MIDTOWN
MCNICHOLS

MT. ELLIOTT
SOUTHWEST

SECONDARY
DISTRICTS

REMAINDER OF CITY

EMPLOYMENT DISTRICTS

PRIMARY EMPLOYMENT DISTRICTS

- DIGITAL / CREATIVE
- EDS & MEDS AND DIGITAL / CREATIVE
- INDUSTRIAL / CREATIVE
- GLOBAL TRADE / INDUSTRIAL

SECONDARY EMPLOYMENT DISTRICTS

- INDUSTRIAL / CREATIVE
- INDUSTRIAL

The DWP Framework identifies seven primary Employment Districts that provide the best opportunity for large-scale job growth. Located across the city, these districts represent a diverse cross-section of Detroit's economy.

Source: DWPLTP Planning Team

THE ECONOMIC GROWTH ELEMENT

TRANSFORMATIVE IDEAS

 1 A CITY OF ROBUST JOB GROWTH

 2 A CITY OF EQUITABLE ECONOMIC GROWTH

 3 A CITY OF PHYSICALLY AND STRATEGICALLY ALIGNED ECONOMIC ASSETS

 4 A LEADER IN URBAN INDUSTRIAL ACTIVITY

 5 A CITY OF REGIONAL AND GLOBAL ECONOMIC ASSETS

 6 A CITY THAT ENCOURAGES MINORITY BUSINESS ENTERPRISES

7 A CITY OF IMMEDIATE AND LONG-RANGING STRATEGIES FOR RESIDENT PROSPERITY

WE MUST RE-ENERGIZE DETROIT'S ECONOMY TO INCREASE JOB OPPORTUNITIES FOR DETROITERS WITHIN THE CITY AND STRENGTHEN THE TAX BASE.

WE MUST SUPPORT OUR CURRENT RESIDENTS AND ATTRACT NEW RESIDENTS.

IMPLEMENTATION STRATEGIES AND ACTIONS

A SUPPORT FOUR KEY ECONOMIC PILLARS
1 Align cluster strategies with the Detroit Strategic Framework.
2 Establish cluster-based collaboration with labor market intermediaries.

B USE A PLACE-BASED STRATEGY FOR GROWTH
1 Align public, private, and philanthropic investments in employment districts.
2 Develop detailed action plans for primary employment districts.
3 Encourage industrial business improvement districts (IBIDS).
4 Become a national leader in green industrial districts.

C ENCOURAGE LOCAL ENTREPRENEURSHIP AND MINORITY BUSINESS PARTICIPATION
1 Promote short-term approaches to increase the number and success of MBEs* and DBEs** in the city.
2 Support the development of low-cost, shared spaces for clusters with high levels of self employment.
3 Provide young Detroiters with exposure to and experience in Digital / Creative and other new economy clusters.
4 Develop a comprehensive long-term strategy to increase and strengthen the city's MBEs.

D IMPROVE SKILLS AND SUPPORT EDUCATION REFORM
1 "Hire Detroit": strengthen local hiring practices.
2 Link workforce investments to transportation.
3 Coordinate workforce development best practices.
4 Revitalize incumbent workforce training.
5 Expand public-private partnerships for workforce development.
6 Commission a study to identify levers to improve graduation rates and poor labor market outcomes of Detroiters.

E LAND REGULATIONS, TRANSACTIONS, AND ENVIRONMENTAL ACTIONS
1 Create an industrial side-lot program.
2 Create a priority permitting process for employment districts.
3 Focus on land banking industrial and commercial property.
4 Identify alternative capital sources for real estate development.
5 Articulate a reverse change-of-use policy.
6 Create master-planned industrial hubs.
7 Address underutilization of industrial building space and land.
8 Address weaknesses in the local brokerage sector.

*Minority business enterprises
**Disadvantaged business enterprises

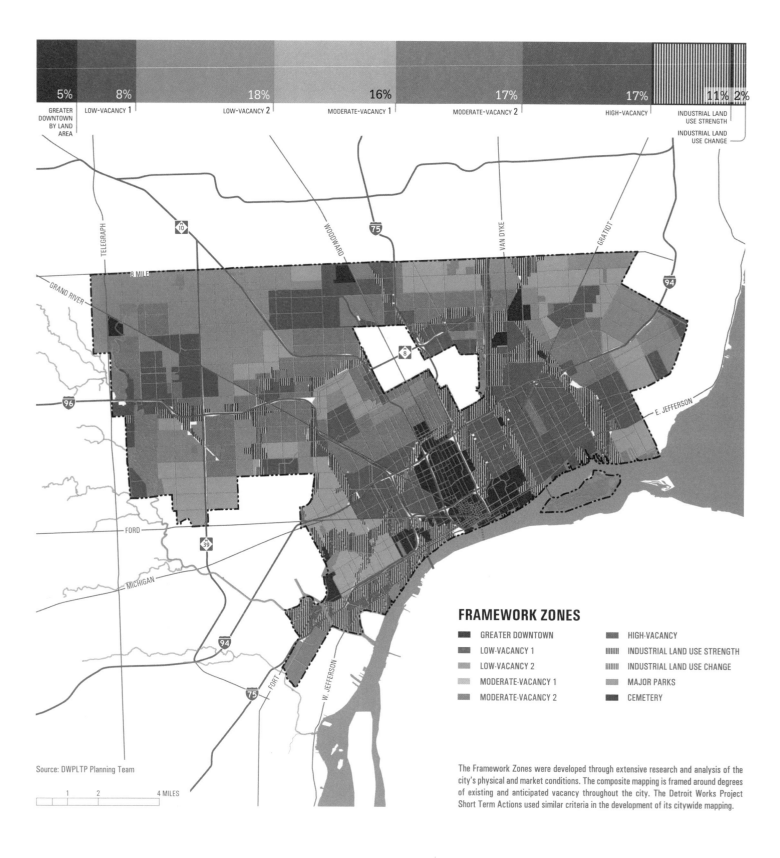

5%	8%	18%	16%	17%	17%	11%	2%
GREATER DOWNTOWN BY LAND AREA	LOW-VACANCY 1	LOW-VACANCY 2	MODERATE-VACANCY 1	MODERATE-VACANCY 2	HIGH-VACANCY	INDUSTRIAL LAND USE STRENGTH	INDUSTRIAL LAND USE CHANGE

FRAMEWORK ZONES

- GREATER DOWNTOWN
- LOW-VACANCY 1
- LOW-VACANCY 2
- MODERATE-VACANCY 1
- MODERATE-VACANCY 2
- HIGH-VACANCY
- INDUSTRIAL LAND USE STRENGTH
- INDUSTRIAL LAND USE CHANGE
- MAJOR PARKS
- CEMETERY

Source: DWPLTP Planning Team

1   2   4 MILES

The Framework Zones were developed through extensive research and analysis of the city's physical and market conditions. The composite mapping is framed around degrees of existing and anticipated vacancy throughout the city. The Detroit Works Project Short Term Actions used similar criteria in the development of its citywide mapping.

THE LAND USE ELEMENT

TRANSFORMATIVE IDEAS

1 A CITY OF MULTIPLE EMPLOYMENT DISTRICTS

2 A CITY CONNECTING PEOPLE TO OPPORTUNITY

3 A GREEN CITY WHERE LANDSCAPES CONTRIBUTE TO HEALTH

4 A CITY OF DISTINCT, ATTRACTIVE NEIGHBORHOODS

WE MUST USE INNOVATIVE APPROACHES TO **TRANSFORM OUR VACANT LAND** IN WAYS THAT **INCREASE ITS VALUE AND PRODUCTIVITY** AND PROMOTE LONG-TERM SUSTAINABILITY.

WE MUST USE OUR OPEN SPACE TO **IMPROVE THE HEALTH** OF ALL DETROIT RESIDENTS.

IMPLEMENTATION STRATEGIES AND ACTIONS

A — CREATE A CITYWIDE FRAMEWORK FOR GROWTH AND INVESTMENT

1. Establish framework zones and future land use scenarios as the basis for public, private and philanthropic investment.
2. Base land use decisions on the fundamental physical and market conditions of the city: low-vacancy, moderate-vacancy, high-vacancy and Greater Downtown areas.
3. Update framework zones map on a 5-year basis to reflect changes to physical and market conditions.

B — SUPPORT A NETWORK OF NEW AND EXISTING NEIGHBORHOOD TYPES

1. Establish land use typologies as the vision for the future city.
2. Reorganize land use around neighborhoods, industry, and landscape.

C — INTRODUCE NEW FORMS OF DEVELOPMENT

1. Align framework zones and future land use typologies to determine appropriate locations and types of development across the city.
2. Introduce new and innovative landscape-based development types.
3. Introduce form-based development criteria.

D — CREATE A NEW AND DIVERSE OPEN SPACE SYSTEM FOR THE CITY

1. Implement blue and green infrastructure projects.
2. Encourage reuse of vacant land with productive landscapes.
3. Diversify park networks.
4. Encourage partnerships between universities and firms in productive landscapes to conduct research and provide job training opportunities.

E — REDEFINE CORRIDORS AND COMPLETE STREETS

1. Develop tiered transit network that ties into regional system.
2. Incorporate multi-modal transit design into all street improvements.
3. Focus commercial development in walkable nodes or auto-oriented strips based on physical/market conditions and future land use vision.
4. Introduce blue and green infrastructure as integral to corridor development.
5. Implement blue infrastructure along arterial and other roads.

F — ENACT INNOVATIVE REGULATORY REFORM

1. Phase land use vision over the 10-, 20-, and 50-year horizons.
2. Revise/amend the City Master Plan of Policies and Zoning Ordinance.
3. Update public, private, and philanthropic policy-guiding documents.

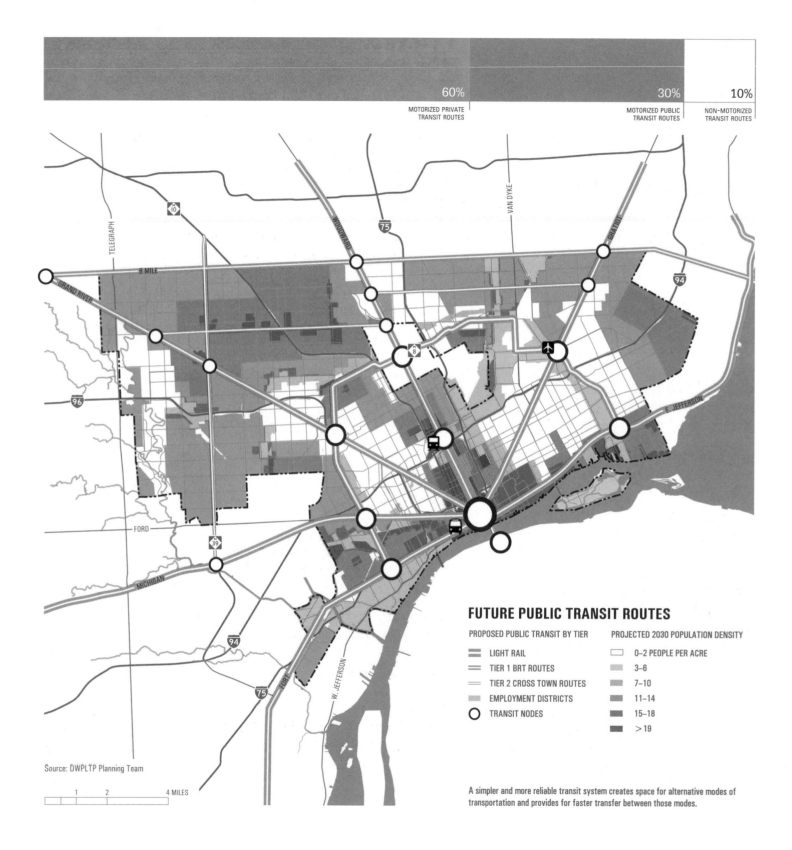

60%

MOTORIZED PRIVATE
TRANSIT ROUTES

30%

MOTORIZED PUBLIC
TRANSIT ROUTES

10%

NON-MOTORIZED
TRANSIT ROUTES

FUTURE PUBLIC TRANSIT ROUTES

PROPOSED PUBLIC TRANSIT BY TIER

LIGHT RAIL
TIER 1 BRT ROUTES
TIER 2 CROSS TOWN ROUTES
EMPLOYMENT DISTRICTS
TRANSIT NODES

PROJECTED 2030 POPULATION DENSITY

0–2 PEOPLE PER ACRE
3–6
7–10
11–14
15–18
> 19

Source: DWPLTP Planning Team

1   2   4 MILES

A simpler and more reliable transit system creates space for alternative modes of
transportation and provides for faster transfer between those modes.

THE CITY SYSTEMS ELEMENT

TRANSFORMATIVE IDEAS

 1 STRATEGIC INFRASTRUCTURE RENEWAL

 2 LANDSCAPE AS 21ST CENTURY INFRASTRUCTURE

 3 DIVERSIFIED TRANSPORTATION FOR DETROIT AND THE REGION

WE MUST FOCUS ON **SIZING THE NETWORKS** FOR A SMALLER POPULATION, MAKING THEM MORE EFFICIENT, MORE AFFORDABLE, AND BETTER PERFORMING.

WE MUST **REALIGN CITY SYSTEMS** IN WAYS THAT PROMOTE AREAS OF ECONOMIC POTENTIAL, ENCOURAGE THRIVING COMMUNITIES, AND IMPROVE ENVIRONMENTAL AND HUMAN HEALTH CONDITIONS.

IMPLEMENTATION STRATEGIES AND ACTIONS

A REFORM DELIVERY SYSTEM

1. Use the Framework to create certainty around residential and employment density in each area of the city.
2. Right-size systems so that network capacity matches residential and employment demand for each area in the medium term.
3. Balance investment in areas of greatest need with investment in areas of greatest potential.
4. Address equity: ensure that a good standard of core services are provided to all groups in all areas, including high-vacancy areas.

B CREATE LANDSCAPES THAT WORK

1. Deploy surplus land as multifunctional infrastructure landscapes, primarily addressing flood water mitigation and air quality.
2. Bring health and social benefits associated with landscapes and green facilities to lower income groups with poor access to transportation.

C RECONFIGURE TRANSPORTATION

1. Realign city road hierarchy to provide faster connections between employment, district, and neighborhood centers.
2. Enhance transit service and increased ridership by realigning Detroit's current transit system to provide an integrated network based on fast connections between regional employment centers, supported by feeder services from residential areas.
3. For higher-vacancy areas, provide smaller-scale, flexible on-demand services.
4. Align pattern of development in centers and neighborhoods to support greater number of walking and cycling trips, including promotion of greenways.
5. Support freight and logistics industries through the upgrades of key routes and provisions of enhanced connections across the border to Canada.
6. Provide large-scale multimodal freight interchange facilities to support local industry and overall city logistics.

D ENHANCE COMMUNICATIONS ACCESS

1. Ensure high-speed data networks are in place to serve existing and new economic sectors and the wider community.
2. Develop e-government platform to maximize the efficiency of social service delivery.
3. Utilize the improved data network to develop smart infrastructure systems which deliver improved service with smaller capacity infrastructure.

E IMPROVE LIGHTING EFFICIENCY

1. Reduce the total number of lights and upgrade all remaining lights to low-energy LED models.
2. In high-vacancy areas, take some parts of the network off-grid, using solar power for generation.
3. Transfer ownership of the network to a new Public Lighting Authority which can procure services from the private sector competitively.

F REDUCE WASTE AND INCREASE RECYCLING

1. Reduce total levels of waste through citizen education and work with packaging industries.
2. Develop targeted and citywide curbside recycling program.
3. Ensure that incinerator emissions remain at or below US EPA standards and international best practice.

G ACTIVELY MANAGE CHANGE

1. Adopt Strategic Framework Plan as basis for systems transformation and put in place rolling review program.
2. Create an interagency platform to coordinate change across public and private sector bodies.
3. Communicate with affected communities and monitor processes for emerging success and unforeseen adverse impacts.

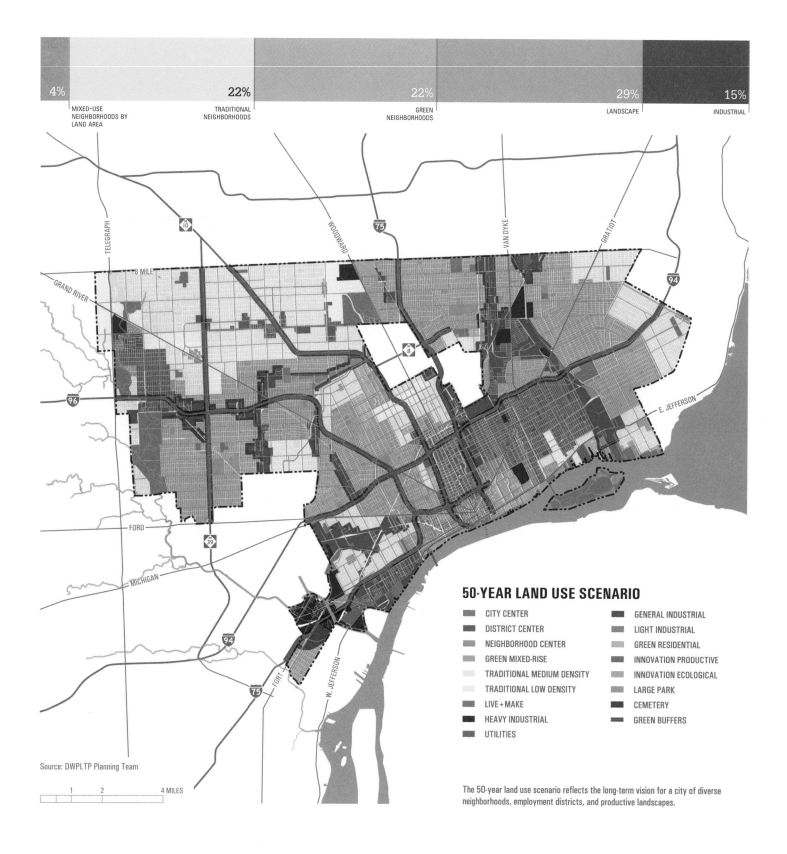

4%	22%	22%	29%	15%
MIXED-USE NEIGHBORHOODS BY LAND AREA	TRADITIONAL NEIGHBORHOODS	GREEN NEIGHBORHOODS	LANDSCAPE	INDUSTRIAL

50-YEAR LAND USE SCENARIO

- CITY CENTER
- DISTRICT CENTER
- NEIGHBORHOOD CENTER
- GREEN MIXED-RISE
- TRADITIONAL MEDIUM DENSITY
- TRADITIONAL LOW DENSITY
- LIVE+MAKE
- HEAVY INDUSTRIAL
- UTILITIES

- GENERAL INDUSTRIAL
- LIGHT INDUSTRIAL
- GREEN RESIDENTIAL
- INNOVATION PRODUCTIVE
- INNOVATION ECOLOGICAL
- LARGE PARK
- CEMETERY
- GREEN BUFFERS

Source: DWPLTP Planning Team

1   2   4 MILES

The 50-year land use scenario reflects the long-term vision for a city of diverse neighborhoods, employment districts, and productive landscapes.

THE NEIGHBORHOOD ELEMENT

TRANSFORMATIVE IDEAS

 1 A CITY OF MANY KEY ASSETS

 2 A CITY OF NEIGHBORHOOD CHOICES

 3 A CITY OF DIFFERENT STRATEGIES FOR DIFFERENT NEIGHBORHOODS

 4 A CITY OF DIVERSE HOUSING TYPES FOR DIVERSE POPULATIONS

 5 A CITY OF RESIDENTS WHO ENGAGE IN THEIR OWN FUTURES

WE MUST PROMOTE A RANGE OF SUSTAINABLE RESIDENTIAL DENSITIES.

IMPLEMENTATION STRATEGIES AND ACTIONS

A ADDRESS QUALITY OF LIFE CHALLENGES THAT AFFECT ALL DETROITERS
1. Realign public safety network to reinforce neighborhood stability.
2. Establish neighborhood-based/community-based schools as neighborhood anchors.
3. Develop strategies to address the divide between high taxation rates and low-quality city services.
   Develop regional transit system.
4. Support programs that promote diverse, mixed-income communities.

B CREATE DENSE, WALKABLE, MIXED-USE NEIGHBORHOODS
1. Stimulate residential market demand (LIVE programs, equity insurance, etc.)
2. Establish dedicated public, private and philanthropic gap funding sources.
3. Create financial and regulatory density incentives.
   Develop walkable retail nodes.
4. Guide development to reinforce transit/public space investment (TOD).

C REGENERATE NEIGHBORHOODS THROUGH FUSION OF ART AND INDUSTRY
1. Relax business start-up and use regulations to stimulate entrepreneurship.
2. Develop comprehensive start-up incentives and support packages for small businesses.
3. Support training and skills development programs to unique local industries (advanced manufacturing, urban agriculture, green tech).
4. Create tailored development package for industrial adaptive reuse including brownfield remediation costs.
5. Develop a variety of co-location spaces for residential, artistic and entrepreneurial uses.
6. Incorporate local arts into comprehensive public space master plans.

D REPURPOSE VACANT LAND TO CREATE GREEN NEIGHBORHOODS
1. Undertake massive demolition/deconstruction program.
2. Create community-based open space master plans.
3. Deploy a variety of low cost, low maintenance open space improvements.
4. Assemble large areas of public land for green reuse.
5. Prioritize rehabilitation of historic or significant structures.
6. Integrate blue and green infrastructure as part of open space plans.

E RENEW TRADITIONAL NEIGHBORHOODS
1. Prioritize safety initiatives including streetlight renewal in target areas.
2. Prioritize city services maintenance and renewal in target areas.
3. Prioritize neighborhood stabilization within 1/2 mile of schools.
4. Co-locate services and amenities at schools to anchor neighborhoods.
5. Target code enforcement on absentee property owners and landlords.
6. Incentivize neighborhood retail nodes with links to transit network.

F UTILIZE PRODUCTIVE LANDSCAPES AS THE BASIS FOR A SUSTAINABLE CITY
1. Establish voluntary house-to-house program.
2. Assemble large contiguous areas of public land for productive reuse.
3. Revise regulatory framework to allow wider range of landscape-based uses.

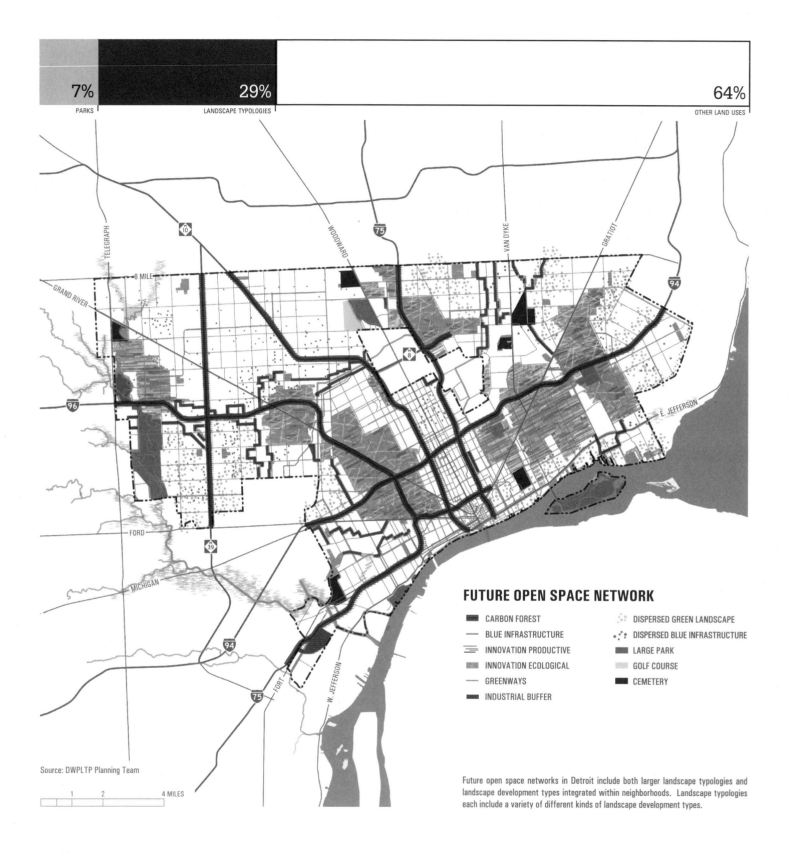

7%	29%	64%
PARKS	LANDSCAPE TYPOLOGIES	OTHER LAND USES

TELEGRAPH

GRAND RIVER

8 MILE

WOODWARD

VAN DYKE

GRATIOT

E. JEFFERSON

FORD

MICHIGAN

W. JEFFERSON

FORT

FUTURE OPEN SPACE NETWORK

- CARBON FOREST
- BLUE INFRASTRUCTURE
- INNOVATION PRODUCTIVE
- INNOVATION ECOLOGICAL
- GREENWAYS
- INDUSTRIAL BUFFER

- DISPERSED GREEN LANDSCAPE
- DISPERSED BLUE INFRASTRUCTURE
- LARGE PARK
- GOLF COURSE
- CEMETERY

Source: DWPLTP Planning Team

1   2   4 MILES

Future open space networks in Detroit include both larger landscape typologies and landscape development types integrated within neighborhoods. Landscape typologies each include a variety of different kinds of landscape development types.

THE LAND AND BUILDINGS ASSETS ELEMENT

TRANSFORMATIVE IDEAS

 1 A CITY THAT SHARES A VISION: COORDINATING THE MANAGEMENT OF VACANT LAND

 2 A CITY WHERE EVERYTHING IS CONNECTED: VIEWING VACANT AND PROBLEM PROPERTIES WITHIN ONE INTERRELATED SYSTEM

 3 A CITY OF STRATEGIC APPROACHES: RECOGNIZING THE UNIQUENESS OF EACH PROPERTY'S VALUE AND CHALLENGES

 4 A NEW URBAN LANDSCAPE: USING LAND FOR INFRASTRUCTURE AND INNOVATION

 5 A CITY WHERE PUBLIC FACILITY INVESTMENTS COUNT: ALIGNING PUBLIC FACILITIES WITH LAND USE TRANSFORMATION

WE MUST BE **STRATEGIC AND COORDINATED** IN OUR USE OF LAND.

IMPLEMENTATION STRATEGIES AND ACTIONS

A TARGET VACANT LAND AND BUILDINGS IN EMPLOYMENT DISTRICTS FOR ECONOMIC GROWTH

1. Identify strategic targets for acquisition of properties by public entities.
2. Adopt policies for targeted disposition and holding of properties in economic growth areas.
3. Increase the cost of holding vacant property.
4. Adopt program to foster greater use of underused buildings.

B USE VACANT LAND AS A TOOL FOR NEIGHBORHOOD STABILIZATION

1. Reuse vacant lots to enhance neighborhood stability.
2. Adopt targeted demolition strategy based on stabilization priorities.
3. Address problem landlords.
4. Increase the cost of holding vacant property.
5. Pursue targeted neighborhood stabilization strategies.

C TRANSFORM LARGELY VACANT AREAS THROUGH BLUE AND GREEN INFRASTRUCTURE

1. Hold land between interstates/industrial areas and neighborhoods for green infrastructure (do not release for future residential development).
2. Acquire available land for blue infrastructure in key locations.

D LINK PUBLIC FACILITY AND PROPERTY DECISIONS TO LARGER STRATEGIES

1. Create priority system for public land acquisition.
2. Create joint policies and systems for disposition of public property.
3. Adopt coordinated maintenance strategy for public land.
4. Adopt targeted demolition strategy based on stabilization priorities.
5. Use new and upgraded schools as community anchors for stabilization.
6. Review criteria for school closing to reflect neighborhood stability factors.
7. Update parks and recreation facilities planning to reflect current and future populations and budgets (update aspects of 2006 Strategic Master Plan by the Detroit Recreation Department).
8. Parks and recreation planning at neighborhood scales: refine citywide strategy of Detroit Strategic Framework through smaller-scaled analysis.

E MAKE LANDSCAPE INTERVENTIONS CENTRAL TO DETROIT'S RENEWAL

1. Adjust city maintenance standards, strategies, and practices to vary by framework zone and future land use (do not mow all vacant lots in city regardless of location, but instead adopt different lower-cost maintenance strategies in different areas); look for partnerships to help with land maintenance.
2. Form partnerships with community groups and other organizations, businesses, and individuals to help maintain land.
3. Refine set of landscape maintenance typologies and develop cost estimates to implement.

F USE AGGRESSIVE REGULATORY TOOLS TO REINFORCE LAND DEVELOPMENT, REUSE, AND MANAGEMENT STRATEGIES

1. Increase the cost of holding vacant property.
2. Address problem landlords.
3. Create formal partnership with Wayne County Treasurer for tax foreclosure auctions.

IMPLEMENTATION HORIZONS FOR CHANGE

> **THE NEXT 5 YEARS** > **YEARS 5-10**

NOW HORIZON 1 STABILIZE

Over the next five years, residents and stakeholders of Detroit will believe a new future is possible if they begin to see an elevated level of reliable and quality services to meet their basic needs, as well as stabilization of physical conditions through more efficient operational reforms, strategic investments, and stabilization or modest improvement in the economic conditions in the city.

A 21st century city must have 21st century regulations that recognize the changing needs of the city's demographics and their requirements for new forms of land use and the long-term sustainability of those uses. Zoning, land use, and land disposition policies and regulations must be realigned to accommodate these needs and opportunities. Other signs of stability in Detroit would include:

- Increased efforts to expand existing businesses in the target economic sectors of industry, education, medical, information technology, creative industries, and local entrepreneurial development, especially among minority-owned businesses and independent sole proprietors who could move from the informal economy to create businesses that have the capacity to grow and to hire.

- Education reform is passed and critical workforce development funding is preserved.

- The necessary land use regulations are revised to make the vision legal.

- The rates of blight and home foreclosures are visibly slowed.

- Essential public facilities have been co-located and programming has been enhanced to meet the needs of residents in convenient locations.

- All public land dispositions are aligned and coordinated with the Framework.

- Pilot projects that are testing new ideas for infrastructure, land maintenance, housing, environmental remediation, urban agriculture, cooperative retailing, and others are underway in neighborhoods throughout the city.

- Local governance has been stabilized.

- An implementation organization has been identified and is working to ensure the vision of the Framework is achieved with local, regional, and national partners.

2020 HORIZON 2 IMPROVE

Over the next 10 years, Detroit will begin to see the results of preparing residents and business (existing and new) for economic growth opportunities and household prosperity by growing, recruiting, educating, and training in traditional and emerging economic sectors. Residents find it a more affordable place to live and are beginning to find job opportunities in town.

- Public land is positioned for new development of businesses, retail and housing, especially in areas with the potential for employment growth.

- Growth in local entrepreneurship is measurably increasing, especially among African Americans and young people.

- Traditional neighborhoods and the more mixed-use urban centers of the city are starting to increase in residential and population density.

- The demotion program has slowed and is transitioning to reconstruction and rehabilitation.

- A visible increase in mature landscapes for recreation and infrastructure are emerging throughout the city.

- Reliable and scheduled public transit is in place along the busiest transit routes in the city and region.

- Infrastructure upgrades to areas of growth are underway.

YEARS 10-20 > YEARS 20-50

2030 SUSTAIN
HORIZON 3

Within 20 years time, Detroit should see a more stabilized population and an increase in local jobs per resident. As such, the city should be well on its way to implementing innovative, 21st-century systems of infrastructure and transportation, stormwater management, power, and waste management to support new growth.

- The population has stabilized, and net loss in population has slowed.

- The gap between the number of jobs per resident is decreasing, with unemployment declining.

- The first generation of youth coming out of education reform are entering the workforce with jobs in the city.

- All neighborhoods have become regionally competitive places to live because of housing and transportation affordability.

- New and convenient public transit options have been expanded to all parts of the city.

- Strategic upgrades to water, energy, and telecommunication networks are advanced.

- The city is visibly more green, with air, land, and water quality metrics improving.

2050 TRANSFORM
HORIZON 4

Detroit regains its position as one of the most competitive cities in the nation, the top employment center in the region, and a global leader in technology and innovation, creating a healthy and sustainable jobs-to-resident ratio and economic opportunities for a broad range of residents. Traditional and mixed-use neighborhoods of the city, including City Center, District Centers and Live+Make areas, have filled their density capacities. Opportunities for new residential growth can be expanded into green residential areas. Productive and ecological landscapes are now firmly established as the new form and image of the city.

THE ECONOMIC GROWTH ELEMENT

THE EQUITABLE CITY

A Day in the Life *Fulfilling our Economic Potential*

Darius lives in Northwest Detroit with his wife Barbara, a medical technician, and his two kids Bakari, 17, and Hope, 15. It's been a tough decade, but things are looking up. Not too long ago Darius was unemployed because of cutbacks at the auto factory he'd worked at since high school. The only job Barbara could find was in the suburbs, and her daily commute began at 4:30 a.m. by bus so Darius could have the car.

How'd they recover? In 2012, the city government and its business partners began focusing on four key areas of job growth, including 21st century industrial work. Through a new training partnership between a local university and a foundation, Darius touched up his advanced-technology skills and landed a job within 60 days of receiving his certificate. Jobs in the city were picking up rapidly, since the city had focused its business development in seven strategic employment districts. Businesses locating in these districts attracted others in similar fields, and all of them were hiring.

Barbara soon got a job, too, at a new clinic in the "Eds and Meds" district in the McNichols corridor. She takes one of the city's rapid bus lines to work now, getting there in about 20 minutes. Bakari and Hope take the rapid bus to school, too, and they even take the bus to after-school activities at the library (SAT practice for Bakari, digital photography for Hope). With everyone's commute time cut, dinner begins at 6 p.m. sharp: Just in time for a family report on everyone's day.

TRANSFORMATIVE IDEAS
ECONOMIC GROWTH

Unlike many of the country's struggling cities, Detroit is challenged not with the creation of a new set of economic assets but with a geographic and strategic alignment of existing assets. While it is true that the city's original land patterns cannot efficiently serve its current residents, the real challenge is this: **Detroit is not too big, its economy is too small.**

The challenge of growing Detroit's economy comes with an important imperative: the need to enhance equity by creating job opportunities for Detroiters of all backgrounds and skill levels. This is not only a desirable output—the right thing to do for people—but a key input for the city's sustainable economic future—the smart thing to do for business.

The good news is that Detroit's economy is changing, and its economic base is diverse, if modest. Four "pillars" of employment now account for well over half of Detroit's employment base: education and medical employment ("Eds and Meds"), digital and creative jobs, industrial employment (both traditional and new technologies, large-scale and artisanal, manufacture and processes), and local entrepreneurship. All of these are promising areas of employment, and local entrepreneurship in particular is the "sleeping giant" that could change the economic landscape of Detroit, especially in the areas of business-to-business services (B2B), food processing, and construction/demolition/engineering/repurposing (CDER).

Physical corridors of strength and investment have emerged within the city's checkerboard development patterns. The Strategic Framework proposes an economic strategy that builds on existing trends and unique characteristics in seven employment districts in the city of Detroit, which will serve as strategic areas for investment and new growth, attracting residents and companies to exchange interests, ideas, and innovations. **These seven primary employment districts account for about half of the city's total employment but take up less than 15% of the city's land.** Detroit's physical transformation is intended to create additional job opportunities and tap the incredible potential inherent in the very "problem" that has plagued the city: its miles of vacant and underused spaces. Two emerging industries for Detroit are most promising in this context: food production (taking advantage of Detroit's resident urban farming movement, the ingenuity of its people, and a growing nationwide interest in locally sourced food); and CDER (construction/demolition/engineering/repurposing, which builds on Detroit's industrial skills base and makes a virtue of the very necessity to change the landscape). Both of these emerging industries, coupled with Detroit's existing strength in TDL (transportation, distribution, and logistics), will likely provide thousands of new jobs and entrepreneurial opportunities for Detroiters of all backgrounds and skill levels.

Every job—and every resident—is important to Detroit's future. **For the city's economic alignment to yield its full potential, economic growth in Detroit must be fair and must benefit all of the city's residents.** This plan recognizes equitable growth not only because it is the right thing to do, but because it makes good business sense: By increasing Detroiters' access to employment and entrepreneurship, the city will grow its base of workers and business owners, while increasing incentives for and investment in further education and training.

As Detroit strengthens the key actors and assets within the city, it will also be able to tighten the linkages between the city and regional economies, maintaining its position as a global trade center. The vision of the Strategic Framework is a strong, equitable urban economy that anchors the revitalization of the larger metropolitan economy.

The Framework is also designed to be adaptable to the conditions in the regional, national, and international economies. The intent was to provide a framework for action that is flexible and dynamic, yet establishes a strong structure to support both growth and equal opportunities.

7 ECONOMIC GROWTH TRANSFORMATIVE IDEAS

COMPARATIVE CITY PRIVATE SECTOR EMPLOYMENT RATIOS

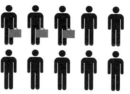

DETROIT

27 JOBS PER 100 RESIDENTS

POPULATION: 714,000
SIZE: 139 SQ. MILES
JOBS: 193,000

PHILADELPHIA

35 JOBS PER 100 RESIDENTS

POPULATION: 1,526,000
SIZE: 134 SQ. MILES
JOBS: 535,000

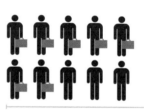

ATLANTA

73 JOBS PER 100 RESIDENTS

POPULATION: 420,000
SIZE: 133 SQ. MILES
JOBS: 307,000

PORTLAND

55 JOBS PER 100 RESIDENTS

POPULATION: 584,000
SIZE: 133 SQ. MILES
JOBS: 321,000

DENVER

60 JOBS PER 100 RESIDENTS

POPULATION 600,000
SIZE: 153 SQ. MILES
JOBS: 360,000

While the population in the city has declined over the past 60 years the number of jobs located in the city has fallen at a sharper rate. This has left Detroit with relatively few private sector jobs for the number of people who reside here. Of the top 100 cities, only 5 have fewer jobs per resident.

Data Sources: 2010 LEHD—On the Map, 2010 SF1 Census, ICIC Analysis

ECONOMIC PILLARS   GLOBAL TRADE / INDUSTRIAL • DIGITAL / CREATIVE • LOCAL ENTREPRENEURSHIP • EDUCATION & MEDICAL

Half of Detroit's employment base can be found in these four economic pillars. These sectors present the opportunity to provided equitable employment growth for Detroiters of all skill levels.

 A CITY OF ROBUST JOB GROWTH

 A CITY OF EQUITABLE ECONOMIC GROWTH

DESPITE SIX DECADES OF POPULATION LOSS, DETROIT'S FUTURE WILL BE DRIVEN BY ITS ABILITY TO INCREASE EMPLOYMENT IN THE CITY. Most discussions about Detroit's future to date have focused on land area and population. Yet if we compare Detroit with similar-sized cities, the number of jobs per resident is far more telling than the number of residents itself. Of the four cities closest in size to Detroit, only one has more residents, but all four have many more jobs and a higher ratio of jobs to residents. In fact, this is true for most American cities: only 5 of the top 100 cities have fewer jobs per resident than Detroit.

It is true that Detroit's dramatic loss of population will call for reconfiguration and repositioning of its infrastructure and land assets to create a new city form of diverse neighborhood types and land uses that are easier to serve, The key to fiscal sustainability and a better quality of life for Detroit is not simply higher population, although population increases would be welcome. **Increasing the ratio of jobs to residents will contribute to the financial stability of the city while creating economic opportunity for the city's residents.**

DETROIT'S ECONOMIC GROWTH MUST BE BASED ON FAIRNESS AND EQUITY. Detroit's diversifying economy should be developed toward job growth for a variety of skill demands and business types. This approach will not only enhance equity, but will also foster growth by tapping underutilized human capital, increasing local incomes and consumer demand, improving educational outcomes, and reducing fiscal, social, and human costs associated with poverty.[1] More than half of Detroit's current employment base comes from four economic pillars that are well suited to creating jobs for people of all skills and backgrounds: education and medical employment ("Eds and Meds"); digital and creative jobs; industrial employment (both traditional and new technologies, large-scale and artisanal, manufacture and processes); and local entrepreneurship.

Within each of these key employment "pillars", job opportunities and professional growth should be cultivated for people with a variety of educational backgrounds, skills, and interests. For example, in Eds and Meds, the innovative capacity of all workers— from medical staff, faculty, and researchers to maintenance, kitchen, and housekeeping staff—should be utilized and rewarded. In the small-scale industrial sector, and especially in the food sector, shared production spaces can offer low-cost options for local entrepreneurs and more broad-based ownership or sharing of business assets. Shared creative space is certainly vital to the information exchange and resource sharing necessary in the creative/digital fields, and can open up opportunities for training and career development, especially among youth and among adults seeking to start a second career.

A crucial step toward equitable job growth will also be the explicit recognition and dismantling of current barriers facing Detroit residents in terms of access to skills development and employment and entrepreneurship opportunities. In fact, those very barriers have forced many Detroiters into the informal economy as entrepreneurs, which in turn offers an opportunity to create new pathways to prosperity and job growth for an unknown number of sole proprietors who might one day be employers themselves. This is discussed in further detail in the Strategies section of this chapter.

Text Sources: 1) Pastor, Manuel, and Chris Benner. "Been Down So Long: Weak-Market Cities and Regional Equity." In Richard M. McGahey and Jennifer S. Vey, eds., *Retooling for Growth*. New York: American Assembly and Columbia University, 2008; Katherine S. Newman, James B. Knapp Dean of the Arts and Sciences, Johns Hopkins University, Testimony to the Senate Finance Committee, Hearing on "Drivers of Intergenerational Mobility and the Tax Code," July 10, 2012; Robert Weissbourd. Strengthening Communities for Regional Prosperity. The Living Cities Policy Series, 2006; Porter, Michael, Orson W. Watson, and Alvin Kwan. The Changing Models of Inner City Grocery Retailing. Initiative for a Competitive Inner City, 1998.

LOCATION QUOTIENT RANKING AMONG 100 LARGEST CITIES

Detroit's economy is already unique. Compared to other cities, Detroit's diverse economic base has an established foothold in traditional industrial activity and anchor institutions as well as substantial growth in new economy jobs.

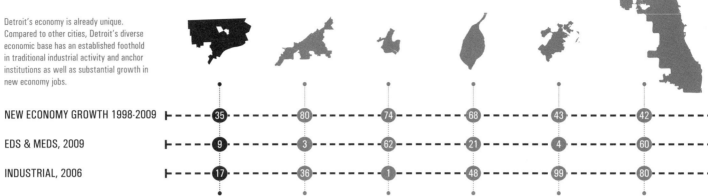

	DETROIT, MI	CLEVELAND, OH	NEWARK, NJ	ST LOUIS, MO	BOSTON, MA	CHICAGO, IL
NEW ECONOMY GROWTH 1998-2009	35	80	74	68	43	42
EDS & MEDS, 2009	9	3	62	21	4	60
INDUSTRIAL, 2006	17	36	1	48	99	80

Data Source: SICE; ICIC analysis

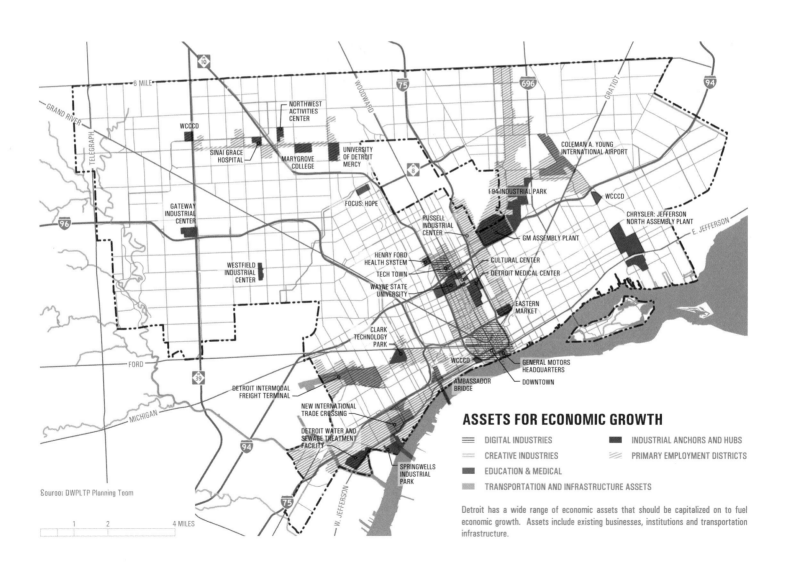

Source: DWPLTP Planning Team

ASSETS FOR ECONOMIC GROWTH

- DIGITAL INDUSTRIES
- CREATIVE INDUSTRIES
- EDUCATION & MEDICAL
- TRANSPORTATION AND INFRASTRUCTURE ASSETS
- INDUSTRIAL ANCHORS AND HUBS
- PRIMARY EMPLOYMENT DISTRICTS

Detroit has a wide range of economic assets that should be capitalized on to fuel economic growth. Assets include existing businesses, institutions and transportation infrastructure.

1.

2.

3 A CITY OF PHYSICALLY AND STRATEGICALLY ALIGNED ECONOMIC ASSETS

DETROIT'S ECONOMY DOES NOT REQUIRE ENTIRELY NEW ECONOMIC ASSETS, BUT THE PHYSICAL AND STRATEGIC ALIGNMENT OF EXISTING ONES. As in all successful cities, fostering economic strength and stability in Detroit will require a constant renewal and realignment of key business assets, education and workforce development, innovation potential, and infrastructure.

On the side of land use and physical assets, tools such as zoning, public land disposition, incentives, and specific strategies can be used to promote concentrated employment districts as focal points around which to pool public, private, and philanthropic investment. The implications will be far-reaching and have the potential to improve the cost structure, innovative capacity, and competitive position of the city's businesses in regional, national, and international markets. Important efforts to create districts of economic activity already exist, most notably in the food cluster around Eastern Market and the education and health-related clusters in Midtown. Existing efforts must be supported and expanded to include Detroit's most important traditional and emerging economic strengths.

Organizational linkages must also be strengthened and sustained among city government and neighborhoods, business support organizations, employers and employees, and businesses and their suppliers. Although too many key companies and organizations today are islands, physically, they have a strong interest in re-knitting the physical, social, and cultural fabric that made Detroit's economy great.

4 A LEADER IN URBAN INDUSTRIAL ACTIVITY

Across the country, many have come to realize the critical role of manufacturing activity in promoting and sustaining innovation, especially in clusters where product and process are tightly linked, such as high-end apparel and biotech.[2] Detroit has a unique combination of educational and medical institutions, information technology companies, low-cost industrial land, and an "industrial commons" that support manufacturing and industrial activity of all kinds. Detroit also has a skilled workforce, managers with operations experience, and broad design and engineering expertise among its residents. **With proactive and coordinated investment, Detroit can remain an innovative hub for production.**

In the food cluster, for example, Detroit has the assets and knowledge to lead in the design and production of urban farming tools. In the medical cluster, the Henry Ford Innovation Institute is focused on user-based innovation that translates insights from the city's medical practitioners into the next generation of surgical tools and medical devices. These are but two examples of the ways in which Detroit can build on its legacy of industrial activity, while creating new pathways to industrial and supporting jobs.

Text Source: 2) Gary P. Pisano and Willy C. Shih, "Does America Really Need Manufacturing?" *Harvard Business Review,* March 2012.

Image Sources: 1) Marvin Shaouni; 2) Paul Sancya/AP

3.

5 A CITY OF REGIONAL AND GLOBAL ECONOMIC ASSETS

Recently, the American automotive sector has revitalized, and the role of Southeast Michigan in global automotive research and development expanded. The automotive renaissance in the region is part of a larger story in which U.S. manufacturing has become more competitive globally. One of the country's most influential consultancies, Boston Consulting Group (BCG), recently estimated that due to improved competitiveness, the U.S. is likely to add between 2.5 and 5 million jobs in manufacturing and support industries by 2020.[3]

DETROIT HAS A DIVERSE BASE OF BUSINESSES, ORGANIZATIONS, AND INSTITUTIONS THAT ARE ESSENTIAL TO BUILDING AND MAINTAINING A COMPETITIVE EDGE FOR SOUTHEAST MICHIGAN IN THE 21ST CENTURY. Beginning more than a decade ago, many public, private, and philanthropic leaders recognized that economic decline in the city and region was not temporary but reflected a broader crisis in local economic assets and capabilities. These leaders and their organizations invested in the ideas, assets, institutions, and culture to enable growth in innovation-driven clusters like education and technology, while also remaking traditional economic clusters like food to better serve local needs. Huge investments were made in expanding the city's institutions and economy: The College for Creative Studies added major new buildings, an MFA program, and a high school; the Detroit Creative Corridor Center opened; Next Energy was founded; the education and medical institutions in Midtown became national models for maximizing local economic impact; Henry Ford Hospital opened an Innovation Institute to capture and commercialize the innovative capacity of medical practitioners; Wayne State University opened TechTown and announced a $93 million biotech hub; and a local son returned to Detroit with 7,000 workers and triggered a new wave of information technology growth in Downtown. Concurrently, local leaders remade traditional industries, including the Detroit Food Policy Council and Detroit Black Community Food Security's work in creating a vision for the national movement in food justice and food security issues. Local organizations such as New Economy Initiative and DEGC are working to promote local procurement and entrepreneurship opportunities across the city.

4.

5.

6 A CITY THAT SUPPORTS MINORITY BUSINESS ENTERPRISES

Business ownership shapes the location of opportunity and power in an economy: Business owners strongly influence organizational practices such as hiring, wage setting, and procurement and often serve in positions of civic and social leadership. One reason minority-owned business enterprises (MBEs) are so important to Detroit is that they are more likely to hire minority employees and utilize minority suppliers, thus increasing opportunity for a large number of Detroiters.[4]

Minorities in Detroit already account for 89% of the city's population; however, the firms they own account for only 15% of private company revenues. African-American-owned businesses account for 94% of the city's MBEs, yet few of these companies grow enough to hire even one employee: Only one in thirty African-American companies in the city has at least one employee compared to one in three white-owned businesses.

These numbers reflect the enormous challenges to the MBE community in Detroit (as well as its potential). In a comparison of 25 U.S. cities, Detroit ranked seventh in African-American self-employment per capita. **Strengthening business ownership in the city's largest population group is one of the best ways to grow businesses in the city.**

7 A CITY OF IMMEDIATE AND LONG-RANGING STRATEGIES FOR RESIDENT PROSPERITY

Although Detroit has an urgent need to support and develop high-quality education and skills to prosper in the 21st century, there is little evidence for the oft-stated claim that "Detroit can't fix its economy until it fixes K-12." **In fact, improving education and increasing economic opportunity are complementary strategies: providing economic opportunities for Detroit's adults will improve fiscal conditions in the city, support the academic performance of their children, and create the incentives for children and adults alike to invest in education and skills development.**

The dramatic downturn in the regional economy has curtailed opportunities for lower-skilled workers across the region. This opportunity gap must be addressed alongside the skills gap. In fact, the lack of job opportunities seems to have profoundly weakened the link between educational attainment and prosperity for Detroiters. Nationwide, high school graduation reduces the chance of living in poverty by 56%, and going on to earn a two-year degree reduces poverty by an additional 51%. Yet in Detroit, the corresponding reductions are much smaller (39% and 33%).

Strategies to combat the city's poverty must acknowledge the need for a dual approach. Public, private, and philanthropic priorities should support a concurrent approach to the creation of new job opportunities along with educational improvements.

Text Sources: 3) Boston Consulting Group, "Why America's Export Surge Is Just Beginning," September 12, 2012 and "U.S. Manufacturing Nears the Tipping Point: Which Industries, Why, and How Much?," March 22, 2012; 4) Based on Fairlie and Robb (2008)

Image Sources: 3) PAC Jeff Hall, Wikimedia Commons; 4) www.modeldmedia.com; 5) CNS Photo/ Jim West

ACCESS AND MOBILITY

61%
61% OF EMPLOYED DETROITERS WORK OUTSIDE THE CITY

21%
21.5% OF DETROITERS DO NOT HAVE ACCESS TO A PRIVATE VEHICLE[2]

30%
30% OF DETROIT JOBS ARE HELD BY DETROITERS

39%
39% OF EMPLOYED DETROITERS WORK WITHIN THE CITY[1]

70%
70% OF DETROIT JOBS ARE HELD BY COMMUTERS[3]

EDUCATION AND EMPLOYMENT

300K
300,000 NEW JOBS ARE PROJECTED FOR SOUTHEAST MICHIGAN BY 2040[4]

2%
DETROIT IS PROJECTED TO RECEIVE ONLY 2% OF THESE NEW REGIONAL JOBS[5]

27 JOBS PER 100 RESIDENTS
THERE ARE CURRENTLY 27 PRIVATE SECTOR JOBS WITHIN THE CITY PER 100 DETROIT RESIDENTS[6]

20% POVERTY
DETROITERS EXPERIENCE HIGH POVERTY RATES AT EVERY LEVEL OF EDUCATION. EVEN 20% OF TWO-YEAR DEGREE HOLDERS LIVE IN POVERTY[7]

68%
68% OF DETROITERS WITHOUT A HIGH SCHOOL DIPLOMA ARE UNEMPLOYED OR DO NOT PARTICIPATE IN THE LABOR FORCE[8]

RACE AND ECONOMIC STAKE

2% OTHER
6% HISPANIC
9% WHITE
83% AFRICAN AMERICAN

DETROIT'S POTENTIAL WORKFORCE DEMOGRAPHICS (AGES 25-64)[9]

85% $12.2B
WHITE

3% $450M
OTHER

12% $1.7B
AFRICAN AMERICAN

BREAK DOWN OF REVENUE AT ALL DETROIT FIRMS[10]

15%
15% OF DETROIT'S PRIVATE EMPLOYER FIRMS ARE OWNED BY AFRICAN AMERICANS[11]

23RD RANKED
DETROIT IS RANKED 23RD OUT OF 25 U.S. CITIES IN AFRICAN AMERICAN OWNERSHIP OF FIRMS WITH EMPLOYEES*

RANKED 8TH
IN A COMPARISON OF 25 U.S. CITIES, DETROIT RANKS 8TH IN TERMS OF AFRICAN AMERICAN BUSINESS OWNERSHIP RELATIVE TO THE SIZE OF BLACK/AFRICAN AMERICAN POPULATION*

*The 25 cities used to rank Detroit were picked based on variables including population size, minority concentration and geography. The 25 cities are: 1) Detroit, MI; 2) Birmingham, AL; 3) Baltimore, MD; 4) Memphis, TN; 5) New Orleans, LA; 6) Atlanta, GA; 7) Cleveland, OH; 8) Washington, D.C.; 9) St. Louis, MO; 10) Philadelphia, PA; 11) Charlotte, NC; 12) Chicago, IL; 13) Columbus, OH; 14) Indianapolis, IN; 15) New York, NY; 16) Boston, MA; 17) Houston, TX; 18) Miami, FL; 19) Fort Worth, TX; 20) Los Angeles, CA; 21) Austin, TX; 22) San Antonio, TX; 23) San Diego, CA; 24) Phoenix, AZ; 25) El Paso, TX
Sources: US Census 2010, 2007 Survey of Business Owners

REALITIES
THE STATE OF DETROIT'S ECONOMY

Detroit confronts major challenges to its revitalization, including issues with workforce preparedness and employment opportunities for Detroiters; the need to strengthen the performance of the city's companies, including small- and minority-owned companies; and the need to translate the city's available land and buildings into affordable, usable spaces that can accommodate growing companies and attract new ones to the city.

EDUCATIONAL ATTAINMENT. As in many areas that have historically relied on manufacturing to drive the economy, education levels among working-age Detroiters are well below the national average:

- 20% do not have a high school degree;
- 35% have a high school degree but no further training;
- 33% have a high school degree and at least some college; and
- 12% have a bachelor's degree.

The proportion of Detroit's population between the ages of 25 and 64 who do not have a high school degree is 60% higher than the U.S. rate of 13%, while the proportion of population holding a four-year degree is 60% lower than the average for the United States.

But education alone is not the only indicator of Detroit's workforce challenge: There is a stronger emphasis on education among Detroiters than is often assumed. Of those with a high school degree, 57% have at least some college, comparable to the rest of the United States (68%). Completion rates are lower than the national average, however: Among Detroiters with at least some college, only 42% have completed a two- or four-year degree compared to 64% across the United States.

Data Sources: 1) US Census 2010 Longitudinal Employer-Household Dynamics; 2) American Community Survey 2010 5-Year; 3) US Census 2010 Longitudinal Employer-Household Dynamics; 4,5) SEMCOG 2012; 6) Initiative for a Competitive Inner City (ICIC) State of Inner City Economies (SICE) database, US Census 2010; 7,8) American Community Survey 2010 5-Year, Integrated Public Use Microdata Series (IPUMS); 9) US Census 2010; 10) US Census 2010 Longitudinal Employer-Household Dynamics; 11) ICIC

LABOR FORCE PARTICIPATION. Among working-age residents in Detroit, labor force participation rates (LFPRs) are low relative to the rest of the region and the United States. In the rest of the region, the participation rate is 79%, nearly identical to the U.S. rate of 78%. If Detroit achieved national participation rates at each education level, about 38,000 additional Detroiters would be in the labor force and the city's overall participation rate would be 75%. The participation rate of Detroiters without a high school degree is low, but this group accounts for only a small portion of the adult population. The greatest opportunity for impact in labor force participation is among those with a high school degree and/or some college (but not a four-year degree), who account for two-thirds of working-age Detroiters. Consequently, if Detroiters without a high school degree participated in the labor force at national rates, the city's overall participation rate would increase from 65% to 68%; if Detroiters with a high school degree and/or some college matched national rates, the city's overall participation rate would increase from 65% to 72%, just below the regional average of 75%.

SCHOOL QUALITY. One oft-cited reason for poor labor force outcomes among Detroiters is the low quality of the city's public schools. Although Detroit's school system has some high performers like Cass Technical High School, Renaissance High School, and the Bates Academy, the majority of schools under-perform relative to those in neighboring school districts. The Michigan Department of Education's "Top-to-Bottom Ranking" of the state's schools shows that in terms of statewide percentile ranking, schools in the Detroit Public Schools district averaged in the 12th percentile. Detroit school performance is also weak by the standards of urban school districts across the United States. In the most recent Trial Urban District Assessment of reading, mathematics, science, and writing skills of 4th and 8th graders in 22 cities, Detroit ranked last, but did show improvement over the previous assessment.

WEAKENED INCENTIVES AND CONNECTIONS. In all groups in all parts of the country, labor force participation rates are sensitive to the costs and rewards of employment, including wages and commuting times. Detroiters of all education levels have wages that are lower than regional and national averages, with the largest gap for those workers without a high school degree and the smallest for the college-educated. This would help explain why labor force activity is so low among the city's least educated residents. Similarly, the challenges of using public transportation to commute to suburban job centers disproportionately harms less educated, lower-income individuals, who are less likely to own cars.

PERCENT OF DETROIT WORKERS WITH A HIGH SCHOOL DEGREE OR LESS BY TARGET CLUSTER: 2009

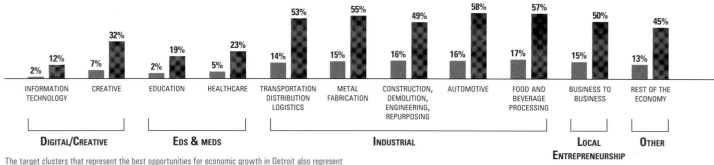

The target clusters that represent the best opportunities for economic growth in Detroit also represent opportunities to employ individuals with different education and skill levels. The importance of education and skills training can't be understated as businesses hire significantly higher percentages of people with a high school degree than without.

■ DETROITERS WITH LESS THAN A HIGH SCHOOL DEGREE
■ DETROITERS WITH LESS THAN OR EQUAL TO A HIGH SCHOOL DEGREE

Data Source: BLS, Employment Projections Program; ICIC

REGIONAL COMPETITION. Between 2002 and 2010, the proportion of Detroit jobs held by Detroit residents fell from 42% to 30%. Changing skill demands do not seem to be the main culprit: The share of city jobs held by Detroiters declined almost as much for jobs paying less than $1,250 per month as for jobs paying greater than $3,333 per month. What did change during those years was the region's unemployment rate. During the 2000s, the region lost more than 400,000 jobs, 100,000 more than any other U.S. region, suggesting that the region's jobs crisis has severely undercut opportunities for less educated workers.

The least educated workers faced competition for jobs from better-educated job-seekers: in the city but also across the region, those without high school degrees participate in the labor force at rates well below the national average. The gap between regional and national labor force participation narrows with increasing education levels until it more or less disappears for the region's residents who hold at least a bachelor's degree.

INEQUITY EVEN WITH EDUCATION. For all the discussion about the importance of education in addressing the city's poverty, the disconnect between educational attainment and prosperity is profound for many Detroiters. At all education levels, Detroiters suffer much higher poverty rates than peers in the region and country:

- 31% of Detroiters with a high school degree and no college live in poverty, compared to 13% of identically educated Americans;

- A Detroiter with a two-year college degree is 50% more likely to live in poverty than the average American with only a high school degree; and

- A Detroiter with a four-year college degree is more likely to live in poverty than the average American with a two-year degree.

In fact, if every working-age Detroiter invested in a two-year degree, the poverty rate in this group would still be almost 21%, higher than overall poverty rates in 70% of U.S. cities.

MINORITY BUSINESS OWNERSHIP HOLDS GREAT POTENTIAL. Although it is true that a large number of Detroiters have dropped out of the labor force, it is also true that many Detroiters have responded to the shortage of formal job opportunities by starting businesses, becoming self-employed, or moving into the informal economy. African-Americans in Detroit are 15% more likely than their counterparts nationally to be formally self-employed. Overall, there are about 50,000 people who are formally self-employed or own businesses with employees in Detroit, and perhaps as many as 100,000 more who are engaged in the informal economy, either as their only source of income or in addition to formal and/or self-employment.[5]

Minority residents are strongly represented in "nonemployer firms," which generally represent formally self-employed persons. These businesses pay taxes and are part of the formal economy but do not have the scale to hire employees. In Detroit, there are about 60 self-employed firms per 1,000 residents:

- 74% are owned by an African-American, 25% have white ownership, and 1% is owned by a member of another group.

- African-American-owned self-employed businesses average about $14,000 in sales, compared to $32,000 for white-owned self-employed businesses in Detroit.

- Among private businesses with employees, 15% are owned by African-Americans, 78% have white ownership, and the remaining 7% fall under primarily Asian ownership.

- White-owned businesses with employees average $2.4 million in revenues, African-American-owned businesses average $1.3 million in revenue, and businesses with "other" (primarily Asian) ownership average $600,000.

- When businesses with and without employees are included, the average revenue of all private businesses in Detroit is about $300,000; within this, the average for white-owned businesses is $780,000, for Asian businesses, $240,000, and for African-American-owned businesses about $50,000.

The gap between white- and black-owned businesses in Detroit can largely be explained by the set of industries in which Detroit's MBEs operate. MBEs across the United States tend to select less capital-intensive industries, and thus face lower overhead but also lower overall growth prospects than white-owned businesses.

PRIVATELY OWNED FIRMS WITH EMPLOYEES

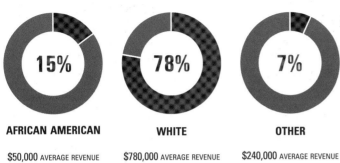

AFRICAN AMERICAN	WHITE	OTHER
15%	78%	7%
$50,000 AVERAGE REVENUE	$780,000 AVERAGE REVENUE	$240,000 AVERAGE REVENUE
1/6 OF CITY AVERAGE	2.6x OF CITY AVERAGE	4/5 OF CITY AVERAGE

Minority groups account for 89% of Detroit's population but only 17% of total private firm revenue.

Data Sources: SBO 2007; ICIC Analysis

81%

OF VACANT INDUSTRIAL PARCELS ARE LESS THAN 1 ACRE IN SIZE

6.8%

6.8% OF THE CITY'S VACANT INDUSTRIAL LAND IS PUBLICLY-OWNED

Data Source: Interface Studio, Detroit Industrial Land Inventory

The selected industries are often oriented toward local rather than regional, national, or international markets; they also have higher failure rates.[6] MBEs often select these industries because of their own work and business experience, but also because of lower levels of personal wealth than their white counterparts. MBEs also are more likely than their white counterparts to experience "real and perceived challenges in securing external capital."[7]

Increasing the number and performance of MBEs must address short-term strategies to increase demand for the goods and services provided by MBEs, and provide assistance with business development and finance options. Longer-term strategies must increase minority participation in high-growth, capital-intensive sectors and address structural barriers to capital access.

LAND IS DETROIT'S GREATEST—AND MOST CHALLENGING—ASSET. Land in Detroit is a potential asset for long-term economic development. Unlike in many U.S. cities, Detroit does not currently suffer from residential encroachment on job-producing land or face supply limitations that preclude growth in industrial sectors. However, the character, configuration, and spatial patterns of vacancy and neglect on formerly job-producing land represent a significant challenge to economic development in the city.

In 2010, vacancies accounted for 22% of Detroit's industrial land, a portion that has likely increased with the further decline in manufacturing activity. Many of these sites are located along industrial corridors that have ceased to be competitive and now sit derelict and empty, contributing to and aggravating surrounding neighborhood blight. Of the sites that are located in more active and vibrant industrial areas—corridors with a "critical mass" of industrial activity—a significant portion consists of small, isolated, inaccessible, or oddly-shaped parcels with very limited potential for viable industrial or commercial redevelopment. More than 95% of the vacant industrial parcels in the city's employment districts are less than one acre in size. The remaining parcels that are well-located and large enough to accommodate viable modern industrial development are often so blighted, contaminated, or in need of demolition that the anticipated costs can deter investment indefinitely.

The major challenge in addressing issues of blight and land assembly in the industrial areas is the patterns of ownership. Unlike in the city's residential areas, where there is significant public ownership of sites, the overwhelming majority of land in the industrial and commercial areas is privately held. Public ownership of vacant or

otherwise re-developable land in the industrial zones, for example, amounts to only 6.8% of the city's total industrial land supply, with most of this found in residential parcels in Delray and formerly residential sites around the I-94 Industrial Park. With so few opportunities to assemble property directly from public agencies, and limited resources to outright acquire private property, other strategies must be considered to stimulate more productive use of vacant and vastly underutilized, privately held, commercial and industrial sites. The depth and breadth of challenges stemming from the condition, location, and configuration of Detroit's job-producing lands will have to be met with a variety of strategies to improve the quality, availability, and productivity of private and public commercial and industrial land.

Text Sources: 5) By definition, the informal economy is very difficult to measure. One study estimates that in Los Angeles County, 9% to 29% of total employment is in the informal economy (Losby, et al., 2002). Using this range, the number of people employed in the informal economy in Detroit would be about 25,000 to 105,000. The estimated range is as wide as 3% to 4% of the U.S. workforce (Nightingale and Wandner, 2011). Lower-income areas tend to have higher levels of informal activity, so Detroit would likely be on the higher end of any estimate. SOURCES: Losby, Jan L., John F. Else, Marcia E. Kingslow, Elaine L. Edgcomb, Erica T. Malm, and Vivian Kao, "Informal Economy Literature Review," ISED Consulting and Research and The Aspen Institute, December 2002; Nightingale, Demetria Smith, and Stephen A. Wandner, "Informal and Nonstandard Employment in the United States: Implications for Low-Income Working Families," The Urban Institute, Brief 20, August 2011.

6,7) Timothy Bates, "Entrepreneur Human Capital Endowments and Minority Business Viability," 1985; Fairlie and Robb, 2008, p 134. Teresa Lynch and Lois Rho, "Capital Availability in Inner Cities: What Role for Federal Policy?" Presented at the "Small Business and Entrepreneurship during an Economic Recovery Conference," Washington, D.C., November 9-10, 2011.

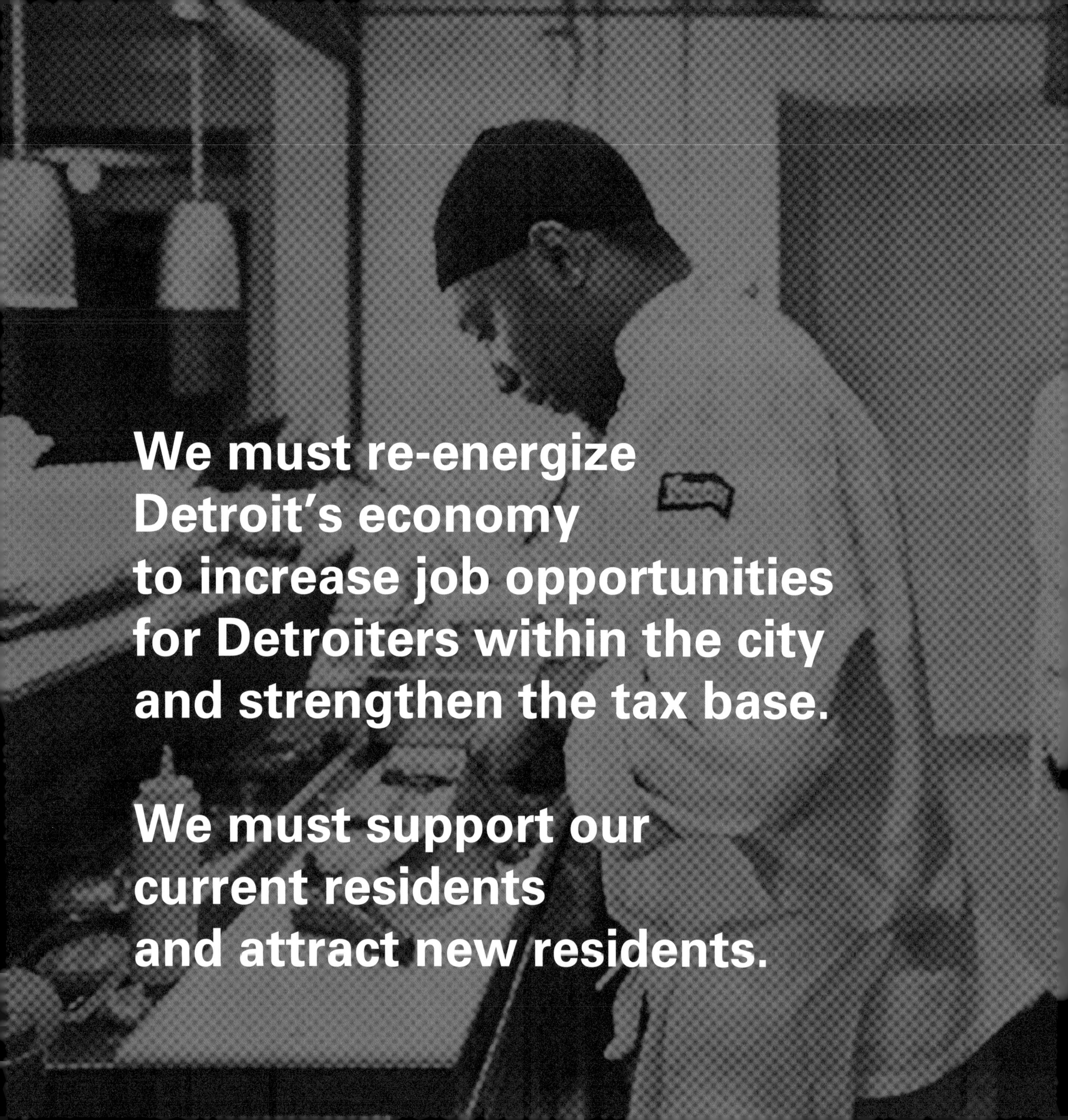

We must re-energize
Detroit's economy
to increase job opportunities
for Detroiters within the city
and strengthen the tax base.

We must support our
current residents
and attract new residents.

IMPERATIVES AND QUALITY OF BUSINESS
ECONOMIC GROWTH ACTIONS AND IMPACT

Detroit has been losing population and employment for decades, and years of fiscal challenges have hollowed out local government capacity. Detroit today provides a challenging business environment marred by high levels of blight, security issues, and significant gaps in local government services. Potential buyers driving to inspect available industrial sites are often deterred by the visible levels of blight before they have even arrived at the property. These factors often frustrate existing business owners and employees, increase costs, and deter investment. Businesses, like residents, desire a secure, attractive environment and a larger, vibrant business community. For Detroit to thrive as a city, the quality of the business environment must be considered as important as the quality of residential life. This will require improvements in the following areas:

 COST: The operating cost environment for businesses compared to regional and peer cities.

 NETWORK: Proximity to related businesses, suppliers, and business services are a key ingredient in location decisions and operating success.

 INFORMATION: There are many information gaps that need to be filled to align businesses with workforce, incentives, and public services.

 SERVICES: Effective and reliable government services are needed to support existing and new businesses.

 ACCESS: Detroit has a legacy of quality, and diverse infrastructure. Strategic improvements are needed to ensure efficient access via highway, rail, ports, and local streets.

 REGULATIONS: Permitting, zoning, and other codes need to be reconfigured to support local job and business growth.

 SAFETY: Safety and security of people and buildings is often cited as a key concern by business owners.

WHAT WE LEARNED FROM CIVIC ENGAGEMENT FEEDBACK

- Survey respondents ranked the "RE-ENERGIZE DETROIT'S ECONOMY" as the most important of the 12 Imperatives
- Survey respondents ranked EDUCATION as the most important investment for Detroit's future
- Top economic strategies recorded from DWP participants included:
  - SUPPORT SMALL BUSINESSES - especially small, new, and resident-owned businesses
  - IMPROVE RESIDENTS' WORKFORCE READINESS for better, well-paying jobs in the future

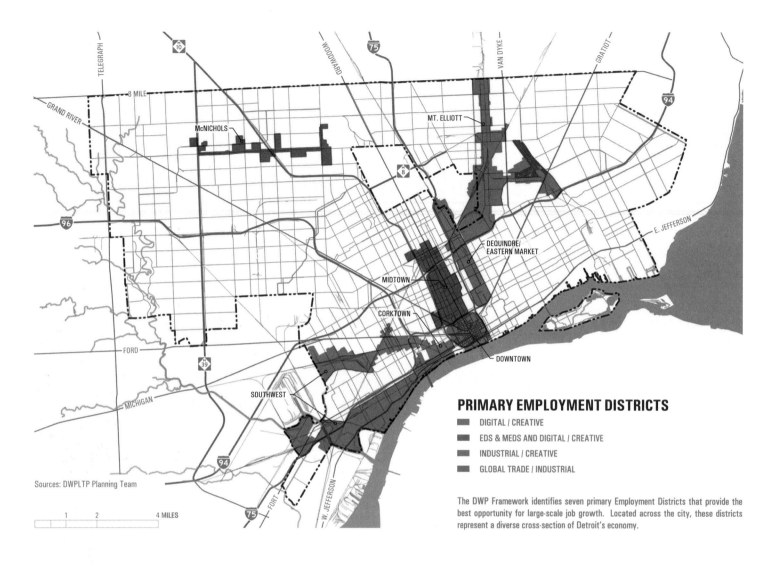

PRIMARY EMPLOYMENT DISTRICTS

- DIGITAL / CREATIVE
- EDS & MEDS AND DIGITAL / CREATIVE
- INDUSTRIAL / CREATIVE
- GLOBAL TRADE / INDUSTRIAL

The DWP Framework identifies seven primary Employment Districts that provide the best opportunity for large-scale job growth. Located across the city, these districts represent a diverse cross-section of Detroit's economy.

Sources: DWPLTP Planning Team

PRIMARY EMPLOYMENT DISTRICT DESCRIPTIONS AND LOCATIONS			
DIGITAL / CREATIVE	**EDS & MEDS / DIGITAL AND CREATIVE**	**INDUSTRIAL / CREATIVE**	**GLOBAL TRADE / INDUSTRIAL**
DESCRIPTION Districts characterized by economic opportunities in information technology and creative businesses such as design & advertising.	Districts characterized by economic opportunities in education, healthcare, research, technology and creative enterprises.	Districts characterized by economic opportunities in industrial activity like food processing and automotive manufacturing as well as creative enterprises and local entrepreneurship.	Districts characterized by economic opportunities in global industrial activity including automotive, metals and logistics.
LOCATIONS Downtown	Midtown McNichols	Dequindre/Eastern Market Corktown	Southwest Mt. Elliott

STRATEGIES AND IMPLEMENTATION
PLANS FOR ACTION

The Strategic Framework proposes five strategies to grow an equitable economy for Detroit:

- Support the Four Key Economic Growth Pillars that have already demonstrated promising job growth: education and medical employment ("Eds and Meds"), digital and creative jobs, industrial employment (both traditional and new technologies, large-scale and artisanal, manufacture, and processes), and local entrepreneurship.

- Use place-based strategies to create core investment and employment corridors, focusing on seven employment districts where job growth is already occurring;

- Encourage local entrepreneurship and minority-owned business;

- Improve education and skills development; and

- Transform the city's land into an economic asset.

Each strategy is designed to address specific challenges but also to reinforce the other four strategies. These strategies are also designed to be flexible to actual economic conditions and changing needs in the city and region, and thus are not tied to specific horizons or timelines. They are consistent, however, with the Strategic Framework's vision for stabilization and transformation over a period of 20 to 50 years. Detroit's public, private, civic and philanthropic stakeholders should align their investments and programmatic initiatives with the broader Framework and with each other's objectives.

The core mechanism for this coordination is strengthening seven existing employment districts in the city. Information from land surveys, data on the city's economy, and interviews with key stakeholders formed the basis for mapping these districts. The unique characteristics of each district are identified not only for their economic potential, but for the diverse opportunities each offers to employ people with a broad range of interests and skills.

The Framework recommends:

- Formalizing the importance of these districts through land use and zoning changes; and

- Encouraging public, private, and philanthropic investments in infrastructure and real estate to support these districts.

The strategies also emphasize strengthening the city's minority business community through expanded opportunities for business ownership and growth. Finally, the plan attempts to create linkages between education and training and opportunities to utilize newly developed skills and address skills gaps and opportunity gaps together, efficiently and fairly.

The success of the plan will rest on the capacity of the strategies to unlock the vast potential of the city's land assets. Through preferential zoning, targeted infrastructure investments, attraction of new capital into the city, and innovative approaches to address under-utilization of land, the strategy aims to increase the value of and investments in the city's highest-potential jobs-producing land. If successful, the city's available land can become its greatest economic asset.

"When we lost the jobs and saw the increase in crime, that sense of common purpose/community was lost."

Seniors Working Session, 2/15/2012

"Create and cultivate a more dense, active vibrant city from which businesses can flourish and grow."

Entrepreneurs Summit

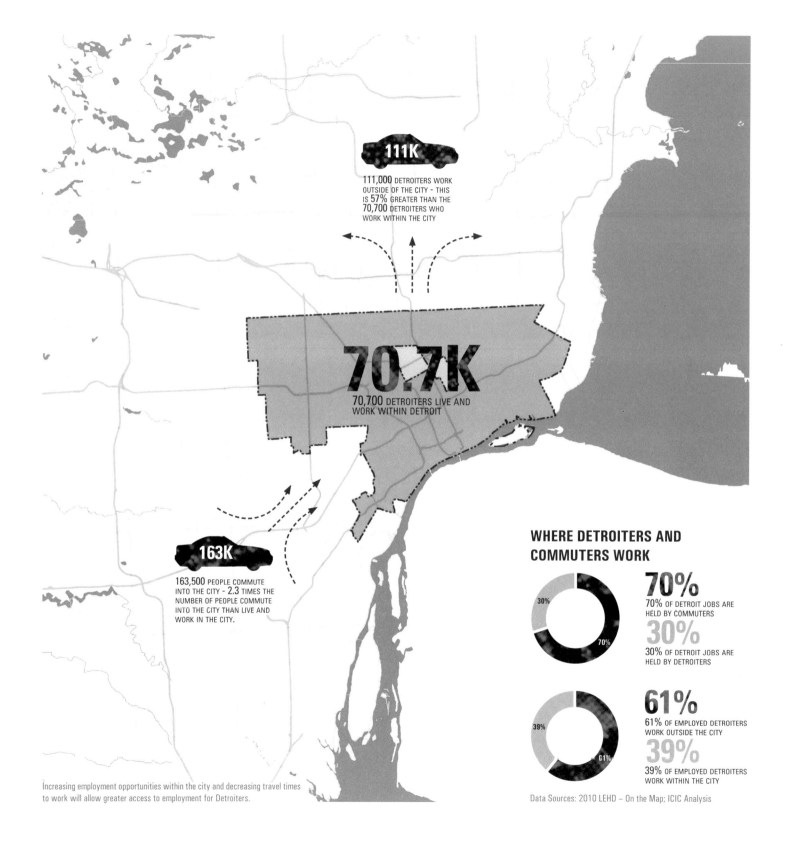

111K

111,000 DETROITERS WORK OUTSIDE OF THE CITY - THIS IS **57%** GREATER THAN THE 70,700 DETROITERS WHO WORK WITHIN THE CITY

70.7K

70,700 DETROITERS LIVE AND WORK WITHIN DETROIT

163K

163,500 PEOPLE COMMUTE INTO THE CITY - **2.3** TIMES THE NUMBER OF PEOPLE COMMUTE INTO THE CITY THAN LIVE AND WORK IN THE CITY.

WHERE DETROITERS AND COMMUTERS WORK

30%

70%

70%
70% OF DETROIT JOBS ARE HELD BY COMMUTERS

30%
30% OF DETROIT JOBS ARE HELD BY DETROITERS

39%

61%

61%
61% OF EMPLOYED DETROITERS WORK OUTSIDE THE CITY

39%
39% OF EMPLOYED DETROITERS WORK WITHIN THE CITY

Increasing employment opportunities within the city and decreasing travel times to work will allow greater access to employment for Detroiters.

Data Sources: 2010 LEHD – On the Map; ICIC Analysis

SEVEN TRANSFORMATIVE IDEAS : FIVE IMPLEMENTATION STRATEGIES

A SUPPORT FOUR KEY ECONOMIC PILLARS

B USE A PLACE-BASED STRATEGY FOR GROWTH

51

A strategy that targets the sectors of the economy that are most likely to generate broad-based economic growth will allow the public, private, and philanthropic sectors to align strategies and resources around economic growth "pillars" that can create jobs, foster economic opportunity and social equity, and best utilize the city's land assets. These opportunities fall into four broad categories: Education and Medical; Industrial; Digital/Creative; and Local Entrepreneurship.

The most recent 30-year regional employment forecast for Detroit, developed by the Southeast Michigan Council of Governments (SEMCOG), shows some employment growth in Detroit between 2010 and 2015, followed by a leveling off after 2015. For the entire 2010-2040 period, SEMCOG projects the entire Southeast Michigan regional economy will add 300,000 net new jobs, of which just over 7,000 will land in the City of Detroit. Although these projections provide an important sightline into the dynamics of the city's and region's economies, and can be used as a baseline for understanding future job growth, they suffer from an unavoidable flaw: They were developed assuming "business as usual."

The "business as usual" projections do not account for or anticipate the potential impact of aligning future investments with existing major civic investments in the four pillar economic areas. Coupled with critical changes in the city's productive landscape— including the resurgence of the downtown district and the emergence of the city as a hub for digital and creative businesses—these investments indicate that continued, intentional investment in the Four Key Economic Growth Pillars will yield potent benefits.

Seven specific employment districts have the greatest potential to unleash large-scale job creation in Detroit. These districts will promote a deliberate spatial pattern to business activity, generate multiple benefits to the economy, and help alleviate critical fiscal and social issues in the city. Reinvesting in specific employment districts will create the scale required for efficient investments in infrastructure and services; allow development of effective strategies for building demolition and land assembly; and create dense employment nodes that can facilitate transportation connections between Detroit residents and businesses, an issue that currently plagues the least-advantaged Detroiters but also employers who would benefit from a larger labor pool with more reliable transportation options. This concept will have a secondary (but critical) effect of raising property values in the employment districts, thus reducing the required subsidy for new construction and creating conditions to support private real estate activity.

These efforts will rely on an alignment among all levels of government (city, state, federal), the private sector, and the philanthropic community. Many in the private sector have voiced support for concentrating economic activity, with the understanding that it will increase the feasibility and efficiency of private-sector attempts to address shortcomings in the existing operating environment. Some private companies already pool resources to fund shared security and emergency services. Concentrating activity would make these investments more efficient and could create conditions for private-public-philanthropic partnerships to address other critical issues like transportation linkages between residents and employment opportunities. To help target resources and develop effective infrastructure, land use, and worker-support policies, each employment district will require a menu of strategies and investments tailored to the opportunities they present.

IMPLEMENTATION ACTIONS

1 Align cluster strategies with the Detroit Strategic Framework.

2 Establish cluster-based collaboration with labor market intermediaries.

IMPLEMENTATION ACTIONS

1 Align public, private, and philanthropic investments in employment districts.

2 Develop detailed action plans for primary employment districts.

3 Encourage industrial business improvement districts (IBIDS).

4 Become a national leader in green industrial districts.

THE ECONOMIC GROWTH ELEMENT : THE EQUITABLE CITY

C — ENCOURAGE LOCAL ENTREPRENEURSHIP AND MINORITY BUSINESS PARTICIPATION

As many Detroit leaders have recognized, growing the base of the city's entrepreneurs is a great opportunity for employment and wealth creation. Opportunities for the self-employed and small businesses are likely to increase over time: Nationally, employment growth has been fastest in those parts of the economy that serve local markets rather than national and international ("traded") markets. These opportunities will grow as consumers turn increasingly to local products and larger national and international companies continue to outsource secondary functions, such as building and facilities maintenance. These are significant but often overlooked opportunities. For example, the Local Business Services cluster ("Local B2B") in Detroit employs about 25,000 people (including self-employed) and could employ thousands more if local demand for these services was met by Detroit-based companies. The opportunities that exist in Detroit today can support different forms of enterprise, self-employment, small business ownership, and scaling of existing businesses.

The local business clusters are also a good opportunity to diversify the city's base of businesses. Many of the opportunities in the local clusters do not require large amounts of start-up capital, yet offer proximity to a large and broad base of customers. Moreover, some of the infrastructure to support these initiatives has already been built. The Midtown educational and medical institutions are national leaders in identifying opportunities for local suppliers, and DEGC has started a multi-year Local B2B initiative to increase local opportunities in this cluster. Broadening and deepening existing efforts and identifying new opportunities could lead to the creation of thousands of jobs in the city.

IMPLEMENTATION ACTIONS

1. Promote short-term approaches to increase the number and success of MBEs and DBEs in the City.
2. Support the development of low-cost, shared spaces for clusters with high levels of self employment.
3. Provide young Detroiters with exposure to and experience in Digital / Creative and other new economy clusters.
4. Develop a comprehensive long-term strategy to increase and strengthen the City's MBEs.

D — IMPROVE SKILLS AND SUPPORT EDUCATION REFORM

Skills building and education reform are key factors driving economic growth in Detroit. Even more important, they shape opportunity, incomes, and quality of life for Detroiters. Although the Framework does not discuss K-12 reform, the strategies here will complement K-12 improvement in the city's public schools by increasing high school graduation rates and improving the value of two-year degrees held by Detroiters; better linking the needs of employers with workforce training investments, a direction already underway among the city's workforce training providers and community colleges; increasing training opportunities for degreed Detroiters already in the workforce; developing strategies to address challenges faced by African American high school graduates nationally in securing full-time employment opportunities;[8] and in general, increasing overall opportunities for Detroiters by better linking residents to Detroit jobs as well as overcoming challenges with physical access to workforce opportunities by better aligning employment and training locations with residential areas in the city.

This approach attempts to increase the opportunities and means for Detroiters to improve their education and skills levels, then reward these investments with job opportunities, career paths, and higher wages. The approach recognizes that education and skills are the primary determinants of economic quality of life and must be matched with opportunities to utilize these skills and be rewarded.

IMPLEMENTATION ACTIONS

1. "Hire Detroit": Strengthen local hiring practices.
2. Link workforce investments to transportation.
3. Coordinate workforce development best practices.
4. Revitalize incumbent workforce training.
5. Expand public-private partnerships for workforce development.
6. Commission a study to identify levers to improve graduation rates and poor labor market outcomes of Detroiters.

Text Source: 8) Margaret Simms and Marla McDaniel, "The Black-White Jobless Gap," *Philadelphia Inquirer*, September 5, 2010.

E LAND REGULATIONS, TRANSACTIONS, AND ENVIRONMENTAL ACTIONS

The condition, location, and configuration of Detroit's job-producing land presents many challenges that are critical to address in order to generate economic activity and jobs for all Detroiters. The regulation of land in employment districts can have far-reaching impacts, including blight reduction, improved safety, and ultimately a surge in private investment.

A critical opportunity lies in developing and popularizing organizational and funding mechanisms for "clean and safe" programs to dramatically improve the character and security of Detroit's industrial and commercial zones and employment centers. Perception is reality, so focusing on the look and feel of key employment areas is essential to their success. Branding and character campaigns can also dramatically improve the allure of certain areas to specific economic clusters, while conceptual site and district planning exercises can help brokers and developers to concretely envision the potential of an area and plan for land assembly as appropriate. In addition, attention to the natural environment will create modern and green employment districts that improve the health of workers and nearby residents.

IMPLEMENTATION ACTIONS

1 Create an industrial side-lot program.

2 Create a priority permitting process for employment districts.

3 Focus on land banking industrial and commercial property.

4 Identify alternative capital sources for real estate development.

5 Articulate a reverse change-of-use policy.

6 Create master-planned industrial hubs.

7 Address underutilization of industrial building space and land.

8 Address weaknesses in the local brokerage sector.

CIVIC ENGAGEMENT FEEDBACK AND PUBLIC PERCEPTIONS

- Ensure economic development improves RESIDENTS' quality of life - BEYOND PROSPERITY AND INCOME ALONE

- Target industries that will provide jobs and also improve quality of life throughout the city: recycling, deconstruction, retrofitting/rehabbing/weatherization, senior care & services, urban agriculture, clean/sustainable energy (solar, geothermal, wind)

"While everybody is looking at Detroit today and saying, 'Oh, thank God we are not Detroit,' I say many people in America are going to wake up 10 years from now surprised that Detroit is rewriting the new chapter of what an American city looks like."

Omar Blaik, Urban Development Expert

"If this strategy includes reaching into the communities, recruiting the residents who have the skills and training those who don't, then it will contribute."

Maria, Economic Growth Open House, 8/7/2012

"Focus on providing services and products for the needs [of] under resourced families. 1) Agriculture to provide food products. 2) Construction for low-cost efficient home ownership. 3) Deconstruction and reuse of materials from homes."

Jeff, Economic Growth Open House, 8/7/2012

"This strategy [continuing to grow and support four key economic growth pillars] builds upon existing industries that current and aspiring Detroiters are familiar with, yet also allows for expansion and innovation."

Angie, Economic Growth Open House, 8/7/2012

"Provide 'turn-key' start up food production and processing opportunities and housing opportunities that entrepreneurs could lease if successful."

Economic Growth Open House, 8/7/2012

KEY ECONOMIC GROWTH CLUSTER	CURRENT EMPLOYMENT*	PROJECTED GROWTH (2011-2020)	REPRESENTATIVE JOBS
LOCAL ENTREPRENEURSHIP: Local Business to Business (B2B)	23,000	13%	Accounting, landscaping, facilities maintenance, short haul trucking, wholesale activities, recruiting, and delivery
TARGET INDUSTRIAL: Automotive Food and Beverage (F&B) Metal Fabrication (MF) Transportation, Distribution and Repair (TDL) Construction, Demolition, Engineering and Repurposing (CDER)	32,000	13%	Assembly, fabrication, engineering, processing, packaging, trucking, rail operation, construction trades, management
DIGITAL / CREATIVE: Digital Industries (DI) Creative Industries (CI)	15,000	9%	Programming, engineering, industrial design, IT repair, web services, fashion, graphic design, arts
EDUCATION & MEDICAL: Education Healthcare	59,000	13%	Teaching, administration, medical services, research, vocational training, dentistry, medical manufacturing
PUBLIC ADMINISTRATION AND OTHER NON-PRIVATE EMPLOYMENT	49,000	N/A	
OTHER: Retail Real Estate Finance	100,000	16%	Retail management and sales, stocking, headquarters activity, public service, nonprofit management

*Includes private, non-private, and self-employment
Table Sources: Estimated by project team based on QWI, LEHD – On the Map, NETS, and Census Bureau Nonemployer Statistics, and BLS employment projections

---

FOUR KEY ECONOMIC GROWTH PILLARS
THE IMPORTANCE OF THE FOUR ECONOMIC PILLARS

THE ECONOMIC GROWTH ELEMENT : THE EQUITABLE CITY

To provide a broader picture for Detroit's economic growth, the Framework relies on three sets of 20-year scenarios for the city's employment. The first scenario directly borrows SEMCOG's projections for Detroit, resulting in total city job growth of 1.5% over 20 years. The second scenario applies SEMCOG's growth rates for Wayne County to Detroit, resulting in about 4% job growth over the period. The third scenario applies projected U.S. growth rates to the city of Detroit, resulting in almost 20% job growth over 20 years, the equivalent of about 50,000 new jobs in the city. Just as important, in this scenario, job growth in the city keeps pace with that in the region and contributes to a more vibrant regional economy.

LOCAL ENTREPRENEURSHIP includes a range of potential transformative agendas including formalizing the informal sector; improving the economic lives of the self-employed by increasing their net wages and/or helping them to transition from self-employed to small business owner; and aiding in business creation and expansion for Detroit's entrepreneurs and would-be entrepreneurs. One of the largest opportunities for entrepreneurs is in Local Business Services, i.e., "Local B2B," a broad category that captures the opportunity for small- and mid-sized local businesses to provide goods and services to other, usually larger businesses. Local B2B firms perform professional and support services like accounting, printing, and employee recruiting; local logistical services like short-haul trucking and courier services; and facilities management functions including security, janitorial, and landscaping services. Local B2B companies can be successful at many scales, including sole proprietorships and very small companies. There is a tremendous opportunity in this cluster today—Detroit currently has a Local B2B "gap" of about 10,000 jobs that could be supported by existing activity—and the cluster is expected to grow all across the United States in the next decade.

EDUCATION AND MEDICAL, also known as "Eds and Meds" or the "anchor institutions", includes hospitals, health clinics, and health-related manufacturing like medical devices, as well as universities, community colleges, and some research organizations. Together, these organizations employ 50,000 people in Detroit, with concentrations of activity in the Midtown area and in the northwest around McNichols Road. In the city of Detroit, hospitals make up approximately 60% of the employment in Eds and Meds. Henry Ford Hospital is the largest with more than 10,000 employees. Detroit's colleges, universities, and professional schools employ over 8,000 while educating 65,000 people per year. In addition, many of Michigan's major universities now have Detroit offices or programs. Health-related organizations like home health care services and outpatient clinics also create large numbers of jobs.

INDUSTRIAL includes those clusters in which processing, assembly, manufacturing, repair, or distribution of physical goods is a central activity. A core set of industrial clusters is thought to drive to Detroit's current and future economy: automotive; construction/demolition/engineering/repurposing (CDER); food; metals and machinery; and transportation, distribution, and logistics (TDL). The physical transformation of the city will spur significant job and business growth in the CDER cluster and create additional opportunity in the food cluster as more land becomes available for productive use. Together, companies in these clusters employ 27,000 people in industrial activity in the city and thousands more in non-industrial positions. Many jobs in the industrial clusters do not require high levels of formal education but do pay above-average wages. There are three primary industrial areas—Dequindre/ Eastern Market, Mt. Elliott, and Southwest—and multiple secondary industrial areas.

DIGITAL/CREATIVE includes companies in Information Technology (IT) but more broadly, companies that use web-based technologies and platforms to deliver service. The Digital clusters are centered around a few large downtown companies that specialize in IT outsourcing for large corporate clients (GalaxE, Strategic Staffing Solutions, VisionIT) but also Quicken, a mortgage lending company that revolutionized the use of on-line platforms in consumer lending; and Crain Communications, which makes broad use of digital media. The downtown New Economy cluster is part of a larger regional cluster that includes the IT divisions of global companies like General Motors and General Electric. Although still small relative to its potential, Detroit has one of the fastest-growing IT clusters in the country and is a key reason why the Detroit metro area led the United States in tech-related job growth in 2010. Detroit's creative cluster, which specializes in areas like design, advertising, and talent management, can be found in every part of the city but is most highly concentrated along the so-called Creative Corridor and in Northwest around McNichols Road.

DETROIT AS A PERCENTAGE OF REGIONAL EMPLOYMENT

14% REGIONAL EMPLOYMENT

■ DETROIT ■ SOUTHEAST MICHIGAN

DETROIT'S EMPLOYMENT CLUSTERS

30% FOOD INDUSTRY

29% EDUCATION

22% HEALTHCARE

17% CREATIVE INDUSTRY

■ DETROIT ■ SOUTHEAST MICHIGAN

Data Source: Quarterly Workforce Indicators (QWI), 2011

REGIONAL AUTO ASSEMBLY

ORION ASSEMBLY

STERLING HEIGHTS ASSEMBLY

WARREN TRUCK

JEFFERSON NORTH ASSEMBLY

DEARBORN TRUCK

WINDSOR ASSEMBLY

MICHIGAN ASSEMBLY

WOODHAVEN STAMPING

AUTO ALLIANCE INTERNATIONAL

3.5   7   14 MILES

REGIONAL AUTO ASSEMBLY

AUTO ASSEMBLY PLANTS ◉

DETROIT

WAYNE COUNTY

COUNTY BOUNDARIES – –

Source: Interface Studio

Detroit has been and continues to be the center of the industrial network in Southeast Michigan. The geographic location of the city at the center of the region and a larger international trade hub is a strategic asset that can be leveraged to revitalize Detroit's economy and increase opportunities for the city's residents.

DETROIT POPULATION / NATIONAL INSTITUTES OF HEALTH (NIH) GRANTS

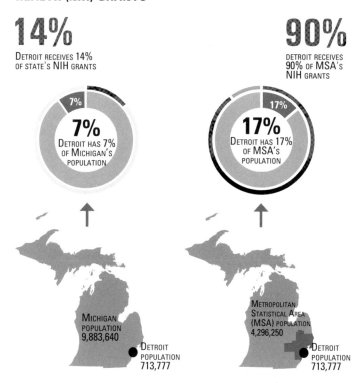

14%
DETROIT RECEIVES 14% OF STATE'S NIH GRANTS

90%
DETROIT RECEIVES 90% OF MSA'S NIH GRANTS

7%

7%
DETROIT HAS 7% OF MICHIGAN'S POPULATION

17%

17%
DETROIT HAS 17% OF MSA'S POPULATION

MICHIGAN POPULATION 9,883,640

DETROIT POPULATION 713,777

METROPOLITAN STATISTICAL AREA (MSA) POPULATION 4,296,250

DETROIT POPULATION 713,777

Data Sources: US Census 2010; National Institute of Health, Research Portfolio Online Reporting Tools; ICIC Analysis

Due to the strength of institutions in Detroit, the city receives a large proportion of the state's NIH Grants. This puts Detroit at the center of medical research for the Region with the city receiving 90 percent of grants by NIH in the metro area.

FOUR KEY ECONOMIC GROWTH PILLARS: STRATEGIES

A.1 ALIGN CLUSTER STRATEGIES WITH THE STRATEGIC FRAMEWORK

The city and regional economies are loosely organized into clusters with strong, but not always coordinated, local and regional intermediaries in the education, medical, creative, digital and food clusters; as well as some coordination of the traditional industrial clusters. This diverse set of organizations should create new strategies, or update existing ones, to reflect the priorities and actions in the Detroit Strategic Framework, which will the space for cooperation within and across clusters on common issues like workforce training, transportation, and security. Cluster organization and strategy development are perhaps the key mechanism for identifying areas of cooperation and investment that mutually benefit the city and regional economies and create strong and durable linkages between city and regional stakeholders.

Given the current citywide shortage of available, turnkey, low-cost space, each cluster strategy should include a real estate component that identifies real estate options, including shared-space options, for cluster companies and the self-employed. In addition, each cluster strategy should identify a portfolio of capital options for funding necessary real estate investments and business development and growth. In short, cluster leaders should look to cooperate with traditional and non-traditional capital sources to align resources with growth clusters and activities. Finally, each cluster strategy should outline a comprehensive approach for inclusion that ensures low-income and minority populations participate in and benefit from cluster growth.

A.2 ESTABLISH COLLABORATION WITH LABOR MARKET INTERMEDIARIES IN EACH ECONOMIC CLUSTER

The profound changes in city and regional labor markets have been accompanied by a change in the workforce infrastructure and the role of various intermediaries. One of the key changes is the growing importance of temp agencies in identifying and placing potential workers. Temp agencies' role in placing workers in manufacturing and technology-related firms has expanded greatly in Detroit and nationally. Today, employers utilize temp agencies to screen for new hires that produce value in a short window of time. As such, cluster leaders should coordinate and create linkages between labor market intermediaries and the private sector in order to develop a Detroit labor pool that can produce short- and long-term value for companies. Detroit residents' placement into jobs will be enhanced through tighter linkages between temp agencies and traditional training intermediaries, and between the large suburban temp agencies looking for workers and the city residents looking for jobs.

IMPLEMENTATION ACTIONS

1   Align cluster strategies with the Detroit Strategic Framework.

2   Establish cluster-based collaboration with labor market intermediaries.

	DETROIT ECONOMIC ANCHORS	BUSINESS STRENGTH		LAND OPPORTUNITY[3]		
		2010 ESTIMATED NUMBER OF BUSINESSES[1]	2010 ESTIMATED EMPLOYMENT[2]	VACANT (ACRES)	UNDER-UTILIZED (ACRES)	JOB CAPACITY AT VACANT SITES > 1 ACRE
INDUSTRIAL — SOUTHWEST	Detroit Water and Sewerage, Detroit Intermodal Freight Terminal, Ambassador Bridge and Customs Complex Marathon Refinery	850	9,100	405	588	4,500
INDUSTRIAL — MT. ELLIOT	GM Detroit Hamtramck Assembly Plant, I-94 Industrial Park, Detroit Chassis, Chrysler Axle, Chrysler Tool & Die, Cassens Transport	1,700	10,000	423	181	3,900
INDUSTRIAL / NEW ECONOMY — E. MARKET	Eastern Market, Russell Industrial Complex, Greater Detroit Resource Recovery Facility, Pepsi Bottling, Wolverine Packing	650	4,400	307	42	4,600
INDUSTRIAL / NEW ECONOMY — CORKTOWN	DHL, Michigan Avenue retail, Ponyride, UPS	750	2,600	124	8	1,600*
DIGITAL / CREATIVE — DOWNTOWN	Quicken Loans/Bedrock, Renaissance Center, Comerica Park, Ford Field, MGM Grand, Cobo Hall, Riverfront, Municipal Center, Compuware, Blue Cross Blue Shield, GM Headquarters, DTE Energy, Greektown, Olympia Entertainment	7,150	61,400	N/A**	N/A**	N/A**
EDUCATION AND MEDICAL — MIDTOWN	Wayne State University, Tech Town, Henry Ford Health System, Detroit Medical Center, College for Creative Studies	3,400	50,900	N/A**	N/A**	N/A**
EDUCATION AND MEDICAL — McNICHOLS	Sinai Grace Hospital, WCCCD, Marygrove College, University of Detroit Mercy, Livernois Avenue retail	1,900	5,500	N/A**	N/A**	N/A**
INDUSTRIAL — SECONDARY	Legacy businesses in each district	1,850	11,600	683	372	8,200

Notes: *Corktown statistic is only for the redevelopment of industrial vacant land.
**Survey data on vacancies and underutilized sites are not available.

Table Sources: 1) NETS 2010 Estimates
2) Private sector employment from QWI; non-private employment from LEHD—On the Map. Private sector employment was apportioned to districts using NETS data for 2010.
3) Interface Studio, Detroit Industrial Land Use Inventory

USE A PLACE-BASED STRATEGY FOR GROWTH INVESTING IN EMPLOYMENT DISTRICTS B

THE ECONOMIC GROWTH ELEMENT : THE EQUITABLE CITY

Detroit was built around a diverse and distributed collection of employment corridors. Concentrations of large institutions, including universities and medical centers, formed in Midtown and along McNichols Road (6 Mile); and Downtown was built as a hub for business and entertainment. Industrial uses, long associated with Detroit's innovative spirit, were developed alongside the city's infrastructure networks (notably rail, the Port and, more recently, highways). Some formerly active areas of industrial employment have indeed experienced the worst of the city's decline. Fortunately, other areas remain strong today and provide the framing for creating concentrations of business activity. Detroit's established employment corridors, therefore, face very different futures.

The fundamental challenge for economic development strategy and growth is not a matter of the physical scale of the city, as is often claimed, but the lack of employment density. Attracting investors, new businesses, and employees to Detroit is now inhibited by physical deterioration, limited services, and aging infrastructure that comes with the reduction in the number of companies and employees in a given area. Similarly, potential public investments in key infrastructure like transportation are difficult to deploy efficiently because of the checkerboard pattern of business activity in the city. Detroit must strategically boost employment density to fuel economic growth and investment and provide targets and a rationale for public investments to strengthen the economy.

Based on the existing patterns of business activity, potential for future growth, location of key economic assets, and land availability and ownership patterns, three categories of employment districts have been identified. These include:

CORE EMPLOYMENT DISTRICTS. Seven employment districts across the city represent the best opportunities to leverage existing land and infrastructure and support sustainable economic development. Core employment districts are defined by the presence of significant economic anchors to build upon including major legacy businesses or institutions, a diversity of economic activity, excellent infrastructure access, a recognized niche or brand that can help to attract additional businesses, and relatively vibrant existing employment activity. It is in these districts where focused and proactive public investment can have the greatest impact. Given their importance to the overall economic health of Detroit, core employment districts should be the target of efforts to assemble and redevelop land, improve and upgrade infrastructure; and test and develop initiatives designed to maximize private investment and improve workforce training. In an era of limited resources, Detroit's economic growth should be built upon the future of these districts.

SECONDARY EMPLOYMENT DISTRICTS. Not all existing economic activity occurs within the core employment districts. Other locations in Detroit provide valuable jobs, just not at the same density or scale as the core districts. These secondary districts represent many of Detroit's remaining industrial areas and are characterized by established industrial businesses but also higher vacancy rates. Due to the presence of larger tracts of vacant land, a few of these districts present some significant opportunities for redevelopment. However, due to location, infrastructure, and the level of investment needed to bring these sites to market, they have remained vacant. While valuable to the city's economy, the secondary districts lack a distinct niche or marketing identity that could help to spur additional private investment, and—in a world of limited resources— should generally not absorb public or philanthropic dollars for new infrastructure or programmatic investments. The strategy for these districts should include maintenance of existing infrastructure, retention of existing businesses, and flexibility to allow public and philanthropic dollars to follow the lead in the event of large-scale private-sector investment.

TRANSITIONING INDUSTRIAL DISTRICTS. Some industrial land is no longer suitable for modern industrial use due to a combination of different factors including a high concentration of vacant land and buildings, buildable sites that are too small to attract investment, and poor truck or rail access. In a handful of cases, what was formerly industrial is now institutional or commercial, all but eliminating the likelihood of new industrial development. Like many cities, Detroit needs to change land use policy to enable a full transition of these unmarketable industrial areas to alternative uses as identified in the Land Use and Land and Building Assets Element chapters of this Strategic Framework.

IMPLEMENTATION ACTIONS
1   Align public, private, and philanthropic investments in employment districts.
2   Develop detailed action plans for primary employment districts.
3   Encourage industrial business improvement districts (IBIDS).
4   Become a national leader in green industrial districts.

PRECEDENT
1   Los Angeles Downtown Industrial District (LADID): Los Angeles, CA

PILOT PROJECTS
1   Action Plans for Primary Employment Districts
2   Industrial Buffers

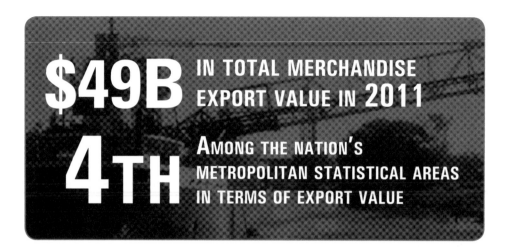

$49B IN TOTAL MERCHANDISE EXPORT VALUE IN **2011**

4TH AMONG THE NATION'S METROPOLITAN STATISTICAL AREAS IN TERMS OF EXPORT VALUE

6.

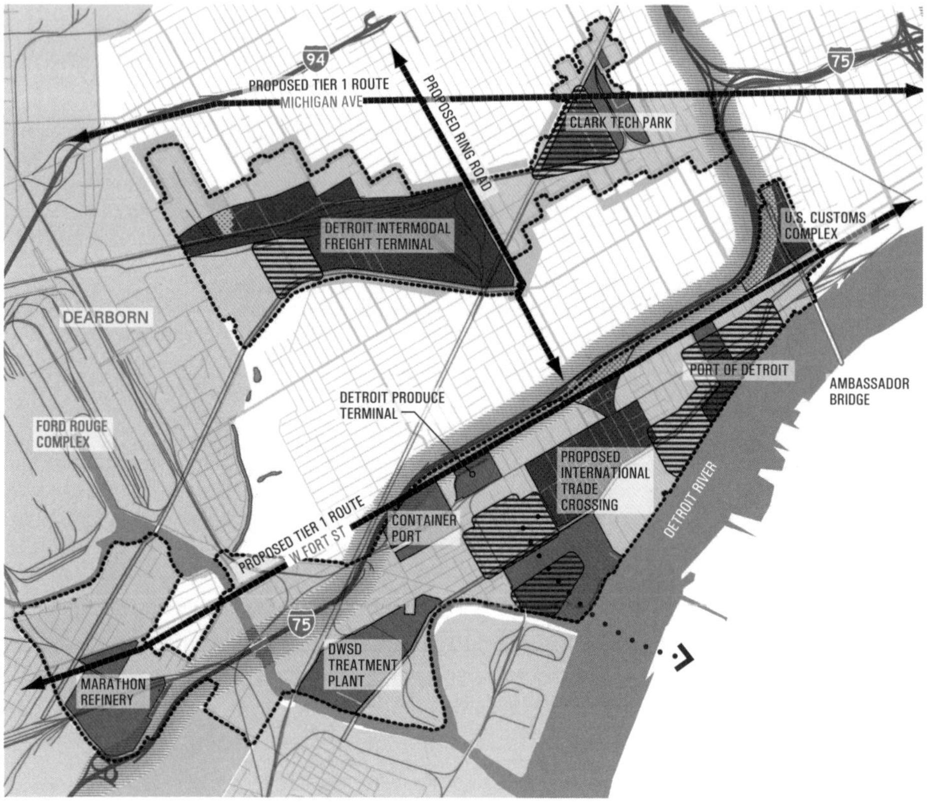

SOUTHWEST EMPLOYMENT DISTRICT

ECONOMIC ASSETS AND OPPORTUNITIES

::::: CORE EMPLOYMENT DISTRICT

▨ INDUSTRIAL ANCHOR / ASSET

▨ INFRASTRUCTURAL ANCHOR / ASSET

≡ POTENTIAL BUSINESS INVESTMENT OPPORTUNITIES

NETWORK INFRASTRUCTURE AND OPPORTUNITIES

← PROPOSED TRANSIT ROUTES

▨ FREEWAY CARBON FOREST

▨ GREEN INDUSTRIAL BUFFERS

The map labels:

- PROPOSED TIER 1 ROUTE MICHIGAN AVE
- PROPOSED RING ROAD
- CLARK TECH PARK
- DETROIT INTERMODAL FREIGHT TERMINAL
- U.S. CUSTOMS COMPLEX
- DEARBORN
- DETROIT PRODUCE TERMINAL
- PORT OF DETROIT
- AMBASSADOR BRIDGE
- FORD ROUGE COMPLEX
- PROPOSED INTERNATIONAL TRADE CROSSING
- DETROIT RIVER
- PROPOSED TIER 1 ROUTE W FORT ST
- CONTAINER PORT
- MARATHON REFINERY
- DWSD TREATMENT PLANT

Source: DWPLTP Planning Team

0.25 0.5 1 MILE

"Don't pigeonhole other areas – people live in SW Detroit; it is a desirable place still for people to move...There's a place for both [industry and neighborhood amenities]."

DWP Website, 8/2012

Data Source: International Trade Administration

Image Source: 6) Little House on the Urban Prairie blog

1 2   4 MILES

INDUSTRIAL
SOUTHWEST
CAPITALIZING ON INTERNATIONAL TRADE

THE ECONOMIC GROWTH ELEMENT : THE EQUITABLE CITY

DISTRICT VITALS

LAND AND INFRASTRUCTURE

SIZE (acres)	2,694
VACANCY (acres)	405
UNDERUTILIZED (acres)	588
% VACANT AND PUBLICLY OWNED	6%
INFRASTRUCTURE ASSETS	I-75, NS Container Port, Ambassador Bridge, Port of Detroit, Fort Street, DIFT Intermodal Hub
PLANNED INFRASTRUCTURE INVESTMENTS	Michigan Central Railway Tunnel expansion, DIFT expansion, New International Trade Crossing

BUSINESS AND ECONOMY

ECONOMIC ANCHORS	Refer to adjacent map
TOTAL NUMBER OF BUSINESSES[1]	850
CURRENT EMPLOYEES[2]	9,100
TYPES OF JOBS	Stock clerks and order fillers, truck drivers, first line supervisors and managers, carpenters, civil engineers, accountants

Table Sources: 1) NETS 2010 Estimates; 2) Private sector employment from QWI; non-private employment from LEHD— On the Map. Private sector employment was apportioned to districts using NETS data for 2010

DISTRICT VISION. Southwest Detroit has unparalleled access to infrastructure and represents a signature opportunity for Detroit. Through investments to the area's port, rail yards, international crossings, and main streets, Southwest will be positioned to become the country's largest, non-coastal transportation, logistics, and distribution (TDL) hub and an integral node for national and international trade. Expansion of TDL operations will transform blighted land into jobs-producing assets that provide economic opportunity for Detroiters of all backgrounds and skill levels. To protect both industrial activity and the nearby communities, industrial land uses will be consolidated south of I-75 and around the proposed Detroit International Freight Terminal (DIFT). Landscape buffers will be created to reduce noise, visibility, and pollution impacts on nearby communities. A proposed ring-road that connects employment districts across the city as well as the Coleman A. Young Airport will help to fuel additional demand for TDL activities in Southwest from local businesses.

DISTRICT DETAILS. Southwest Detroit is a compact industrial corridor radiating from the Corktown neighborhood along the Detroit River on the south and along the rail corridor leading to the proposed Detroit Intermodal Freight Terminal (DIFT) on the north. Nearby residential and commercial districts are located in Mexicantown, Hubbard Farms, Springwells, and Delray neighborhoods, along with major civic assets such as Historic Fort Wayne, and Riverside Park.

Southwest's unique concentration of industrial assets includes the newly expanded and consolidated DIFT and three international border crossings at the combined Ambassador Bridge / new Customs complex; the Michigan Central Railway Tunnel (slated for replacement); and the proposed New International Trade Crossing (NITC). These crossings supplement the major infrastructure assets: the Rouge and Detroit River Marine Terminals; access to I-75 and I-94, proposed rail track upgrades to West Detroit Junction; the reconstruction of southwest Fort Street and its River Rouge Bridge; and numerous freight rail hubs and drayage trucking links to the DIFT Southwest. Southwest is thus the ideal location for a range of industrial activity, including the region's only oil refinery (being upgraded to include "heavy crude" capability), a DWSD Wastewater Treatment Plant, the Detroit Produce Terminal, and two industrial parks: Springwells and the Clark Technology Park. The proposed infrastructure investments are essential for Southwest to reach its potential for economic growth, but only if accompanied by complementary efforts to strategically assemble land that supports global trade and logistics activities. Although there are opportunities for redevelopment in the Springwells and Clark Technology Parks, the most promising assembly areas lie just west of the NITC project area in Delray, the area adjacent to the DIFT expansion, and the land around the Port of Detroit.

The TDL, automotive, and CDER clusters currently dominate the district with a mix of large operations and small- to mid-sized firms. Southwest is the second-largest industrial corridor in the city by employment, with more than 7,500 employees, and companies currently operating are able to add 3,000 more jobs.

16K 16,000 CHEVY VOLTS WERE SOLD IN THE FIRST **9** MONTHS OF **2012**

1ST AMONG ELECTRIC CARS SOLD IN THE U.S.

7.

MT. ELLIOTT EMPLOYMENT DISTRICT

ECONOMIC ASSETS AND OPPORTUNITIES

- ::::: CORE EMPLOYMENT DISTRICT
- ▨ INDUSTRIAL ANCHOR / ASSET
- ▨ INFRASTRUCTURAL ANCHOR / ASSET
- ≡ POTENTIAL BUSINESS INVESTMENT OPPORTUNITIES

NETWORK INFRASTRUCTURE AND OPPORTUNITIES

- ◄ PROPOSED TRANSIT ROUTES
- ▤ FREEWAY CARBON FOREST
- ▤ GREEN INDUSTRIAL BUFFERS

Map labels: CHRYSLER TOOL & DIE, CHRYSLER ASSEMBLY, OUTER DRIVE, CONANT, VAN DYKE, PROPOSED CROSSTOWN ROUTE 7 MILE, HAYES, MT. ELLIOTT, MT. OLIVET CEMETERY, McNICHOLS, PROPOSED RING ROAD, DAVISON, PROPOSED TIER 1 ROUTE, GRATIOT, OUTER DRIVE, COLEMAN A. YOUNG INTERNATIONAL AIRPORT, HIGHLAND PARK, 75, CHRYSLER AXLE, HAMTRAMCK, I-94 INDUSTRIAL PARK, WOODWARD, 94, GM ASSEMBLY PLANT, WARREN, CHRYSLER ASSEMBLY PLANT

Source: DWPLTP Planning Team

0.25   0.5   1 MILE

"I am trying to work where I live and volunteer where I live: Van Dyke and Mt. Elliott, E. Seven Mile. I'd love to see both chain and local shops of all kinds on [these] corridors. Coffee shops, boutiques, restaurants with patios, pop-ups, retail, etc."

Angie, Economic Growth Open House, 8/7/2012

Data Source: http://www.clean-greencars.com/chevy-green-cars.html
Image Source: 7) General Motors/John F. Martin/Jeffrey Sauger

1 2   4 MILES

THE ECONOMIC GROWTH ELEMENT : THE EQUITABLE CITY

INDUSTRIAL
MT. ELLIOTT
CREATING A MODERN INDUSTRIAL AND INTERMODAL FREIGHT DISTRICT

DISTRICT VITALS

LAND AND INFRASTRUCTURE

SIZE (acres)	3,203
VACANCY (acres)	423
UNDERUTILIZED (acres)	181
% VACANT AND PUBLICLY OWNED	11%
INFRASTRUCTURE ASSETS	I-94, Detroit North Rail Yard and Freight Rail, Coleman A. Young International Airport
PLANNED INFRASTRUCTURE INVESTMENTS	Coleman A. Young International Airport expansion, I-94 widening

BUSINESS AND ECONOMY

ECONOMIC ANCHORS	Refer to adjacent map
TOTAL NUMBER OF BUSINESSES[1]	1,700
CURRENT EMPLOYEES[2]	10,000
TYPES OF JOBS	Assemblers and fabricators, machinists, truck drivers, accountants, civil engineers

Table Sources: 1) NETS 2010 Estimates; 2) Private sector employment from QWI; non-private employment from LEHD— On the Map. Private sector employment was apportioned to districts using NETS data for 2010

DISTRICT VISION. The Mt. Elliott employment district was built around automotive and metals activity. The vision is to upgrade Mt. Elliott as an intense and attractive industrial area designed to accommodate modern, large-format industrial development; provide ample employment opportunities for Detroiters; and reinforce the region's role as a global hub for manufacturing. Expansion of the Coleman A. Young Airport will serve to support the local auto and metals industries but also provide additional opportunities in aerospace activities that align with many skills already in place to serve auto production. A new ring-road will connect this district directly with Chrysler to the south along with logistics activities, the Port, and the international crossing in Southwest Detroit.

The contraction of the auto industry in 2008-2010 set the stage for a new wave of growth and diversification in Mt. Elliott by opening up large tracts of land. The three largest land development assets in the corridor include the nearly complete I-94 Industrial Park, the large parcel vacancies centered on the former Chrysler Detroit Axle Plant and the Trident Huber site to the south, and the vast—and largely vacant—residential area between Forest Lawn Cemetery and the Coleman A. Young Airport. In addition, with moderate land assembly efforts, four additional mid-sized parcels could be created out of current vacancies. With the resurgence of the auto industry and the assemblers' and suppliers' new and evolving research and training needs, this district can be positioned for innovative education and training facilities and can support smaller-scale tech center research and development for smaller and lower-tier suppliers.

DISTRICT DETAILS. The Mt. Elliott employment district runs from the center of Detroit north to the city limits at Eight Mile. It lies in the heart of the region's automotive manufacturing corridor that runs through the city and into the suburbs by way of the Chrysler Warren Truck Plant and the GM Powertrain and Tech Centers. Mt. Elliot is Detroit's manufacturing heartland and its potential is bolstered by its proximity to major infrastructure assets such as Coleman A. Young Airport, freight rail and rail yards, and direct access to I-94. The area is slated for further infrastructure investment in the form of rail improvements, bridge construction, and the widening of I-94 through the area to four lanes.

The automotive, metals, and TDL clusters dominate this district's economy, with large stakeholders such as the GM Detroit Hamtramck Assembly Plant, Detroit Chassis, and Chrysler Tool and Die interacting closely with metal manufacturers, fabricators, and shippers. Mt. Elliott is the single largest industrial corridor in the city by employment— and the third largest industrial or non-industrial employment district in Detroit—with an estimated 10,000 employees within its boundaries as of 2010. Companies currently operating in the district are able to add 4,000 jobs.

$1.5B DEMAND FOR FOOD IN DETROIT AMOUNTS TO $1.6 BILLION

DETROIT HAS ONE OF THE LARGEST AND HIGHEST-QUALITY WATER SYSTEMS IN THE WORLD TO SUPPORT

8.

Source: DWPLTP Planning Team

0.25   0.5   1 MILE

DEQUINDRE / EASTERN MARKET EMPLOYMENT DISTRICT

ECONOMIC ASSETS AND OPPORTUNITIES

⋮⋮⋮⋮⋮ CORE EMPLOYMENT DISTRICT

▮ INDUSTRIAL ANCHOR / ASSET

▮ INFRASTRUCTURAL ANCHOR / ASSET

≡ POTENTIAL BUSINESS INVESTMENT OPPORTUNITIES

NETWORK INFRASTRUCTURE AND OPPORTUNITIES

◄ PROPOSED TRANSIT ROUTES

▨ FREEWAY CARBON FOREST

▨ GREEN INDUSTRIAL BUFFERS

◄ DEQUINDRE CUT GREENWAY

"Eastern Market is a great example of a fresh & thriving market place, and more areas like it need to spring up throughout the city."

Detroit 24/7, 5/2012

Data Source: ICIC, et al., "Designing an Inner City Food Cluster Strategy," Submission to EDA, October 13, 2011
Image Source: 8) Marvin Shaouni

1 2   4 MILES

INDUSTRIAL AND CREATIVE
DEQUINDRE/EASTERN MARKET
ESTABLISHING A CENTER FOR FOOD-RELATED JOBS AND PRODUCTION IN THE REGION

DISTRICT VITALS

LAND AND INFRASTRUCTURE

SIZE (acres)	1,130
VACANCY (acres)	307
UNDERUTILIZED (acres)	42
% VACANT AND PUBLICLY OWNED	8%
INFRASTRUCTURE ASSETS	I-94, I-75, freight rail, Dequindre Cut
PLANNED INFRASTRUCTURE INVESTMENTS	I-94 widening, Dequindre Cut Phase II

BUSINESS AND ECONOMY

ECONOMIC ANCHORS	Refer to adjacent map
TOTAL NUMBER OF BUSINESSES[1]	650
CURRENT EMPLOYEES[2]	4,400
TYPES OF JOBS	Packing and filling machine operators, assemblers and fabricators, advertising sales agents, lawyers

Table Sources: 1) NETS 2010 Estimates; 2) Private sector employment from QWI; non-private employment from LEHD— On the Map. Private sector employment was apportioned to districts using NETS data for 2010

DISTRICT VISION. Building on local assets, Dequindre/Eastern Market is envisioned as the center for food in Detroit and the region, with uses that support retail, wholesaling, packaging, and food/beverage processing. Investment will leverage this activity and grow additional food-related businesses. This district exhibits a visible connection to the land, with urban farms and the popular indoor/outdoor market that gives the district its name, where as many as 40,000 Detroiters come from across the city each week for locally grown produce and locally made food. Productive landscapes proposed to the east of the district provide the opportunity to create a full-year growing cycle, which would ensure Detroiters have better access to fresh food and feed the processing and packaging activities that provide the greatest number of jobs in the food cluster.

Eastern Market is an intense mixed-use district. Investments should seek to not only grow food cluster activities but also reinforce local retail and creative production. Above I-94, investments should continue to strengthen the auto cluster. Unlike other districts, Dequindre/Eastern Market will become a combination of Live+Make activities, light, and general industrial typologies.

New businesses focused on food and beverage processing and the expansion of existing facilities should be a priority in this district. These activities should be linked to the expansion of local food production, as proposed in the Productive Landscapes typology in the Detroit Strategic Framework's Land Use Element. For the auto cluster north of I-94, the successful redevelopment of the American Axle site is key to the district's success. At nearly 170 acres, this sprawling complex actually includes a large area of vacant acreage that American Axle was "banking" for future development. The site could be redeveloped into a modern, multi-tenant industrial park.

DISTRICT DETAILS. The diverse corridor extending from Eastern Market on the south up through the freight rail node of Milwaukee Junction to the massive former American Axle site comprises the Dequindre/Eastern Market Employment Center. The district has good access to major highways (I-75, I-94) and perhaps most crucially, proximity to the innovation corridor in Midtown Detroit. On its south end, the corridor also abuts the Dequindre Cut Greenway, soon to be extended through Eastern Market to the north, which serves as an important and highly visible neighborhood and recreational amenity in Detroit. Phase II of this "rails to trails" conversion will lie cheek-by-jowl with active industrial uses, setting an important precedent for the mingling of clean, low-impact modern industrial uses with recreational and residential priorities in Detroit.

This unique, mixed-sector corridor is currently dominated by several clusters, most notably food. The southern part of the district is anchored by the multitude of wholesalers, suppliers, and processors based in the Eastern Market, as well as a handful of large food-related plants, including Pepsi Bottling and Wolverine Packing. Near the intersection of I-75 and I-94 lies the Detroit branch of the Federal Reserve Bank of Chicago as well as a large collection of city industrial functions, including a DPS maintenance facility, the Greater Detroit Resource Recovery Facility, a Detroit Transportation Department yard, DTE's Trombley Service Center, and the Detroit Household Hazardous collection center. Metals cluster activity is interspersed throughout this area and extending north to the former American Axle site. The district's Russell Industrial Center has become a hub for design, arts, artisanal craft activities, and entrepreneurs. With the closing of American Axle, employment in Dequindre/Eastern Market fell dramatically. As of 2010, there were about 6,000 jobs in the district and firm utilization rates were about 50%, largely because of the dramatic downsizing at American Axle.

CORKTOWN IS HOME TO
2.5K JOBS IN A MIX OF LOGISTICS, CREATIVE ENTERPRISES AND RETAIL*
$4M HAS BEEN EARMARKED FOR REDEVELOPMENT EFFORTS, INCLUDING THE FORMER TIGER STADIUM SITE**

9.

CORKTOWN EMPLOYMENT DISTRICT
ECONOMIC ASSETS AND OPPORTUNITIES

▦ CORE EMPLOYMENT DISTRICT
▬ INDUSTRIAL ANCHOR / ASSET
▬ INFRASTRUCTURAL ANCHOR / ASSET
≡ POTENTIAL BUSINESS INVESTMENT OPPORTUNITIES
▨ NEIGHBORHOOD INVESTMENT & STABILIZATION
▩ ARTS AND ENTERTAINMENT ASSETS
▦ CIVIC ASSETS

NETWORK INFRASTRUCTURE AND OPPORTUNITIES

◄ PROPOSED TRANSIT ROUTES
▤ FREEWAY CARBON FOREST

Map labels:
MGM GRAND CASINO
TIGER STADIUM SITE
PROPOSED TIER 1 ROUTE
MICHIGAN AVE
DPW YARD
NEIGHBORHOOD INVESTMENT & STABILIZATION
MATRIX THEATRE
MICHIGAN CENTRAL STATION
COMMUNITY HEALTH AWARENESS GROUP
DETROIT HISPANIC DEVELOPMENT CORP.
INTERNATIONAL PORT OF ENTRY
NEIGHBORHOOD INVESTMENT & STABILIZATION
PENSKE LOGISTICS
UPS
U.S. POST OFFICE
SALVATION ARMY
AMBASSADOR BRIDGE U.S. CUSTOMS COMPLEX
PROPOSED TIER 1 ROUTE
FORT ST.
FORT ST. GALLERY
MICHIGAN CENTRAL RAIL TUNNEL REPLACEMENT
JEFFERSON
ROSA PARKS
TRUMBULL
LAFAYETTE
96
75
10

Source: DWPLTP Planning Team

0.25   0.5   1 MILE

"...By creating concentrations of new industry and business entrepreneurship in community, we can make it easier to meet the needs of businesses and developers, employees. It possible present opportunities to use our vacant buildings in more productive ways."

Economic Growth Open House, 8/7/2012

Data Sources: *2.5K stat from 2010 NETS; SEMCOG; QWI.; **http://www.mlive.com/news/detroit/index.ssf/2011/08/old_tiger_stadium_conservancy.html
Image Source: 9) Marvin Shaouni

1 2   4 MILES

INDUSTRIAL AND LOCAL ENTREPRENEURSHIP
CORKTOWN
A NEW ENTREPRENEURIAL DISTRICT

DISTRICT VITALS

LAND AND INFRASTRUCTURE

SIZE (acres)	509
VACANCY (acres)	124
UNDERUTILIZED (acres)	8
% VACANT AND PUBLICLY OWNED	3%
INFRASTRUCTURE ASSETS	I-75, Ambassador Bridge, freight rail, Fort Street
PLANNED INFRASTRUCTURE INVESTMENTS	Michigan Central Railway Tunnel expansion

BUSINESS AND ECONOMY

ECONOMIC ANCHORS	Refer to adjacent map
TOTAL NUMBER OF BUSINESSES	750
CURRENT EMPLOYEES	2,600
TYPES OF JOBS	Laborers and freight, stock and material movers, stock clerks and order fillers, truck drivers, editors, advertising sales agents

Table Sources: 1) NETS 2010 Estimates; 2) Private sector employment from QWI; non-private employment from LEHD— On the Map. Private sector employment was apportioned to districts using NETS data for 2010

DISTRICT VISION. At the edge of Downtown, Corktown is envisioned as one of the City's most desirable Live+Make neighborhoods. New small businesses and creative enterprises will mix with existing industrial uses to further attract both national and global talent. New housing and continued revitalization along Michigan Avenue will provide a walkable environment for businesses with new services, entertainment, and housing.

At the heart of Corktown's future is a network of community leaders, volunteers, and business entrepreneurs who can undertake neighborhood improvements and reclaim vacant lots as productive community spaces. Such groups include the Corktown Historical Society, Greater Corktown Residents Council, Detroit Hispanic Development Corporation, Greater Corktown Development Corporation, Old Tiger Stadium Conservancy, the Roosevelt Park Conservancy, Most Holy Trinity Church, and The Greening of Detroit, among others. Corktown's resurgence has attracted new businesses and entrepreneurs, and has gained momentum through the interest of funders and investors.

With existing companies operating close to capacity, additional employment in Corktown will come through the strategic repurposing of vacant buildings and new construction on targeted sites. Similarly, with a housing shortage in the community, future growth of Corktown will be accommodated by the development of critical parcels of land currently held by speculators and other private land owners.

To realize this vision, investment should be coordinated closely with community leaders to promote new business and housing development. Initial investments should leverage projects and programs underway, including: the $3.8 million federal earmark awarded to help redevelop the old Tiger Stadium; the Detroit RiverWalk, funded with over $40 million to connect Corktown and the Ambassador Bridge to Belle Isle; and the recently established program to promote business in Corktown, funding up to $50,000 or 25% of total development/capital improvements.

DISTRICT DETAILS. A National Register Historic District, Corktown is Detroit's oldest neighborhood. Established by Irish immigrants in the wake of the Potato Famine of the 1840s, this once-industrial area is now home to key local and regional assets and popular eateries and shops, including Slow's Barbecue, Honey Bee Market, and Mudgie's Deli. Green spaces include Murphy Playlot and Roosevelt Park. Additionally, the Welcome Center and Mercado act as vital economic anchors in the neighborhood.

Corktown is convenient for freight and people alike, providing access to the Detroit riverfront, the International Ambassador Bridge, the International Michigan Central Railway Tunnel, and all major highways. MDOT has made streetscape Improvements to make Corktown's retail district inviting for pedestrians and bicyclists.

Corktown is home to about 2,500 private-sector jobs, as well as thousands of public sector jobs, including public works employment, Wayne County Community College District (WCCCD) faculty and staff jobs, and hundreds of local logistics jobs through major employer Penske Logistics and others. A 30,000-square-foot creative business incubator, Pony Ride, currently provides almost 20 creative firms with shared space at reasonable rents.

DETROIT IS RANKED

2ND

AMONG THE **100** LARGEST CITIES FOR GROWTH IN INFORMATION TECHNOLOGY BUSINESSES BETWEEN **1998-2009**[*]

19M

VISITORS COME TO DOWNTOWN DETROIT EVERY YEAR[**]

10.

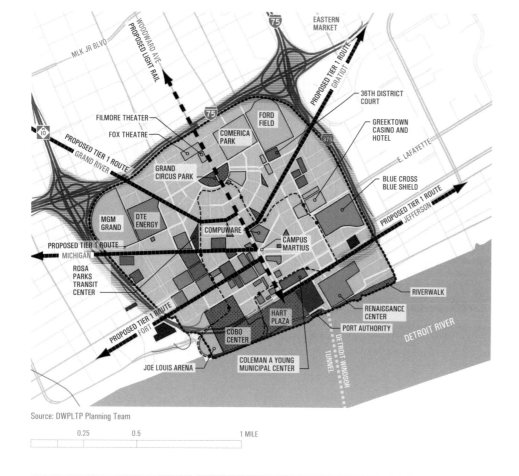

Source: DWPLTP Planning Team

0.25   0.5   1 MILE

DOWNTOWN EMPLOYMENT DISTRICT

ECONOMIC ASSETS AND OPPORTUNITIES

- CORE EMPLOYMENT DISTRICT
- ARTS AND ENTERTAINMENT ASSETS
- EDUCATIONAL ANCHORS
- GOVERNMENT
- CIVIC ASSETS
- ECONOMIC ANCHORS
- INFRASTRUCTURAL ANCHOR / ASSET

NETWORK INFRASTRUCTURE AND OPPORTUNITIES

- ◄ PROPOSED TRANSIT ROUTES
- FREEWAY CARBON FOREST
- ◄-●- DETROIT PEOPLE MOVER

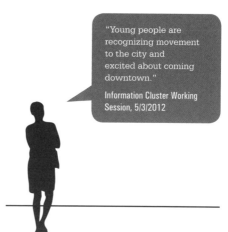

"Young people are recognizing movement to the city and excited about coming downtown."

Information Cluster Working Session, 5/3/2012

Data Sources: [*]ICIC SICE Database; [**]Detroit Economic Growth Corporation
Image Source: 10) Marvin Shaouni

1 2 MILES

DIGITAL AND CREATIVE
DOWNTOWN
RECREATING DETROIT'S CITY CENTER AS AN INFORMATION TECHNOLOGY HUB

THE ECONOMIC GROWTH ELEMENT : THE EQUITABLE CITY

DISTRICT VITALS

LAND AND INFRASTRUCTURE

SIZE (acres)	723
VACANCY (acres)	N/A (survey data on vacant and underutilized sites not available)
UNDERUTILIZED (acres)	N/A
% VACANT AND PUBLICLY OWNED	3%
INFRASTRUCTURE ASSETS	I-75, M-10, I-375, Woodward Avenue
PLANNED INFRASTRUCTURE INVESTMENTS	M-1 Rail

BUSINESS AND ECONOMY

ECONOMIC ANCHORS	Refer to adjacent map
TOTAL NUMBER OF BUSINESSES[1]	7,150
CURRENT EMPLOYEES[2]	61,400
TYPES OF JOBS	Computer programmers, computer support specialists, editors

Table Sources: 1) NETS 2010 Estimates; 2) Private sector employment from QWI; non-private employment from LEHD— On the Map. Private sector employment was apportioned to districts using NETS data for 2010

DISTRICT VISION. The seat of government for the City of Detroit and Wayne County, Downtown is already an important hub for employment and a symbol of Detroit. It is also a major convention and entertainment destination for the region, with a major convention center, the nation's largest automobile show, three sports teams, and casinos, along with other attractions. Downtown is poised to become the best location in the state for medium- and large-sized corporations, the center of the region's burgeoning digital/creative cluster, and a nationally known center for entertainment. Vacant buildings in Downtown, often characterized by striking architecture, will be rehabilitated and occupied with new creative, digital, and professional services companies. Light rail along Woodward will connect Downtown to other employment centers and services, while the Detroit River will continue to provide a unique asset for Downtown residents, workers, and visitors. Over time, new development will complement the existing Downtown fabric to fill in the gaps and create a mixed-use and flourishing city center.

This vision is already underway, with a surge in downtown employment as a result of major corporate relocations including Quicken Loans and Blue Cross Blue Shield. Recent investment includes a public-private partnership to develop three historic buildings for mixed-use space in Capitol Park as well as the renovation of the historic Broderick Tower and David Whitney Building for residential reuse. Potentially the largest driver of the Downtown transformation is Quicken Loans' acquisition of over 2 million square feet of office space. Under the banner of Opportunity Detroit, Quicken Loans has successfully attracted a broad range of digital and creative entrepreneurs and start-ups, establishing the Downtown as a nationally and internationally recognized technology hub.

DISTRICT DETAILS. Downtown Detroit is a major employment center that enjoys a number of key regional and national assets, including the region's highest concentration of entertainment venue: Three professional sports stadiums, three full-service casinos, and the Detroit riverfront. As a National Register Historic District since 1978, the district includes over 50 Nationally Registered Historic Places, such as the Fox Theatre and Detroit Opera House. Downtown Detroit is the largest employment hub in the city of Detroit and among the largest in the region, with about 40,000 employees. Existing companies could add 11,500 jobs, suggesting that current companies have space to grow.

The digital and creative clusters are well-represented in this district, as are regional and global headquarters of large companies such General Motors, Blue Cross Blue Shield, Compuware, Quicken Loans, and DTE. The headquarters activity is attracted to the availability of affordable and abundant Class-A office space. The high density of office jobs and close proximity to local retail amenities have created the conditions for intercompany cooperation and the branding of the area. Examples of collaborative efforts include the "WEBward Initiative" led by Quicken Loans and the "Outsource to Detroit" campaign by GalaxE Solutions.

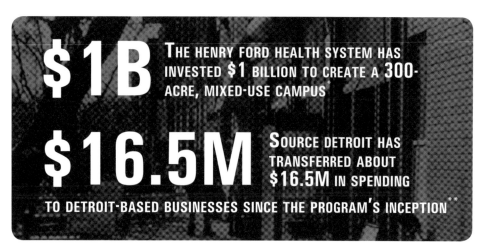

$1B THE HENRY FORD HEALTH SYSTEM HAS INVESTED $1 BILLION TO CREATE A 300-ACRE, MIXED-USE CAMPUS*

$16.5M SOURCE DETROIT HAS TRANSFERRED ABOUT $16.5M IN SPENDING

TO DETROIT-BASED BUSINESSES SINCE THE PROGRAM'S INCEPTION**

11.

MIDTOWN EMPLOYMENT DISTRICT

ECONOMIC ASSETS AND OPPORTUNITIES

- CORE EMPLOYMENT DISTRICT
- ARTS AND ENTERTAINMENT ASSETS
- MEDICAL ANCHOR / ASSET
- EDUCATIONAL ANCHORS
- NEIGHBORHOOD STABILIZATION AND INVESTMENT

NETWORK INFRASTRUCTURE AND OPPORTUNITIES

- PROPOSED TRANSIT ROUTES
- FREEWAY CARBON FOREST

Source: DWPLTP Planning Team

0.25   0.5   1 MILE

> ". . .there [has been] a culture shift in the university to recognize that Wayne [State University] and Detroit are linked."
>
> Education Cluster Working Session 5/2/2012

Data Sources: *Greene, Jay. "Henry Ford lands first tenant for health park in Midtown." *Crain's Detroit Business.* 03 June 2012;
**sourcedetroit.com
Image Source: 11) dbpedia.org

1 2   4 MILES

EDUCATION, MEDICAL, DIGITAL, AND CREATIVE
MIDTOWN
BUILDING UPON LOCAL EDUCATIONAL, MEDICAL, AND CREATIVE INSTITUTIONS

DISTRICT VITALS

LAND AND INFRASTRUCTURE

SIZE (acres)	1,534
VACANCY (acres)	N/A (survey data on vacant and underutilized sites not available)
UNDERUTILIZED (acres)	N/A
% VACANT AND PUBLICLY OWNED	6%
INFRASTRUCTURE ASSETS	I-75, M-10, I-94, freight rail
PLANNED INFRASTRUCTURE INVESTMENTS	M-1 Rail / BRT, Midtown Shuttle

BUSINESS AND ECONOMY

ECONOMIC ANCHORS	Refer to adjacent map
NUMBER OF BUSINESSES[1]	3,400
CURRENT EMPLOYEES[2]	50,900
TYPES OF JOBS	Janitors and cleaners, secretaries, registered nurses, computer support specialists

Table Sources: 1) NETS 2010 Estimates; 2) Private sector employment from QWI; non-private employment from LEHD—On the Map. Private sector employment was apportioned to districts using NETS data for 2010

DISTRICT VISION. With an unprecedented level of public/private cooperation that builds on the local skills, resources, and knowledge base of the district's major institutions, Midtown serves as a national model for anchor-based revitalization in distressed urban areas. With the advent of the Henry Ford Innovation Institute and myriad collaborative ventures across the College of Creative Studies, Wayne State, and the medical institutions, Midtown has the potential to be a national model for innovation-based economic growth. The staging of tech-based growth companies and the creation of flex space to absorb second-generation growth from TechTown and the hospitals and universities will promote knowledge spillovers and fuel multiple scales of entrepreneurial activity—further leveraged by the proposed light rail system on Woodward Avenue and the Woodward Corridor Initiative, a collaborative effort between Midtown Inc. and Living Cities Integration Initiative to attract local residents and businesses.

Despite the positive momentum and national attention, barriers to this vision remain. Midtown is a very large district and, although many assets are in place, there is no real or symbolic center of activity. Places like TechTown need a recognizable, physical district to help attract and retain knowledge workers. There is also too little low-cost flex space for creative firms. Targeted redevelopment activity is needed to support the small, creative and IT firms as well as B2B operations that support and serve the large local institutions like Wayne State University and Henry Ford Medical Center.

DISTRICT DETAILS. Midtown is comprised of the traditional Midtown, North End, and New Center neighborhoods. This district is home to a number of key regional assets, including four of the region's most celebrated hospitals that collectively represent 23,000 jobs; an agglomeration of post-secondary institutions; renowned Cass Tech High School; the Charles H. Wright Museum of African American History; the Detroit Public Library; community groups such as the Detroit Parent Network and Black Family Development; and three up-and-coming incubators that leverage Midtown's position as Detroit's core innovation corridor. The district also includes over 70 sites on the National Register of Historic Places, including the Detroit Institute of Arts (DIA), the Whitney Restaurant, and the world's largest Masonic temple, the Detroit Masonic Temple.

The education and medical clusters are the economic anchors in this district, while creative sector activity from organizations like Detroit Creative Corridor, TechTown, Museum of Contemporary Art Detroit (MOCAD), Detroit Symphony Orchestra (DSO), and Mosaic Youth Theater are some of the most tangible representations of the broad set of skills in the city and region. Collaborative efforts include the $93M "Bio-Tech Hub" led by Wayne State University with participation from the Detroit Medical Center (DMC) and Henry Ford Health System (HFHS); and Live Midtown—a wildly successful $1.2M program that provides incentives for Midtown's institutional employees to purchase, rent, or improve residential property in Midtown.

As the second largest employment hub in the city of Detroit, Midtown Detroit is also the fastest-growing non-industrial employment district. Existing companies could add 16,000 jobs, suggesting that they have space to grow. Larger anchors are helping to give the area a facelift with DMC and HFHS planning to spend over $1B in facility upgrades over the next few years. These anchors are also leveraging their balance sheets to build out facilities for suppliers and other complementary companies. One anchor institution recently agreed to build a $25M medical warehouse to house supplies it uses regularly and plans to procure additional acreage in Midtown, where one-third of the available land is currently owned by the City.

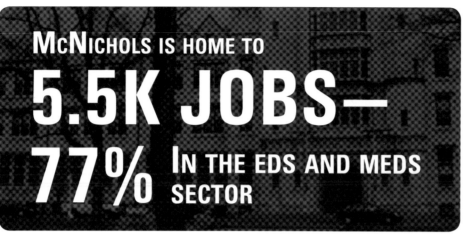

McNICHOLS IS HOME TO
5.5K JOBS—
77% IN THE EDS AND MEDS SECTOR

12.

13.

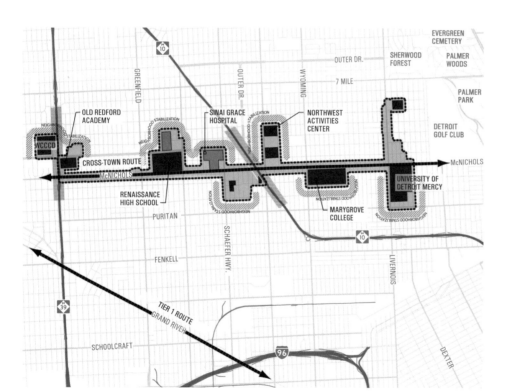

Source: DWPLTP Planning Team

0.25   0.5   1 MILE

McNICHOLS EMPLOYMENT DISTRICT

ECONOMIC ASSETS AND OPPORTUNITIES

- CORE EMPLOYMENT DISTRICT
- MEDICAL ANCHOR / ASSET
- EDUCATIONAL ASSET
- NEIGHBORHOOD STABILIZATION AND INVESTMENT

NETWORK INFRASTRUCTURE AND OPPORTUNITIES

- PROPOSED TRANSIT ROUTES
- FREEWAY CARBON FOREST

Data Sources: 2010 NETS; SEMCOG; QWI
Image Sources: 12) Dwight Burdette, Wikimedia Commons; 13) Hamilton Anderson Associates

1 2   4 MILES

EDUCATION AND MEDICAL AND CREATIVE
McNICHOLS
ESTABLISHING DETROIT'S SECOND EDS AND MEDS CORRIDOR

DISTRICT VITALS

LAND AND INFRASTRUCTURE

SIZE (acres)	962
VACANCY (acres)	N/A (survey data on vacant and underutilized sites not available)
UNDERUTILIZED (acres)	N/A
% VACANT AND PUBLICLY OWNED	2%
INFRASTRUCTURE ASSETS	Southfield Freeway, M-10
PLANNED INFRASTRUCTURE INVESTMENTS	M-10 improvements

BUSINESS AND ECONOMY

ECONOMIC ANCHORS	Refer to adjacent map
NUMBER OF BUSINESSES[1]	1,900
CURRENT EMPLOYEES[2]	5,500
TYPES OF JOBS	Janitors and cleaners, security guards, secretaries, registered nurses, editors, post-secondary teachers, physicians and surgeons

Table Sources: 1) NETS 2010 Estimates; 2) Private sector employment from QWI; non-private employment from LEHD— On the Map. Private sector employment was apportioned to districts using NETS data for 2010

DISTRICT VISION. The vision for McNichols is to connect its education and medical institutions, as well as creative enterprises, into a revitalized McNichols Road corridor that will serve as home to a mix of new small businesses, retail, and supporting services. While redevelopment and expansion opportunities are predominantly located within existing campuses, McNichols Road will serve as an attractive front door, improved to provide a unifying character and brand focused on Eds/Meds, creative businesses, and retail. Targeted investments will strengthen existing retail along Livernois Avenue and new programs will support housing and neighborhood stabilization around the district. The major employment opportunities, quality of the surrounding housing, and location near the city border position McNichols as an ideal district to attract new businesses or residents that may otherwise choose the suburbs. McNichols could also become the city's second key district for growth of creative firms.

Active partnership among the district's primary employers is necessary to enact this vision. Although large land holdings by Jesuit and other publicly minded organizations foster a well-kept, pastoral feeling in the district, McNichols is currently comprised of islands of major institutions that feel disjointed from one another, which inhibits efforts to capitalize on this concentration of employment, pool money for improvements, or market the district and its services. The key to success for this district rests in the ability to tackle the nuts and bolts of revitalizing a commercial corridor to attract businesses, manage parking, and improve the physical character of McNichols Road (including improved lighting, sidewalks, landscaping, signage, and public art). The major institutions will need to develop a comprehensive strategy beyond the boundaries of any one campus to create a much-needed center of gravity, which will benefit them all by providing attractive options for faculty, staff, and students to live and play. Marygrove College and University of Detroit Mercy are positioned to lead this district forward, as Wayne State University is a leader in the revitalization of Midtown.

DISTRICT DETAILS. The McNichols employment district extends from Greenfield road to Woodward, (east and west), and from Puritan to 8 Mile, (north and south). Local assets include two turn-of-the-century post-secondary institutions that were historically the schools of choice for much of Detroit's homegrown talent; a 36-hole private golf course, designed by Scottish golf-pro Donald Ross with a clubhouse designed by famed architect Albert Kahn; a 18-hole public golf course; the Michigan State Fairgrounds, a sprawling 160-acre site that was home to the oldest state fair in the United States. The district also boasts the most expansive concentration of high-quality housing stock in the city and a rich network of faith-based organizations who work with community groups to address neighborhood challenges and opportunities.

The Eds and Meds clusters contribute just under 65% of the economic activity as measured by employment. Sinai Grace, a Detroit Medical Center affiliate, recently began a $77M renovation project. Additional large-scale activity can be seen in the District's unveiling of the 36-acre Gateway Marketplace retail development. Local retail and personal services range from local restaurant gems like La Dolce Vita, home to Ronald Reagan's former personal Chef Matteo, to the Swanson Funeral Home, which has handled the "going-home" arrangements for everyone from Detroit Mayor Coleman Young to Rosa Parks. Local groups like University Commons are drafting strategic initiatives and building internal capacity to leverage dollars for economic development through programs like Re$tore Detroit.

SECONDARY EMPLOYMENT DISTRICTS

- INDUSTRIAL
- INDUSTRIAL / CREATIVE
- PRIMARY EMPLOYMENT DISTRICTS

Source: DWPLTP Planning Team

1   2   4 MILES

In addition to Detroit's primary Employment Districts there are six secondary Employment Areas. These areas are home to a wide range of employment opportunities and currently contain 1,850 businesses and 11,500 jobs.

INDUSTRIAL

I-96	WESTFIELD	LIVERNOIS	UPPER CONNER CREEK	LOWER CONNER CREEK
Near Detroit's western city limits, this area is anchored by the CP Oak Yard, soon to be consolidated into the DIFT to the south, the Gateway Industrial Center on I-96, Sherwood Food Distributors, and a number of TDL, metal fabrication, and engineering companies. The most significant redevelopment opportunity here lies to the south of the CP Oak Yard and I-96 on the large site of the former Farmer Jack Distribution Center.	South of the freeway and east of the I-96 Employment Area, Westfield is centered along a north-south freight rail corridor anchored by PVS Nolwood Chemicals, the Westfield Industrial Centers, the Joy Road Distribution Center, and a number of other construction, chemical, metal fabrication, and TDL companies. A great deal of space is available in the Westfield Industrial Center, and to the north around the former Chrysler office complex at Plymouth and Freeland Streets.	Centered along a freight rail spur south of I-96 and north of I-94, the Livernois Employment Area is anchored by three large industrial users: the DTE Warren Service Center, Coca-Cola Bottling Plant, and ThyssenKrupp Steel Distribution Center, that receives and processes rolled and billet steel from the Port of Detroit bound for regional Auto cluster firms. Large and significant redevelopment and land assembly opportunities exist in the areas adjacent to ThyssenKrupp between Warren Ave and I-94.	One of the smallest Secondary Employment Areas, Upper Conner Creek is significant for its industrial anchors—the Chrysler Conner Avenue Assembly Plant, a DWSD Filter Station, and W Industries. In addition, Upper Conner Creek is located at the base of an extensive industrial corridor radiating north into Warren along M-97. A moderate redevelopment potential also exists around a land assembly opportunity at East State Fair and Hoover Streets.	Lower Conner Creek is a legacy industrial corridor anchored by the Chrysler Jefferson North Assembly Plant on Conner Ave and the Mack Avenue Engine Plant. Lower Conner Creek retains tremendous development and redevelopment potential in the form of the stalled Riverside Industrial Park, located between Jefferson and Freud Streets south of the Chrysler assembly plant, which is partially assembled and developed.

DISTRICT VITALS

LAND AND INFRASTRUCTURE

SIZE (acres)	3,752 acres
VACANCY (acres)	683 acres
UNDERUTILIZED (acres)	372 acres
% VACANT AND PUBLICLY OWNED	6%

BUSINESS AND ECONOMY

NUMBER OF BUSINESSES[1]	1,850
CURRENT EMPLOYEES[2]	11,600
TYPES OF JOBS	Machinists, assemblers and fabricators, inspectors, testers, sorters, samplers, weighers, truck drivers

Table Sources: 1) NETS 2010 Estimates; 2) Private sector employment from QWI; non-private employment from LEHD— On the Map. Private sector employment was apportioned to districts using NETS data for 2010

INDUSTRIAL/CREATIVE

LYNDON

The Lyndon corridor is a unique and vibrant collection of smaller industrial companies from many different clusters that occupy the garages and shops of Lyndon Avenue from Livernois, west to Schaefer Highway. The few larger anchor businesses in the area include DDOT's Coolidge Terminal, DTE MichCon Gas Company's Coolidge Station, and a Comcast Yard. A smattering of smaller redevelopment opportunities exist in Lyndon that would strengthen the corridor. The eastern portion of the corridor is anchored by Focus: HOPE, a multifaceted career training community advocate and industrial innovation center.

EDUCATION & MEDICAL AND CREATIVE
SECONDARY EMPLOYMENT DISTRICTS
REINFORCING INDUSTRIAL JOBS

VISION. In addition to Detroit's primary employment centers, a number of peripheral nodes of industrial activity comprise a smaller, less intensive, but important set of secondary employment centers. As they contain many active and viable businesses that employ Detroiters, the vision is to stabilize and maintain these centers going forward. Each district offers potential development opportunities to further strengthen the city's auto, metals, TDL, and CDER clusters if led by private interest and investment. Proposed investments in infrastructure include targeted industrial buffers to protect nearby communities promoted for stabilization and growth and a new ring-road designed to connect employment districts across the city with infrastructure assets in the Southwest.

DETAILS. These secondary employment centers are scattered across Detroit, primarily following highways and rail corridors. Four of these centers—I-96, Westfield, Lyndon, and Livernois—are located in northwest Detroit, while the remaining two—Upper and Lower Conner Creek—extend to the north and south of the Coleman A. Young Airport, respectively, on the city's east side. Home to 1,850 businesses and a combined industrial employment of more than 11,500, these districts comprise a significant proportion of Detroit's overall industrial activity.

At the root of an expansive and vibrant industrial corridor that extends west out of Detroit into neighboring Livonia and beyond, the four northwestern Secondary Employment Centers all lie within a short distance of I-96 and active freight rails. They contain a mix of cluster activities, from TDL uses—including an active intermodal yard that is currently being consolidated into the DIFT expansion in Southwest Detroit—to metal fabrication and CDER. These corridors historically contained many larger, rail-adjacent industrial properties which have become fragmented in the intervening years due to continuous subdivision. Many of the remaining properties are currently underutilized and these employment centers suffer from a lack of "critical mass" of industrial diversity or anchor activity. However, three of Detroit's largest multi-tenant industrial buildings are located here. In contrast, Upper and Lower Conner Creek are driven primarily by auto cluster anchors, including the large Chrysler Jefferson North Assembly Plant in the south, and Chrysler's Conner Avenue Assembly Plant in Upper Conner Creek near Eight Mile. These infrastructural and anchor assets underpin the redevelopment and intensification potential of these secondary employment districts.

LOS ANGELES DOWNTOWN INDUSTRIAL DISTRICT (LADID)

LADID is a 44-block industrial business improvement district administered by the Central City East Association. The district provides public safety, maintenance and trash services, and abandoned property removal.

14.

A PLACE-BASED STRATEGY FOR GROWTH: STRATEGIES

ACTION PLANS FOR PRIMARY EMPLOYMENT DISTRICTS

Utilizing the data collected through the Detroit Works process, detailed action plans should be created for each employment district. These plans will identify relevant land assemblies, infrastructure investments, and other public improvements may be needed.

15.

B.1 ALIGN PUBLIC, PRIVATE, AND PHILANTHROPIC INVESTMENTS IN EMPLOYMENT DISTRICTS

Employment districts provide targets for private, public, and philanthropic investments, including local and national philanthropy, and city, state, and federal government investments. By concentrating investments and economic activity, Detroit can create the economic density associated with more successful cities, and provide a framework for the effective and efficient allocation of public and philanthropic investments. For example, road funds can be strategically deployed to support employment districts; investments in and operation of public transportation can prioritize employment districts; and workforce and training facilities can be concentrated in neighborhoods and employment districts. One-stop centers in each of the primary employment districts could offer practical services to working parents, such as high-quality daycare and help with applying for the Earned Income Tax Credit and other support for lower-income working parents. Funding for similar centers across the country has come from some combination of employment consortia and public and philanthropic funds.[9] Policy makers should focus on investing in infrastructure that guides public, private, and philanthropic investments to employment districts, tracks cumulative investments, and identifies and addresses any operational issues that arise. These district boundaries need to be formally adopted by relevant organizations and staffed with the appropriate internal capacity. The coordination of city and state investments is paramount. A formal mechanism for this coordination should be considered.

B.2 DEVELOP DETAILED ACTION PLANS FOR PRIMARY EMPLOYMENT DISTRICTS

An important step is to develop detailed action plans and a prioritized list of actions and investments for specific land assembly opportunities, infrastructure investments, public realm improvements, and facilities to provide assistance with pre- and post-employment support for workers to address issues like transportation and childcare. Drawing on the data collected for the development of the Strategic Framework, as well as the work of entities working on the ground in these districts, the planning must rely on an active dialogue with existing businesses and adjacent communities to set priorities for actions and investments that will grow the base of economic activity in each district as well as opportunities for Detroit workers. The plans must strive to brand core employment districts with a clear identity that can be reinforced and marketed to prospective employers. For areas lacking a clear identity or requiring a change in direction to best leverage assets and business climate, the plans must detail necessary steps to reposition such districts.

INDUSTRIAL BUFFERS

Industrial Buffers are forested areas that repurpose vacant land around industry to clean air, block light/glare, and provide a visual barrier for adjacent residential neighborhoods. Buffers also limit land use conflicts and create a more attractive, healthy business environment.

16.

"I can easily remember the busy restaurants and shops along Grand River…updated versions of those places are really important to creative and entrepreneurial work… need to be located all over the city, but especially in the targeted areas."

David, DWP Website, 8/2012

B.3 ENCOURAGE INDUSTRIAL BUSINESS IMPROVEMENT DISTRICTS (IBIDS)

Cities across the country utilize Business Improvement Districts (BIDS) to supplement city services and ensure an attractive and safe business environment through a nominal yearly tax. Detroit's industrial districts would greatly benefit from a similar approach. Led by local business representatives, an IBID would focus its activities on the needs of each specific district. Likely IBID activities would include improving safety, reducing blight, maintenance, coordinated marketing initiatives and offering shared services unique to local businesses, such as job training. An IBID would help to build business leadership across the city, and create a more secure environment in which to invest. BID legislation is in place; however, the process of organizing local businesses to create a BID is often a difficult challenge to overcome. A pilot IBID is needed to help demonstrate the benefits of this approach to businesses across the city. The pilot IBID should target an employment district with strong existing leadership willing to work with the public sector to enable the organization and establish its mission and activities.

B.4 BECOME A NATIONAL LEADER IN GREEN INDUSTRIAL DISTRICTS

A series of landscape initiatives can improve and integrate employment districts into the fabric of the city, boosting economic growth and improving neighborhoods. Currently, industrial areas and major transportation infrastructure (interstates and rail corridors) directly abut residential neighborhoods in many areas of the city. As a result, pollution, noise, and light/glare from industry and infrastructure threaten resident health and comfort. In particular, emissions from these land uses degrade air quality and contribute to a number of health problems for nearby residents, including cardiovascular, respiratory, and other diseases.

Industrial buffers, carbon forests, and setback requirements are proposed solutions aimed at reducing the impact of these uses on residential neighborhoods by cleaning air, reducing sound, blocking light/glare and providing a visual barrier. Specific strategies for these approaches are discussed in the City Systems, Land Use, and Land and Building Assets Elements of this Strategy.

Text Source: 9) Karin Martinson and Pamela Holcomb, "Innovative Employment Approaches and Programs for Low-Income Families." The Urban Institute Center on Labor, Human Services, and Population. February 2007.

Image Sources: 14) Eric Richardson; 15) Hamilton Anderson Associates; 16) Bing Maps

CIVIC ENGAGEMENT FEEDBACK AND PUBLIC PERCEPTIONS

- Relate economic development and land use: target different industries and businesses in different areas of the city

- Plan for and develop retail in certain areas – along commercial corridors

- Using existing buildings and infrastructure (convenience stores, etc.) to sell fresh/healthy food

- Update zoning codes to support small businesses (don't "over-zone" for commercial, ensure residential zoning densities match/support nearby commercial or mixed use)

ENCOURAGE LOCAL ENTREPRENEURSHIP AND MINORITY BUSINESS OWNERSHIP
EXPANDING OPPORTUNITIES TO CREATE NEW BUSINESSES

C

C.1 PROMOTE SHORT-TERM APPROACHES TO INCREASE THE NUMBER AND SUCCESS OF MBES IN THE CITY

Successfully promoting minority business enterprises (MBEs) requires short- and long-term strategies. Short-term strategies should promote growth in sectors of the economy that serve local markets, have low capital requirements, or are known to have a strong MBE presence. These characteristics are prevalent in the city's Local B2B cluster, which should be an early target for MBE growth. In addition to increasing opportunities for MBEs, business and economic development organizations should create a specific toolbox to help MBEs to address financing and business development challenges.

Over the longer term, strategies must attempt to address the larger social and economic factors that curtail MBE creation and growth, including lower average personal wealth, less experience with family businesses, lower average education levels, and challenges with access to capital.

C.2 SUPPORT THE DEVELOPMENT OF LOW-COST, SHARED SPACES FOR CLUSTERS WITH HIGH LEVELS OF SELF-EMPLOYMENT

Detroit should develop new models of shared space for entrepreneurs and small businesses in clusters with high levels of entrepreneurship and for which there are currently few models that include local business services and construction. Like some of the shared and incubator models that exist, these spaces would provide small businesses and entrepreneurs with low-cost office space with shared services and access to relevant expertise, including cost estimation, contract negotiation, accounts receivable, and business development planning. Unlike most shared and incubator spaces, however, this concept would also provide areas for businesses to store equipment, tools, products, and so forth.

CIVIC ENGAGEMENT FEEDBACK AND PUBLIC PERCEPTIONS

- SUPPORT SMALL, NEW, AND RESIDENT-OWNED BUSINESSES
- Provide more resources for existing and small businesses via collaboration with and among universities, funding – e.g. grants and competitive tax breaks – at City, State, and Federal levels, and resources for specific types of businesses, e.g. Black-owned and home-based businesses
- Create a physical environment that makes it easy to operate a business (safe, clean, properly zoned, accessible)

IMPLEMENTATION ACTIONS

1. Promote short-term approaches to increase the number and success of MBEs and disadvantaged business enterprises (DBEs) in the City.

2. Support the development of low-cost, shared spaces for clusters with high levels of self employment.

3. Provide young Detroiters with exposure to and experience in Digital / Creative and other new economy clusters.

4. Develop a comprehensive long-term strategy to increase and strengthen the City's MBEs.

PRECEDENT

1. Minority Business Enterprise-Focused Funding

C.3 PROVIDE YOUNG DETROITERS WITH EXPERIENCE IN DIGITAL/ CREATIVE CLUSTERS AND THE NEW INNOVATION ECONOMY

Business ownership tends to follow generational patterns: People with relatives who were entrepreneurs are more likely to own businesses and often have more tools to grow those businesses. Moreover, those who start businesses tend to concentrate in areas of the economy with which they are most familiar. In some cases, this can make it difficult for MBEs to break into some of the highest-growth, most profitable segments of the economy. To strengthen the number and performance of MBEs in the city, children and young adults without these advantages will need to be given a similar set of experiences and skills. A consortium of business leaders in digital and other sectors, Detroit schools, and the city's leading business incubators should work together to expose young Detroiters to employment and entrepreneurship in the city's high-growth Digital/Creative clusters.

The traditional clusters, like automotive and food, are also important not only for job growth in the city and region but for innovation to address national challenges. For example, Southeast Michigan was a global center for automotive research and development even before the region's automakers recently agreed to double average vehicle fuel economy by 2025. Students in Detroit's high schools should be contributing to these goals and preparing for careers in the leading innovative segments of the economy. The public schools already offer specializations in most of the city's major economic clusters, and some of the programs work with businesses in the city and region. By more closely linking cluster development with the innovation pipeline and education reform, Detroit can create a national model while preparing its students to succeed in the new economy.

"We should have Detroit designated a regional center for the purposes of investor visas and encourage entrepreneurs from all over the world to come to Detroit to start businesses."

Richard, Planning Cluster-based Meetings, 1/2011 - 3/2011

"Support small businesses with grants to get to the next level."

Planning Cluster-based Meetings, 1/2011- 3/2011

C.4 DEVELOP A COMPREHENSIVE LONG-TERM STRATEGY TO INCREASE AND STRENGTHEN THE CITY'S MBES

Detroit must develop strategies to increase the participation of minority populations in all modes of entrepreneurship, including self-employment, business ownership, and communal models such as cooperatives. Getting there will require a comprehensive strategy that addresses the particular opportunities and challenges facing MBE growth in the city of Detroit—such as the city's high rate of minority self-employment and its very low rate of graduation from self-employment to hiring employees. Where possible, a comprehensive strategy will need to address common challenges that face MBE development and growth as described above in Strategy C.1. Such a strategy should include a cluster-by-cluster assessment of opportunities and roadblocks to more and stronger MBEs in the city; assessment of the variety of models that promote local and minority ownership of economic assets; and an assessment of the capital needs and challenges facing the city's MBEs. Some of the country's leading experts on MBEs are in Detroit's universities; their expertise should be tapped.

To help interested Detroiters transition from informal to formal activity will likely require a menu of strategies. Some Detroiters have been excluded from formal sector activity by strict licensing requirements for a range of occupations, an issue that has received attention at the state level. Michigan Department of Licensing and Regulatory Affairs recently proposed dropping licensing requirements associated with 18 occupations, although few seem to be in the occupations that have been identified by national groups as limiting options for lower-income workers.[10] However, a bill to loosen requirements for barbers was recently introduced in the Michigan House.[11] Detroit stakeholders could be important voices in policy discussions around occupational access for lower-income and populations.

In addition to licensing, strategies to graduate informal workers into the formal sector and help the self-employed scale their businesses must address capital challenges and regulatory burdens. Increasing the availability of capital, especially micro-loans that small businesses often require, can create incentives for informal businesses to transition for formal activity and can provide the self-employed with needed capital to scale their activities.[12] Similarly, changes in the regulatory environment that reduce costs of registering or maintaining businesses can also foster formalization of activity. Finally, additional strategies must be employed to help those with criminal records, poor credit history, or other factors that create real or perceived barriers to licenses, capital, and other factors that contribute to entrepreneurial success.[13]

Text Sources: 10) Turner, Mike, State Office of Regulatory Reinvention report: Deregulate 18 occupations, kill 9 boards," Detroit Free Press, April 16, 2012. Michigan Office of Regulatory Reinvention, "Recommendations of the Office of Regulatory Reinvention Regarding Occupational Licensing," February 17, 2012; Carpenter, Dick M., II, Lisa Knepper, Angela C. Erickson and John K. Ross, License to Work: A National Study of Burdens from Occupational Licensing, Institute for Justice, May 2012. 11)"2012 House Bill 5517: Repeal barber licensure mandate" on http://www. michiganvotes.org/; 12) Klapper, Leora, Raphael Amit, Mauro F. Guillén, and Juan Manuel Quesada, "Entrepreneurship and Firm Formation Across Countries, "The World Bank, Development Research Group, Finance and Private Sector Team, Policy Research Working Paper 4313, August 2007; 13) Losby, Jan L., Marcia E. Kingslow, and John F. Else, "The Informal Economy: Experiences of African Americans," ISED Solutions, September, 2003.

Image Sources: 17) Flickr.com Girl.in.tha.D; 18) Bob'o Cloooio Kioko Facebook; 10) Norah's Vintage Loft—Facebook; 20) www.grnnamdi.com; 21) Definitive Style Exclusives (DSE); 22) Broderick Tower Blog/AngelaH; 23) Marvin Shaouni; 24) Spiral Collective—Facebook; 25) http://detroitfunk.com; 26) Diseños Ornamental Iron; 27) Future Net Group; 28) http://hothiphopdetroit.com; 29) www. theimgexperience.com; 30) www.realtimesmedia.com; 31) Velocity Cow; 32) Alter Ego Management

EXAMPLES OF DETROIT MINORITY-OWNED BUSINESSES BY ECONOMIC PILLAR

LOCAL ENTREPRENEURSHIP

CAFÉ CON LECHE
17.

BOB'S CLASSIC KICKS
18.

NORAH'S VINTAGE LOFT
19.

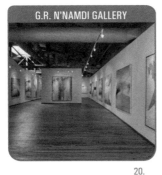
G.R. N'NAMDI GALLERY
20.

DSE
21.

HONEYBEE MARKET
22.

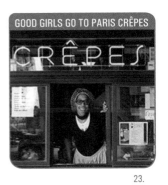
GOOD GIRLS GO TO PARIS CRÊPES
23.

SPIRAL COLLECTIVE
24.

INDUSTRIAL

NEW CENTER STAMPING
25.

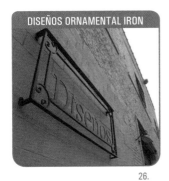
DISEÑOS ORNAMENTAL IRON
26.

FUTURE NET GROUP
27.

OAKLAND STAMPING
28.

DIGITAL / CREATIVE

IGNITION MEDIA GROUP
29.

REAL TIMES MEDIA, LLC
30.

VELOCITY COW
31.

ALTER EGO MANAGEMENT
32.

"Help create a plan for building new, viable, self-sustaining communities of the future with an emphasis on changing the culture of our youth... by promoting the development of a community workforce that will help improve the quality of life for city residents within their neighborhoods and communities. The goal is to build healthy, strong, vibrant, self-sustaining neighborhoods and communities in Detroit."

Ann, Planning Cluster Meeting, 2/5/2011

"The single most important thing the City can do is better workforce training."

Entrepreneurs Working Session

"Most of the innovative entrepreneurship programs I am aware of are already here in Detroit (even national/international ones)."

Angie, Economic Growth Open House, 8/7/2012

"Connect . . . transit lines with a much-expanded international airport hub. Build a big enough hub for Detroit and it will inevitably regain its massive export capacity. Watch the jobs pour in..."

John, Facebook Comment

The strategies for building skills aim at increasing skills and opportunities for Detroiters by improving access to training institutions, aligning training with cluster strategies, increasing the number of local opportunities, and addressing current roadblocks to training and employment, especially transportation.

D.1 "HIRE DETROIT": STRENGTHEN LOCAL HIRING PRACTICES

Shared prosperity will depend on the ability of Detroit residents to secure employment at the major institutions and corporations in the city, which will largely depend on a continued shift towards demand-driven models of workforce training. These must be accompanied by clear mechanisms for recruitment and hiring of Detroit residents, and even roundtable discussions with local employers regarding perceptions and misperceptions of Detroit workers and benefits of local hiring. The Midtown education and medical institutions are already at the national forefront of "hire local" efforts. Best practices include the following: targeting specific positions with the greatest potential for local resident recruitment and documenting education, training, and experience requirements; developing screening and referral partnerships in the community and setting targets for local applicants to be interviewed and hired; creating strategies to retain and retrain incumbent workers through flexible scheduling and on-line training modules; and formulating incentives for managers to hire locally. These efforts should be scaled first within Midtown to organizations not currently involved, and then expanded citywide.

IMPROVE SKILLS BUILDING AND EDUCATION REFORM
PREPARING THE WORKFORCE FOR A DIVERSE ECONOMY

D.2 LINK WORKFORCE INVESTMENTS TO TRANSPORTATION

Transportation accessibility remains a key issue for Detroiters looking for employment. Many of the city's households do not have access to private vehicles and public transportation options do not usually succeed in reliably linking Detroiters to employment centers. Over the longer term, these issues can be addressed through the development of employment districts and the alignment of new public transportation investments around them. In the shorter term, innovative public-private models must be explored. All workforce investments, especially for unemployed or lower-skilled workers, should be linked to a transportation solution.

Innovative models to better link workers and jobs have been successful in other cities. For example, the Lake Cook Shuttle Bug Program in Chicago is a public-private partnership that serves 1,300 riders per day by shuttling them from commuter rail stations to employers.[14] The program, which is currently funded by private employers and the metropolitan transportation authorities, began with vans that brought employees directly from public transportation stops to work sites then expanded to buses as demand grew; this scalability makes it a good model for Detroit. Developing public-private partnerships to better link workers to employers in Detroit will be made more feasible by the strengthening of employment districts that better concentrate jobs in the city.

D.3 COORDINATE WORKFORCE DEVELOPMENT BEST PRACTICES

Workforce conditions and challenges in Detroit and the surrounding region are unique among American cities: The scale of job loss over the last decade is unparalleled, job sprawl is more pronounced than in any other region, and the returns on education appear to be low, especially for male Detroiters. The civic and philanthropic communities recognize that these unique conditions require innovation and experimentation. There is also recognition that sharing information and experiences is critical, yet stories exist about the replication of unsuccessful models. Stakeholders in workforce development need to double down on efforts to coordinate investments, share findings from innovation, and replicate successful models. Development and dissemination of a shared fact sheet on the Detroit workforce, hiring trends, and successful models can be used to track progress and develop the pipeline of talent to meet employer needs.

IMPLEMENTATION ACTIONS

1   "Hire Detroit": Strengthen local hiring practices.
2   Link workforce investments to transportation.
3   Coordinate workforce development best practices.
4   Revitalize incumbent workforce training.
5   Expand public-private partnerships for workforce development.
6   Commission a study to improve graduation rates and poor labor market outcomes of Detroiters.

PRECEDENT

1   Focus: HOPE: Detroit, MI

Text Source: 14) Barbara Ladner, "Blending Public/Private Funding Sources for Employment Transportation." Accessed at http://joblinksencore.ctaa.org/presentations/panel_3. June 2008.

D.4 REVITALIZE INCUMBENT WORKFORCE TRAINING

The greatest opportunity for changing the quality of life for Detroiters is to improve employment options, increase wages, and reduce commuting time for those who already hold jobs. Over 60% of Detroiters who hold jobs commute to the suburbs; of these, 40% make less than $1,250 per month or less than $15,000 per year. In other words, 25% of Detroit's working population faces long commutes for low wages. The majority of this group of Detroiters has at least a high school degree, and a significant segment has at least some college. By virtue of their employment status, many of these Detroiters already possess the so-called "soft" skills needed to find and secure employment.

For these workers, training to advance in their current jobs or secure better-paid employment is critical. Unfortunately, federal funds for incumbent workforce training have evaporated. Philanthropic funding can be aligned with cluster-based growth strategies to better leverage the existing pool of Detroit labor and talent. These funds are the key to the "forgotten middle" in Detroit's workforce.

D.5 EXPAND INNOVATIVE PARTNERSHIPS FOR WORKFORCE DEVELOPMENT

Innovative partnerships have the potential to address challenging workforce issues. For example, the public-private partnership "Michigan Shifting Code" was launched in January 2012 by the Michigan Economic Development Corporation in order to address critical labor shortages in the areas of computer programming and information technology (IT)-related occupations. Designed as demand-driven training modules, each Shifting Code program responds to specific market needs by relying heavily on local IT employers in partnership with local community colleges. Public-philanthropic partnerships have also shown promise. The statewide "Earn and Learn" program works to place the chronically unemployed, including the formerly incarcerated, into long-term employment. The local partner, Southwest Solutions, aims to help over 1,000 metropolitan residents by the end of 2013. The city's strong set of faith-based organizations (FBOs), which already contribute to community and economic development, can also be important partners in workforce development programs, especially for harder-to-serve populations such as the formerly incarcerated.

PRECEDENT

FOCUS: HOPE

Focus: HOPE operates two flagship programs: the Machinist Training Institute and the Information Technologies Center, which have jointly trained and certified thousands of machine and CNC operators, and IT professionals in specific areas like network administration and small office operations.

33.

"I believe that you can make a greater impact with job training and educating people of all walks of life."

Sonja, DWP Website, 8/2012

D.6 COMMISSION STUDY TO IDENTIFY LEVERS TO IMPROVE GRADUATION RATES AND POOR LABOR MARKET OUTCOMES OF DETROITERS

The strong correlation between educational attainment and future employment prospects highlights the need to better understand how to increase high school graduation rates, improve the quality of GED preparation, and address poor labor market outcomes for those with two-year degrees. Studies of GED recipients in recent years demonstrate that while they fare better in terms of college acceptance than those who drop out of high school, only 31 percent of them enroll, mostly in two-year colleges, and 77% percent of them last no longer than one semester. GED recipients who do not enroll in college tend to earn salaries on par with high school dropouts of similar ability.[15] The study should also examine trends in high school graduation rates and in particular, the recent dramatic decrease in high school graduation rates of young black men in Detroit. Finally, the study should examine the relatively poor economic outcomes of Detroiters with two-year college degrees who, as a group, suffer from 16 percent unemployment and poverty rates of more than 20 percent, both well above the national average for Associate's degree holders.

"Education is an economic tool. It is good business."

Nonprofit and Community Development Roundtable

"If you mention training on a lot of campuses there's a negative sentiment. But if you mention education there's a positive response. Are you training people to function in the work pool, or are you training people to be thinkers?"

Education Cluster Working Session, 5/2/2012

Text Source: 15) Margaret Becker Patterson, Wei Song, and Jizhi Zhang. GED candidates and their postsecondary educational outcomes: A pilot study. Research Studies 2009-5, GED Testing Service, Washington, DC, December 2009. James J. Heckman, John Eric Humphries, Nicholas S. Mader, The GED, NBER Working Paper No. 16064, June 2010

Image Source: 33) Focus: HOPE

43E EXPEDITED PERMITTING

This Massachusetts program promotes expedited permitting of development projects on sites with dual designation as "Priority Development Sites." The program requires permitting bodies to review and take final action within 180-210 days of receiving a permit application.

34.

PRIORITY PERMITTING IN EMPLOYMENT DISTRICTS

In cities and states across the country, priority permitting has been used as a catalyst in economic development. This approach would streamline the permitting process and create incentives to shift investment and development patterns towards these districts.

35.

CLEVELAND INDUSTRIAL-COMMERCIAL LAND BANK

This land bank allows the City of Cleveland to strategically assemble properties and create long-term economic and community investments. The City aggressively pursues assessments, acquisition, demolition, and remediation of identified properties.

36.

Land regulation strategies recognize the key role that private markets must play in unlocking the city's potentially vast real estate assets. Unlike in residential areas, almost all of the jobs-producing land in the city, including the vast amounts of vacant and underutilized land, is held privately. With so few opportunities to date to assemble property directly from public agencies or land banks and limited resources to outright acquire private property, other strategies must be considered to affect change on stagnant, privately held commercial and industrial sites. Markets right now are locked because of speculation, the age and quality of the building stock, gaps between development costs and rents, and other financing challenges. Land regulations need to encourage the private market through a combination of strategic land assembly and consolidation where appropriate while also focusing on long-term management tools that provide healthy, safe, and attractive employment districts.

INDUSTRIAL SIDE LOT PROGRAM

- ▢ COMBINED SITE
- ▨ LARGE SITE
- ▰ SMALL SITE

The vast majority of vacant industrial sites are less than one acre in size and have few prospects for redevelopment. Similar to the residential side-lot program, this program would transfer these small sites to the adjacent business.

LAND REGULATIONS
ENCOURAGING PRIVATE INVESTMENT AND ENVIRONMENTAL ACTIONS

E.1 CREATE AN INDUSTRIAL SIDE LOT PROGRAM

The vast majority of industrial vacancies are very small (under 1 acre) parcels, for which there are few industrial development opportunities in Detroit today. The goal of this program would be to dramatically reduce the number of these parcels. Modeled on the residential side lot approach, this program would transfer property rights of small (under 1 acre) industrial lots to an adjacent owner with the proviso that the lots be combined into one larger parcel.

E.2 CREATE A PRIORITY PERMITTING PROCESS FOR EMPLOYMENT DISTRICTS

In cities and states across the country, priority permitting has been used to facilitate investments that will have significant economic development or community impacts. Detroit should adopt expedited permitting in employment districts. This approach would create incentives to shift investment and development patterns towards the employment districts and, by reducing construction time and risk, would increase overall investment in the districts and the city. Models for priority and expedited permitting, including pre-permitting, have been successfully utilized in Chicago, Washington, D.C., and at the state level in Florida, Massachusetts, New York, and Rhode Island.

E.3 FOCUS ON LAND BANKING INDUSTRIAL AND COMMERCIAL PROPERTY

Detroit must take the lead among cities in America's manufacturing heartland that have established a land banking process dedicated to the acquisition, assembly, and disposition of property for industrial and commercial development. The Detroit Land Bank Authority has substantial statutory powers to flexibly acquire and convey property. To date, land bank activities have focused on the challenges associated with vacant and tax delinquent residential property. An arm of the Detroit Land Bank Authority focused on industrial-commercial land would build upon these activities and serve to address the challenges associated with redevelopment within designated employment districts. Such a program, designed with DEGC, would allow the City of Detroit to proactively assemble and transfer properties to attract businesses and create long-term economic growth.

"To help industrial development, there should be pre-assembled sites for development and obsolete/blighted structures torn down."

For Profit Real Estate Developer and Broker Working Session, 1/27/2012

Image Sources: 34) http://mass.gov; 35) Marvin Shaouni; 36) www.city.Cleveland.oh.us

"Detroit is a good place to own a business because of the opportunity, openness, and the spirit of the people. You can't do elsewhere what you can do in Detroit."

Entrepreneurs Working Session

PRECEDENT

VOLKSWAGEN CHATTANOOGA SUPPLIER PARK

Volkswagen's new supplier park is key to powering the success of the Chattanooga assembly plant. Once completed, seven VW supplier companies will assemble parts and ready them for use in the park. Five hundred new jobs will also be created.

37.

E.4 IDENTIFY ALTERNATIVE CAPITAL SOURCES FOR REAL ESTATE DEVELOPMENT

Detroit is in desperate need of capital and subsidies for commercial and industrial building construction that New Markets Tax Credits (NMTC) provide. Nationally, 21 NMTC allocatees include Michigan in their service area but only one, Invest Detroit, is headquartered in the state of Michigan. An annual report and convening of NMTC allocatees would promote Detroit to non-Michigan organizations. In addition, the potential for philanthropic program-related investments (PRIs) in a Detroit-centric real estate investment trust (REIT) and solicitation of non-Michigan REITs should be explored.

E.5 ARTICULATE A REVERSE CHANGE-OF-USE POLICY

In many U.S. cities, a steady erosion of valuable industrial land has been underway through piecemeal conversion of formerly industrial parcels to commercial or residential uses. Detroit, however, is in the unique position of being able to rezone land for jobs producing uses in and around the city's most valuable jobs-producing areas. A clearly articulated reverse change-of-use mechanism should be established to effectively return vacant, abandoned or foreclosed residential or commercial properties adjacent to key employment centers to productive use. As a minimum threshold of properties is reached, such a mechanism could be utilized by the city or land bank to extend adjacent productive land use and zoning designations to the target properties. Long term, the future land use map proposed in the Land Use element chapter identifies and recommends converting formerly commercial and residential lands to industrial zoning in areas that have the greatest potential to create new job and business growth.

E.6 CREATE MASTER-PLANNED INDUSTRIAL HUBS

The most innovative trend in industrial development in recent years has been the emergence of holistic, master-planned industrial hubs such as Supplier Parks, Inland Port developments, Distribution Parks, Workforce Development Hubs, and Eco-Industrial Centers. Such developments often concentrate synergistic industrial activities in close proximity, providing many benefits to tenant companies and clients (including large manufacturers), including closer supply-chain integration, shared services, and more effective innovation and product development. As such, these developments offer major competitive advantages over traditional, dispersed, industrial development models. The feasibility of specific applications within the City of Detroit should be explored in detail.

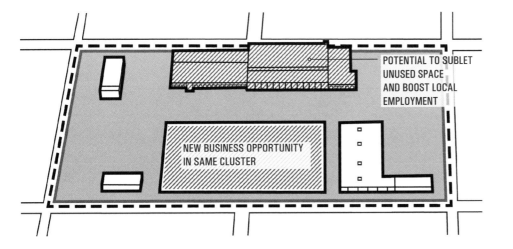

POTENTIAL TO SUBLET UNUSED SPACE AND BOOST LOCAL EMPLOYMENT

NEW BUSINESS OPPORTUNITY IN SAME CLUSTER

UNDERUTILIZED FACILITY

∷ COMBINED SITE

▭ LARGE SITE

≋ SMALL SITE

The challenge of underutilized land requires a long-term initiative designed to boost employment at existing firms. This example demonstrates a common condition: underutilized facilities that used to employ many more Detroiters.

E.7 ADDRESS UNDERUTILIZATION OF INDUSTRIAL BUILDING SPACE AND LAND

Many industrial buildings and sites are simply underutilized, with too few workers given the building and parcel size and location. These are generally the result of long-term employment loss that leaves companies with only a fraction of the company's peak-level workforce. Companies suffer because of the high space and utility costs they must absorb; growth in the city is stifled because these large sites are not available for more productive use. This program would evaluate potential strategies to create a market for subletting unused space to smaller companies and entrepreneurs and in extreme cases, to "right size" companies by moving them to smaller sites in the city.

E.8 ADDRESS WEAKNESSES IN THE LOCAL BROKERAGE SECTOR

As in many cities with dramatic employment loss, Detroit suffers gaps in local business services. In residential real estate, few brokers focus on Detroit, but several strong existing organizations with deep knowledge of the city could be tapped to expand into residential services. In commercial/industrial real estate, an entire regional infrastructure exists but there is too little incentive to show Detroit properties given the glut of space in the region. The Framework recommends working with key downtown organizations to develop programs to strengthen and coordinate information about residential real estate options and the development of an incentive pool to encourage commercial/industrial brokers to show Detroit properties.

IMPLEMENTATION ACTIONS

1. Create an industrial side lot program.
2. Create a priority permitting process for employment districts.
3. Focus on land banking industrial and commercial property.
4. Identify alternative capital sources for real estate development.
5. Articulate a reverse change-of-use policy.
6. Create master-planned industrial hubs.
7. Address underutilization of industrial building space and land.
8. Address weaknesses in the local brokerage sector.

PRECEDENTS

1. 43E Expedited Permitting: Massachusetts
2. Cleveland Industrial-Commercial Land Bank: Cleveland, OH
3. Volkswagen Chattanooga Supplier Park: Chattanooga, TN

PILOT PROJECTS

1. Priority Permitting in Employment Districts
2. Industrial Side Lot Program

Many industrial sites are underutilized and could accommodate many additional jobs.

Data Sources: Interface Studio
Image Source: 37) www.gray.com

EMPLOYMENT DENSITY

HISTORIC EMPLOYMENT DENSITY

CURRENT EMPLOYMENT DENSITY

5 EMPLOYEES PER ACRE

3 EMPLOYEES PER ACRE

60% UTILIZATION RATIO

093

TRANSFORMATIVE IDEAS

099

REALITIES

101

IMPERATIVES

103

**STRATEGIES AND
IMPLEMENTATION**

THE LAND USE
ELEMENT
THE IMAGE OF THE CITY

A Day in the Life *Transforming the Use of Land*

Antonio grew up in the house his grandfather bought in a once-thriving neighborhood. As a little boy, he sat for hours on the driveway while his Papi tinkered with the motorboat that was his pride and joy. Some weekends, when Papi wasn't working, the family hooked the boat up to their Cutlass Supreme and drove to the marina for a day of relaxation and fun.

The boat was sold years ago, and his grandfather passed away in 1986, but the house remains in the family. Antonio swore he'd never leave, but five years ago he was ready to give up and sell out. About 20 out of 50 houses remained occupied on his block, and it felt like the city had forgotten them. Streetlights that went out stayed out, police calls took longer and longer, and every spring meant flooded basements and gutters. As worried as he was for himself and his family, Antonio was more worried for his neighbor Sarah, who was 75 and had no family left in the city.

Things started to change when the Detroit Strategic Framework was released. The City soon put routine city services and maintenance on a regular schedule in response to community requests, and police and fire services have improved. Although it is no secret that the neighborhood will never return to its former days, a new kind of neighborhood is being proposed, and planned with the neighbors' collaboration—a Green Residential area that will be organized around a city pond that Antonio will be able to see from his window. Not everyone will stay: Sarah is taking advantage of Detroit's new "house swap" incentive program, trading her house for a townhome in a senior living community in Midtown, close to shopping, health care, and other activities, all accessible by transit.

Better than that is something Antonio never dreamed of for his home: The City of Detroit and Wayne County have created a plan together to stabilize values for remaining homeowners, while creating a new park, bike path, and water-retention pond to take a burden from the city's aging infrastructure.

So Antonio is staying. Because by the time his own kids give him grandchildren, he's going to have something to show them, something he wishes his own grandfather could see: A view of green space every day of the week, from his own home.

TRANSFORMATIVE IDEAS
LAND USE

LAND IS DETROIT'S GREATEST LIABILITY AND ITS GREATEST ASSET. The preoccupation with *what to do with all that land* has driven the discussion about land use and led to oversimplified strategies. In fact, Detroit's population density is still similar to that of cities like Portland, Atlanta, and Denver. **To be sure, a traditional "build it and they will come" approach is not going to work for Detroit.**

Detroit's image and identity have evolved through three major eras, each tied to a particular aspect of the city's economy. First, the early period of riverfront trade and commerce set the tone for downtown's majestic Beaux Arts buildings and formal street pattern. Then as the city grew during the Auto Age, an extensive industrial ring grew up around the city core. New modes of industrial production decentralized the city still more, with a combination of rail and highways serving the sprawling outer reaches of Detroit. During the third phase of Detroit's identity, large neighborhoods of single-family detached homes spread out across the city. Once a sign of the American Dream, these neighborhoods were never as efficient to serve as more mixed-use, compact neighborhoods would have been. Both the neighborhoods, and the over-scaled systems that serve them, fell on hard times as the city lost population and revenue.

This plan outlines a fourth idea for the city: A stronger, greener, and more socially and economically vital Detroit, where neighborhoods feature a wide variety of residential styles from apartments to houses, and where residents are connected to jobs and services by many transportation options (and especially a regional network of transit) in a "canvas of green" that features stately boulevards, open green space, urban woodlands, ponds and streams, and new uses of natural landscape to clean the air, restore ecological habitats, and produce locally sourced food. Such a Future Detroit will not have a single "hub and spoke" pattern with one downtown, but many centers and neighborhoods that each have a distinctive identity and a character all their own. One of the newest and most ambitious aspects of this change will be the network of productive and working landscapes that actively maintain a higher quality of public health for Detroit, while offering beauty and a wholly new way to experience an urban environment. **Detroit actually has the opportunity to lead the region in creating a new urban form, becoming a model for other North American cities. Here, in the midst of tremendous challenge, is the opportunity to transform the city's form and function in new and exciting ways.**

Some initial efforts can start immediately, through small- or large-scale demonstration projects. A sustained and sustainable transformation of Detroit calls for even more: connected land use and design strategies that stimulate economic growth, align city systems, provide open space, and strengthen neighborhoods, supported by an entirely new framework for decision making and regulation that can respond rapidly to business opportunities, urgent public health needs, and the imperative of job growth and residents' quality of life. The Strategic Framework's new physical vision for the city taps the potential of Detroit's land-rich environment, supports existing areas of growth and stability, and sets forth specific recommendations for serving current residents where they live and work right now.

4

LAND USE TRANSFORMATIVE IDEAS

PEER CITY DENSITY COMPARISON BY AREA

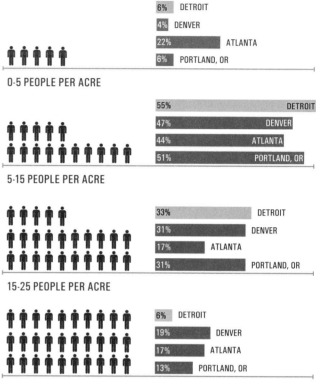

0-5 PEOPLE PER ACRE

6%	DETROIT
4%	DENVER
22%	ATLANTA
6%	PORTLAND, OR

5-15 PEOPLE PER ACRE

55%	DETROIT
47%	DENVER
44%	ATLANTA
51%	PORTLAND, OR

15-25 PEOPLE PER ACRE

33%	DETROIT
31%	DENVER
17%	ATLANTA
31%	PORTLAND, OR

30 + PEOPLE PER ACRE

6%	DETROIT
19%	DENVER
17%	ATLANTA
13%	PORTLAND, OR

Even with many parts of Detroit experiencing high land vacancy, the percentage of Detroit's low-density areas is comparable to peer cities. However, Detroit lacks high density areas as a percentage of its overall land area when compared to peer cities; only 6% of Detroit's land area is high density compared to 13-19% of peer U.S. cities. Source: US Census 2010

DENSITY AND TAX REVENUE

$19K/ACRE/YEAR

8 HOUSEHOLDS PER ACRE   ESTIMATED TAX REVENUE[1]

$4.7K/ACRE/YEAR

2 HOUSEHOLDS PER ACRE   ESTIMATED TAX REVENUE[1]

Density directly impacts the financial condition of the city. Areas of the city with high land vacancy only generate a fraction of the tax revenue that higher density areas produce. The problem is compounded when city systems, originally sized for a higher density, must be maintained and renewed for a population that is significantly smaller. Source: Hamilton Anderson Associates

[1] Based on a household income of $30,000, and a housing value of $50,000. The Detroit resident income tax rate is 2.5%, and the current millage rate for the City of Detroit is 65.14 per 1,000.

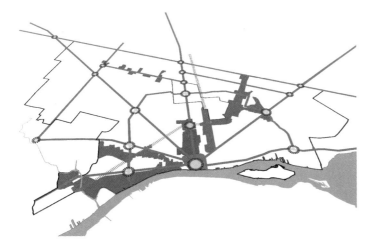

A CITY OF MULTIPLE EMPLOYMENT DISTRICTS

A CITY CONNECTING PEOPLE TO OPPORTUNITY

The Strategic Framework's employment-district strategy addresses the key economic issue in Detroit: not the size of the city's physical footprint, but the scale of the city relative to current levels of economic activity and job and business growth. By promoting focused growth in seven districts, the city can create employment levels typically associated with more prosperous cities, while creating viable strategies for addressing the physical deterioration, limited services, and aging infrastructure across the city.

Each district will have a unique scale and character suited to its function and existing or potential assets, development pattern, and building styles. For example, the McNichols corridor will leverage its institutional assets, including the University of Detroit Mercy, Marygrove College, Sinai-Grace Hospital, and Wayne County Community College District, to expand Eds and Meds employment opportunities, attract employees to live in the area, and improve a diverse range of neighborhoods abutting the corridor from the historic University District to the creation of new multi-family apartment buildings directly fronting McNichols and Palmer Park.

A new network of transportation corridors will connect employment centers to neighborhood districts, allow for new bicycle routes and bus rapid transit corridors, reinforce economic and neighborhood centers, and provide a range of infrastructural services in sustainable natural landscapes that filter stormwater (blue infrastructure) and clean the air of transportation and industrial emissions (green infrastructure). **Existing proposals for enhanced transportation systems in Detroit can be modified to create a transformed network that connects people to jobs and services within the city and to employment centers beyond the city limits.** The transformed network needs to respond to today's metropolitan region while actively contributing to the planned growth of employment districts and localized needs within the city. The key principle behind the transformation is the creation of a clear hierarchy of corridors, ranging from high-capacity and high-speed arterials and highways to intermediate thoroughfares, and lower-capacity neighborhood strips with frequent stopping services. Transportation networks will be conceived in concert with planning for retail amenities and services at the regional and residential scale, with neighborhood-level transportation routes designed as "complete streets" that allow bicycling, walking, and a broader range of approaches to getting places.

Efficient movement of goods and waste in and through Detroit is key to the economic and environmental health of the city. For freight as well as personal transit, the interchanges between hierarchy tiers or different modes of transportation are as important as the routes that run between them. The type of interchange required will have an important impact on the land use in that area. A transit interchange will offer a range of higher-density land uses that can offer services to those passing through. A freight interchange may require large amounts of space and therefore should be considered for areas expected to stabilize at lower residential densities or even change land use altogether.

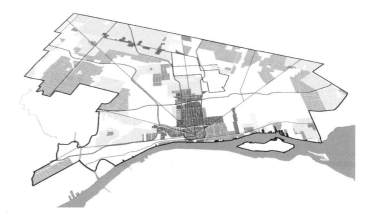

 3   A GREEN CITY WHERE LANDSCAPES CONTRIBUTE TO HEALTH

4   A CITY OF DISTINCT, ATTRACTIVE NEIGHBORHOODS

Unlike other cities pressed to find space for transformative landscapes, Detroit has an abundance of available land resources that can be leveraged to create a new green and sustainable city unlike any other in the world. **Landscape has enormous potential to structure or foster social and cultural relationships through adapted and productive ecologies that will give rise to a new urban form.**

Landscapes are inevitable: If you do nothing else, landscape will re-establish itself even in the most built-up areas. Relative to other forms of infrastructural or urban development, then, landscape strategies are very affordable. Landscapes also adapt well to different conditions, so they can require different types and lower intensities of maintenance to sustain them.

Landscapes are productive and multi-functional. They clean air and water and soil; they make urban environments healthier; and they generate food, jobs, energy, commerce, and habitat. In this way, they cultivate new kinds of urban landscapes and experiences. They are also effective grounds for research and experimentation. New ideas can be safely and effectively tested in landscape settings for later application across the city and in other cities like Detroit.

Landscapes are the original "green" land use: they can reduce the resources necessary to sustain the city. Landscapes enrich communities by improving the health of the environment and of the people in it, and also create a lush, rich image and identity for the city—one which competing cities would love to have.

Because they work most effectively across large scales, with the ability to connect and coordinate seemingly unrelated entities, landscapes also have the potential to reconnect Detroit with its regional context. Landscapes of this type are already in place in Detroit, including the William G. Milliken State Park and Harbor, Detroit RiverWalk, and Belle Isle.

Detroit has room to offer many neighborhood types and lifestyle choices for residents who want to stay in the city, while welcoming new residents looking to make Detroit their home. To achieve this, a series of traditional and innovative neighborhood typologies have been established to directly engage existing challenges within the city, and to leverage the strengths and assets of existing neighborhoods and places with unique characteristics. Guiding the development of these neighborhoods are a series of development targets and performance measures to define neighborhood goals and measure their success in meeting those goals—which are in turn tied to the goal of a high quality of life for all residents.

While Detroit's traditional neighborhoods offer a compelling starting point for this transformation, many other areas—some of which are not necessarily recognized as viable neighborhoods today—offer a significant long-term opportunity for Detroit to be a leader in establishing a new urban form.

For Detroit, this new urban form includes areas in which vacant and underutilized land and defunct industrial building stock provide the material for innovative residential environments. Green residential and green mixed-rise neighborhoods transform existing land vacancy into integrated landscapes, providing recreational, ecological, and productive functions. Mixed-use neighborhoods for living and making not only transform parts of Detroit's unutilized industrial and residential areas, they also capitalize on Detroit's production philosophy, where ideas are developed, and become real.

CREATING A 50-YEAR LAND USE VISION

A CITY OF MULTIPLE
EMPLOYMENT DISTRICTS

A CITY CONNECTING PEOPLE
TO OPPORTUNITY

A GREEN CITY WHERE LANDSCAPES
CONTRIBUTE TO HEALTH

A CITY OF DISTINCT,
ATTRACTIVE NEIGHBORHOODS

50 YEAR LAND USE VISION

The four transformative ideas provide the
basis for the future land use vision.

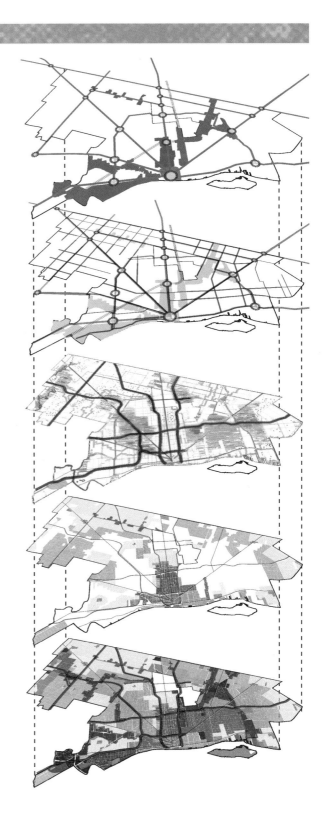

THE LAND USE ELEMENT : THE IMAGE OF THE CITY

98

POPULATION & LAND

21
IN 1950, DETROIT HAD AN AVERAGE OF 21 RESIDENTS PER ACRE[1]

1950

61%
DETROIT LOST 61% OF ITS POPULATION BETWEEN 1950-2010

2010

8
IN 2010, DETROIT HAD AN AVERAGE OF 8 RESIDENTS PER ACRE[3]

5.7 AVG
IN 1950, DETROIT HAD AN AVERAGE OF 5.7 OCCUPIED HOUSING UNITS PER ACRE[2]

3
IN 2010, DETROIT HAD AN AVERAGE OF 3 OCCUPIED HOUSING UNITS PER ACRE[4]

UNDERUTILIZED LAND

72 SUPERFUND SITES IN DETROIT
SUPERFUND IS A PROGRAM ESTABLISHED TO ADDRESS HAZARDOUS WASTES CAUSED BY INDUSTRIAL ACTIVITIES & ABANDONED SITES[5]

80K
OF DETROIT'S 349,170 TOTAL HOUSING UNITS, 79,725 ARE VACANT[6]

22%
22% OF DETROIT'S INDUSTRIAL ZONED LAND IS VACANT[7]

VACANT LAND 20 SQ MILES
APPROXIMATELY 20 SQUARE MILES OF DETROIT'S OCCUPIABLE LAND AREA IS VACANT[8]

36%
36% OF DETROIT'S COMMERCIAL PARCELS ARE VACANT[9]

UNMET DEMAND

583K SQ FT
THE AMOUNT OF MONEY SPENT ON GROCERIES OUTSIDE THE CITY COULD SUPPORT APPROXIMATELY 583,000 SQUARE FEET OF ADDITIONAL GROCERY RETAIL SPACE IN DETROIT[10]

6.7 ACRES
PARK SPACE PER PERSON
DETROIT FALLS BELOW THE NATIONAL RECREATION AND PARK ASSOCIATION RECOMMENDATION OF 10 ACRES OF PARK SPACE PER 1,000 RESIDENTS[11]

65%
65% OF TOTAL CITYWIDE HOUSING SUPPLY IS SINGLE FAMILY DETACHED[12]

66%
66% OF TOTAL HOUSING DEMAND IN DETROIT'S GREATER DOWNTOWN IS FOR MULTI-FAMILY[13]

REALITIES
THE STATE OF DETROIT'S LAND USE

UNDERUTILIZATION OF LAND. The breathtaking growth that defined Detroit's emergence into the American industrial age is now a distant memory. In the last 10 years the total number of vacant housing units has doubled while the population has declined by 25 percent. Today, approximately 20 square miles of Detroit's occupiable land area are vacant. Within this context, the City of Detroit finds itself insolvent and struggling to provide the core services Detroiters need. With projected population decline in the city extending to 2040, and low workforce participation, the reutilization of Detroit's land must also navigate within an anemic market and environmental challenges while fulfilling currently unmet demands of Detroit's residents and employees.

CHALLENGING MARKET. While the consideration of Detroit's market challenges is often framed within the context of declining population, the resulting disinvestment has left 36 percent of the city's commercial parcels and 80,000 homes vacant. Within Detroit's struggling market, such vacancy quickly becomes abandonment, blight, and a public safety risk. These realities represent real, physical hurdles to Detroit's redevelopment, and demonstrate a diminished quality of life. For those who remain in the city, the ability to obtain amenities and services remains strained, particularly for Detroiters without a private vehicle. The result is unmet demand, loss of revenue, and inequity.

Detroit has far to go if it is to recapture its competitive edge in the region and the state of Michigan. Ultimately, $1.5 billion in annual Detroit retail spending is lost to surrounding cities, including $200 million alone in unmet retail food demand that dramatically undermines Detroiters' access to fresh, healthy food. Although there is demand for apartments and multi-family homes in Detroit, most of the city's housing choices are large, single-family homes that cannot compete with similar home choices in the suburbs. Further contributing to market struggle and health concerns are the 72 Superfund sites located in Detroit where the unmanaged industrial legacy of the city has created a range of areas with measurable hazardous waste that must be cleaned up before the land can be reused.

UNHEALTHY ENVIRONMENT FOR RESIDENTS. Combined Sewer Overflows (CSO) and Sanitary Sewer Overflows (SSO) pollute rivers several dozen times per year on average, far in excess of state and national clean water standards. Heavy rainfalls also cause flooding, which shuts down roads, interrupts transportation and business, and threatens human health and safety. Air quality and soil quality are typically low due to a legacy of past industrial uses, current pollution releases, and lead contamination.

Not everyone in Detroit bears the burden equally. Past decisions, policies, and practices placed disproportionate environmental and health burdens on poorer neighborhoods. A new approach to land use must now correct these inequities.

OVERSCALED, NON-SUSTAINABLE INFRASTRUCTURES. Current infrastructural systems (including open spaces and recreational facilities, school, etc.) were built to accommodate populations more than twice the size of current-day Detroit. These systems are too big and maintenance-intensive—and they consequently cost too much to sustain. Built at a time when sustainable practices were not prevalent, they also can harm the environment, as in the case of CSOs.

NEED FOR MORE OPEN SPACE AND RECREATIONAL RESOURCES. For all the discussion about vacancy and surplus land, Detroit still falls well below the national average for park space acreage per resident. The still-new 31-acre William G. Milliken State Park and Harbor, as well as historic Belle Isle and Campus Martius, offer a glimpse into what is possible for Detroit's transformation into a greener city of beautiful vistas, playing fields, urban woodlands, bicycle paths and walking trails, as well as lakes and ponds, streams, playgrounds, and pocket parks.

Today, however, Detroit lags behind national standards and comparable cities in park availability. Parks and recreation centers are also poorly distributed across the city, relative to population densities: Areas of high-vacancy often have an abundance of open space that is being underused, while more populated areas lack enough parks to serve their residents. Care for parks and playgrounds is also an issue: Most current open spaces designed for traditional, high levels of maintenance, which is not affordable for limited park budgets.

1,2) US Census 1950; 3,4) US Census 2010; 5) US Environmental Protection Agency; 6) US Census 2010; 7) Interface Studio; 8) Detroit Planning & Development Department (P&DD), Hamilton Anderson Associates; 9) Wayne State University Department of Urban Studies & Planning, Pⅅ 10) Social Compact 2010; 11) Trust for Public Land; 12) American Community Survey 2010 5-Year; 13) Zimmerman & Volk

We must use innovative approaches to transform our vacant land in ways that increase its value and productivity and promote long-term sustainability.

We must use our open space to improve the health of all Detroit residents.

IMPERATIVES
LAND USE ACTIONS AND IMPACT

The Detroit Strategic Framework provides specific land use typologies to properly guide investment and land use decisions for achieving a sustainable, equitable, and healthy city. The Strategic Framework's identification and development of innovative land use forms and patterns was shaped by the quality-of-life and quality-of-business elements identified during the public process to engage with residents, employers, and other civic leaders. These elements not only guide the land use recommendations of the Strategic Framework, but also form the basis for long-term measurement of how well these proposed land uses are meeting the needs of residents, employees, and the city at large.

The future land uses, integrated with coordinated investment strategies, will demonstrate opportunities to fulfill needs for employment districts, neighborhoods, city systems, and open space. Among other objectives, they achieve sustainable densities and forms, effectively connecting to city transit corridors, integrating open spaces and services within neighborhoods, and using green and blue infrastructure to improve system performance and cost. Each approach defines an urban form to more efficiently use Detroit's land-rich environment to improve quality of life and business in the city. In some cases, these approaches leverage existing forms of development, but in others they deploy more innovative urban forms that create new models for land and facilities reuse by transforming existing buildings and land area into productive contributors to a sustainable Detroit.

WHAT WE LEARNED FROM CIVIC ENGAGEMENT FEEDBACK

- Survey respondents' top choice for where they would like to do activities in the future was "Within walking distance from my home".

- Survey respondents' top choices for neighborhood types to develop in the next five years were less traditional neighborhood typologies:

  - Green Residential

  - Green Mixed-Rise

  - Live+Make

- Top land use strategies recorded from DWP participants included:

  - Prioritize green and natural areas

  - Develop a wider range of safe, affordable, and diverse housing

  - Remediate, maintain, clean-up, and utilize land more effectively—including currently vacant, City-owned, and privately-owned land

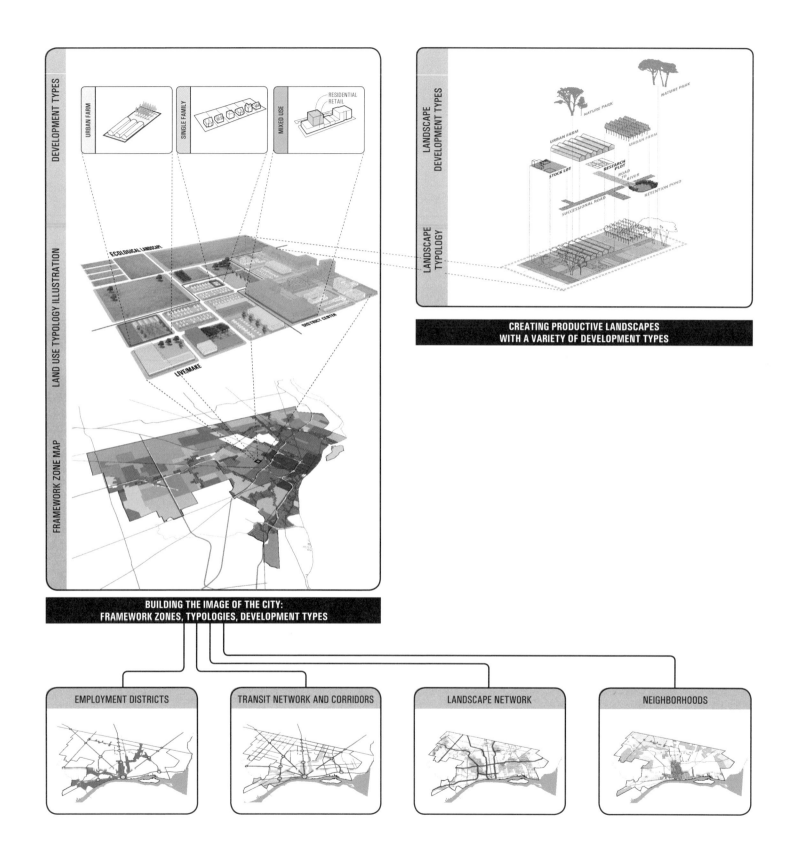

DEVELOPMENT TYPES

URBAN FARM

SINGLE FAMILY

MIXED USE

RESIDENTIAL RETAIL

LAND USE TYPOLOGY ILLUSTRATION

ECOLOGICAL LANDSCAPE

DISTRICT CENTER

LIVE/MAKE

FRAMEWORK ZONE MAP

LANDSCAPE DEVELOPMENT TYPES

NATURE PARK

NATURE PARK

URBAN FARM

URBAN FARM

STOCK LOT

RESEARCH PLOT

ROAD TO RIVER

RETENTION POND

SUCCESSIONAL ROAD

LANDSCAPE TYPOLOGY

CREATING PRODUCTIVE LANDSCAPES WITH A VARIETY OF DEVELOPMENT TYPES

BUILDING THE IMAGE OF THE CITY: FRAMEWORK ZONES, TYPOLOGIES, DEVELOPMENT TYPES

EMPLOYMENT DISTRICTS

TRANSIT NETWORK AND CORRIDORS

LANDSCAPE NETWORK

NEIGHBORHOODS

STRATEGIES AND IMPLEMENTATION

Detroit's successful transformation will rely on its ability to retain current residents, businesses, and institutions while attracting new ones. Because Detroit did not arrive at its current condition overnight, its turnaround will require considerable time, and a willingness to adapt and try new solutions. Putting the proper tools and resources in place today can ensure more coordinated, flexible, and effective actions in the future.

The appropriate land use strategies to fulfill this objective are situated between the city's existing conditions and a range of preferred futures. The Detroit Strategic Framework organizes a wide variety of potential land use types within three levels of scale and purpose:

FRAMEWORK ZONES are meant to guide citywide and investment decisions in terms of the best ways to make positive change in areas with differing characteristics. These zones seek to categorize the city's residential, commercial, and industrial land based on similar physical and market characteristics. The most influential characteristic is vacancy, because of its drastic effect on physical and market conditions of an area.

LAND USE TYPOLOGIES provide the future vision for land use within the city. They are divided into three primary categories: neighborhood, industrial, and landscape. Land use typologies are used within the framework zones to provide the next-highest-level tool for decision making. They also provide the basis for the city's future land use map and zoning districts. Instead of standard zoning practices that classify each property within the city, land use typologies seek to generate complete neighborhoods by prescribing densities and allowable development types for larger areas. To illustrate, each neighborhood typology aims for specific ratios and types of residential, commercial, and landscape uses that will allow residents and employees to live, work, and play within every unique neighborhood.

DEVELOPMENT TYPES are the physical development of buildings and landscape that may occur within a particular land use typology. They are divided into four major categories: residential, commercial, landscape, and industrial. For example, a development type may be a single family home, a retail strip, a stormwater retention pond, or a warehouse. Development type suitability and use criteria are determined by the land use typology.

The focus of the land use strategies is to recognize these three levels of consideration as a fundamental set of reference points for investment and future directions. In addition, the Detroit Strategic Framework recommends the following supportive strategies for land use:

- Create a new and diverse open space system for the city.
- Redefine corridors and complete streets.
- Develop innovative regulatory reform.

FOUR TRANSFORMATIVE IDEAS : SIX IMPLEMENTATION STRATEGIES

A — CREATE A CITYWIDE FRAMEWORK FOR GROWTH AND INVESTMENT

The public, private, and philanthropic sectors need a tool to assess the city's land use conditions and develop strategic approaches to investments that will improve quality of life across all parts of the city. Based on comprehensive research and analysis of the physical and market conditions of the city, the Framework Zones map will help assesses the condition of Detroit's districts and neighborhoods in terms of degrees of vacancy, from low to moderate to high. From this fact-based mapping, decision makers from city leaders to neighborhood organizations have the ability to take a more strategic approach to the opportunities and challenges facing neighborhoods, and to place those challenges in the context of the city at large. The discussion of vacancies in this broad, citywide context does not attribute "strength" or "weakness" to neighborhoods only on the basis of vacancy: Every neighborhood within the city is at risk, and every effort needs to be made to stabilize and transform the existing conditions to improve quality of life in all parts of the city.

IMPLEMENTATION ACTIONS

1   Establish framework zones and future land use maps as the basis for public, private, and philanthropic investment.

2   Base land use decisions on the fundamental physical and market conditions of the city: low-vacancy, moderate-vacancy, high-vacancy and Greater Downtown areas.

3   Update framework zones map on a 5-year basis to reflect changes to physical and market conditions.

B — SUPPORT A NETWORK OF NEW AND EXISTING NEIGHBORHOOD TYPES

The Detroit Strategic Framework introduces a new set of land use typologies that combine to represent the future land use vision for the city, from traditional forms that now characterize Detroit to entirely new departures. These are organized in three major categories: Neighborhoods, Industry, and Landscape. Each typology is scaled to the district or neighborhood level, and includes a range of strategic interventions and development types to support the larger vision for Detroit's new form. In addition to more conventional land use typologies, such as Traditional Residential Neighborhoods or General Industrial Districts, the Detroit Strategic Framework introduces new typologies that repurpose vacant land or obsolete industrial areas for innovative or productive uses, such as Innovation Ecological landscapes and Live+Make districts.

IMPLEMENTATION ACTIONS

1   Establish land use typologies as the vision for the future city.

2   Reorganize land use around neighborhoods, industry, and landscape.

C — INTRODUCE NEW FORMS OF DEVELOPMENT

Areas of high, moderate, and low-vacancy all hold the potential to be assets in the reinvention of the city. As part of the land use vision, the Detroit Strategic Framework posits two key points regarding development: First, not all development can occur in all places; and second, new forms of development can affirm the city's assets and address existing physical conditions. New residential and commercial development must reinforce areas of strength and increase densities there. At the same time, areas with significant population loss and high degrees of vacancy can be the sites of new, innovative, and productive development types that improve quality of life for city residents.

IMPLEMENTATION ACTIONS

1   Align framework zones and future land use typologies to determine appropriate locations and types of development across the city.

2   Introduce new and innovative landscape-based development types.

3   Introduce form-based development criteria.

D — CREATE A NEW AND DIVERSE OPEN SPACE SYSTEM FOR THE CITY

Landscape, open space, and environmental systems are envisioned as a new, healthy, green, and productive structure for the city of Detroit. Large-scale ecological and productive landscapes will take the place of vacant lots, and begin their work cleansing the water, the air, and the soil, all the while putting people to work. They also become a center for improving public health, sustaining Detroit's rich mix of cultures, and strengthening social connections in neighborhoods and across the city.

IMPLEMENTATION ACTIONS

1 Implement blue and green infrastructure.

2 Encourage reuse of vacant land with productive landscapes.

3 Diversify park network.

4 Encourage partnerships between universities and firms in productive landscapes to conduct research and provide job training opportunities.

E — REDEFINE CORRIDORS AND CREATE COMPLETE STREETS

Similar to its residential land, Detroit's commercial and transportation corridors have seen massive disinvestment over the last 50 years. The city's reduced population has left its roadways oversized for the population they serve. The space left behind holds the potential for rethinking the city's corridors. In fact, we cannot afford to continue to think of transportation and other city systems as "mono-functional"—Detroit has the opportunity and the imperative to combine many services and functions in repurposed corridors that can accommodate different types of transit, bicycling, and walking. Doing so will create a network of "complete streets" that offer an efficient set of transportation options and also address the need for green space and high-quality street design. Excess space within the right-of-way can accommodate blue infrastructure such as swales to collect stormwater run-off. Within areas of low-vacancy, land can be assembled in nodes to create walkable retail districts or new residential development that reinforces adjacent neighborhoods.

IMPLEMENTATION ACTIONS

1 Develop tiered transit network that ties into regional system.

2 Incorporate multi-modal transit design into all street improvements.

3 Focus commercial development in walkable nodes or auto-oriented strips based on physical/market conditions and future land use vision.

4 Implement green infrastructure along highway corridors.

5 Implement blue infrastructure along arterial and other roads.

F — ENACT INNOVATIVE REGULATORY REFORM

The overlay of Framework Zones, land use typologies, and development types provide the basis for a revised regulatory framework that the City of Detroit should formally adopt. The City's anticipated adoption and codification of the Detroit Strategic Framework will also call for multiple layers of policy guidance documents within City departments and other public agencies, so that they can align implementation with the citywide vision for Detroit's new image. The Detroit Strategic Framework also offers an important opportunity to provide a fully coordinated basis for regional and state decision making about land use and public investment, recognizing the importance of the city within a larger regional, state and national context.

IMPLEMENTATION ACTIONS

1 Phase land use vision over 3 horizons (stabilize/improve, sustain, transform).

2 Revise/amend City Master Plan of Policies and Zoning Ordinance.

3 Update public, private, and philanthropic policy guiding documents.

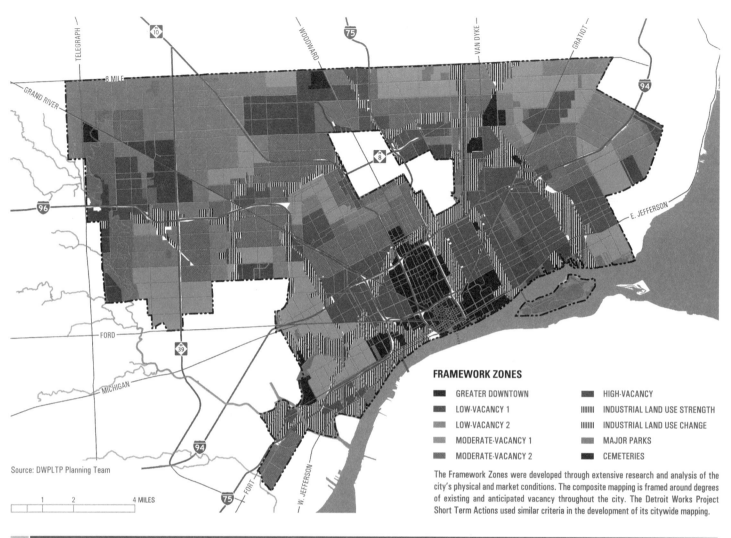

FRAMEWORK ZONES

- ███ GREATER DOWNTOWN
- ███ LOW-VACANCY 1
- ███ LOW-VACANCY 2
- ███ MODERATE-VACANCY 1
- ███ MODERATE-VACANCY 2
- ███ HIGH-VACANCY
- ▍▍▍ INDUSTRIAL LAND USE STRENGTH
- ▍▍▍ INDUSTRIAL LAND USE CHANGE
- ███ MAJOR PARKS
- ███ CEMETERIES

The Framework Zones were developed through extensive research and analysis of the city's physical and market conditions. The composite mapping is framed around degrees of existing and anticipated vacancy throughout the city. The Detroit Works Project Short Term Actions used similar criteria in the development of its citywide mapping.

Source: DWPLTP Planning Team

1   2   4 MILES

ANALYSES THAT INFLUENCED THE FRAMEWORK FOR DECISION MAKING		
RESIDENTIAL PHYSICAL CONDITION ANALYSIS	**MARKET VALUE ANALYSIS**	**DWP SHORT TERM ACTIONS INTEGRATED ANALYSIS**
DESCRIPTION Evaluation of prevailing physical conditions and household occupancy trends in residential areas across the city, identifying areas sharing common characteristics to inform decision making and strategy.	Evaluation of market factors and trends across the city, identifying areas sharing common market value characteristics to inform decision making and strategy.	Designation of general market types by the City of Detroit based on physical conditions and market value characteristics, articulating specific short-term governmental roles for intervention.
INDICATORS Percent change in households 2000-2010; vacant land; vacant housing; housing condition	Median housing unit sales price 2009-2010; sales price coefficient of variance; percent residential properties in REO; subsidized rental stock; vacant lots; vacant, open, and dangerous buildings; foreclosures; commercial/residential ratio; owner occupancy	Residential Physical Condition Analysis; Market Value Analysis
SOURCES Hamilton Anderson Associates; Data Driven Detroit; US Census 2000-2010	The Reinvestment Fund; Southeast Michigan Council of Governments (SEMCOG); US Census 2010; Data Driven Detroit; US Department of Housing and Urban Development (HUD); Wayne County Assessor's Office	Detroit Planning and Development Department; The Reinvestment Fund; Hamilton Anderson Associates

CREATE A CITYWIDE FRAMEWORK FOR GROWTH AND INVESTMENT
LAND USE FRAMEWORK ZONES

Public, private nonprofit, and philanthropic decision makers urgently need a thorough understanding of existing and anticipated land use conditions throughout Detroit to guide strategic investment for long-term strength and viability. The fundamental tool for this is the Framework Zones map, developed through comprehensive research and mapping of both the physical and market conditions of the city's residential, industrial, and commercial land. On the basis of existing and anticipated degrees of vacancy, the Framework Zones map aids developing the most appropriate range of strategies to inform land use decision making and investment, as well as citywide decision making for city system infrastructure, public land, and facilities.

The boundaries of the Framework Zones were determined not only by vacancy conditions, but also by neighborhood identity and physical separation created by major pieces of infrastructure or variations in land use. The goal was to analyze districts and neighborhoods in their entirety, not on the basis of parcel-level or block-level conditions. Previous mappings of the city–including the Community Development Advocates of Detroit's (CDAD) Strategic Framework map—aggregated data to the block level. While block level analysis is critical to neighborhood-based planning, it is less effective in determining direction for citywide decision making, particular where conditions may vary significantly from block to block as is common in the city today. The Framework Zones map should be understood to work in concert with these and future finer-grain maps: the Framework Zones provide the basis for citywide decision making; finer grain mapping provides the basis for individual neighborhood planning efforts.

The Framework Zones define four main composite characteristics across the city, and where those characteristics may be found. This composite is defined typically by degrees of overall land and structural vacancy. These include Low-Vacancy, Moderate-Vacancy, High-Vacancy, and Greater Downtown. Greater Downtown stands out distinctly because while it does have considerable land vacancy, its market characteristics remain the strongest in the city, and may incorporate different long-term goals and opportunities.

Areas with the highest degree of vacancy represent areas in which the existing residential fabric has been significantly eroded and land is often lying fallow and unused. Transformational approaches to areas with the highest degree of vacant land represent opportunities to dramatically improve the quality of life for those who currently live there, while ensuring future land use is more productive,

ecologically beneficial, and manageable from the standpoint of city systems.

In the middle of the Framework Zones spectrum are the moderate-vacancy areas. These areas represent both the largest overall land area and largest population of the framework zones. They also represent degrees of vacancy and market condition that range considerably across their geographies, posing challenges to stabilization and long-term land use transformation. In many ways, these are the areas that tell the most compelling stories of the city's growth, losses, and resilience: It is in these areas where the most innovative land use strategies can stabilize residential neighborhoods and define new types of neighborhoods to seamlessly integrate landscape and neighborhood.

The areas of lowest vacancy are neighborhoods that have historically been stable in terms of population and housing values, making them more competitive with their regional counterparts. Similar to the areas of moderate-vacancy, these neighborhoods continue to house a large percentage the city's population. With the deployment of near-term strategies that help to stabilize the housing market, forestall the rate of foreclosures and maintain improvement levels of neighborhood appearance and public safety, these neighborhoods can offer some of the best traditional urban housing options in the region.

The range of conditions found throughout Detroit provides the opportunity for creative reinvention of this land while simultaneously aligning scarce resources to have the greatest effect. Each Framework Zone should be seen in terms of its opportunity, with the differences lying only in the range of strategies available to achieve transformation.

IMPLEMENTATION ACTIONS

1   Establish framework zones and future land use maps as the basis for public, private, and philanthropic investment.

2   Base land use decisions on the fundamental physical and market conditions of the city: Low-Vacancy, Moderate-Vacancy, High-Vacancy, and Greater Downtown areas.

3   Update framework zones map on a 5-year basis to reflect changes to physical and market conditions.

LOCATIONS

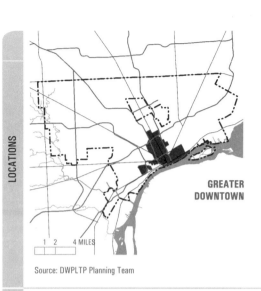

GREATER DOWNTOWN

1 2   4 MILES

Source: DWPLTP Planning Team

LOW-VACANCY

LOW-VACANCY 1

LOW-VACANCY 2

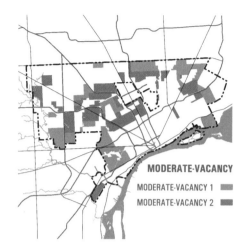

MODERATE-VACANCY

MODERATE-VACANCY 1

MODERATE-VACANCY 2

EXAMPLE AREA

OCCUPIED   VACANT

DESCRIPTION AND STATISTICS

POPULATION: 45,279   MEAN INCOME: $32,652

21%

32%

14% PO

5% OF CITY

HOUSING VACANCY

VACANT PARCELS: PUBLICLY OWNED

LAND AREA

GREATER DOWNTOWN is broken out as a separate framework zone due to its role as the commercial core of the city and its unique physical form and zoning, which support higher densities and mixed-use development. It is characterized by moderate amounts of land and building vacancy. As a result, it has the highest capacity for increased commercial and residential growth due to significant amounts of buildable land and an existing multi-story building fabric. Greater Downtown has the strongest market demand in the city for additional residential and commercial uses. It also has low rates of foreclosure, relative to the rest of the city.

POPULATION: 254,260   MEAN INCOME: $48.509

16%

7%

3% PO

26% OF CITY

HOUSING VACANCY

VACANT PARCELS: PUBLICLY OWNED

LAND AREA

LOW-VACANCY 1 neighborhoods have very low land and building vacancy. They also have the strongest residential markets relative to the rest of the city. Despite falling market values, they have maintained steady demand, accounting for their low-vacancy rates. Relative to the rest of the city they have had lower rates of home foreclosure. They include many of the city's historic districts.

LOW-VACANCY 2 neighborhoods have low land and building vacancy and by all appearances retain their identity as intact traditional residential neighborhoods. However, the residential markets in these areas have shown elevated rates of home vacancy as well as high rates of home foreclosure. Falling home values and weakening demand have made them vulnerable to future depopulation and increased vacancy.

POPULATION: 318,140   MEAN INCOME: $35,821

26%

22%

15% PO

33% OF CITY

HOUSING VACANCY

VACANT PARCELS: PUBLICLY OWNED

LAND AREA

MODERATE-VACANCY 1 neighborhoods have moderate land and building vacancy. The traditional residential fabric in these neighborhoods is punctuated by interspersed vacant land and buildings. Market conditions in most instances are weak, showing vulnerability with low demand and high foreclosure rates. Many Moderate-Vacancy 1 areas, due to their proximity to Low-Vacancy neighborhoods, show greater potential for stabilization than Moderate-Vacancy 2 areas.

MODERATE-VACANCY 2 neighborhoods show an extreme variation of vacancy conditions from moderate to high. As a result, many Moderate-Vacancy 2 areas are on the verge of losing their largely residential character. These areas have weak residential markets with very low demand and high foreclosure rates. They tend to be located adjacent to areas of High-Vacancy.

HIGH-VACANCY

INDUSTRIAL LAND USE STRENGTH

INDUSTRIAL LAND USE CHANGE

1 2 4 MILES

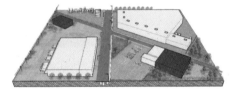

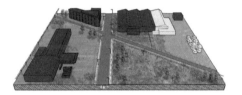

POPULATION: 88,255   MEAN INCOME: $28,082

30%

HOUSING
VACANCY

56%
39%

VACANT PARCELS:
PUBLICLY OWNED

17%
OF CITY

LAND AREA

POPULATION: N/A   MEAN INCOME: N/A

44%
21%

VACANT PARCELS*:
PUBLICLY OWNED

21%
14%

VACANT LAND AREA:
PUBLICLY OWNED

POPULATION: N/A   MEAN INCOME: N/A

47%
21%

VACANT PARCELS*:
PUBLICLY OWNED

32%
16%

VACANT LAND AREA:
PUBLICLY OWNED

HIGH-VACANCY neighborhoods have very high rates of both land and building vacancy. These areas have largely lost their residential character. Residential structures are often isolated in a larger field of maintained or unmaintained vacant land. These areas have experienced high rates of illegal dumping and other forms of neglect. They exhibit very weak to no market outside of speculative land purchases adjacent to key city assets. A very high percentage of vacant land in High-Vacancy areas is in public ownership.

INDUSTRIAL LAND USE STRENGTH areas contain Detroit's industrial lands that hold the most promise for productive use going forward. At the heart of these zones lie Detroit's strongest and most diverse existing industrial nodes, which act as anchors for other industrial and commercial activity. These areas combine higher employment density with good infrastructure access, a variety of appropriate development sites, and buffering from residential land uses. These corridors have the best potential for meeting the needs of current and future advanced and traditional industrial sectors.

INDUSTRIAL LAND USE CHANGE areas are formerly industrial corridors and nodes in Detroit where an industrial critical mass is gone, or nearly so. The topography of viable industrial activity in Detroit has evolved in tandem with technological advances and market globalization, and these changes are reflected in industrial firms' individual and collective land use decisions. As a result, certain areas once appropriate for industrial use are no longer so and should be reassessed and ultimately transitioned to land uses more beneficial to Detroit communities.

*Note: Vacant Land was coded in the Detroit Industrial Land Inventory as 1) vacant site; abandoned or 2) vacant site; empty

EXISTING DETROIT LAND USE TYPOLOGY EXAMPLES

RESIDENTIAL TYPOLOGIES

GREEN RESIDENTIAL
1.

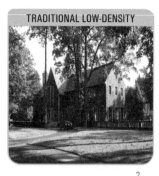
TRADITIONAL LOW-DENSITY
2.

TRADITIONAL MEDIUM-DENSITY
3.

GREEN MIXED-RISE
4.

MIXED-USE TYPOLOGIES

NEIGHBORHOOD CENTER
5.

DISTRICT CENTER
6.

CITY CENTER
7.

LIVE+MAKE
8.

INDUSTRIAL TYPOLOGIES

HEAVY INDUSTRIAL / UTILITIES
9.

GENERAL INDUSTRIAL
10.

LIGHT INDUSTRIAL
11.

"Given the prevalence of high-vacancy neighborhoods and industrial areas with abandoned warehouses, it would seem that the Green Residential and the Live+Make typologies would be . . . particularly beneficial."

Alexandra, Community Conversation #3, 9/2012

LANDSCAPE TYPOLOGIES

INNOVATION PRODUCTIVE
12.

INNOVATION ECOLOGICAL
13.

LARGE PARKS
14.

SUPPORT A NETWORK OF NEW AND EXISTING NEIGHBORHOOD TYPES
LAND USE TYPOLOGIES

Land use typologies comprise the building blocks for the future land use map. They provide the vision and strategic direction for specific districts and neighborhoods throughout the city, while simultaneously addressing the existing and anticipated land use conditions presented within the Framework Zones. The three major categories of land use typologies—Neighborhoods, Industrial, and Landscape—work together within the Framework Zones to guide strategic decision making that contributes to a more sustainable city and improves quality of life for residents.

NEIGHBORHOOD TYPOLOGIES. Detroit's neighborhoods must be regionally competitive to retain current residents, attract new residents, and provide the quality of life everyone deserves. Such neighborhoods should not only fulfill multiple resident lifestyle needs, they must also contribute to a neighborhood model that establishes sustainable densities for the city at large. The neighborhood typologies range from recognizable, traditional forms to non-traditional and innovative prototypes that offer opportunities for new mixed-use communities and the integration of residential structures with transformative landscapes. In some instances, such neighborhood development will leverage existing assets to stimulate greater market demand that could support higher density housing types.

LANDSCAPE TYPOLOGIES. Not all areas of the city that were historically traditional residential neighborhoods can remain as such. In areas with high levels of vacancy, eroding physical condition, diminished quality of life, and virtually nonexistent market demand, new investment in residential uses cannot be recommended. No resident should be forced to move, however. The Detroit Strategic Framework recommends a range of approaches to serving residents in these areas, while preparing for the transformation of these areas as residential population declines. New and productive land uses in these areas can provide needed jobs to Detroit residents, and allow land that no longer serves a productive purpose to return to a maintained version of its natural state.

These areas can be re-imagined as landscapes for economic growth, infrastructure, and ecology. In each, landscapes provide a unique opportunity to address existing challenges of environmental justice and environmental decline. New landscapes can provide needed jobs to Detroit residents, perform infrastructural functions like capturing stormwater and cleaning air, provide habitat to local wildlife and migrating birds, and decrease maintenance costs. Landscape typologies also include large parks like Belle Isle and Palmer Park, which provide important recreational opportunities and ecological functions for the city and region.

INDUSTRIAL TYPOLOGIES. The proposed industrial typologies recognize that Detroit's economic and productive uses vary significantly in terms of their scale, intensity, and impacts. The amount of vacant land around many industrial areas also provides unique design opportunities that are integrated into the typologies.

Modern industrial activity is essential to Detroit's economic growth but it needs to be carefully planned to maximize the use of existing land and infrastructure while creating an attractive and healthy environment for both businesses and adjacent neighborhoods. This includes an opportunity to establish a new era for making things in the city, with cleaner, more sustainable measures that support research, cultivation, assembly, and artisanal uses.

Detroit's market for industrial land and real estate is unique in several ways when compared to the markets for other typologies. Users often choose their space and location based on purely pragmatic criteria such as access to transportation infrastructure and workforce, number of loading docks, ceiling clearances, and floor loads. These recognized real estate standards for modern industry need to be accommodated in the design of Detroit's industrial typologies to ensure they are regionally competitive.

Proposed industrial activity is categorized into five distinct typologies that outline standards for density and use. A critical consideration for the design of the industrial typologies is the proposed interface between industrial activity and other, nearby non-industrial uses. The Live+Make typology, for instance, is intended to encourage a wide range of uses from small-scale manufacturing to housing and can therefore be designed in the context of existing economic districts and neighborhoods. On the other hand, the Heavy Industrial typology recognizes that some industrial uses require a significant distance and buffering from other uses. The result is a range of typologies that enable the opportunity to either integrate small-scale industrial activity into communities, or buffer higher-impact uses in a way that supports economic activity.

Image Sources: 1,2) Hamilton Anderson Associates; 3,4) Marvin Shaouni; 5) Hamilton Anderson Associates; 6) Parkerdr, Wikimedia Commons; 7) Marvin Shaouni; 8,9) Hamilton Anderson Associates; 10) Connie Johnson; 11) Interface Studio; 12) Marvin Shaouni; 13) Suzanne Temple, blogspot.com; 14) Mike Russell

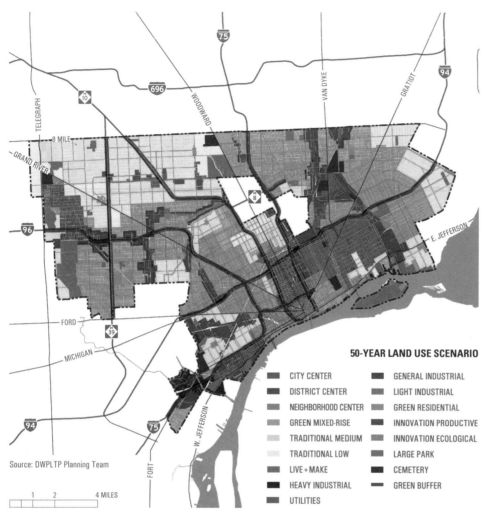

50-YEAR LAND USE SCENARIO

- CITY CENTER
- DISTRICT CENTER
- NEIGHBORHOOD CENTER
- GREEN MIXED-RISE
- TRADITIONAL MEDIUM
- TRADITIONAL LOW
- LIVE + MAKE
- HEAVY INDUSTRIAL
- UTILITIES
- GENERAL INDUSTRIAL
- LIGHT INDUSTRIAL
- GREEN RESIDENTIAL
- INNOVATION PRODUCTIVE
- INNOVATION ECOLOGICAL
- LARGE PARK
- CEMETERY
- GREEN BUFFER

Source: DWPLTP Planning Team

1   2   4 MILES

The 50-year land use scenario is built from the land use typologies. There are three major categories of land use typologies: Neighborhoods, Industrial, and Landscape. Within each of these major categories is a range of potential typologies, each providing the vision for returning vacant land to productive uses.

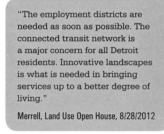

"The employment districts are needed as soon as possible. The connected transit network is a major concern for all Detroit residents. Innovative landscapes is what is needed in bringing services up to a better degree of living."

Merrell, Land Use Open House, 8/28/2012

NEIGHBORHOOD LAND USE TYPOLOGIES: RESIDENTIAL

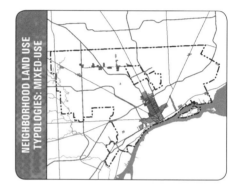

NEIGHBORHOOD LAND USE TYPOLOGIES: MIXED-USE

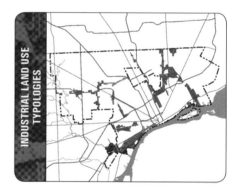

INDUSTRIAL LAND USE TYPOLOGIES

LANDSCAPE LAND USE TYPOLOGIES

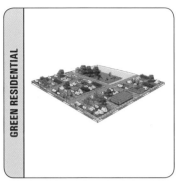

GREEN RESIDENTIAL

TRADITIONAL LOW-DENSITY

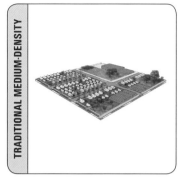

TRADITIONAL MEDIUM-DENSITY

GREEN MIXED-RISE

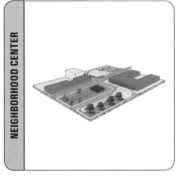

NEIGHBORHOOD CENTER

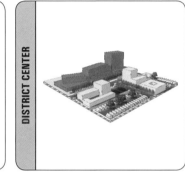

DISTRICT CENTER

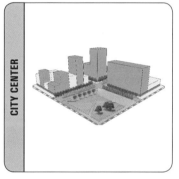

CITY CENTER

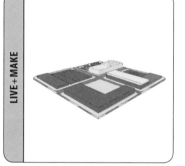

LIVE+MAKE

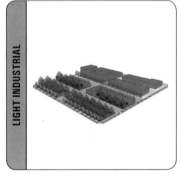

LIGHT INDUSTRIAL

GENERAL INDUSTRIAL

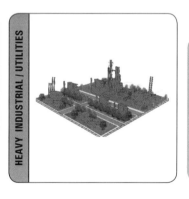

HEAVY INDUSTRIAL / UTILITIES

"It seems neighborhood centers would most provide what's missing. They'd bring in needed services and foster community, which is vital to connection, safety, life, and excitement . . . I appreciate adding the green aspects to each for true sustainability, especially buffering the industrial areas."

Karen, Email Comment, 9/2012

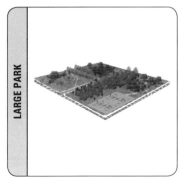

LARGE PARK

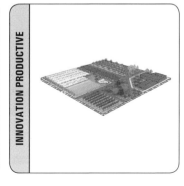

INNOVATION PRODUCTIVE

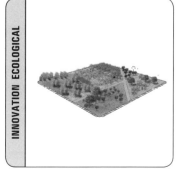

INNOVATION ECOLOGICAL

113

THE LAND USE ELEMENT : THE IMAGE OF THE CITY

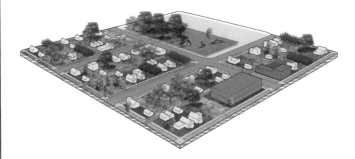

GREEN RESIDENTIAL areas illustrate one of the more profound ways in which Detroit may become a leader in sustainable land use, responding to neighborhood disinvestment and population loss by creating a new urban identity integrated with landscape. The Green Residential typology proposes transformed, landscape-based neighborhoods that transform Detroit's vacant and underutilized land into a canvas of green, supporting single- and multi-family residential along with community-maintained recreational spaces, productive landscapes, and blue/green infrastructure.

GREEN RESIDENTIAL TRANSITIONAL use shares the same set of strategic interventions as the Green Residential typology, but defers city systems renewal decisions until residential densities have achieved long-term stability.

TRADITIONAL LOW-DENSITY defines several of Detroit's historic districts. The predominant housing type in these areas is the detached single-family house on a 45-foot-wide (or larger) parcel, placed within a range of urban grids or lower-density meandering suburban streets. A limited mix of commercial retail types may be located at the periphery. Public space is provided by neighborhood parks, schools, or recreation centers. Future development of a similar size and scale should be reviewed carefully to confirm sustainable densities, and suitable cost/revenue ratio to provide services. Traditional Low-Density neighborhoods rely upon relatively better market strength compared with other Detroit neighborhoods, and have correspondingly higher taxable valuable and revenues to sustain cost-effective delivery of services.

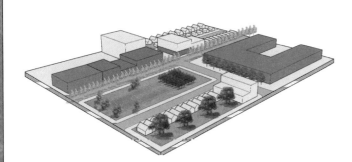

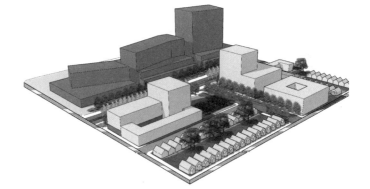

NEIGHBORHOOD CENTERS are vibrant mixed-use environments that are hubs for commercial, community, and recreational activities for adjacent residential areas. These neighborhoods incorporate a limited mix of commercial employment and retail uses, and support a diverse range of residential housing types from multi-family to townhouse to detached single-family. Neighborhood retail is integrated into the residential fabric in nodes or along commercial strips. Public spaces include neighborhood parks or squares, as well as integrated landscapes. Schools, recreation centers, libraries, cultural centers, or places of worship provide institutional anchors.

DISTRICT CENTERS are active, medium-to-high density, mixed-use areas that provide an even split of residential and employment uses. They are typically anchored by a major commercial or institutional employer such as a university or medical center. Residential areas incorporate a mix of housing types from multi-family to townhouse to detached single-family. Multiple medium-density residential neighborhoods typically surround a District Center. District and neighborhood center retail types cater to resident and employee populations. Major civic cultural institutions and public spaces provide regional and neighborhood destinations.

LAND USE COLOR CODE

▬ OFFICE   ▬ RESIDENTIAL   ▬ INSTITUTIONAL   ▬ RETAIL   ▬ INDUSTRIAL

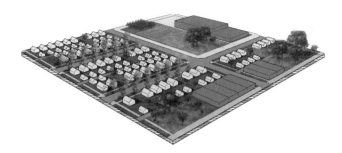

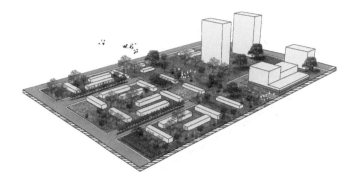

TRADITIONAL MEDIUM-DENSITY areas are primarily residential, with peripheral retail and other commercial uses. Traditional medium-density areas typify the dominant residential pattern throughout the city. The predominant housing type is the detached single-family house on a 30- to 45-footwide parcel within a conventional urban street grid, but may also include attached duplex and townhouse structures. A mix of retail types is located in commercial strips or nodes at the periphery of these neighborhoods. Public space is provided by neighborhood parks, schools, or recreation centers. At full density, Traditional Medium-Density Residential neighborhoods maintain a sustainable cost to provide services.

GREEN MIXED-RISE presents an innovative new residential neighborhood that combines medium- and high-density multi-family housing (both low- and high-rise) within a landscape setting. This landscape context can favor more productive characteristics (such as community gardens and forests), or more ecological characteristics (such as blue and green infrastructures and new urban habitats). Commercial retail and employment may be interspersed within the development area or at the periphery along corridors. Green Mixed-Rise neighborhoods demonstrate a unique way for Detroit to incorporate and attract greater density by capitalizing on existing physical assets– such as the east riverfront, and especially areas susceptible to flooding—while fostering a more symbiotic relationship with the natural environment. The relatively high density of the Green Mixed-Rise neighborhood achieves a low cost to provide services.

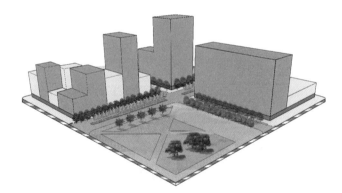

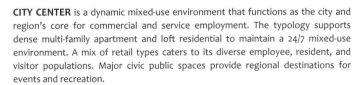

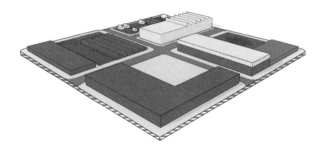

CITY CENTER is a dynamic mixed-use environment that functions as the city and region's core for commercial and service employment. The typology supports dense multi-family apartment and loft residential to maintain a 24/7 mixed-use environment. A mix of retail types caters to its diverse employee, resident, and visitor populations. Major civic public spaces provide regional destinations for events and recreation.

LIVE+MAKE presents another opportunity for Detroit to become a change leader in innovative urban design. Repurposed historic industrial structures and land that fosters a blend of smaller scale, low-impact production activity is combined with a diversity of other land uses. This typology provides a framework for true live-work in Detroit by allowing artisanal and small manufacturing, fabrication, assembly, and workshop uses compatible with housing and retail. The scale of industrial use is relatively fine grained, with a range of overall forms, including occupying multi-story, former industrial structures as well the development of new building types. Any adaptive reuse or new construction should be encouraged to have space set aside for productive activities.

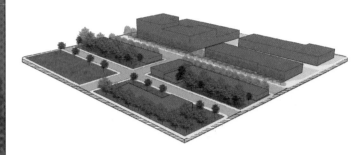

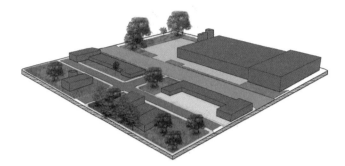

LIGHT INDUSTRIAL areas incorporate modern, light industrial uses that provide attractive environments for jobs and are compatible with nearby neighborhoods. They accommodate light industrial business and technology parks, food processing and wholesaling, advanced manufacturing, and research and development facilities on high-value urban land in an attractive, low-impact environment. Design guidelines, performance standards, and a percentage of by-right office uses would provide for an environment competitive with suburban business and technology parks, with the added advantage of proximity to educational and health assets located in the city. Low-impact light industrial users– fabricators, wholesalers, and small distributors—would be typical of the market for this typology, which features higher building coverages, urban street patterns, and small or subdivided lots.

GENERAL INDUSTRIAL areas incorporate the bulk of Detroit's non-infrastructural industrial lands. They provide job centers to accommodate a wide range of production and distribution activities, buffered from other uses with blue/green infrastructure. The impact of the activities located here is lower than those found in heavy industrial areas, and many general industrial zones already abut residential neighborhoods. Higher building coverages, large lots, and building footprints and truck circulation areas are found in this zone, which comprises the most appropriate territory for retention and growth of modern industrial facilities. Urban design standards should be employed to achieve the quality business environment required to make these sites more competitive and marketable. Manufacturing, processing, wholesale, and distribution uses with moderate noise, vibration, odor, and traffic impacts would be typical in this zone.

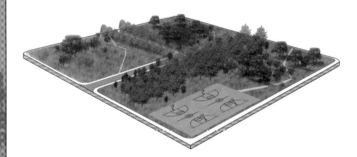

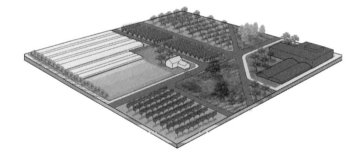

LARGE PARKS are traditional large open spaces across the city that provide recreational opportunities and environmental benefits locally and regionally. This typology includes parks, cemeteries, golf courses, and any other traditional landscapes 4 acres or greater in size. These public spaces are typically managed by the Detroit Recreation Department, but other organizations may contribute to programming and maintenance.

INNOVATION PRODUCTIVE areas are landscapes of innovation where productive development types predominate. These landscapes put vacant land to productive, active uses: growing food and productive forests, reducing maintenance costs, cleaning soil, generating new knowledge, and reshaping public perceptions of vacant land. These innovative landscapes primarily include flowering fields that clean contaminated soils, research plots to test ideas, urban farms with greenhouses or cultivated forests (silviculture), and aquaculture and algae-culture facilities. A portion of these areas is devoted to blue infrastructures to manage stormwater, and ecological landscapes are also found here as a tertiary use of innovation, where working+productive development types predominate. The minimum size would be 2 acres, with some large-scale commercial sites being potentially much larger.

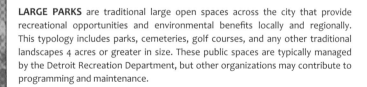

LAND USE COLOR CODE

OFFICE   RESIDENTIAL   INSTITUTIONAL   RETAIL   INDUSTRIAL

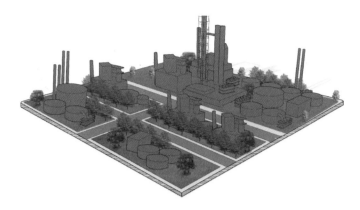

HEAVY INDUSTRIAL districts accommodate high-impact industrial activity isolated from other residential and commercial uses. Low building coverage– often lacking enclosed activity—accommodates industrial activity like storage tanks, pipelines, and material yards in this zone. Heavy industrial zones are more permissive of high impacts such as noise, vibration, odor, traffic, and activity in order to provide for functional and secure space in the city required by petrochemical tank farms, refineries, gasification plants, asphalt, and concrete plants. Additional areas for community-serving heavy industrial activities– including scrap yards, salvage yards, recycling, waste transfer and heavy equipment maintenance or repair—may be designated within existing industrial districts via a community planning process where necessary.

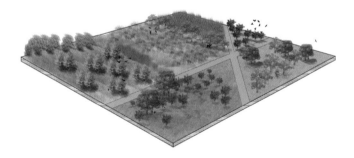

INNOVATION ECOLOGICAL areas are landscapes of innovation, where ecological development types predominate. Here forests, meadows, and other landscapes develop gradually over time and cost very little (or nothing!) to "construct" and maintain. Flowering meadows gradually give way to forests, and the changing landscape supports a variety of plant and animal life, including birds like pheasants. These landscapes can develop on their own, or can be guided to different types of desirable landscapes, which may be especially suitable for a particular species, or more appropriate for stormwater management, or a quick-growing forest that shades out tall grasses and prevents them from growing, improving visibility and eliminating need for mowing. A portion of these areas is devoted to blue infrastructures to manage stormwater, and working+productive landscape development types are also found here as a tertiary use, occupying no more than 10% of the land area not allocated to blue infrastructure.

"We need to grow more of our own food, clean our air and water through strategic use of plants, produce energy from renewable sources."

Mary Lou, Land Use Open House, 8/28/2012

"While I don't know all neighborhoods well enough to determine if the land use typologies designated in the given maps is the best choice, I think defining land use typologies and looking at where they best fit will be potentially very beneficial."

Alexandra, DWP Community Conversation, 9/12/2012

IMPLEMENTATION ACTIONS

1 Establish land use typologies as the vision for the future city.

2 Reorganize land use around neighborhoods, industry, and landscape.

117

THE LAND USE ELEMENT : THE IMAGE OF THE CITY

EXISTING: CURRENT LAND USE

58%	7%	17%	8%	10%
RESIDENTIAL	COMMERCIAL	INDUSTRIAL	PARKS	INSTITUTIONAL

LEGEND

- RESIDENTIAL
- COMMERCIAL
- INDUSTRIAL
- PARKS AND OPEN SPACE
- INSTITUTIONAL
- TRANSPORTATION, COMMUNICATIONS, AND UTILITIES

Source: SEMCOG

1   2   4 MILES

PROPOSED: 50-YEAR LAND USE SCENARIO

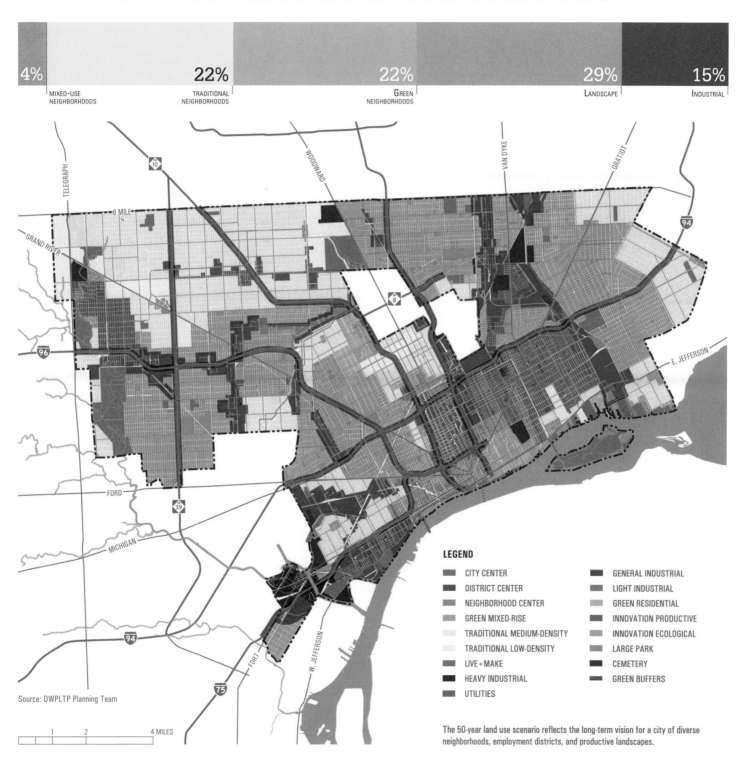

4%	22%	22%	29%	15%
MIXED-USE NEIGHBORHOODS	TRADITIONAL NEIGHBORHOODS	GREEN NEIGHBORHOODS	LANDSCAPE	INDUSTRIAL

LEGEND

- CITY CENTER
- DISTRICT CENTER
- NEIGHBORHOOD CENTER
- GREEN MIXED-RISE
- TRADITIONAL MEDIUM-DENSITY
- TRADITIONAL LOW-DENSITY
- LIVE+MAKE
- HEAVY INDUSTRIAL
- UTILITIES

- GENERAL INDUSTRIAL
- LIGHT INDUSTRIAL
- GREEN RESIDENTIAL
- INNOVATION PRODUCTIVE
- INNOVATION ECOLOGICAL
- LARGE PARK
- CEMETERY
- GREEN BUFFERS

Source: DWPLTP Planning Team

The 50-year land use scenario reflects the long-term vision for a city of diverse neighborhoods, employment districts, and productive landscapes.

THE LAND USE ELEMENT : THE IMAGE OF THE CITY

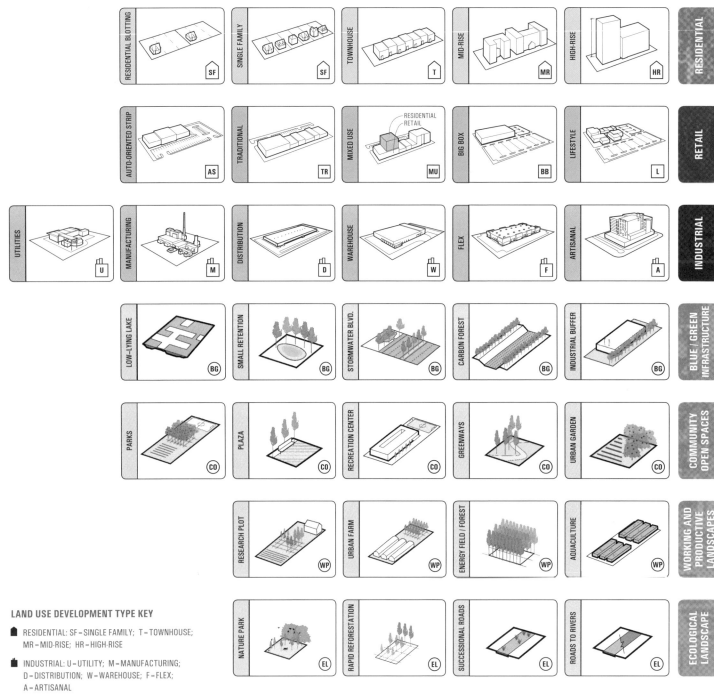

RESIDENTIAL

RESIDENTIAL BLOTTING — SF

SINGLE FAMILY — SF

TOWNHOUSE — T

MID-RISE — MR

HIGH-RISE — HR

RETAIL

AUTO-ORIENTED STRIP — AS

TRADITIONAL — TR

MIXED USE — MU

RESIDENTIAL
RETAIL

BIG BOX — BB

LIFESTYLE — L

INDUSTRIAL

UTILITIES

MANUFACTURING — M

DISTRIBUTION — D

WAREHOUSE — W

FLEX — F

ARTISANAL — A

U

BLUE / GREEN INFRASTRUCTURE

LOW-LYING LAKE — BG

SMALL RETENTION — BG

STORMWATER BLVD. — BG

CARBON FOREST — BG

INDUSTRIAL BUFFER — BG

COMMUNITY OPEN SPACES

PARKS — CO

PLAZA — CO

RECREATION CENTER — CO

GREENWAYS — CO

URBAN GARDEN — CO

WORKING AND PRODUCTIVE LANDSCAPES

RESEARCH PLOT — WP

URBAN FARM — WP

ENERGY FIELD / FOREST — WP

AQUACULTURE — WP

ECOLOGICAL LANDSCAPE

NATURE PARK — EL

RAPID REFORESTATION — EL

SUCCESSIONAL ROADS — EL

ROADS TO RIVERS — EL

TRANSITIONAL LANDSCAPES

EVENT LANDSCAPES — TL

ARTSCAPES — TL

PHYTOREMEDIATION — TL

URBAN MEADOW — TL

LAND USE DEVELOPMENT TYPE KEY

- RESIDENTIAL: SF = SINGLE FAMILY; T = TOWNHOUSE; MR = MID-RISE; HR = HIGH-RISE
- INDUSTRIAL: U = UTILITY; M = MANUFACTURING; D = DISTRIBUTION; W = WAREHOUSE; F = FLEX; A = ARTISANAL
- RETAIL: AS = AUTO-ORIENTED STRIP; TR = TRADITIONAL; MU = MIXED USE; BB = BIG BOX; L = LIFESTYLE CENTER
- LANDSCAPE: BG = BLUE / GREEN INFRASTRUCTURE; CO = COMMUNITY OPEN SPACES; EL = ECOLOGICAL LANDSCAPES; TL = TRANSITIONAL LANDSCAPES; WP = WORKING AND PRODUCTIVE LANDSCAPES

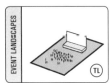
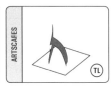
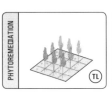
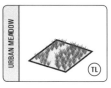

INTRODUCE NEW FORMS OF DEVELOPMENT
LAND USE DEVELOPMENT TYPES

While the Framework Zones map provides a framework for decision making based on the physical and market conditions of the city, and the land use typologies provide the vision for how land and neighborhoods should evolve to improve quality of life, development types provide the range of possible developments within the city. These development types work within the framework zones and the land use typologies to help guide investment and development to the most appropriate areas of the city.

There are four major categories of development types: Residential, Commercial/Retail, Industrial, and Landscape. Within each of these major categories is a wide range of possible development types. Each land use typology is made up of a combination of possible development types. For instance, within High-Vacancy areas, there are only a limited number of allowable land use typologies. These typologies consist of a wide array of primarily landscape-based development types. However given the physical and market conditions described in High-Vacancy areas and the land use vision described in the range of High-Vacancy typologies, future residential or commercial uses would be excluded from future development.

The matrix on the following pages reflects the reality that **although not all forms of investment can occur in all parts of the city, all parts of the city will need some form of investment to achieve its land use potential.** Development types provide the range of development allowed within a given land use typology. The land use typologies provide the vision for how land is to be redeveloped. The framework zones situate the land use typologies to steer development to the most appropriate parts of the city. This nesting becomes the basis of recommended future zoning ordinance revisions.

INTRODUCE NEW AND INNOVATIVE FORMS OF DEVELOPMENT. While there is a strong regulatory component to steering development to its most appropriate location, the Detroit Strategic Framework also advocates for a much wider array of allowable uses to encourage experimentation, entrepreneurship, and innovation. Although conventional residential, commercial/retail and industrial development types form the building blocks for growth within a diverse range of employment districts and mixed-use neighborhoods, the landscape-based development types provides Detroit with a unique opportunity to reframe its future around its landscape and open spaces. Multiple scales of blue and green infrastructure, from small retention ponds to low-lying lakes, can be interspersed within more conventional development to address the need for stormwater

management and quality amenities for residents. Carbon forest and industrial buffer development types can help cleanse the air around major areas of pollution. Research plots, urban farms, aquaculture, and energy field development types can help return vacant land to productive uses and provide needed jobs for Detroit residents. Event landscapes and artscapes can help establish Detroit as an international destination for arts and culture around its creative use of land. Detroit's future lies in the opportunity these new and innovative uses provide to transform the city's vacant land for productive and creative purposes.

IMPLEMENTATION ACTIONS

1   Align framework zones and future land use typologies to determine appropriate locations and types of development across the city.

2   Introduce new and innovative landscape-based development types.

3   Introduce form-based development criteria.

THE LAND USE ELEMENT : THE IMAGE OF THE CITY

122

LAND USE TYPOLOGIES

| GREEN RESIDENTIAL | GREEN RESIDENTIAL TRANSITIONAL | TRADITIONAL LOW-DENSITY | TRADITIONAL MEDIUM-DENSITY | GREEN MIXED-RISE | NEIGHBORHOOD CENTER | DISTRICT CENTER |

NEIGHBORHOOD TYPOLOGIES

FRAMEWORK ZONES

The matrix (FRAMEWORK ZONES rows: GREATER DOWNTOWN, LOW-VACANCY 1, LOW-VACANCY 2, MODERATE-VACANCY 1, MODERATE-VACANCY 2, HIGH-VACANCY, INDUSTRIAL STRENGTH, INDUSTRIAL CHANGE):

- **GREATER DOWNTOWN** — Green Mixed-Rise: T MR HR MU BB LS BG CO; Neighborhood Center: T MR TR MU BG CO; District Center: T MR HR TR MU BG CO A
- **LOW-VACANCY 1** — Traditional Low-Density: SF TR CO BG; Traditional Medium-Density: SF T AS TR BB LS BG CO; Green Mixed-Rise: T MR HR MU BB LS BG CO; Neighborhood Center: T MR TR MU BG CO A; District Center: T MR TR MU BG CO F A
- **LOW-VACANCY 2** — Green Residential Transitional: AS TR BG CO; Traditional Medium-Density: SF T AS TR BB LS BG CO; Green Mixed-Rise: T MR HR MU BB LS BG CO; Neighborhood Center: T MR TR MU BG CO A
- **MODERATE-VACANCY 1** — Green Residential: AS TR BB BG CO TL; Green Residential Transitional: AS TR BB BG CO TL; Traditional Medium-Density: SF T AS TR BB BG CO TL; Green Mixed-Rise: T MR HR MU BB LS BG CO TL; Neighborhood Center: T MR TR MU BG CO A
- **MODERATE-VACANCY 2** — Green Residential: AS TR BB BG CO TL

HOW TO READ THE LAND USE DEVELOPMENT TYPE MATRIX

The Land Use Development Type Matrix illustrates how development will be guided by framework zone and typology to achieve a future vision for the city. The matrix illustrates which typologies are appropriate for each framework zone and the development types that are appropriate for each typology and framework zone. For example, if an area of the city is classified Moderate-Vacancy 1, there are 5 appropriate typologies: Green Residential, Green Residential Transitional, Traditional Medium-Density, Green Mixed-Rise and Neighborhood Center. If the desired typology is Green Residential there are then 5 appropriate development types: Neighborhood and Auto-Oriented Strip retail development types, Blue Green Infrastructure, Community Open Spaces, and Transitional Landscapes landscape development types.

LAND USE DEVELOPMENT TYPE LEGEND

- RESIDENTIAL: SF = SINGLE FAMILY; T = TOWNHOUSE; MR = MID-RISE; HR = HIGH-RISE
- INDUSTRIAL: U = UTILITY; M = MANUFACTURING; D = DISTRIBUTION; W = WAREHOUSE; F = FLEX; A = ARTISANAL
- RETAIL: AS = AUTO-ORIENTED STRIP; TR = TRADITIONAL; MU = MIXED USE; BB = BIG BOX; L = LIFESTYLE CENTER
- LANDSCAPE: BG = BLUE / GREEN INFRASTRUCTURE; CO = COMMUNITY OPEN SPACES; EL = ECOLOGICAL LANDSCAPES; TL = TRANSITIONAL LANDSCAPES; WP = WORKING & PRODUCTIVE LANDSCAPES

- ● BY RIGHT
- ○ CONDITIONAL

CITY CENTER

LIVE+MAKE

LIGHT INDUSTRIAL

GENERAL
INDUSTRIAL

HEAVY INDUSTRY /
UTILITIES

INNOVATION
PRODUCTIVE

INNOVATION
ECOLOGICAL

LARGE PARKS

INDUSTRIAL TYPOLOGIES		LANDSCAPE TYPOLOGIES	

123

THE LAND USE ELEMENT : THE IMAGE OF THE CITY

REGIONAL PARK NETWORK

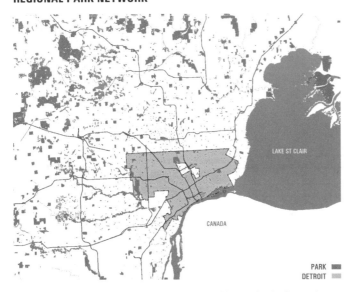

LAKE ST CLAIR

CANADA

PARK
DETROIT

Detroit's largest open spaces are currently large parks, which link to a regional park network.

STORMWATER / SEWER MANAGEMENT

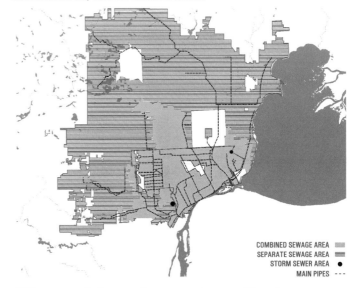

COMBINED SEWAGE AREA
SEPARATE SEWAGE AREA
STORM SEWER AREA •
MAIN PIPES ---

DWSD operates a regional stormwater/sewage system that covers a 946 sq mile area.

MAJOR BIRD MIGRATION ROUTES

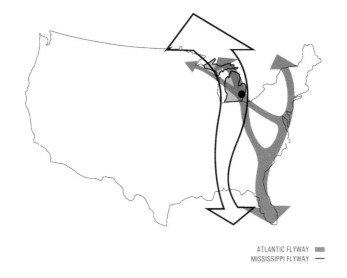

ATLANTIC FLYWAY
MISSISSIPPI FLYWAY

Detroit is located at the intersection of the Atlantic and Mississippi flyways, key migration paths for birds that stretch across North America.

GREAT LAKES WATERSHED

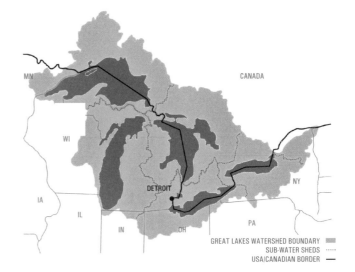

MN
CANADA
WI
DETROIT
NY
IA
IL
IN
OH
PA

GREAT LAKES WATERSHED BOUNDARY
SUB-WATER SHEDS .....
USA/CANADIAN BORDER

Michigan, including Detroit, sits within the Great Lakes Watershed. The ecological issues facing the Great Lakes Basin include: land runoff, coastal development & loss of habitat, invasive species, toxic chemicals, climate change, fishing pressure, and water withdrawals.

CREATE A NEW AND DIVERSE OPEN SPACE SYSTEM FOR THE CITY
CONNECTING AND ADDING TO EXISTING OPEN SPACE

NEED FOR NEW KINDS OF LANDSCAPES. The city and its residents have needs that must be met for healthy neighborhoods, convenient access to recreation opportunities, and affordable and reliable city services. Traditional open spaces, infrastructure services, and remediation techniques are too expensive to maintain. Given all this, there is a need to find unconventional strategies:

- to reduce burdens on existing infrastructure networks so they cost less to operate and maintain;

- to provide new, hybridized types of recreation areas that cost less to maintain; and

- to put vacant land to productive use, and to improve the health of the city, its residents, and its ecosystem.

Landscapes and landscape strategies can tackle many of these challenges, and address resident concerns. New open space networks capture and clean stormwater, improve air quality, provide diverse recreation opportunities, provide habitat for local wildlife and migrating birds, clean contaminated soil and improve environmental conditions, and structure sustainable urban design and give new identity to Detroit.

Many of these ideas aren't new; innovative solutions are already underway in Detroit, but face challenges:

- Some uses are illegal.

- Other uses, like events, require multiple, costly permissions and licenses to sponsor.

- Organizations have limited funding and budgets.

- Projects are often undertaken independently; there is no unified vision (inefficient use of limited resources).

- Uncertainties due to soil contamination, regulatory questions, and other factors impede projects. A unified vision for a diverse range of open spaces coupled with regulatory changes can transform Detroit into a 21st century sustainable city.

"We need to transform the city of Detroit into a cleaner, healthier, safer environment."

Oscar, Land Use Open House, 8/28/2012

"There is no one idea for repurposing the open space in the city. Urban farming, successional landscapes, productive water/rain-scapes, buffer zones between neighborhoods—all of them offer promise."

Gary, Detroit 24/7, 5/2012

"Landscape changes alone will not completely address the health challenges. We need to look at policies as well as additional innovative opportunities (i.e., using schools as recreational opportunities)."

Environmental Working Group, 2/6/2012

"Use vacant land for managing water that comes through rainfall (stormwater management) in a systematic and planned manner. The City could identify all those low-lying vacant parcels in the city and integrate that information into a comprehensive stormwater management plan."

Justin, Detroit 24/7, "Environmental Issues," 5/2012

"Support urban agriculture (small-scale, organic, community/ locally driven) through city policies and zoning."

Sarah, Environmental Summit, 5/5/2011

LANDSCAPE DEVELOPMENT TYPES

COMMUNITY OPEN SPACES	ECOLOGICAL LANDSCAPES	BLUE / GREEN INFRASTRUCTURE	WORKING AND PRODUCTIVE LANDSCAPES	TRANSITIONAL LANDSCAPES
Landscapes for recreation, social life, and small-scale food cultivation	Meadows and forests that provide habitat and other environmental benefits	Landscapes that capture stormwater and clean air	Landscapes that generate new knowledge, grow energy and food, and create new urban experiences	Temporary landscapes that clean soil and enable new forms of social life and creative displays
Playground	Nature park	Large lake	Research landscape	Event landscape
Neighborhood park	Industrial nature park	Smaller retention pond	Urban farm	Remediation fields or forest
Sports field	Rapid reforestation	Infiltration park	Aquaculture and hydroponics	Artscape
Regional park	Successional road	Swales and infiltration medians	Algae-culture	Urban meadow
Cemetery (Existing)	Roads to rivers	Roadside pond (along wide roads)	Energy field or forest	
Plaza		Green industry buffer	Homestead	
Recreation center		Carbon forest	Campground	
Trails / greenway				
Urban garden				
Farmers market				

Image Source: Kresge Foundation

Image Source: Suzanne Temple

Image Source: www.inlandbays.org

Image Source: Hamilton Anderson Associates

Image Source: Paul Hitz—Flickr, Wikimedia Commons

LANDSCAPE AS URBAN CATALYST

PRODUCTIVE LANDSCAPES AS URBAN CATALYST. All of these landscapes put vacant land to productive use. "Productive" is used in a very broad sense: These landscapes provide a wide range of benefits:

- **Environmental benefits:** Clean air, improve water quality, capture stormwater, clean soil, provide habitat for local wildlife

- **Economic benefits:** Reduce maintenance and utility costs, perform roles of traditional systems, create jobs, produce food and other tangible products

- **Social benefits:** Allow for recreation and promote other forms of social life; increase property values; improve resident health and comfort. These landscapes function in multiple ways, at multiple scales, over multiple time horizons.

LANDSCAPES FOR ECONOMIC GROWTH. Productive landscapes offer job opportunities; grow food, biomass for energy, and wood products; and clean soil, air, and water. Linked to employment districts, these are places of innovation, where new ideas are tested and imagined.

Future open space networks in Detroit include both larger landscape typologies and landscape development types integrated within neighborhoods. Landscape typologies each include a variety of different kinds of landscape development types.

LANDSCAPES AS TRANSFORMATIVE INFRASTRUCTURES. Landscape strategies can support city infrastructure systems, including stormwater/wastewater, energy, roads/transportation, and waste. Carbon forests along freeways clean air; stormwater boulevards along the city's historic axial roads clean water; industrial buffers mitigate the environmental and public health effects of industry.

LANDSCAPES FOR NEIGHBORHOODS. Small-scale playlots, urban gardens, remediation meadows, and blue infrastructure repurpose vacant lots in neighborhoods. These landscapes provide recreation opportunities, grow fresh fruits and vegetables, clean soil and capture stormwater, increase property values, and improve a sense of community.

LANDSCAPES AS RECREATIONAL AND ECOLOGICAL NETWORKS. Anchored by regional parks and linked by greenways, this network builds off existing, traditional parks, sports fields, and recreation centers, and adds new kinds of parks that cost less to operate and maintain. Additional recreation opportunities like hiking, mountain biking, and bird watching are found with blue and green corridors and larger ecological areas.

PILOT PROJECT

URBAN AGRICULTURE (MEDIUM-SCALE)

Tests an installation of a medium-scale urban agriculture project on the ground. Needed: planning knowledge, capacity and sponsorship. Barriers include contaminated soils and lack of regulatory framework.

Image Source: www.foodshedplanet.com

PILOT PROJECT

INNOVATIVE FOREST CREATION

Tests to understand the lowest cost techniques for agitating the ruderal landscape into an urban woodland. Woodlands create more benefit in terms of stormwater infiltration and particulate filtration for the health of regional air quality.

Image Source: Bobak Ha'Eri, Wikimedia Commons

DETROIT FUTURE CITY | 2012

TELEGRAPH

GRAND RIVER

8 MILE

WOODWARD

VAN DYKE

GRATIOT

94

696

75

10

96

8

E. JEFFERSON

FORD

39

MICHIGAN

W. JEFFERSON

FORT

94

75

FUTURE OPEN SPACE NETWORK

- CARBON FOREST
- BLUE INFRASTRUCTURE
- INNOVATION PRODUCTIVE
- INNOVATION ECOLOGICAL
- GREENWAYS

- INDUSTRIAL BUFFER
- DISPERSED GREEN LANDSCAPE
- DISPERSED BLUE INFRASTRUCTURE
- LARGE PARKS

Source: DWPLTP Planning Team

1   2   4 MILES

Future open space networks in Detroit include both larger landscape typologies and landscape development types integrated within neighborhoods. Landscape typologies each include a variety of different kinds of landscape development types.

A NEW OPEN SPACE NETWORK

"Evaluate and improve ecosystem services: Plant trees, indigenous species, rain gardens. Vegetation can improve the land, provide employment, raise funds through sales, and help sustain the neighborhood."

Northwest Community Conversation 2, 5/7/2012

A NEW SYSTEM OF DIVERSE KINDS OF OPEN SPACE. A new system of innovative landscapes creates a new framework for civic life, reshapes perceptions of Detroit, and creates a new green (and blue) city identity. These landscapes include traditional landscapes like parks of many sizes, but importantly expand the range of landscape typologies to include blue + green corridors, large-scale blue infrastructure, and larger areas for innovation, such as the following:

- Innovative productive includes urban farms – greenhouses, managed forests, and aquaculture facilities; research plots; deconstruction sites; and other active uses.

- Innovative ecological includes meadows, forests, marshes, and other landscapes.

Complementing these larger uses, smaller-scale landscape development types include urban gardens, neighborhood parks, remediation plots, event-scapes, urban meadows, and smaller blue infrastructures.

PRECEDENT

EMSCHER PARKS

A whole series of parks and cultural facilities in the Ruhr Region, Germany, including Landschaftspark, are conversions of very large industrial sites to new uses—regional scale planning relevant in terms of its contemporary thinking on ecology and reuse.

Image Source: Gerd W. Schmölter

IMPLEMENTATION ACTIONS

1 Implement blue and green infrastructure.

2 Encourage reuse of vacant land with productive landscapes.

3 Diversify park network.

4 Encourage partnerships between universities and firms in productive landscapes to conduct research and provide job training opportunities.

PRECEDENTS

1 Emscher Parks, Ruhr Region, Germany

2 Nature Park Südgelände, Berlin, Germany

3 Emerald Necklace, Boston

4 Sweetwater Farms, Milwaukee, WI

5 Salamonie Reservoir, Monument City, IN

6 Point Fraser Wetland, Perth, Australia

PILOT PROJECTS

1 Urban Agriculture (Medium Scale)

2 Innovative Forest Creation

ECOLOGICAL LANDSCAPES AND RIVERFRONTS

Ecological landscapes include forests, meadows, and other landscapes that develop and evolve gradually over time and cost very little to create and maintain. Flowering meadows gradually give way to forests, and the changing landscape supports a variety of plant and animal life, including birds like pheasants or migrating species. These landscapes can develop on their own, or can be guided to different types of desirable landscapes, which may be especially suitable for a particular species, or more appropriate for stormwater management, or a quick-growing forest that shades out tall grasses to improve visibility and eliminate need for mowing. They will often include remnants from previous land uses, which both cuts down on construction costs and alludes to the many histories of each individual site.

In particular, the Detroit and Rouge riverfronts include a mix of landscape uses: parks like River Rouge Park, Belle Isle, and the many others; greenways with walking and bicycling opportunities, like the RiverWalk; marsh parks and blue infrastructure that filter stormwater before it enters the rivers; and green mixed-rise neighborhoods within a water-based landscape framework.

ECOLOGICAL LANDSCAPES AND RIVERFRONTS

- INNOVATION ECOLOGICAL
- RIVERFRONT PARKS

Source: DWPLTP Planning Team

1   2   4 MILES

NATURE PARK SÜDGELÄNDE

This former rail yard site opened in Berlin, Germany in the year 2000. The site was saved from new rail yard development by an active local group of citizens in 1980. The nature park still retains rail tracks and a water tower.

Image Source: http://heijinkg.files.wordpress.com

LARGE PARKS AND NEIGHBORHOOD PARKS / PLAZAS

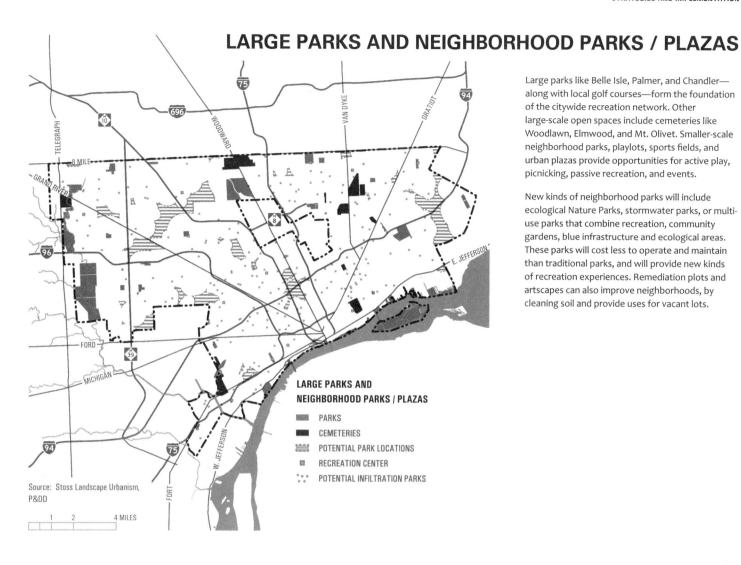

Source: Stoss Landscape Urbanism, P&DD

LARGE PARKS AND NEIGHBORHOOD PARKS / PLAZAS

- PARKS
- CEMETERIES
- POTENTIAL PARK LOCATIONS
- RECREATION CENTER
- POTENTIAL INFILTRATION PARKS

Large parks like Belle Isle, Palmer, and Chandler—along with local golf courses—form the foundation of the citywide recreation network. Other large-scale open spaces include cemeteries like Woodlawn, Elmwood, and Mt. Olivet. Smaller-scale neighborhood parks, playlots, sports fields, and urban plazas provide opportunities for active play, picnicking, passive recreation, and events.

New kinds of neighborhood parks will include ecological Nature Parks, stormwater parks, or multi-use parks that combine recreation, community gardens, blue infrastructure and ecological areas. These parks will cost less to operate and maintain than traditional parks, and will provide new kinds of recreation experiences. Remediation plots and artscapes can also improve neighborhoods, by cleaning soil and provide uses for vacant lots.

131

THE LAND USE ELEMENT : THE IMAGE OF THE CITY

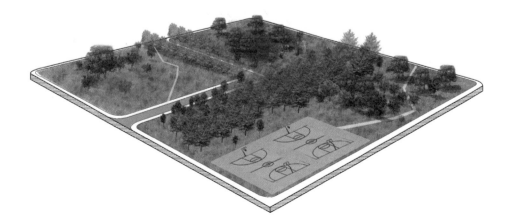

PRECEDENT

EMERALD NECKLACE

Olmstead designed this network of parks in Boston that combines recreational parks, infrastructures (flood control, light rail), and parkways. The Emerald Necklace restructured the city and serves ecological/habitat purposes.

Image Source: Emerald Necklace Conservancy

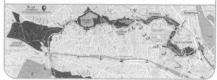

FOOD NETWORK AND PRODUCTIVE LANDSCAPES

Productive landscapes offer many potential links to employment districts, partnership possibilities between institutions and industry, environmental benefits, and products like food, wood, compost, and salvaged building materials for reuse.

The food network includes small-scale urban gardens linked to residents/local farmers markets, and larger-scale urban farms linked to employment districts, the food and beverage processing industry, and food distribution network. Urban farms like large greenhouses offer a local, year-round source of fresh food, which allows a system-wide shift to local food procurement in Detroit. (Currently, local institutions like universities and hospitals do not buy local food because it is not available year-round, preferring instead to contract with a single out-of-town supplier.) This shift will grow food processing and other related industries in the food cluster and also increase access to affordable, fresh foods for all Detroiters.

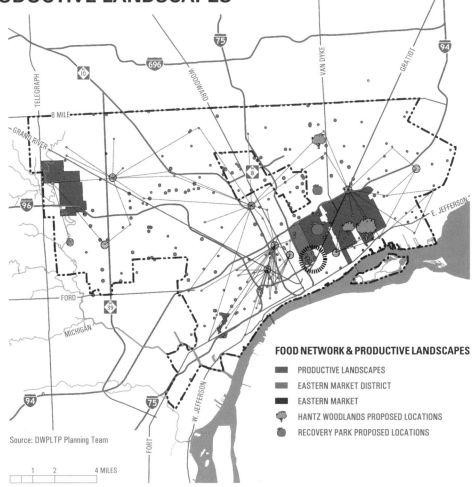

Source: DWPLTP Planning Team

1   2   4 MILES

FOOD NETWORK & PRODUCTIVE LANDSCAPES

- PRODUCTIVE LANDSCAPES
- EASTERN MARKET DISTRICT
- EASTERN MARKET
- HANTZ WOODLANDS PROPOSED LOCATIONS
- RECOVERY PARK PROPOSED LOCATIONS

PRECEDENT

SWEETWATER FARMS

The Sweetwater urban farm in Milwaukee, WI reuses a former industrial building for fish farming and vegetable production. The farm uses a three-tiered, bio-intensive, simulated wetland. In the recirculating systems, the fish waste acts as natural fertilizer for plant growth, and the plants act as a water filter.

Image Source: www.offermation.com

BLUE / GREEN INFRASTRUCTURE

Blue infrastructures—water-based landscapes like swales, retention ponds, and lakes that capture and clean stormwater—provide an active use for vacant land and oversized roads. Green infrastructures – forest landscapes that improve air quality by capturing air-borne pollutants—can buffer industrial areas and high-traffic roadways from neighboring districts; can help connect different parts of the city through greenways; and offer attractive amenities for current and new residents, employers, and visitors.

BLUE / GREEN INFRASTRUCTURE

BLUE INFRASTRUCTURE	GREEN INFRASTRUCTURE
STORMWATER BLVD	CARBON FOREST
SURFACE LAKE	INDUSTRY BUFFERS
WET BUFFER	GREENWAYS
DISTRIBUTED NETWORK	
HIGH CONCENTRATION PONDS	
DISPERSED PONDS	
INFILTRATION PARK	
RIVER MARSHLANDS	

Source: Stoss Landscape Urbanism, P&DD

1 2 4 MILES

THE LAND USE ELEMENT : THE IMAGE OF THE CITY

PRECEDENT

SALAMONIE RESERVOIR

In Monument City, IN, the Army Corps of Engineers currently uses the reservoir for flood control and stormwater runoff collection. Camping, boating, fishing, swimming, hiking, and picnicking occur throughout the park.

Image Source: www.in.gov/dnr/public/mayjuno

PRECEDENT

POINT FRASER WETLAND

Located in Perth, Australia, this wetland was completed in 2006. Designed as stormwater infrastructure, the wetland is a bio-filter of native reeds, sedges, shrubs, and trees that filter water and improves the quality of urban stormwater before discharge back into river.

CURRENT: EXISTING PARKS SYSTEM

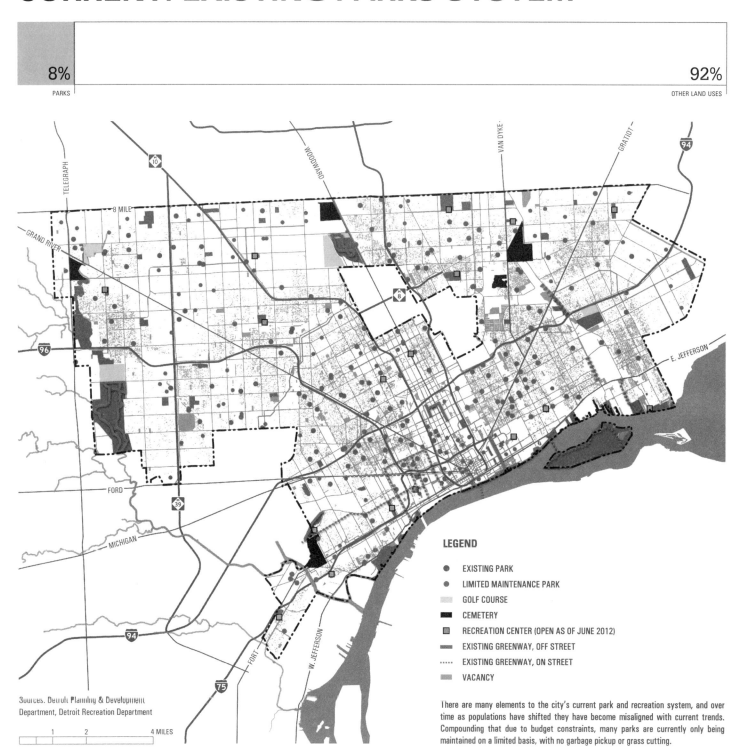

8%

PARKS

92%

OTHER LAND USES

LEGEND

● EXISTING PARK

● LIMITED MAINTENANCE PARK

▨ GOLF COURSE

■ CEMETERY

▣ RECREATION CENTER (OPEN AS OF JUNE 2012)

▬▬ EXISTING GREENWAY, OFF STREET

••••• EXISTING GREENWAY, ON STREET

▬ VACANCY

Sources: Detroit Planning & Development
Department, Detroit Recreation Department

1 2 4 MILES

There are many elements to the city's current park and recreation system, and over
time as populations have shifted they have become misaligned with current trends.
Compounding that due to budget constraints, many parks are currently only being
maintained on a limited basis, with no garbage pickup or grass cutting.

PROPOSED: FUTURE OPEN SPACE SYSTEM

7%	29%	64%
PARKS	LANDSCAPE TYPOLOGIES	OTHER LAND USES

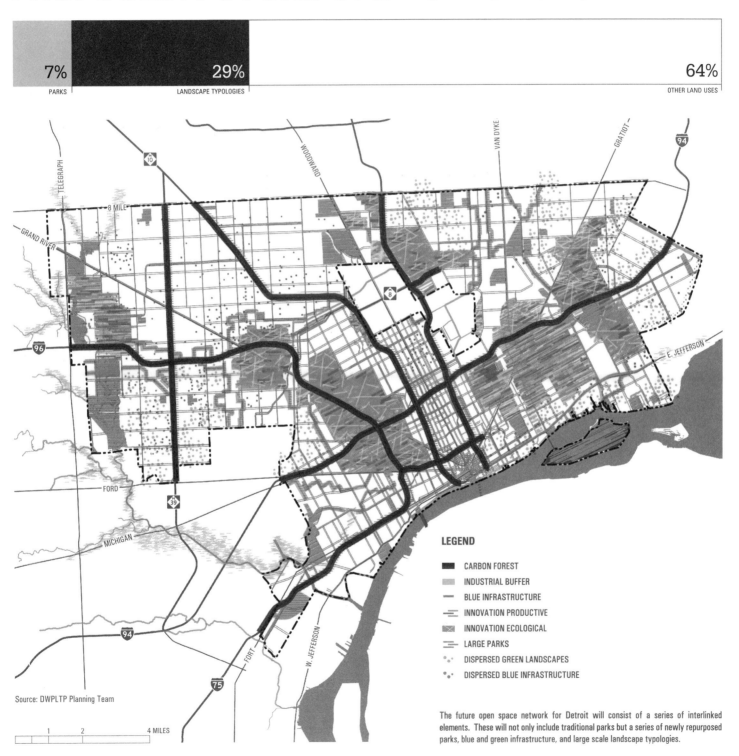

LEGEND

- CARBON FOREST
- INDUSTRIAL BUFFER
- BLUE INFRASTRUCTURE
- INNOVATION PRODUCTIVE
- INNOVATION ECOLOGICAL
- LARGE PARKS
- DISPERSED GREEN LANDSCAPES
- DISPERSED BLUE INFRASTRUCTURE

Source: DWPLTP Planning Team

1   2   4 MILES

The future open space network for Detroit will consist of a series of interlinked elements. These will not only include traditional parks but a series of newly repurposed parks, blue and green infrastructure, and large scale landscape typologies.

HIGHWAYS

CARBON FOREST   HIGHWAY   CARBON FOREST

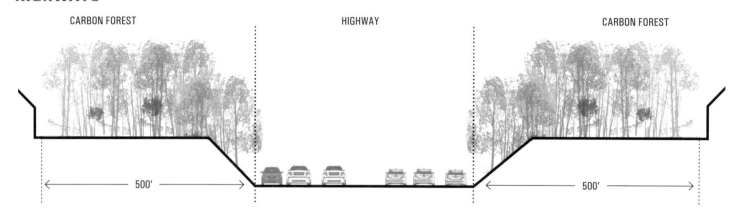

← 500' →   ← 500' →

ARTERIALS

PUBLIC RIGHT-OF-WAY ±100'

ROAD ± 75'

MIXED USE

AUTO-ORIENTED SETBACK | TRADITIONAL

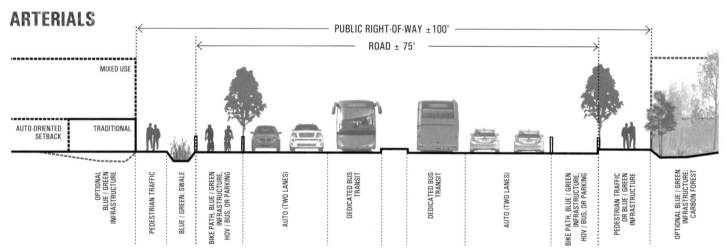

- OPTIONAL BLUE / GREEN INFRASTRUCTURE
- PEDESTRIAN TRAFFIC
- BLUE / GREEN: SWALE
- BIKE PATH, BLUE / GREEN INFRASTRUCTURE, HOV / BUS, OR PARKING
- AUTO (TWO LANES)
- DEDICATED BUS TRANSIT
- DEDICATED BUS TRANSIT
- AUTO (TWO LANES)
- BIKE PATH, BLUE / GREEN INFRASTRUCTURE, HOV / BUS, OR PARKING
- PEDESTRIAN TRAFFIC OR BLUE / GREEN INFRASTRUCTURE
- OPTIONAL BLUE / GREEN INFRASTRUCTURE: CARBON FOREST

MAJOR THOROUGHFARES

PUBLIC RIGHT-OF-WAY ±80'

ROAD ± 45'

MIXED USE

AUTO-ORIENTED SETBACK | TRADITIONAL

- OPTIONAL BLUE / GREEN INFRASTRUCTURE
- PEDESTRIAN TRAFFIC
- BLUE / GREEN: SWALE
- BIKE PATH, BLUE / GREEN INFRASTRUCTURE, HOV / BUS, OR PARKING
- AUTO (TWO LANES)
- BIKE PATH, BLUE / GREEN INFRASTRUCTURE, HOV / BUS, OR PARKING
- PEDESTRIAN TRAFFIC OR BLUE / GREEN INFRASTRUCTURE
- OPTIONAL BLUE / GREEN INFRASTRUCTURE: CARBON FOREST

LOCAL ROADS

PUBLIC RIGHT-OF-WAY ±60'

ROAD ± 25'

- RESIDENTIAL
- UPGRADE / MAINTAIN, RENEW / MAINTAIN, REDUCE/MAINTAIN, OR REPURPOSE, REPLACE OR DECOMMISSION
- RETAIN, RUBBELIZE, DECOMMISSION, GREENWAY, CLOSE, ROAD-TO-RIVERS
- UPGRADE / MAINTAIN, RENEW / MAINTAIN, REDUCE/MAINTAIN, OR REPURPOSE, REPLACE OF DECOMMISSION
- RESIDENTIAL

Cross sections of the four major road types show potential configurations for transit, non-motorized and blue/green infrastructure in support of creating complete streets.

REDEFINE CORRIDORS AND CREATE COMPLETE STREETS
CITYWIDE IDENTITY OF CORRIDORS

A NEW NETWORK OF MULTI-USE, MULTIMODAL CORRIDORS connects employment centers to neighborhood districts, allows for new bicycle routes and bus rapid transit corridors, reinforces economic and neighborhood centers, and provides a range of infrastructural services through sustainable blue and green infrastructures. This network radically reconsiders the idea that all boulevards have retail and commercial space all along them, as this is neither economically sustainable nor necessary. Newly revamped corridors are multi-use and multimodal; they improve efficiency, quality, and character; and they respond sensitively to their newly revamped surrounding contexts.

IMPLEMENTATION ACTIONS

1 Develop tiered transit network that ties into regional system.
2 Incorporate multi-modal transit design into all street improvements.
3 Focus commercial development in walkable nodes or auto-oriented strips based on physical/market conditions and future land use vision.
4 Introduce blue and green infrastructure as integral to corridor development.

EARLY ACTIONS

1 M-1 Rail Streetcar Project
2 Regional Transit Authority
3 Contiguous Greenway System
4 Neighborhood Pop-up Retail
5 DWSD Blue Infrastructure Projects

PILOT PROJECTS

1 Comprehensive Retail District Program
2 Stormwater Boulevard
3 Carbon Forest

Detroit's urban road network is made up of four major types of roads:

HIGHWAYS are the primary regional, state, and national circulation routes for personal vehicles and freight transportation. Due to the speeds, congestion, and pollution generated on the city's freeways, strategies, such as carbon forest planting, will need to be deployed to mitigate negative environmental impacts on neighborhoods.

ARTERIALS include the city's radial boulevards and provide the spine for a larger regional rapid transit system. Many of these roads are currently oversized relative to the amount of traffic they carry. The oversized nature of the arterial roads and adjacent underutilized/vacant commercial land provides the opportunity for both blue infrastructure inside and outside of the public right-of-way, as well as integration of multiple modes of transit to support complete streets. These have also been the sites for continual commercial use. Other land uses, including residential development, should now be developed along these roads. Given the transit-oriented development opportunities around a regional rapid transit system, key nodes are identified for economic development opportunities.

MAJOR THOROUGHFARES include the Mile roads, Warren, and Vernor, among others. These roads provide opportunity for major crosstown transit connections, as well as future commercial or residential development adjacent to low-vacancy neighborhoods or blue infrastructure in higher-vacancy areas.

LOCAL ROADS typically serve residential areas and feed the city's thoroughfares and arterials. In areas of high-vacancy, local roads provide the opportunity for rubbelzation to assist with stormwater run-off or decommissioning in areas that have been completely depopulated and do not feed thoroughfares from populated areas.

To function as a corridor, each road type must serve some combination of three productive uses: transportation network, adjacent development (not only commercial, but also residential and other types of use), and capacity for blue or green infrastructure inside or outside the right-of-way.

REGIONAL TRANSIT AUTHORITY

The authority will create public transit options connecting southeast Michigan localities. Increased public transportation options will reduce road congestion and vehicle emissions in the region. As a regional authority, it would be eligible for certain federal funding.

Image/Text Source: MI House Bill 5309

TIER 1 BUS RAPID TRANSIT ROUTES

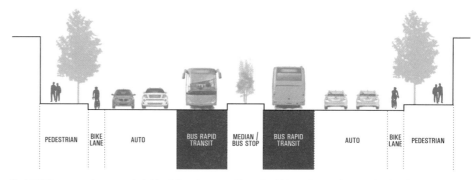

PEDESTRIAN | BIKE LANE | AUTO | BUS RAPID TRANSIT | MEDIAN / BUS STOP | BUS RAPID TRANSIT | AUTO | BIKE LANE | PEDESTRIAN

Tier 1 BRT Routes comprise a network of either dedicated center or side running, high-speed connections to regional employment centers.

CONTIGUOUS GREENWAY SYSTEM

Connecting multiple citywide greenway initiatives, fund the planning and implementation of a fully functioning greenway link/system with the help the Detroit Strategic Framework recommendations.

Image Source: huntsvilleal.gov

TIER 2 CROSSTOWN ROUTES

PARKING | LANDSCAPING OR SWALE | PEDESTRIAN | SWALE | BIKE LANE | AUTO AND BUS (THREE LANES) | BIKE LANE | SWALE | PEDESTRIAN | LANDSCAPING OR SWALE | PARKING

Tier 2 Crosstown Routes run in traffic and connect neighborhoods to Tier 1 BRT routes.

M-1 RAIL STREETCAR PROJECT

The M-1 rail project reestablishes key linkages between downtown, cultural destinations, health and educational facilities, and stadia. It will complement and support intercity passenger rail services and future envisioned bus rapid transit within the region.

Text/Image Source: M-1 Rail

LIGHT RAIL

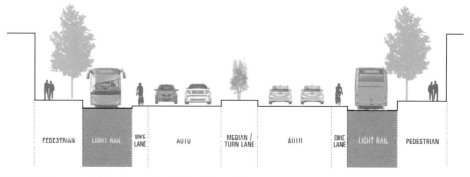

PEDESTRIAN | LIGHT RAIL | BIKE LANE | AUTO | MEDIAN / TURN LANE | AUTO | BIKE LANE | LIGHT RAIL | PEDESTRIAN

Light Rail is a slower speed, side-running transit mode that makes more frequent stops. It is only proposed in the Greater Downtown.

TRANSIT NETWORK: PLANNING FOR MULTIMODAL TRANSPORTATION. The Detroit Strategic Framework supports a Tier One regional transit system with the city's arterials acting as the spine for a bus rapid transit system. An internal ring road is also proposed for bus rapid transit to connect the city's neighborhoods to major employment districts. Crosstown bus routes on the city's major arterials and thoroughfares provide Tier Two connections to the Tier One arterials. These transit nodes hold the potential for associated transit-oriented development. Both fixed and non-fixed route Tier Three buses and paratransit provide access to the larger system from within neighborhoods.

Many of Detroit's streets are too wide for the amount of traffic they now carry. This holds the potential for introducing multiple modes of transit within the right-of-way. Rightsizing the city's roads to meet projected future population densities provides the opportunity for the integration of multiple modes of transit, including dedicated lanes for Bus Rapid Transit (BRT), bike lanes, and wide sidewalks where residential densities are highest. The Detroit Strategic Framework supports the development of Complete Streets wherever practical to fully integrate an accessible and safe transit network for all pedestrians, cyclists, transit riders, and drivers. As part of this effort, the Detroit Strategic Framework supports efforts to create a citywide network of non-motorized greenways.

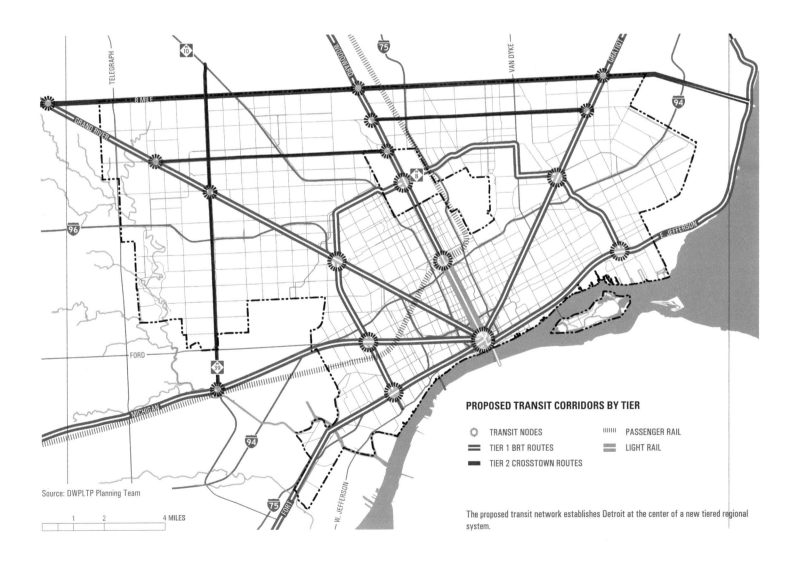

PROPOSED TRANSIT CORRIDORS BY TIER

- TRANSIT NODES
- TIER 1 BRT ROUTES
- TIER 2 CROSSTOWN ROUTES
- PASSENGER RAIL
- LIGHT RAIL

Source: DWPLTP Planning Team

The proposed transit network establishes Detroit at the center of a new tiered regional system.

COMPREHENSIVE RETAIL DISTRICT PROGRAM

Establish comprehensive retail packages that include site selection/acquisition, employee training, interior/exterior renovations, infrastructure improvements, and start-up costs in identified retail districts.

Image Source: Hamilton Anderson Associates

NEIGHBORHOOD POP-UP RETAIL

In the pop-up retail model, businesses set up temporary sales locations to gain exposure, quickly sell limited merchandise, test market potential in a new location, and/or build interest in a specific neighborhood commercial area.

Image Source: Margarita Barry, huffingtonpost.com

CORRIDOR MULTI-USE ZONING REVISION

Revise zoning ordinance to allow expanded range of uses along corridors including blue infrastructure.

Image Source: Hamilton Anderson Associates

MIXED-USE RETAIL NODE OR STRIP

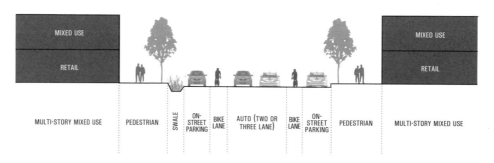

Mixed-use commercial nodes are reserved for City and District Center typologies where there is the greatest potential market for mixed-use development.

TRADITIONAL RETAIL NODE OR STRIP

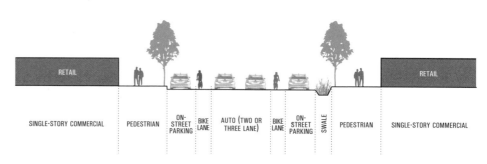

Traditional commercial nodes are used in the Neighborhood Center typology and provide neighborhood amenities in a pedestrian-oriented environment.

AUTO-ORIENTED RETAIL STRIP

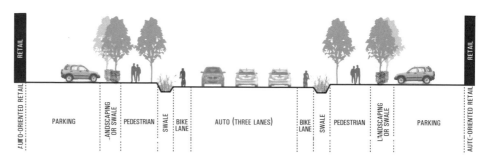

Auto-oriented strip is used along major thoroughfares and is designed to meet the needs of the automobile while creating separation for pedestrians and non-motorized users.

COMMERCIAL CORRIDORS: PROVIDING A NEW MIX OF LAND USES. Detroit has an excess of commercially zoned land along its arterials and major thoroughfares. Much of the land zoned for commercial use is auto-oriented, allowing for large areas of parking between buildings and creating a generally hostile environment for pedestrians. It is estimated that 36% of Detroit's commercially zoned land is currently vacant, and the overall quality of the retail that is serving residents has declined. Although much of this land must be rezoned and repurposed for a range of new productive land uses, the commercial retail needs of the city still must be addressed.

Because retail tends to follow residential density and development, the Detroit Strategic Framework aligns the most appropriate commercial retail development types within a corresponding neighborhood typology that increases the chances for sustainability. The proposed commercial corridor map recommends an overall reduction of the amount of commercially zoned land, principally located along arterials and major thoroughfares. These lands would be rezoned to allow for a broader range of land uses and development types, including residential and blue and green infrastructure.

The Framework recommends clustering commercial development primarily in centers along arterials and thoroughfares with major transit routes. New commercial development within Neighborhood Center, District Center, and City Center typologies should be designed for pedestrians. Retail along major thoroughfares outside of these neighborhood typologies may be a combination of auto- and pedestrian-oriented. Major sites at high-density transit nodes are excellent opportunities for larger-scale retail development (big-box or lifestyle-center types of retail).

Several different commercial retail development types would be allowable within this framework. As introduced earlier in this chapter (page 120), these development types include the following:

TRADITIONAL RETAIL This development type is generally characterized by buildings on small lots, one or two stories in height and built directly up to the street front property line. Traditional retail usually occurs in a linear pattern along several blocks of a corridor, or in a more nodal pattern, clustered closely around one or two key street intersections.

MIXED-USE RETAIL This retail develop is similar to traditional retail in that it can also be found to exist continuously along corridors or clustered as a node at key intersections. The buildings, often two to five stories in height, have larger building footprints, accommodate a mix of upper-floor residential or commercial uses.

AUTO-ORIENTED RETAIL STRIP This development type took root in cities as populations began living further apart, requiring more use of personal automobiles for daily activities. Retailing adjusted to this shift by developing in-line stores set back from the street to easily accommodate parking for shoppers. Given the car culture of the Detroit region, this type of retail development is here to stay. As such, new design guidelines are encouraged to make these developments more pedestrian friendly and respond better to existing community character, including reducing parking requirements and creating landscaped separation between cars and pedestrians.

BIG-BOX RETAIL AND LIFESTYLE CENTERS These mega-retail development types are appropriate for large-scale sites that can adequately accommodate on-site parking. In some instances, big-box development, can be combined into a mixed-use retail and residential development. Downtowns across the country are transforming large former office buildings into mixed-use projects that include well-known big-box retailers such as Target or Bed Bath & Beyond, or grocery stores like Trader Joes, with residential living above. This type of retail is well suited for transit-oriented development sites that take advantage of residential and employment populations.

EXISTING: CURRENT COMMERCIAL CORRIDORS

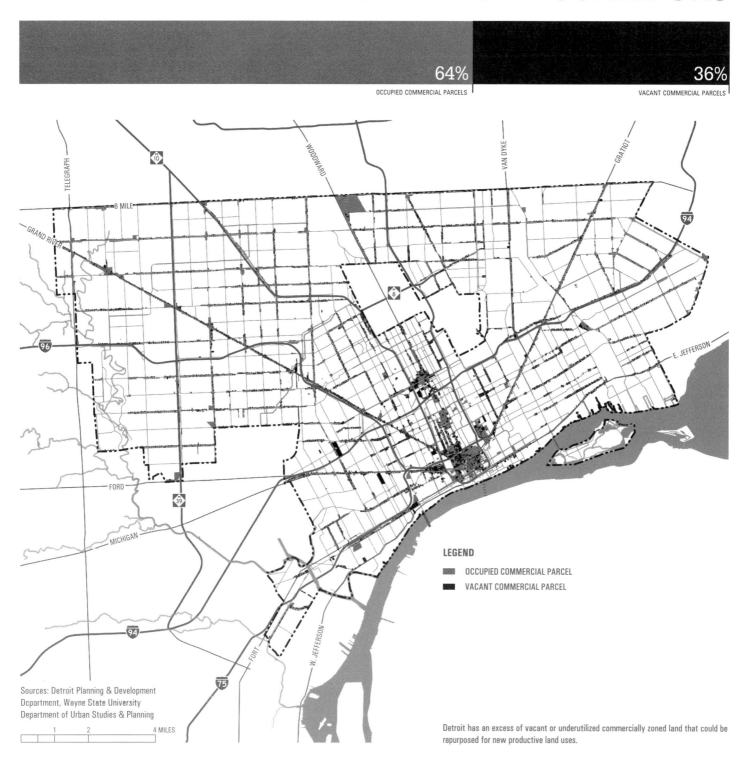

64%	36%
OCCUPIED COMMERCIAL PARCELS	VACANT COMMERCIAL PARCELS

TELEGRAPH

10

WOODWARD

VAN DYKE

GRATIOT

94

8 MILE

GRAND RIVER

96

8

E. JEFFERSON

FORD

39

MICHIGAN

94

FORT

W. JEFFERSON

75

LEGEND

OCCUPIED COMMERCIAL PARCEL

VACANT COMMERCIAL PARCEL

Sources: Detroit Planning & Development
Department, Wayne State University
Department of Urban Studies & Planning

| 1 | 2 | 4 MILES |

Detroit has an excess of vacant or underutilized commercially zoned land that could be repurposed for new productive land uses.

PROPOSED: COMMERCIAL CORRIDORS IN 2030

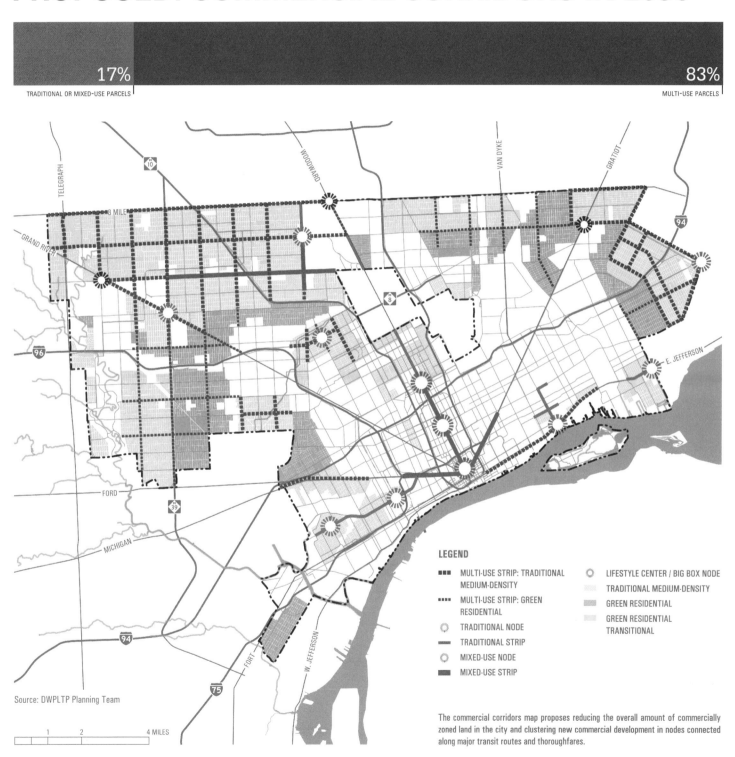

17%
TRADITIONAL OR MIXED-USE PARCELS

83%
MULTI-USE PARCELS

LEGEND

- ▪▪▪▪ MULTI-USE STRIP: TRADITIONAL MEDIUM-DENSITY
- ▪▪▪▪ MULTI-USE STRIP: GREEN RESIDENTIAL
- ⊙ TRADITIONAL NODE
- ── TRADITIONAL STRIP
- ⊙ MIXED-USE NODE
- ▬ MIXED-USE STRIP
- ⊙ LIFESTYLE CENTER / BIG BOX NODE
- ▨ TRADITIONAL MEDIUM-DENSITY
- ▨ GREEN RESIDENTIAL
- ▨ GREEN RESIDENTIAL TRANSITIONAL

Source: DWPLTP Planning Team

1   2   4 MILES

The commercial corridors map proposes reducing the overall amount of commercially zoned land in the city and clustering new commercial development in nodes connected along major transit routes and thoroughfares.

DWSD BLUE INFRASTRUCTURE PROJECTS

DWSD is implementing small-scale blue infrastructure pilot projects in coordination with SEMCOG and Greening of Detroit in northwestern Detroit. Additional blue infrastructure projects should be aligned with their efforts.

Image Source: SEMCOG Low Impact Development Manual

STORMWATER BOULEVARD

In partnership with DWSD and SEMCOG, convert short segment of arterial road to stormwater blvd. Narrow the road, install swales and bicycle lanes, and construct retention ponds on adjacent vacant, publicly owned land.

Image Source: inlandbays.org

CARBON FOREST

Install linear portion of carbon forest along an existing highway. The project should also include short and long-term monitoring, which could be handled by volunteers, professionals, or academic advisors.

Image Source: Bobak Ha'Eri, Wikimedia Commons

BLUE INFRASTRUCTURE WITHIN THE RIGHT-OF-WAY

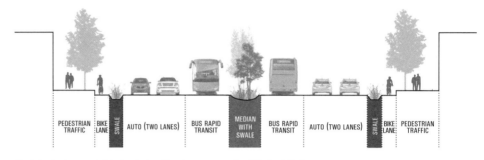

PEDESTRIAN TRAFFIC | BIKE LANE | SWALE | AUTO (TWO LANES) | BUS RAPID TRANSIT | MEDIAN WITH SWALE | BUS RAPID TRANSIT | AUTO (TWO LANES) | SWALE | BIKE LANE | PEDESTRIAN TRAFFIC

Blue infrastructure may be introduced where there is excess capacity within the right-of-way.

BLUE INFRASTRUCTURE OUTSIDE OF THE RIGHT-OF-WAY

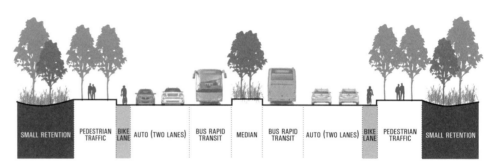

SMALL RETENTION | PEDESTRIAN TRAFFIC | BIKE LANE | AUTO (TWO LANES) | BUS RAPID TRANSIT | MEDIAN | BUS RAPID TRANSIT | AUTO (TWO LANES) | BIKE LANE | PEDESTRIAN TRAFFIC | SMALL RETENTION

Blue infrastructure outside the right-of-way is best suited for Green Residential and Landscape typologies.

CARBON FOREST

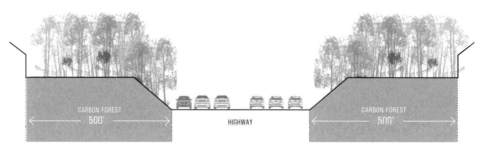

CARBON FOREST 500' | HIGHWAY | CARBON FOREST 500'

The carbon forest proposal calls for a 500' separation between highways and neighborhoods. Planting area includes embankments and vacant parcels.

CORRIDORS FOR 21ST CENTURY INFRASTRUCTURE. Given the excess vehicular capacity within the right-of-way and the vast amount of vacant commercial land adjacent to the right-of-way, land should be prioritized for the development of new blue and green infrastructure. Blue infrastructure should be fully integrated into a multimodal street section and create an amenity for pedestrians, cyclists, and drivers. Green infrastructure should be implemented along all major highways in the city to improve air quality within Detroit's neighborhoods. By planting trees on vacant land within 500' of the highway right-of-way, the carbon forest will act to absorb CO_2 emissions from automobiles and prevent pollutants from reaching adjacent residents. Simultaneously, carbon forests will act as a visual amenity for passing traffic in areas along the highway that frequently have some of the city's highest levels of vacancy.

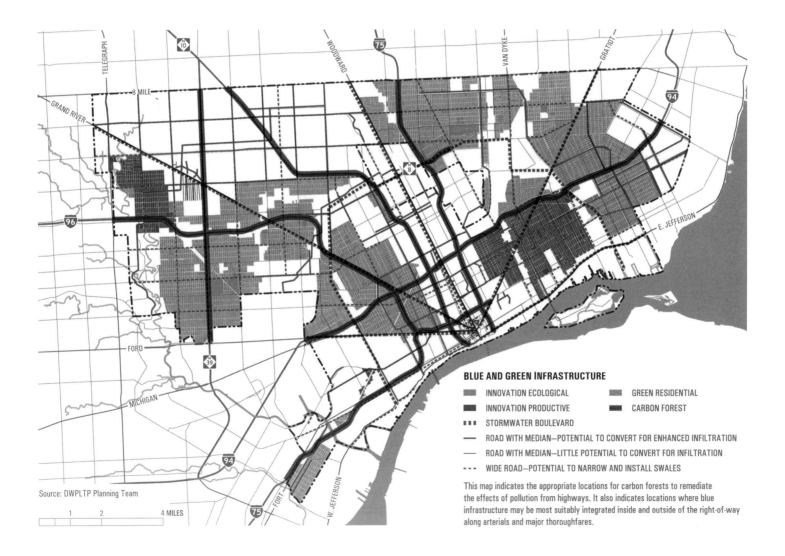

BLUE AND GREEN INFRASTRUCTURE

- INNOVATION ECOLOGICAL
- INNOVATION PRODUCTIVE
- STORMWATER BOULEVARD
- GREEN RESIDENTIAL
- CARBON FOREST
- ROAD WITH MEDIAN—POTENTIAL TO CONVERT FOR ENHANCED INFILTRATION
- ROAD WITH MEDIAN—LITTLE POTENTIAL TO CONVERT FOR INFILTRATION
- WIDE ROAD—POTENTIAL TO NARROW AND INSTALL SWALES

This map indicates the appropriate locations for carbon forests to remediate the effects of pollution from highways. It also indicates locations where blue infrastructure may be most suitably integrated inside and outside of the right-of-way along arterials and major thoroughfares.

Source: DWPLTP Planning Team

1 2 4 MILES

THE LAND USE ELEMENT : THE IMAGE OF THE CITY

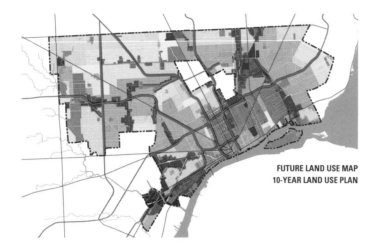

**FUTURE LAND USE MAP
10-YEAR LAND USE PLAN**

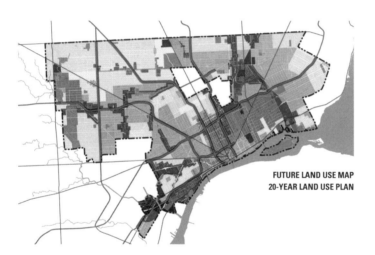

**FUTURE LAND USE MAP
20-YEAR LAND USE PLAN**

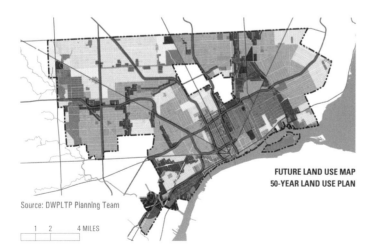

Source: DWPLTP Planning Team

**FUTURE LAND USE MAP
50-YEAR LAND USE PLAN**

1   2   4 MILES

STABILIZE AND IMPROVE: 10-YEAR LAND USE PLAN

- Establish 7 major employment districts

- Target population growth in the Greater Downtown

- Stimulate market demand to stabilize population in targeted traditional neighborhoods

- Stabilize or reconfigure areas where housing vacancy, land vacancy, and population growth are in flux through demolitions and vacant land management

- Introduce new and innovative land use typologies in high-vacancy residential and industrial areas

- Introduce green buffers to mitigate the effects of highway and industrial pollutants

- Introduce new blue infrastructure to address stormwater management issues

SUSTAIN: 20-YEAR LAND USE PLAN

- Continue growth of 7 major employment districts

- Extend targeted population growth to mixed-use centers outside of the Greater Downtown

- Identify areas for strategic growth of traditional neighborhoods around key assets (such as universities), adjacencies (such as strong surrounding communities) and arriving populations (such as growing immigrant populations)

- Continue ongoing stabilization and reconfiguration efforts in areas experiencing shifts in population or increased land and housing vacancy

- Introduce Green Mixed-Rise residential development adjacent to parks, rivers, and natural amenities

- Expand new and innovative land use typologies in areas of high-vacancy

- Expand use of carbon forest and industrial buffers

- Expand blue infrastructure in networked system of stormwater management

TRANSFORM: 50-YEAR LAND USE PLAN

- Complete build-out of 7 major employment districts

- Approach capacity densities in citywide mixed-use centers

- Expand areas for strategic growth of traditional neighborhoods around key assets (such as universities), adjacencies (such as strong surrounding communities), and arriving populations (such as growing immigrant populations)

- Renew infrastructure at lower capacity in Green Residential areas where residential population is not anticipated to return to capacity

- Expand Green Mixed-Rise residential development adjacent to parks, rivers, and natural amenities

- Complete blue and green infrastructure development

ENACT INNOVATIVE REGULATORY REFORM
CHANGING THE PARADIGM OF PLANNING FOR DETROIT

A NEW APPROACH TO THE FUTURE LAND USE MAP. Land use change does not happen in a day or even a year, but is incremental over the course of years and decades. The preparation and adoption of a Future Land Use Map must be done in recognition of this, as well as with an understanding that changing land use requires many different, coordinated actions and investments. Most city planning frameworks produce a single long-range map, projecting a growth pattern 20, 30, or 50 years out, leaving the average resident or investor to speculate about what change might look like during in the intervening years. Rather than a singular map, the Detroit Strategic Framework instead proposes that 10-year milestones for growth should be documented to both assess progress and adjust strategies based on the evolution of the city.

The future land use maps developed for the Detroit Strategic Framework represent the aspirational goals laid out in the Horizons: Stabilize and Improve (10-year), Sustain (20-year), and Transform (50-year). The 10-year land use map is built on the existing and anticipated vacancy conditions of the Framework Zones map, and lays out the initial steps to stabilize neighborhoods and establish a long-term trajectory for sustainable growth. Critical components of the plan include establishing the seven employment districts and a tiered transit hierarchy, stimulating market demand in strategic neighborhoods, and reducing blight and introducing landscape-based productive land uses to stabilize population decline.

The 20-year land use map builds on the 10-year map, identifying areas to increase population density, but also allocating additional land to be repurposed for landscape-based reuse. By the 20-year horizon, city systems should be upgraded, renewed, reduced, or decommissioned to support target population densities across the city. The employment districts should be fully defined and connected through a regional and citywide transit system. A new environmentally sustainable open space network comprised of blue infrastructure, green industrial and highway buffers, and alternative productive land uses should be fully established within the fabric of the city.

The 50-year land use map represents the completed vision for land use transformation. The city is comprised of a diverse range of neighborhood types, each with a unique identity and structured to accommodate sustainable densities. Strategic districts and neighborhoods are established to receive future population growth in a rapidly urbanizing nation and world. Through the growth of the employment districts, the ratio of residents to jobs is fiscally sustainable at 2 to 1. The city's identity is internationally recognized for its integration of landscape and urban form as a 21st century model of industrial reinvention and environmental sustainability.

WHY DOES LAND USE POLICY AND REGULATION MATTER? Change in a city takes place over time. It is organic and influenced by many people and businesses making decisions every day that affect the landscape of the city, but it is also prescribed through laws, codes, and regulations designed to protect the public good, maximize public benefit, and allow for the creation of both public and private value. Planning for and administering this change is the role of city planning departments, who use the tools of future land use plans, comprehensive citywide plans, neighborhood plans, and zoning to affect and guide change. These tools help steer a citywide vision for future development, and are fundamental to implementing the recommendations of the Detroit Strategic Framework.

FUTURE LAND USE MAP LEGEND

CITY CENTER	LIVE+MAKE	GREEN RESIDENTIAL TRANSITIONAL
DISTRICT CENTER	HEAVY INDUSTRIAL	
NEIGHBORHOOD CENTER	UTILITIES	INNOVATION PRODUCTIVE
GREEN MIXED-RISE	GENERAL INDUSTRIAL	INNOVATION ECOLOGICAL
TRADITIONAL MEDIUM-DENSITY	LIGHT INDUSTRIAL	LARGE PARK
	GREEN RESIDENTIAL	CEMETERY
TRADITIONAL LOW-DENSITY		GREEN BUFFERS

WHAT IS THE MASTER PLAN OF POLICIES?

From the Michigan Planning Enabling Act, Section 33 (1-3) of PA 33 of 2008 (Sec. 33).

(1) A master plan shall address land use and infrastructure issues and may project 20 years or more into the future. A master plan shall include maps, plats, charts, and descriptive, explanatory, and other related matter and shall show the planning commission's recommendations for the physical development of the planning jurisdiction.

(2) A master plan shall also include those of the following subjects that reasonably can be considered as pertinent to the future development of the planning jurisdiction:

(a) A land use plan that consists in part of a classification and allocation of land for agriculture, residences, commerce, industry, recreation, ways and grounds, subject to subsection (5), public transportation facilities, public buildings, schools, soil conservation, forests, woodlots, open space, wildlife refuges, and other uses and purposes. If a county has not adopted a zoning ordinance under former 1943 PA 183 or the Michigan zoning enabling act, 2006 PA 110, MCL 125.3101 to 125.3702, a land use plan and program for the county may be a general plan with a generalized future land use map.

(b) The general location, character, and extent of all of the following:

(i) All components of a transportation system and their inter-connectivity including streets and bridges, public transit including public transportation facilities and routes, bicycle facilities, pedestrian ways, freight facilities and routes, port facilities, railroad facilities, and airports, to provide for the safe and efficient movement of people and goods in a manner that is appropriate to the context of the community and, as applicable, considers all legal users of the public right-of-way.

(ii) Waterways and waterfront developments.

(iii) Sanitary sewers and water supply systems.

(iv) Facilities for flood prevention, drainage, pollution prevention, and maintenance of water levels.

(v) Public utilities and structures.

(c) Recommendations as to the general character, extent, and layout of redevelopment or rehabilitation of blighted areas; and the removal, relocation, widening, narrowing, vacating, abandonment, change of use, or extension of streets, grounds, open spaces, buildings, utilities, or other facilities.

(d) For a local unit of government that has adopted a zoning ordinance, a zoning plan for various zoning districts controlling the height, area, bulk, location, and use of buildings and premises. The zoning plan shall include an explanation of how the land use categories on the future land use map relate to the districts on the zoning map.

(e) Recommendations for implementing any of the master plan's proposals.

(3) If a master plan is or includes a master street plan or 1 or more elements described in subsection (2)(b)(i), the means for implementing the master street plan or elements in cooperation with the county road commission and the state transportation department shall be specified in the master street plan in a manner consistent with the respective powers and duties of and any written agreements between these entities and the municipality.

Two documents specifically lay out the legal framework for citywide policy and regulation, and must be prioritized for alignment with the Strategic Framework: the City's Master Plan of Policies (MPP) and the City Zoning Ordinance. Additionally, there exists an array of city, regional, and state policy and regulatory documents that also inform and guide the city's growth, including these:

- City Green Infrastructure and Sustainable Technologies Report and Plan
- Planning and Development Department Strategic Plan
- Detroit Water and Sewerage Department Stormwater Management Plan
- Detroit Public Works Department Solid Waste Plan
- City Capital Agenda and Budget
- Detroit Economic Growth Corporation Strategic Plans
- SEMCOG Transportation Improvement Plan
- Michigan State Housing Development Authority Qualified Application Plan
- Michigan Department of Natural Resources Urban Initiatives program
- State Strategic Plan
- Michigan Economic Development Corporation strategic plans

Each of these must be amended to recognize the recommendations of the Detroit Strategic Framework in order to establish a fully aligned and coordinated city, regional, and state approach to the city's long-term transformation.

A MASTER PLAN OF POLICIES THAT ACCEPTS A SMALLER POPULATION, LARGER ECONOMY, AND NEW LAND USES. The city's current Master Plan of Policies does not adequately acknowledge the city's permanent population decline and increased vacancy. Recognition of these pervasive conditions requires the city's land use policy and regulatory frameworks to introduce new land uses that can repurpose today's vacant land into new productive uses that contribute to long-term economic, social, and environmental sustainability. The Detroit Strategic Framework recommends a series of specific changes to the Master Plan of Policies and the City Zoning Ordinance in order to both recognize the current prevailing conditions of the city and lay out a vision for the future city. They are as follows:

1. Acknowledge land vacancy in policy and regulatory documents as both a fundamental challenge and opportunity.

Land vacancy poses the fundamental challenge to policy-related land use decisions in Detroit. It is the dominant physical characteristic of many areas of the city and has a profound impact on residents' quality of life, as well as the quality of business in Detroit. To this end, the City's guiding policy and regulatory documents must go much further to address land vacancy as the greatest challenge and opportunity facing the city in the 21st century. The City's Master Plan of Policies should include a section specifically addressing land vacancy, and all other land use policy-related sections will need to be framed by conditions of vacancy.

2. Define and expand landscape uses in policy and regulatory documents.

To the extent that land vacancy poses the fundamental challenge facing land use policy, landscape-based reinvention of vacant land to return it to productive reuse presents the greatest opportunity. Policy and regulatory documents need to be rewritten to facilitate the reinvention of vacant land for landscape-based reuse. The Master Plan of Policies and Zoning Ordinance should specifically permit all of the land uses identified and defined by the Strategic Framework, including the many landscape typologies defined in this Land Use Element. Doing so will expedite the process of vacant land renewal.

3. Use regulatory framework to steer development to appropriate areas of the city.

Because existing regulatory documents do not adequately recognize the current physical conditions of the city, specifically land vacancy, they are ineffective in guiding development to reinforce areas of population density or encourage landscape-based reuse in areas of high-vacancy. As a result, new development, while often undertaken with the best intentions, often creates pockets or islands of new development in areas where the overall physical conditions of the area will continue to trend toward increased vacancy. A revised regulatory framework that more effectively steers new development to reinforce density or encourage landscape-based reuse presents one of the strongest tools the city has to support the strategic recommendations of the Detroit Strategic Framework. As a first step, adopting the framework zones map as a citywide zoning overlay will recognize conditions of vacancy to facilitate development within appropriate areas of the city. This will allow the existing zoning district definitions and map to stay in place while a revised Master Plan of Policies and Zoning Ordinance are developed. The long-term goal should be the alignment of the future land use map and the zoning map to achieve the future land use vision. While there will inevitably be legal challenges to this approach, a zoning ordinance revision is critical to establishing a legally binding, codified framework for implementation.

4. Introduce new land use types and expand mix of use zoning district definitions and applications.

While several zoning districts in the current Zoning Ordinance allow for a mix of uses, only the Special Development (SD) Districts are specifically written to address a mixed-use urban environment. Even then, the application of these districts throughout the city is sporadic. The description of these mixed-use districts needs to be updated to better foster the qualities of a vibrant mixed-use environment with particular attention paid to criteria to encourage transit-oriented development and improved walkability. Application of these mixed-use districts should subsequently inform a revision to the zoning map to recognize mixed-use districts as located on the future land use map.

In addition to conventional residential-commercial mixed-use zoning districts, corridor zoning districts should similarly move toward a larger acceptance of a mix of uses. Given the vast quantities of vacant commercially zoned land along corridors, there should be fewer use restrictions placed on land in order to return it to productive use. A new Multi-Use Strip Designation should allow for a wide range of commercial, residential, or blue infrastructure uses to redefine the identities of vacant and underutilized commercial corridors.

5. Incorporate aspects of a form-based code.

Simultaneously, while certain zoning districts should be modified or created to encourage a greater mix of uses, use restrictions in the zoning ordinance should transition to more form-based development criteria. The Development Types described in the report appendix begin to lay out the form and use criteria that may be applied within the various future land use typologies. Rather than allow or restrict specific uses, they attempt to appropriately locate broader use categories within their typological context. For example, within mixed-use land use typologies, commercial development types are limited to those that encourage walkability by building to the right-of-way, locating parking in the rear of establishments, etc. New zoning districts written around the future land use typologies and corridor types should reference the appropriate form-based development types within those typologies.

NEIGHBORHOOD PLANNING REFORM: THE DETROIT STRATEGIC FRAMEWORK'S RELATIONSHIP TO NEIGHBORHOOD PLANNING. Neighborhood planning efforts can help to land more specific strategies on the ground, meeting the more specific needs of local communities—all within the Strategic Framework neighborhood typologies. The Detroit Strategic Framework recognizes the importance of neighborhood-based planning, as represented by efforts such as those of the Lower Eastside Action Plan (LEAP) and similar Community Development Advocates of Detroit (CDAD) Strategic Framework projects, and believe this type of neighborhood planning will play a critical role in developing the future vision for Detroit's neighborhoods. We maintain that all parts of city will need some form of investment to achieve their potential. The Detroit Strategic Framework provides the parameters within which to focus that investment before more specific, on-the-ground actions are implemented through a neighborhood-based planning process. The Detroit Strategic Framework holds the potential to bridge citywide and neighborhood planning initiatives and leverage the support of the public, private, and philanthropic communities to better realize common goals across multiple scales of planning.

THE MI-PLACE PARTNERSHIP INITIATIVE

The goal of the MI-Place partnership Initiative is to create more jobs, raise incomes and thereby restore prosperity in Michigan at least in part through targeted local and regional placemaking activities. A significant amount of state, regional, and private resources would be marshaled to make significant physical change in a relatively short period of time (2-6 years). Action projects would be planned in collaborative public, private, and nonprofit entity partnerships, and be largely built by the private sectors (in some cases with state financial support or credits).

The types of regional and community placemaking improvements necessary to attract and retain talent and residents include:

- Wide range of housing choices (including workforce, affordable, rental and owner-occupied housing)
- Wide range of transportation choices (including improved transit)
- Quality public infrastructure
- Mixed-use development
- Pedestrian-oriented public spaces
- Amenities (including green and blue infrastructure, bicycle paths and trails, entertainment venues, etc.)

Achievement of these goals requires development toolkits to assist local officials and stakeholders. Direct technical assistance should be provided to those who need and request it, including broad training for state and local government staff members, officials, and key stakeholders about what placemaking is and how to effectively engage in it. Key outcomes include preparation of regional and local strategic action plans for targeted placemaking improvements, community engagement, and specific local project action plans prepared to meet local and state requirements.

CITY GREEN INFRASTRUCTURE AND SUSTAINABLE TECHNOLOGIES REPORT AND PLAN

- Incorporate blue infrastructure recommendations
- Incorporate industrial and carbon forest buffering
- Commit to building a citywide open space network around landscape-based productive reuse of vacant land [reference Future Open Space Network map]

PLANNING AND DEVELOPMENT DEPARTMENT STRATEGIC PLAN

- Develop revised approach to public land holdings based on Land and Buildings Assets Element recommendations
- Restructure and reprioritize land use strategies based on the strategic framework recommendations

DETROIT WATER AND SEWER DEPARTMENT STORMWATER MANAGEMENT PLAN

- Develop comprehensive blue infrastructure master plan as key component of overall stormwater management plan [reference Blue Infrastructure map]

DETROIT PUBLIC WORKS DEPARTMENT SOLID WASTE PLAN

- Develop alternative approaches to waste collection and material recycling based on Framework Zones and future land use vision [reference Framework Zones map and Future Land Use map]

CITY CAPITAL AGENDA AND BUDGET

- Steer public investment based on vacancy conditions and future land use vision [reference Framework Zones map and Future Land Use map]

DETROIT ECONOMIC GROWTH CORPORATION STRATEGIC PLANS

- Recognize employment districts as city's target economic growth areas
- Incorporate transit oriented development as strategic priority
- Prioritize commercial and residential development, including gap financing and subsidies, within City Center and District Center land use typologies; Neighborhood Centers as next tier priority [reference Employment District and Future Land Use map]

SEMCOG TRANSPORTATION IMPROVEMENT PLAN

- Incorporate tiered transportation hierarchy within larger regional transit plan [reference Transit Network map]
- Incorporate carbon forest as part of highway design standards [reference Green Infrastructure map]
- Incorporate complete streets and multi-modal transit as part of regional transit plan
- Coordinate rubblized or decommissioned roads in high-vacancy areas with regional transportation and freight network

MICHIGAN STATE HOUSING DEVELOPMENT AUTHORITY QUALIFIED APPLICATION PLAN

- Steer low income housing tax credit development to reinforce density and support future land use vision [reference Framework Zones and Future Land Use map]

MICHIGAN DEPARTMENT OF NATURAL RESOURCES URBAN INITIATIVES PROGRAM

- Support programs to establish citywide open space network [reference Future Open Space Network map]
- Expand and support wide range of landscape-based uses including blue and green infrastructure and alternative land uses

STATE STRATEGIC PLAN

- Prioritize support for the State's largest city and urban center
- Recognize central position of the Detroit Works Project strategic framework as city's strategy guiding document

MICHIGAN ECONOMIC DEVELOPMENT CORPORATION STRATEGIC PLANS

- Recognize employment districts as city's target growth areas
- Incorporate transit oriented development as strategic priority
- Prioritize commercial and residential development, including gap financing and subsidies, within City Center and District Center land use typologies; Neighborhood Centers as next tier priority [reference Employment District and Future Land Use map]

CONNECTING TO REGIONAL AND STATE CONTEXT: AMENDING CITY AND STATE POLICY AND REGULATORY GUIDING DOCUMENTS. The Detroit Strategic Framework's extensive, multi-year, community-based planning effort lays the groundwork for better interagency coordination at all levels of government: city, county, region, and state. The Detroit Strategic Framework provides a singular vision and sets of strategies to help inform policy-guiding documents at multiple levels of local, regional, and state government. Beyond the fundamental alignment of the City's Master Plan of Policies and Zoning Ordinance, to the following local, regional, and state policy and regulatory documents will need to be aligned with the Detroit Strategic Framework recommendations.

THE STRATEGIC FRAMEWORK ELEMENT RECOMMENDATIONS AND THEIR ALIGNMENT WITH THE CURRENT MASTER PLAN OF POLICIES. The five planning elements of the Strategic Framework—Economic Growth, Land Use, City Systems, Neighborhoods and Land and Buildings—provide a series of policy and implementation approaches that can be integrated into the public policy and action documents listed on the previous pages. The City of Detroit Master Plan of Policies and Zoning Ordinance are two of the most important tools to help move the

Framework's recommendations into action. While these tools do not drive the pace of development change, having a predictable regulatory framework in place will give the private sector greater confidence in making decisions about investing in the city, now and in the future. An updated Master Plan and Zoning Ordinance will also give community greater confidence that development is following a plan that they had a hand in crafting—one that reflects the desires of the city overall and the aspirations for its neighborhoods.

The adjacent chart illustrates how the Framework Elements align with the Master Plan of Policy elements and begins to identify the kinds of updates that will be required to bring the MPP in line with the Strategic Framework.

THE LAND USE ELEMENT : THE IMAGE OF THE CITY

PRECEDENT

SAGINAW MASTER PLAN (2011)

In its recently completed master plan, Saginaw created three new land use classifications to deal with vacancy issues:

- Neighborhood Opportunity Areas
- Urban Venture Areas
- Green Reserve Opportunity Areas

In spite of the large degree of vacancy in many areas of the city, only a small portion was designated "Green Reserve Opportunity Area." Much of this area was previously classified as the Green Zone.

Image/Text Source: Saginaw Master Plan (2011)

PRECEDENT

PHILADELPHIA ZONING ORDINANCE (2012)

Philadelphia revised its zoning ordinance in 2012 to support the recommendations of the city's updated Comprehensive Plan, Philadelphia 2035.

In it, overlaying zoning was consolidated, streamlined and reorganized. The code includes 3 "master overlays": Center City, Neighborhood Commercial Areas, Neighborhood Conservation Areas.

Uses are organized by categories and sub-categories; not by each individual use.

It modernizes uses in preparation for the future and addresses urban agriculture, solar panels, bed and breakfasts, adult day care and community homes.

Updated design standards were included for multi-family, institutional and commercial properties; enhanced landscaping and better protection for natural resources.

It reduces automobile parking requirements and includes off-street parking maximums.

Image/Text Source: www.phila.gov

PRECEDENT

YOUNGSTOWN 2010

To anticipate remaining a smaller city, Youngstown redesignated 30 percent of its residential land in its 2010 Master Plan revision. Much of this land was reclassified as "Industrial Green." Vacant land that had not been previously developed was reclassified as "Open Space."

In the course of rewriting the Zoning Code, however, much of the residential land that was designated to shift away from residential in the Master Plan remained zoned residential in the Zoning Ordinance.

In order to address issues of extreme vacancy, the Zoning Ordinance included a "Limited Services Overlay," designed to steer investment away from heavily disinvested areas. This overlay has yet to be applied to any areas of the city.

Image Source: Youngstown 2010

THE STRATEGIC FRAMEWORK ELEMENT RECOMMENDATIONS AND THEIR ALIGNMENT WITH THE CURRENT MASTER PLAN OF POLICIES.

	CITY OF DETROIT MASTER PLAN OF POLICIES ELEMENTS (MPP)	ALIGNMENT WITH DETROIT WORKS STRATEGIC FRAMEWORK PLAN ELEMENTS	RECOMMENDED UPDATES FOR MASTER PLAN OF POLICIES
EXISTING ELEMENTS	ARTS AND CULTURE	NEIGHBORHOODS LAND USE	• Acknowledge and add Live+Make land use typology and related development types
	ECONOMY	ECONOMIC GROWTH	• Describe primary and secondary employment districts and economic growth strategies
	HEALTH AND SOCIAL SERVICES	NEIGHBORHOODS	• Address role of food systems within the city
	INFRASTRUCTURE	CITY SYSTEMS	• Address strategic renewal of city systems
	PARKS, RECREATION AND OPEN SPACE	LAND USE LAND AND BUILDINGS	• Include a wider range of landscape-based/open space reuse options
	TRANSPORTATION AND MOBILITY	CITY SYSTEMS LAND USE	• Include a wider range of landscape-based/open space reuse options • Update Transportation Network map to show tiered city-regional system
	CITY DESIGN	LAND USE	• Update goals to ensure that new development supports land use vision for each typology • Add land use definitions for landscape typologies: Innovation Ecological and Innovation Productive • Add or modify land use definitions for new neighborhood types: Green Residential, Green Mixed-Rise, Live+Make
	EDUCATION AND LIBRARIES	NEIGHBORHOODS LAND AND BUILDINGS	• Align facilities with neighborhood typologies
	HISTORY, LEGACIES AND PRESERVATION	LAND USE	• Incorporate preservation strategies aligned with neighborhood typologies
	INTERGOVERNMENTAL AFFAIRS	LAND AND BUILDINGS CITY SYSTEMS	• Incorporate intergovernmental strategies reflected in City Systems and Land and Buildings Assets elements
	PUBLIC SAFETY	NEIGHBORHOODS	• Update to reflect the importance of reinforcing proposed density patterns through neighborhood typologies and neighborhood element strategies
	ZONING CONCEPTS	LAND USE	• Update Zoning Concepts to expand range of vacant land reuse options beyond agriculture
	COMMUNITY ORGANIZATIONS	CIVIC ENGAGEMENT	• Update to reflect role of community organizations in neighborhood-based planning
	ENVIRONMENT AND ENERGY	CITY SYSTEMS	• Update to describe blue and green infrastructure • Update to include carbon forest and green buffers
	INDUSTRIAL CENTERS	ECONOMIC GROWTH LAND USE	• Incorporate industrial strategies from Economic Growth chapter
	NEIGHBORHOODS AND HOUSING	NEIGHBORHOODS LAND USE	• Update and expand the range of traditional and innovative neighborhood types • Describe commitment to neighborhood-based planning within a larger citywide framework for decision making
	RETAIL AND LOCAL SERVICES	LAND USE	• Update to include a more strategic prioritization of commercial land in nodes and strips matching the land use corridors recommendations
NEW ELEMENTS	ADD VACANT LAND ELEMENT		• Add Vacant Land Element specifically addressing approaches to vacancy that includes the Framework Zones; to be updated at five-year intervals
	ADD PUBLIC LAND ELEMENT		• Add Public Land Element that specifically addresses a strategic and coordinated approach to acquisition/assembly, disposition and maintenance of city-owned property
	FUTURE LAND USE MAP		• Revise future land use map to address Framework Plan recommendations • Add new land use typologies and development types per the Land Use Element of the Framework Plan • Develop phased future land use map at 10-, 20- and 50-year intervals

TWO OPTIONS FOR REVISING MASTER PLAN AND ZONING:

The process of revising the Master Plan of Policies and Zoning ordinance is not a small undertaking. It requires technical research, testing, and community participation. Detroit's city planning staff recently completed a multi-year Master Plan revision process, beginning in 2004 and finally adopted in 2009, and they are still in the process of creating a new ordinance for urban agriculture. The level of effort is considerable; yet, having a current comprehensive city planning framework and corresponding zoning ordinance is critical to effectively managing the proper growth and preservation of the city's land, buildings, and cultural and historic assets. The Detroit Strategic Framework strongly recommends incorporating its proposals into these two regulatory documents as an essential implementation task of the plan.

To effectively take on this task requires the recognition of current challenges. These include limited staffing capacity (the number of dedicated professional planners on staff to support the effort, as well as limited staff to address both long-term planning and short-term needs); constrained resources to conduct meaningful outreach for public and political support; the length of time to complete the revision and adoption process; the demands of managing market conditions and investments; and the possible "planning fatigue" the community may currently be experiencing. As such, the Framework offers two possible approaches to initiating an adoption process, going forward.

1 FULL REVISION OF MASTER PLAN OF POLICIES AND ZONING ORDINANCE

PROS:
1. The public momentum that will immediately follow the completion of the Strategic Framework, coupled with the revision of the City Charter, puts in place an engaged and informed community that is better prepared to participate in a public hearing and outreach process.
2. The public process required for full adoption can take advantage of the civic engagement infrastructure now in place throughout the city.
3. Taking two to three years now to revise the MPP in total is a more efficient use of staffing resources in the long run.
4. A complete revision now ensures the Framework's recommendations can be adopted within a single political cycle.
5. Funding support is more likely to contribute to a comprehensive approach versus a small-scale change over an undefined period of time
6. Much of the technical research, analysis, and recommendations of the Strategic Framework meet the general requirements of the City Charter and State Planning Enabling Act.

CONS:
1. Will keep existing land use policies and zoning in place that might contribute to development and investments that conflict with the Strategic Framework over the next two to three years.
2. Stretches already thin staff capacities beyond their ability to manage both near- and long-term planning and development needs.
3. Requires broad political (Mayor and City Council) and community support and therefore, a robust civic engagement process.
4. The community might feel a sense of "planning fatigue" and not be willing to participate in another two- to three-year planning implementation process. (The key here is that the adoption process must be framed as an "implementation action," rather than another planning process).
5. The Detroit Planning and Development Department and City Planning Commission completed a full revision just three years ago, a process that took nearly five years to complete.
6. Unless the Strategic Framework recommendations are quickly codified, they run the risk of being lost to changing priorities and/or market conditions.

FULL ZONING AMENDMENT
1. Rewrite zoning ordinance to incorporate new zoning district definitions in alignment with the MPP future land use map.
2. Place greater emphasis on form-based criteria for new districts.
3. Undertake associated map revision to align zoning map with future land use map.

2 PHASED ADOPTION OF MASTER PLAN OF POLICIES AND PRIORITIZED ZONING CODE ORDINANCES

PROS:
1. All public agencies to prioritize the most critical issues that need to be addressed by MPP and zoning revisions, using overlay revisions and individual zoning code additions or revisions.
2. Potentially requires a smaller scale of civic engagement.
3. Revisions are more manageable by a smaller staff.
4. Costs of individual revisions required less funding resource up front.

CONS:
1. Revisions may become piecemeal and detached from a more comprehensive vision.
2. No guarantee the overall amount of time to make all revisions will take less time, in fact, adopting all changes in a phased approach will take longer to complete all changes.
3. Unless the Strategic Framework recommendations are quickly codified, they run the risk of being lost to changing priorities and/or market conditions.

PHASED ZONING AMENDMENTS
1. Adopt Urban Agriculture Zoning Ordinance revision.
2. Rewrite and expand use of mixed-use zoning districts.
3. Adopt Framework Zones overlay to existing Zoning map.
   a. Steer development to the appropriate areas of the city without a full rewriting of the district definitions.
   b. Example: Nonprofit housing developer in High-Vacancy area.
4. Expand landscape use definitions and incorporate into uses associated with Framework Zones overlay.
5. Rewrite commercial corridor zoning to incorporate greater mix of uses including blue infrastructure, incorporating greater emphasis on form-based over use-based zoning criteria as appropriate.

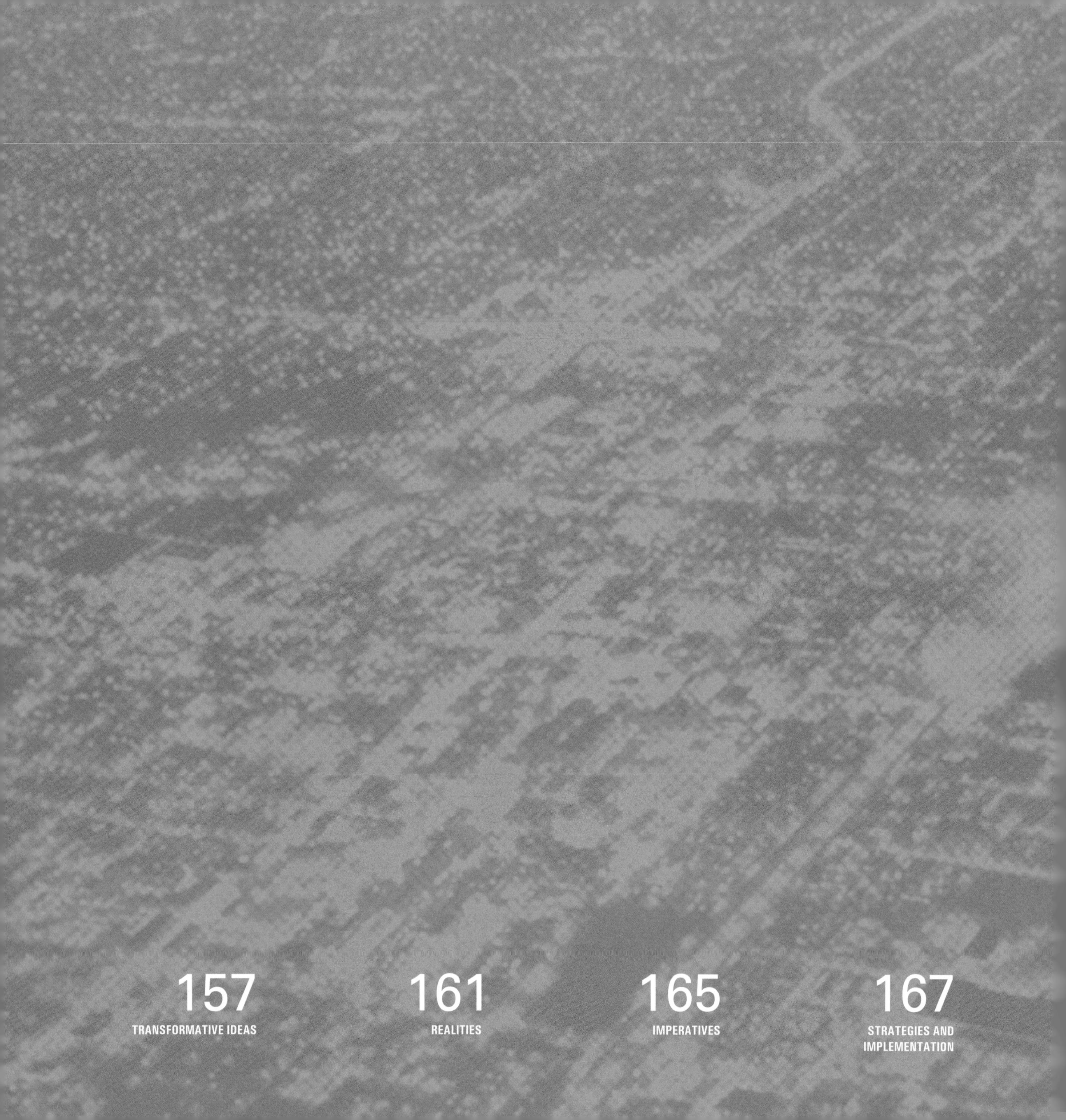

THE CITY
SYSTEMS
ELEMENT
THE SUSTAINABLE CITY

A Day in the Life *Improving City Services*

"You work for Public Lighting? Let me ask you something…"

Demarco used to dread this moment at social gatherings. But in the last year or so, he has had many more answers for the questions that come his way. Instead of trying to provide exactly the same services to the entire city, his department has joined other city departments in a more strategic approach. Public Lighting now bases its upgrades and service decisions on real conditions and needs in each neighborhood. Maintenance schedules have been adjusted, too. As lighting strategies have improved this past year, so has public safety.

This strategy is also working for Demarco on a personal level. His neighborhood, which has had a lot of vacancy and safety problems because many lights had stopped working, is getting new installation of high-efficiency streetlights and is beginning to see a quicker response to other service requests, as well as a significant drop in car break-ins at night. The investment for physical infrastructure is coordinated with other investments in the city, too. For example, renovation of the local elementary school was timed with street improvements and tree plantings. The persistent flooding in Demarco's neighborhood is also being addressed, through a system of attractive marsh-like "swales" beside the streets that collect stormwater runoff from Demarco's neighborhood and connect to a broader system of boulevards with long, linear stormwater gardens and new tree plantings. An unexpected benefit of this change? Aquatic birds and other small native wildlife have found a refuge in parts of the neighborhood. Now if only Demarco can solve his trash pick-up problem: getting his sons to remember the trash schedule as well as the city does.

TRANSFORMATIVE IDEAS
CITY SYSTEMS AND THE ENVIRONMENT

RENEWING AND REALIGNING FOR THE NEW DETROIT. From streetlights and utility networks to waste management and transportation, Detroit's city systems sustain its residents and businesses—but in turn must be sustained by revenues from these users. Yet population and employment loss, and the resulting loss of revenue and disinvestment, have left Detroiters paying more for less.

Even though Detroit's economy is growing in new sectors—such as information technology, finance, communications, and design—the city will likely continue to lose some population over the next 20 years. Reorganizing the city's systems now is critical to meeting the needs of Detroiters who have been paying and waiting for a better day, as well to match and support the future Detroit of connected, diverse neighborhoods and employment centers that encourage new jobs and new neighbors. The city's government, private utility operators, civic and business leaders, and residents face big decisions about improving services while reducing costs, closing an overwhelming budget gap that has burdened the city for decades, and reshaping an over-scaled, underinvested infrastructure into an efficient, environmentally sustainable set of 21st century systems. **If we confront these tough decisions now, we can improve the quality of life for Detroiters and put the city back on the path to financial security within 10 years.**

RECONCILING AND REPLENISHING. Realigning Detroit's city systems is not just important for the sake of efficiency: It is a matter of justice for all. The most economically vulnerable households in Detroit are also the hardest hit by system inefficiencies that harm their health as well as their pocketbooks. In particular, air pollution from industry and car exhaust have contributed to high rates of asthma and other respiratory diseases, especially among children.

Transportation holds an important key to creating a socially and economically just Detroit. The Detroit of today is a driver's city, without enough transit or other transportation choices, and with many jobs well beyond the city limits. The very people who need jobs most are left behind, struggling with transit routes that don't connect them to work, or sharing an old car along with all the upkeep. Detroiters who can't afford a car are also cut off from fair access to healthy food, recreation, health care, and a whole range of necessities for a healthy, balanced life.

The urgency of addressing environmental degradation and residents' quality of life reaches far beyond city limits. Regional economies, transportation, and water and air quality issues connect Detroit to the entire Great Lakes ecosystem. Traditional infrastructures and industry tend to degrade resources, with regional consequences. **New alternative forms of infrastructure, using landscape to clean air and water, can restore environmental balance and improve quality of life and the environment in Detroit and in the entire Great Lakes basin.**

SHAPING THE CITY TO SUIT REAL NEEDS. The Detroit we now live in was designed for nearly 2 million people, and the extra capacity in city systems is not only going to waste, it actually creates a drag on services for the current residents. Just as we can find new ways to manage the abundance of land in the city, we can unlock innovations to manage surplus system capacity and reallocate resources to upgrade and maintain core systems, improve service, and heal the environment. Systems renewal will be coordinated with land use change to better relate neighborhoods and employment districts, as well as the systems that serve them.

The key is to be smart about how and where we locate and reinforce residential areas, employment, and other activities. These decisions must be balanced with the development Detroit has now, and especially with the knowledge that some residents will continue to live in areas that have high-vacancy. The Strategic Framework foresees how the city can evolve from its present pattern—which is spread out and hard to serve—toward a city of connected neighborhoods where employment, residences, and activities are all close by, or are connected in an efficient system of high-speed transit routes and green, landscaped boulevards. Some areas of the city that have already moved away from residential land use will be suited for new land uses and development types, including new green infrastructure that works to clean the air and water and support the health of the whole city and region. Services will be scaled to the number of people and uses in each area of the city.

SYSTEM TRANSFORMATION. Three major transformations underpin the change in Detroit's systems—strategic renewal of infrastructure to suit demand, deploying surplus land as a form of infrastructure (radically changing the image of the city in the process), and changing the culture of transportation (to enhance connections and minimize environmental impact).

The goal of reconfiguring services is to continue to providing core services—including water, sewerage, gas, electricity, and communications services—to all Detroiters wherever they work and live, while also serving all the needs for existing and growing businesses. Delivering the change that has escaped the city in the past will require coordinated effort among all system providers, public and private. This coordination will need to be planned and carried out from a central point of accountability, in order to transform the city's infrastructure and service quality.

3

CITY
SYSTEMS
TRANSFORMATIVE
IDEAS

1 STRATEGIC INFRASTRUCTURE RENEWAL

DIFFERENTIATED AND RELIABLE INVESTMENT. The Strategic Framework proposes a differentiated level of investment across the city, aligning infrastructure capacity to Detroit's future form and continuing to serve people where they live and work now. The potential benefits for economic development and cost reduction are significant, but cannot be achieved instantly. Instead, each area of the city will need an approach to investment that provides certainty and predictability so that systems agencies, businesses, civic groups, and residents can make long-term plans. Moving to a situation where more people live in higher-density areas and fewer people live in lower-density areas (a more efficient distribution) is a critical step in reducing the financial problems faced by service providers and end users.

SYSTEM DIFFERENCES AND INTEGRATION. The five key systems of water, waste, energy, transportation, and communications each have specific issues arising from their installation and ownership history, as well as their unique technical aspects. A proposed investment approach for each area of the city should be coordinated with land use and should prioritize how systems are upgraded or replaced over time. Although each system has its own peculiarities, coordinating the investments in related systems can provide significant efficiencies across all the systems.

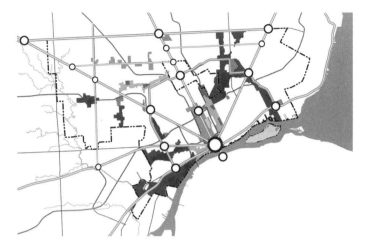

 LANDSCAPE AS 21ST CENTURY INFRASTRUCTURE

DIVERSIFIED TRANSPORTATION FOR DETROIT AND THE REGION

Landscape is an opportunity to address Detroit's critical environmental issues and public health hazards. In particular, blue and green infrastructures are landscapes that cleanse stormwater and improve air quality, respectively. Traditional infrastructural systems are typically focused on delivering only one service at a time, often at the expense of the environment and public health. By contrast, landscape infrastructures serve many functions by providing habitat, offering recreation opportunities, enhancing transportation options through bicycling and walking, and improving neighborhoods by providing beauty and increasing property values—all while serving a practical, environmental function such as retaining or cleansing stormwater.

Landscape systems typically cost less to build and maintain than conventional infrastructure, creating an economic benefit. Landscape infrastructures offer opportunities for interdisciplinary collaboration across agencies, permitting them share or coordinate personnel and budgets in ways that are not possible for conventional infrastructure projects. These systems will have regional ecological benefits, including improved water quality in the Rouge and Detroit Rivers and Lake Erie, as well as increased and improved habitat for local wildlife and migrating birds.

APPLYING NEW TECHNOLOGY TO EXISTING ROADS. The transportation system—especially Detroit's fixed road network—must be substantially reconfigured to suit the currently smaller population within the city, and will also have to adapt to suit emerging needs within the city and region. Because Detroit is also central to the support system for a freight hub of national and global significance—the busiest North American commercial border crossing, and a significant freight employer in its own right—the creation and upgrading of freight routes into and through Detroit need consistent, long-term support. At the same time, residents urgently need more transportation choices beyond driving.

New technologies can be integrated into Detroit's transportation network to serve both commercial and personal transportation. Mobile devices (including cell phones) can be used by users and operators to manage on-demand services that match capacity to demand, improving efficiency and allowing smaller fleets to serve the same number of people. Modest adjustments to the existing road network will greatly facilitate the integration of new technology. The very size of Detroit's existing roads also offers an opportunity to make change with significantly less disruption than in a fast-growing city.

ADDRESSING THE DISTANCE AND DENSITY CHALLENGES. A key challenge in Detroit is how spread out the city is, compared with cities of similar population. The relatively low density and long distances between employment and neighborhoods, coupled with how many commute out from the city every day, will challenge the city and region to devise strategies to increase transit access and use. Bringing more jobs within reach of public transit is only part of the answer. Overhauling the operational practices of the region's transit providers is the other part. Encouraging and supporting greater use of cycling and walking represents a low-cost way to support system-wide change in transportation with a relatively small investment. Key changes will be the development of a 'greenway' network to promote cycling and walking, introduction of bus rapid transit (BRT) operations on main travel routes (within and beyond the city limits), and improved intermodal transfer for passengers and freight.

REVENUE & STRUCTURE MISALIGNMENT

40%

PUBLIC TRANSPORTATION IS RELIANT ON CITY'S GENERAL FUND TO SUBSIDIZE 40% OF REVENUES[1]

-$336M

DETROIT HAS EXPERIENCED A $336 MILLION DECLINE IN PROPERTY TAX REVENUE FROM 1950-2005 (60% DECLINE)[2]

20%

20% OF DETROIT'S POTENTIAL REVENUE GENERATING LAND AREA IS VACANT[3]

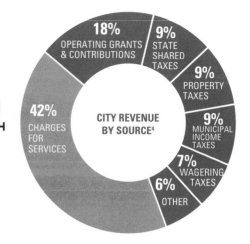

CITY REVENUE BY SOURCE[4]

18% OPERATING GRANTS & CONTRIBUTIONS
9% STATE SHARED TAXES
9% PROPERTY TAXES
9% MUNICIPAL INCOME TAXES
7% WAGERING TAXES
6% OTHER
42% CHARGES FOR SERVICES

UNDERUTILIZED SYSTEMS

32%

IN 2010, DETROIT FAMILIES SPENT AN AVERAGE OF 32% OF THEIR ANNUAL HOUSEHOLD INCOME ON TRANSPORTATION[5]

27%

27% OF DETROIT'S 3000 MILES OF PUBLIC ROADS ARE IN POOR CONDITION[6]

35K WORKING LIGHTS

ONLY 35,000 OF THE EXISTING 88,000 STREET LIGHTS WORK IN DETROIT[7]

ONLY 9% OF DETROITERS USE PUBLIC TRANSIT[8]

BUSES RUN AT 75% CAPACITY DURING PEAK HOURS

BUSES RUN AT 75% CAPACITY DURING PEAK HOURS IN DETROIT. THE NATIONAL AVERAGE CAPACITY FOR UNITED STATES BUSES DURING PEAK TIME IS 105%[9]

ENVIRONMENTAL IMPACT

40% WATER SYSTEM CAPACITY
42B
GALLONS UNACCOUNTED FOR WATER

DETROIT'S WATER SYSTEM OPERATES AT 40% OF ITS OVERALL CAPACITY[10]

DETROIT'S 42 BILLION GALLONS OF WATER CLASSIFIED AS 'UNACCOUNTED FOR WATER' OFTEN RESULTS FROM LEAKS, METER INACCURACIES & HYDRANT USE[11]

4.8K OLYMPIC SIZED SWIMMING POOLS

47.7 BILLION GALLONS OF RAW, UNTREATED SEWAGE WERE DIRECTLY DISCHARGED INTO THE DETROIT RIVER IN 2011. THIS VOLUME IS EQUIVALENT TO 4,800 OLYMPIC-SIZED SWIMMING POOLS[11]

 80%

DTE HAS INCREASED ITS COAL CONSUMPTION BY 80% SINCE 1975[12]

3x
LEAD POISONING ASTHMA

ENVIRONMENTAL HEALTH HAZARDS

DETROIT HAS THREE TIMES HIGHER RATE OF CHILDREN WITH ELEVATED BLOOD LEAD LEVELS THAN THE NATIONAL AVERAGE[13]

DETROIT HAS THREE TIMES HIGHER RATE OF CHILDREN WITH ASTHMA THAN THE NATIONAL AVERAGE[14]

REALITIES
THE STATE OF DETROIT'S CITY SYSTEMS

DETROITERS PAY TOO MUCH FOR TOO LITTLE. As some areas of Detroit have withstood an exodus of more than 80% of residents, those who remained bore the brunt of the cost for services. Yet the revenue from these households was not enough for the major renewal or replacement that would have brought systems in line with modern environmental and efficiency standards. Although the relationships between rates and numbers of residents is more complicated with regard to the private service providers, (because they may operate related services both within and outside of the city limits), for both public and private providers, the fixed costs for services are being spread over a progressively smaller number of residents and businesses. The rates charged for these services are tending to rise and, in some cases, are becoming too expensive for households to maintain. In short, rates for residents are rising, the costs to serve the city are also rising and yet, level and quality of service is tending to fall for most residents.

LEGACY SYSTEMS NO LONGER SERVE THE REAL DETROIT. The city's main systems were planned for larger city with a heavier load of industrial activity than Detroit has today. The legacy systems of Detroit are not right for the new city. The system's capacity far exceeds what is needed today: sometimes usage levels are as low as 30-40% of designed capacity). Not only are the systems mismatched to the restructured (and restructuring) city, they are also aging. Many have already reached the end of their effective design lives and many more will do so during the next twenty years. Aging systems malfunction more often, which when compounded by climate change can have severe economic and personal consequences (flooding is a particular example of this). In many cases the systems are operated and managed following models that are no longer appropriate to the current situation of the city. Personnel shortages and training deficiencies contribute further to these problems.

TRADITIONAL INFRASTRUCTURES ARE NOT SUSTAINABLE. Existing infrastructure systems are struggling in Detroit, placing increasing fiscal burdens on residents and continuing to impact the environment and human health adversely. With aging systems, shrinking budgets, retiring staff, and a declining population, these problems will only grow over time. Addressing these problems cannot be done conventionally; there is a need to find new ways to address city needs. City residents need access to clean air, soil, and water for good health. Local wildlife and migrating birds need access to areas of suitable contiguous habitat.

Changing climatic conditions in the future may cause the problem to worsen, particularly with regard to the stormwater issue in Detroit. Climate change may bring changes in long-term precipitation patterns and an increased frequency and intensity of heavy rainfall events. Short term, very intense rainstorms pose the greatest challenge for Detroit's stormwater system. Detroit's soil conditions, which have very low permeability, lead to high runoff rates, and the Wastewater Treatment Plant cannot handle these sudden, severe spikes in runoff.

1) McKinsey 2010; 2) SEMCOG 2008; 3) Hamilton Anderson Associates, Happold Consulting, Inc. (HCI); 4) HCI; 5) American Community 2010 5-Year, HCI; 6) SEMCOG; 7) The Detroit Free Press; 8) SEMCOG; 9) HCI; 10,11) Detroit Water and Sewerage Department (DWSD); 12) Michigan Department of Environmental Quality; 13) Michigan Department of Community Health; 14) Detroit Alliance for Asthma Awareness

COMPARATIVE DEATH RATES PER 100,000 POPULATION

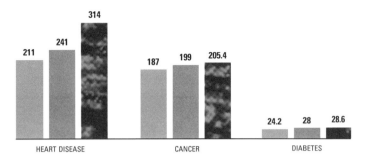

HEART DISEASE: 211, 241, 314
CANCER: 187, 199, 205.4
DIABETES: 24.2, 28, 28.6

Detroiters have a higher incidences of heart disease, cancer, diabetes, adult and childhood asthma, and elevated blood lead levels within children than the national average. Many health problems are correlated with general lifestyle factors including diet and exercise; others are associated with unfavorable environmental conditions.[1]

PREVALENCE RATES PER 100,000 POPULATION

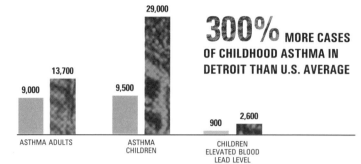

ASTHMA ADULTS: 9,000, 13,700
ASTHMA CHILDREN: 9,500, 29,000
CHILDREN ELEVATED BLOOD LEAD LEVEL: 900, 2,600

300% MORE CASES OF CHILDHOOD ASTHMA IN DETROIT THAN U.S. AVERAGE

TOTAL CANCER RISK AT MONITORING SITES
* SIZE OF CIRCLE INDICATES RELATIVE RISK

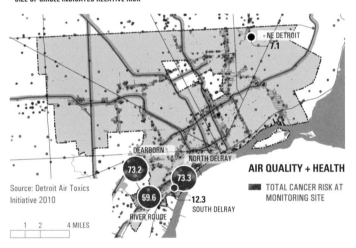

NE DETROIT 7.1
DEARBORN
NORTH DELRAY
73.2
73.3
59.6
12.3
SOUTH DELRAY
RIVER ROUGE

Source: Detroit Air Toxics Initiative 2010

1 2   4 MILES

AIR QUALITY + HEALTH

▪ TOTAL CANCER RISK AT MONITORING SITE

Health risks associated with poor air quality are higher in Southwest Detroit. Michigan Department of Environmental Quality conducted two studies to assess air quality and health risk in Detroit (DATI-1 and DATI-2). The map takes into account air quality measurements from 2006-2007, MDEQ DATI-2.

19.5%

19.5% OF DETROITERS HAVE NO HEALTH INSURANCE COVERAGE, WHILE 32.8% USE PUBLIC HEALTH INSURANCE COVERAGE.[2]

Some areas of the city are less healthy to live in than others because of their proximity to environmental hazards. Low income and minority residents are disproportionately impacted by environmental hazards.

HEALTH HAZARDS. Detroiters have been harmed by dangerous conditions caused or contributed to by the city's inefficient systems. For example, Detroit has a combined wastewater/stormwater system, and when system flows exceed treatment capacity, untreated combined sewage/stormwater overflows into the Detroit and Rouge Rivers. Detroit's wastewater treatment plant is the largest in North America yet cannot handle the stormwater/wastewater flows brought to it during many heavy rain events. These discharges occur at a number of outfall locations along the Detroit and Rouge Rivers, and in 2011, the greatest volumes of diluted (untreated) discharge occurred near downtown.

Poor air quality along transportation and industrial corridors is responsible for significant human health problems. As a result Detroiters have among the highest rates of asthma and related respiratory diseases nationally. African Americans and the poor are disproportionately affected due to the legacy of racially charged policies that targeted these communities as receivers of new highways, incinerators and industrial activity.

THE BURDEN ON LOWER-INCOME RESIDENTS AND CHILDREN. Lower income, minority residents, and children are more frequently exposed to hazards and also more likely to get sick from this exposure. They are more likely to

- live or work near environmental hazards;
- have trouble getting health care and health information because of a wide variety of barriers, including lack of health insurance and problems with transportation; and
- experience difficulties affording and accessing foods to ensure a healthy diet.

Adverse health impacts disproportionately affect children, who are more at risk because their exposure potential is greater (greater likelihood to come into contact with contaminants), exposure can be disproportionately more harmful to their small bodies than to an adult's, and their maturing nervous systems are more susceptible to damage. Lead is a particularly harmful substance for children because exposure at a young age permanently affects their potential to succeed later in life. Lead exposure can impair brain development, impair growth, and cause children to be inattentive, hyperactive, irritable, and have problems with learning, reading, and memory.

30%

FOOD INSECURITY IN DETROIT IS ESTIMATED TO BE DOUBLE THE NATIONAL RATE, APPROXIMATELY 30%.[3]

160 TONS

IN 2010, THE GARDEN RESOURCES PROGRAM COLLABORATIVE ENGAGED MORE THAN 5000 ADULTS AND 10,000 YOUTH IN THE CULTIVATION OF MORE THAN 1,200 VEGETABLE GARDENS - PRODUCING MORE THAN 160 TONS OF FOOD![4]

THE CASE FOR LANDSCAPE. 20th century infrastructures such as highways often divided neighborhoods and degraded environments, but landscape is a new form of infrastructure for the 21st century city that brings people together and functions ecologically.

Landscapes can perform infrastructure functions less expensively than conventional systems. Landscape can be adapted to serve stormwater/wastewater, energy, roads/transportation, and waste infrastructure systems. Blue infrastructures are water-based landscapes like swales, retention ponds, and lakes that capture and clean stormwater, reducing the quantity and improving the quality of water that enters the combined stormwater/sewage system. Reducing water that enters the system will help reduce the frequency and quantity of illegal discharges into the Detroit and Rouge Rivers. Blue infrastructure provides an active use for vacant land and oversized roads. Converting portions of under-used roads to swales reduces road maintenance costs. Green infrastructures are forest landscapes that improve air quality by capturing air-borne pollutants from industry, vehicular exhaust along interstates, and infrastructure facilities like the Detroit Resource Recovery Facility, which incinerates household waste. Green infrastructure also includes greenways, paths and dedicated lanes for bicycling, walking, and running.

Landscape infrastructure can act as multiple kinds of infrastructure at once; blue and green corridors capture stormwater while working with multimodal transit strategies and plugging into employment centers and retail/commercial nodes. In doing so, landscape systems have benefits that carry far beyond the inherent function they serve. Landscape infrastructures provide a wide range of benefits:

- environmental benefits: clean air, improve water quality, capture stormwater, clean soil, provide habitat for local wildlife and migrating birds

- fiscal and economic benefits: reduce maintenance and utility costs, perform roles of traditional systems, create jobs, produce food and other tangible products; create an attractive, unique environment that can draw new businesses to Detroit

- social benefits: allow for recreation and promote other forms of social life; stabilize neighborhoods by acting as an amenity that helps to increase property values; improve resident health and comfort; provide new uses for and management of currently vacant land; remake the image of the city

Landscapes can address environmental justice issues by cleaning contaminated soil, improving air quality, buffering impacts of industry/infrastructure on residents, and reducing the cost of service (by reducing construction and operating costs). In short, landscape can help ensure that environmental burdens are not born disproportionately by Detroit's most vulnerable residents, especially people living on modest incomes or in poverty, and children. Landscapes create healthier neighborhoods for all Detroiters, and a new green image for the city.

Data Sources: 1) Michigan Residents Death File 2007, Division of Vital Records & Health Statistics, MIchigan Department of Community Health, Michigan State Occupational Illness Annual Blood Lead Levels 2009, Asthma Initiative of Michigan, Detroit Alliance for Asthma Awareness, Obesity Stats: Detroit Youth Behaviour Survey 2009, Michigan Department of Community Health 2009; 2) Brender ET. AL. 2011 Residential Proximity to Environmental Hazards and Adverse Health Outcomes, Gochfeld and Burger, Disproportionate Exposures in Environmental Justic and Other Populations: The Importance of Outliers 2011; 3) Detroit Food Policy Council Report 2009-2010; 4) Detroit Food Policy Council Report 2009-2010

THE CITY SYSTEMS ELEMENT : THE SUSTAINABLE CITY

We must focus on sizing the networks for a smaller population, making them more efficient, more affordable, and better performing.

We must realign city systems in ways that promote areas of economic potential, encourage thriving communities, and improve environmental and human health conditions.

IMPERATIVES
CITY SYSTEMS ACTIONS AND IMPACT

Two clear imperatives should guide all actions for reforming city systems. First, future city systems must meet the needs of current residents much better than "business as usual." Second, the city systems must support the needs of the future city.

Detroit has opportunities that other, more constrained cities do not. City system reform offers Detroit not only an improved environment but also a much-needed change in the city's identity. Imagine a day when Detroit is renowned for its efficiency and its form: from its working landscapes that clean the air, soil, and water to its livable neighborhoods and diverse employment and retail districts, all supported by a coordinated system of transportation, utilities, and telecommunications.

"More/better mass transit, especially using alternative fuels, would reduce air pollution."

Maggie, Detroit 24/7 "Making Environmental Sense," 5/2012

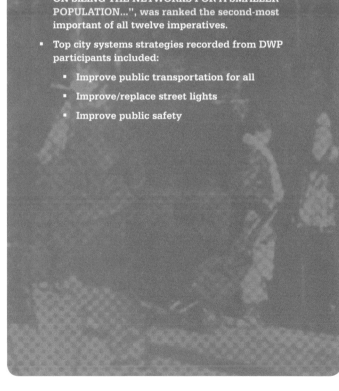

WHAT WE LEARNED FROM CIVIC ENGAGEMENT FEEDBACK

- The City Systems imperative, "WE MUST FOCUS ON SIZING THE NETWORKS FOR A SMALLER POPULATION...", was ranked the second-most important of all twelve imperatives.

- Top city systems strategies recorded from DWP participants included:
  - Improve public transportation for all
  - Improve/replace street lights
  - Improve public safety

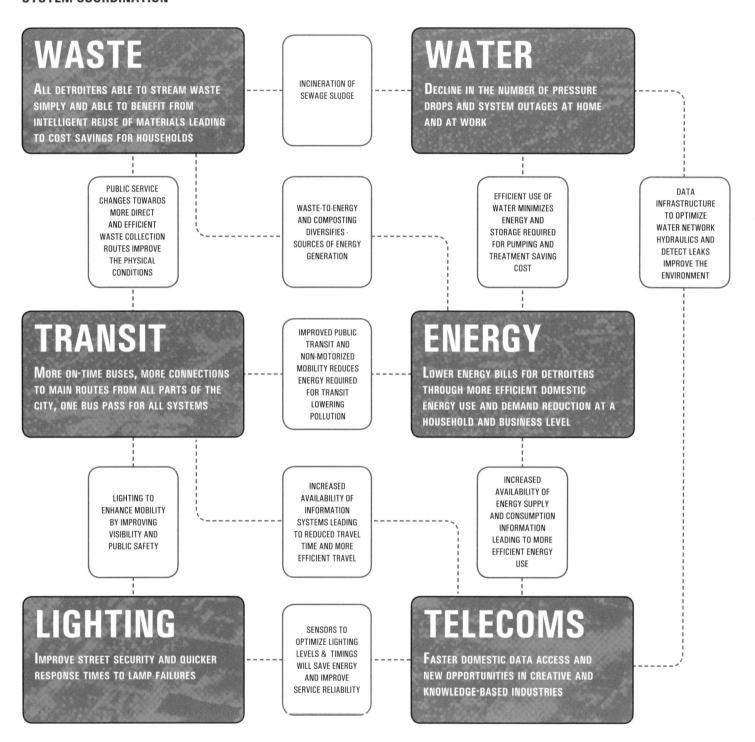

This systems diagram shows the major infrastructure systems in Detroit. Potential multi-system interventions are shown and their associated quality of life benefits.

STRATEGIES AND IMPLEMENTATION

LAND USE AND CITY SYSTEMS. Efficient and cost-effective systems are essential to achieving the vision of a Detroit that supports an excellent quality of life for its residents and attracts a dynamic range of new residents. Detroit's systems must be transformed to

- deliver services at a level that is appropriate for the needs of each neighborhood, employment center, or enterprise;

- be flexible enough to serve the city's current scale and meet the potential for future transformation;

- create a high-quality, accessible, attractive, and environmentally sustainable city environment while reducing resource use and reversing negative environmental impacts; and

- reduce service costs for businesses, residents, and the city government.

Achieving the vision will require changes to all aspects of systems: not only the physical networks but also the legal and regulatory bases for road financing and citywide or regional management of systems, operation and maintenance regimes, and, potentially, organizational and management structures. The Strategic Framework recognizes that systems are linked and interdependent at multiple levels. Changes in one system will often only achieve their full impact when accompanied by complementary changes in others. Furthermore, all systems changes must be directly coordinated with changes in the designation, use, and ownership of land; and in the location and scale of employment and housing.

ACHIEVING CHANGE. No single agency, public or private, can make all the changes necessary to create more sustainable services for the city, including changes governing land use, systems, charging, and taxation. Multiple agencies acting independently are also unlikely to achieve what is needed. Change can only come through a coordinated effort by all systems agencies—both public and private—to achieve overall viability for the city and its systems through measures that reduce cost and increase revenues.

COST REDUCTION: Many City of Detroit departments and agencies are already undergoing significant reform to address management efficiencies. In some cases, maintenance and renewal cycles have also been lengthened to reduce annual expenditures. More fundamental changes may be required soon. For example, mandated service levels and areas may need to be changed to reflect actual need. Bus service for high-vacancy areas may need to be re-patterned. More broadly, as the pattern and intensity of land use changes, so to must planning, regulatory, and investment decisions change to support the city's new urban form. Closely aligned to this, intervention will be required to realign the physical scale and capacity of networks to match the changed land use patterns.

REVENUE RAISING: Direct charges for services and (to a lesser extent) taxation are the primary sources of support for the operation and renewal of systems. Set against Detroit's average household incomes and equivalent rates in peer cities, Detroit's taxation rates and charges for some services are already very high. Raising rates even further will be less successful than, instead, adopting strategies to increase the number of households in a service area. Examples of such strategies include neighborhood stabilization programs that can attract new residents and increase house values and revenues; or establishment of neighborhood retail centers to retain more spending within the city and raise additional employment and sales taxes.

The strategies set out in this chapter utilize all of these 'levers'. However, a fundamental premise of the Strategic Framework is that raising charges and taxation rates and increasing operational efficiency alone will not sustain Detroit's systems. More fundamental realignment is required to adapt to the massive changes that the city has experienced and will experience.

THREE TRANSFORMATIVE IDEAS : SEVEN IMPLEMENTATION STRATEGIES

A REFORM DELIVERY SYSTEM

Detroit's infrastructure renewal strategy addresses the need to allocate limited funds both spatially in the city—where people work and live right now—and temporally over the next twenty years, to encourage new residents and new business. This will mean upgrading network capacity in priority employment centers and neighborhoods, while reducing capacity where there is little or no demand. All investments must be guided by a clear plan that removes uncertainty around future city development and demonstrates the maximum possible cost savings for each dollar spent up front.

Reforming system delivery also means coordinating investment among all of the private and public partners involved, to prevent them from acting without reference to one another, which in turn could prevent them from duplicating efforts or making unnecessary expenditures. It also means being aware of the technical or social constraints and special needs of each particular area, so that restructuring the city is not only cost-effective but also still serves residents' needs.

IMPLEMENTATION ACTIONS

1. Use the framework plan to create certainty around residential and employment density in each area of the city.

2. Right-size systems so that network capacity matches residential and employment demand for each area in the medium term.

3. Balance investment in areas of greatest need with investment in areas of greatest potential.

4. Address equity: ensure that a good standard of core services are provided to all groups in all areas including high-vacancy areas.

B CREATE LANDSCAPES THAT WORK

Although the City of Detroit only accounts for 12.9% of the total Detroit Water and Sewerage Department (DWSD) service area, investing in blue infrastructure within Detroit (rather than elsewhere in the region) is a valuable opportunity for the city

- to emerge as a leader in sustainable water management strategies and technologies;

- to enjoy the multiple benefits blue infrastructure offers to a city (visual amenities, increased property values, and neighborhood stabilization);

- to capture funding opportunities that exist regionally (Great Lakes Restoration Initiative funds, and other grants).

Additional benefits of blue infrastructure include flood mitigation, improved water quality and stream channel health (better for fish and other aquatic life), and recreational opportunities.

Green corridors are proposed as forest buffers that absorb carbon dioxide, particulate matter, and pollutants emitted into the air from vehicular exhaust, industrial uses, or infrastructure facilities. Improved air quality has health benefits for residents who live nearby and can provide a unique setting to attract new businesses.

IMPLEMENTATION ACTIONS

1. Deploy surplus land as multifunctional infrastructure landscapes, primarily addressing flood water mitigation and air quality.

2. Bring health and social benefits associated with landscapes and green facilities to lower income groups with poor access to transportation.

C RECONFIGURE TRANSPORTATION

D ENHANCE COMMUNICATIONS ACCESS

Detroit's transportation systems must be realigned to better serve the emerging needs of the future city. For example, the existing road network has significantly more space than it requires to meet current and projected traffic demand. At the same time, there is a shortage of non-motorized transportation networks for people to walk and cycle on. Paths that do exist are disjointed and less valuable than if they were connected in a single network, particularly for freight efficiency.

Detroit's transit system is in need of major reform to establish bus rapid transit (BRT) links between the main employment centers in the metropolitan area and to orient other transit types as feeders. These faster routes will offer access to a wider range of employment opportunities for Detroiters than at present, and will improve cross-town connections. During initial stages, the proposed adjustments to the network can be made at little or no additional cost. Some changes simply require a different mode of operation using the same fleets and roads—such as designating new express bus routes as a precursor to BRT or light rail. Others can be implemented on a rolling basis so that large up-front costs are avoided. The transportation network (roads and railways, as well as the vehicles that circulate on them) is as important to quality of life as it is to accessing work, services, education, and business opportunities. In addition, Detroit's strategic location on national and international networks makes transportation improvement a potentially important industry in its own right.

The information and communication technology industry (in its wireless incarnation) is sufficiently young that it has not suffered from the decline in Detroit's population in the same way as the other city systems. Telecoms and data companies are, in fact, still expanding their coverage of the city. In this context, Detroit has an opportunity to harness the latest technology for monitoring and real-time balancing or optimizing of city systems. On top of the management of the hard systems there are real benefits available to the delivery of public services through e-governance programs. This is quite apart from the critical support that super-fast data systems provide to some of Detroit's fastest growing industries.

IMPLEMENTATION ACTIONS

1   Realign city road hierarchy to provide faster connections between employment, district, and neighborhood centers.

2   Enhance transit service and increased ridership by realigning transit system to provide integrated network based on fast connections between regional employment centers, supported by feeder services from residential areas.

3   For higher-vacancy areas, provide smaller-scale, flexible on-demand services.

4   Align pattern of development in centers and neighborhoods to support greater number of walking and cycle trips, including promotion of greenways.

5   Support freight and logistics industries through upgrade of key routes and provision of enhanced connections across the border to Canada.

6   Provide large-scale multimodal freight interchange facilities to support local industry and overall city logistics role.

IMPLEMENTATION ACTIONS

1   Ensure high-speed data networks are in place to serve existing and new economic sectors and wider community.

2   Develop e-government platform to maximize efficiency of social service delivery.

3   Utilize improved data network to develop smart infrastructure systems which deliver improved service with smaller capacity infrastructure.

 IMPROVE LIGHTING EFFICIENCY

 REDUCE WASTE AND INCREASE RECYCLING

Of all the public services at stake in Detroit's changing population and land use patterns, public lighting is one of the most potent symbols of the scale of decline in city infrastructures. This being the case, the Public Lighting Department has embarked on an ambitious plan to both rationalize the number of active lamps in the city and to upgrade them to low-energy fittings. This has the potential to be developed further to align to the land use changes set out in the Strategic Development Framework plan. Significant organizational and financial changes—including the establishment of a separate Public Lighting Authority (PLA) to contract out maintenance and operation to a third party—are also being considered to improve service delivery and unlock funding for investment.

Detroit's waste collection and management system is linked to the era of centralized production and distribution. New technologies for collecting and processing, along with restructured form of the city, offer opportunities to decentralize and optimize the city's waste management system. By linking waste management with transportation adjustments and land use changes, Detroit can become cleaner and more efficient. In particular, Detroit could recycle much more of its waste and develop more rigorous recycling programs.

IMPLEMENTATION ACTIONS

1 Reduce number of lights and upgrade all remaining lights to low-energy LED type.

2 In high-vacancy areas, take some parts of the network off-grid, using solar power for generation.

3 Transfer ownership of the network to a new Public Lighting Authority which can procure services from the private sector competitively.

IMPLEMENTATION ACTIONS

1 Reduce total levels of waste through citizen education and work with packaging industry.

2 Develop targeted and citywide curbside recycling program.

3 Ensure that incinerator emissions remain at or below US EPA standards and international best practice.

G — ACTIVELY MANAGE CHANGE

Each of the city system providers has been challenged by the restructuring of the city. Developing a successful response to the challenges will greatly depend on effective coordination among system operators. Such an approach to system consolidation will open up opportunities for a wider number of stakeholders to achieve efficiency and integration of services and systems. These opportunities can be understood as interdependencies (where streamlining one system facilitates operational efficiencies for another), indirect benefits (improving quality of life and environmental justice through more efficient use of space and resources), and interagency agreements (by-products of one system can be used by another).

The regulatory issues that impede effective interagency operation should be tackled, and an interagency platform established to facilitate the kind of coordinated planning that the city will need if it is to move forward from its current predicament. Although distinct, these proposals are linked because one of the best ways to structure change is via the requirements of each agency to file an annual capital investment budget for state approval. Thus, mandated levels and forms of service could be varied to align each system with the others.

Several regulatory changes to support interagency cooperation have been proposed in the past, yet have not been adopted by the city. These changes deserve renewed emphasis. Examples of this are the creation of a Regional Transportation Authority to allow for integrated public transportation policy and funding, adjustment of the current road funding mechanism (Act 51) to meet the future needs of the city, and the creation of a new Public Lighting Authority able to buy its energy from multiple suppliers and outsource maintenance contracts if necessary.

IMPLEMENTATION ACTIONS

1. Adopt Strategic Framework Plan as basis for systems transformation and put in place rolling review program.

2. Create an interagency platform to coordinate change across public and private sector bodies.

3. Communicate with affected communities and monitor processes for emerging success and unforeseen adverse impacts.

"It makes sense to proportion future investment based on where the people are."

City Systems Open House, 8/21/2012

"Land use, lighting, and water interests should be combined as an opportunity to revision our use of roads. If we could reduce the amount of roads, that would reduce the burden/fixed demand on our other systems like lighting and water."

Seniors Working Session, 2/15/2012

"There is no contradiction between a clean environment and prosperity - the new future Detroit must move energetically toward 'green.' The city needs an ordinance for mandatory recycling, both residential & commercial, in order to capture the job potential & economic value of waste stream."

Margaret, Planning Cluster-based Meeting, 2/15/2011

171

THE CITY SYSTEMS ELEMENT : THE SUSTAINABLE CITY

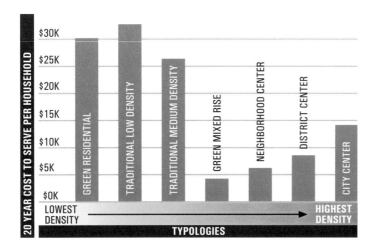

20 YEAR COST TO SERVE PER HOUSEHOLD

Y-axis: $30K, $25K, $20K, $15K, $10K, $5K, $0K

Bars (left to right): GREEN RESIDENTIAL, TRADITIONAL LOW DENSITY, TRADITIONAL MEDIUM DENSITY, GREEN MIXED RISE, NEIGHBORHOOD CENTER, DISTRICT CENTER, CITY CENTER

LOWEST DENSITY → HIGHEST DENSITY

TYPOLOGIES

ESTIMATED NETWORK MAINTENANCE AND RENEWAL PER HOUSEHOLD

The graph at the left illustrates the estimated cost for network maintenance and renewal per household modelled over a 20 year period. The cost of serving dwellings in low density urban areas can be as much as three times the cost of serving dwellings in high density areas.

Source: Happold Consulting, Inc. interviews with public and private service providers, excludes all 'non-network' costs.

ENSURING EFFECTIVE TRANSITION. The strategy for reforming city systems relies on a successful transition from the existing city structures and service networks to a new pattern for meeting the demand for services in Detroit. This change is embodied in both the Land Use Element of the Detroit Strategic Framework and the differentiated investment plan proposed to accompany it.

MODELING LAND USE AND SYSTEMS TOGETHER FOR A MORE SUSTAINABLE CITY. The development of the Land Use Element took place over many months, drawing upon a large amount of data, research analysis, and community feedback. The goal was to develop a proposal for future land use that responds to the city's current needs and imperatives, yet is flexible enough to be adapted to changing realities in terms of where and how people will live and work in the future Detroit.

The Planning Team used modeling techniques to test the viability and implications of different approaches to reforming and managing city systems, as it worked to redefine the way that land is used in Detroit. The team aimed to balance the outcomes for four considerations:

- **Quality of Life / Quality of Business:** Factors that support residents in their life aspirations, and help grow the local economy. Fulfilling these factors requires some physical re-shaping of the city and protection, strengthening, and transformation of neighborhoods over the long term, in order to offer residential and employment choices throughout the city. These aspirations help to set expectations and recommendations for location and levels of service.

- **Cost to Serve:** The cost of operating and maintaining services and utilities. The relative cost of serving an area is determined by the combination of population densities and service levels.

- **Cost to Achieve:** The scale of changes in population patterns, new construction, demolition, upgrade, or other major changes in networks that is implied by the Land Use Element of the Strategic Framework, and associated strategies. Different land use strategies and the systems configurations that serve them require different levels of investment to deliver, based on the current condition.

- **Revenue:** The income generated by fees, charges and taxation that offsets the Cost to Serve and Cost to Achieve. A Revenue strategy seeks to generate more revenue to pay for system services without increasing costs to individual users.

The Land Use Element of the Detroit Strategic Framework represents a blend of these four objectives in a way that is intended to offer the greatest benefits to the residents and businesses of Detroit, and that will be equitable, achievable, and sustainable. Well-established employment centers (around manufacture) are protected while emerging centers (such as the Eds & Meds quarter) are supported. Long-successful residential areas (such as those in northwest Detroit) are consolidated while areas that are less associated with mixed-use residential development (e.g. downtown) are given clear support.

Although the transitions to new and innovative land use types will take 20 years or more, there is a relatively pressing challenge now: In many areas that have experienced long-term loss of people, homes, and businesses, with high-vacancy levels or industrial abandonment, deciding the most appropriate capacity of infrastructure systems in the future cannot be put off indefinitely.

QUALITY OF LIFE / QUALITY OF BUSINESS. A focus on quality of life for residents and businesses is perhaps the most subjective but also the most important approach that the team considered. The team sought to determine how the range of Quality of Life and Quality of Business indicators could be positively supported through the type and distribution of proposed land use typologies and associated strategies.

A Quality of Life strategy focuses on stabilizing and maintaining as much of Detroit's existing urban structure and residential configuration as possible. A range of residential typologies and densities are deployed that encourage gradual changes to existing uses over time. It seeks to minimize the areas where the most dramatic changes in land use are proposed, or where substantial changes to residential densities are required, to support new typologies. Such a strategy seeks to manage transition in a way that offers choices to residents over the future of their neighborhoods. Where possible, areas currently in residential, commercial, or industrial use are preserved and strengthened while areas of relatively high-vacancy would be allowed to remain in transition for longer periods as their future role is determined. Finally, larger areas would be maintained at relatively low population densities over the long term. In adopting such a strategy a greater proportion of investment would be used to support areas that have been in long-term decline and the application of cost reduction strategies (such as reducing, repurposing, or decommissioning city systems) would be more limited in scope.

REFORM SYSTEM DELIVERY A
COORDINATING LAND USE AND SYSTEMS

COST TO SERVE. Low-density neighborhoods (mostly single-family houses, where people usually have to drive to jobs and services) cost more to serve than more compact areas where homes, businesses, and services are located close to one another and are near transit or are accessible on foot or bicycle.

In Detroit the combination of high-vacancy levels and oversized networks operating below their capacities puts great pressure on the ability to deliver efficient, high quality, and cost-effective services. Operating city systems designed for urban populations in areas with suburban, or even rural, population densities drives up the relative cost per household of service delivery to levels that are difficult to sustain.

A Cost to Serve strategy therefore seeks to align investment approaches with the long-term transition of areas into stable residential densities, centers of employment, or alternative land uses. Reductions in capacity in low-density areas and wholesale replacement, repurposing, or even decommissioning of networks in areas that are no longer in residential use will drive cost reductions without the need to reduce the service levels to end users.

COST TO ACHIEVE. The scale of change from existing conditions implies certain levels of new construction, reuse of existing assets, and, potentially, the need for assistance or possibly programs to offer incentives to residents and businesses to locate in particular areas rather than others.

A focus on Cost to Achieve seeks to minimize costly structural changes to the city through the use of land use typologies that are sympathetic to existing conditions and patterns of land use in the city. For example, the size and number of high-density Neighborhood and District Centers would be minimized. Low-density residential typologies would be more widespread, and Innovation Landscapes areas would be restricted to the areas experiencing very high-vacancy levels.

REVENUE. The costs to change systems and deliver services are offset against the charges users pay for services and income from taxation. A large reduction in population and employment over the years has put greater and greater pressure on revenue generation in Detroit. Maintaining aging city systems that are operating below capacity also drives up the costs to users.

A Revenue strategy therefore seeks to increase revenue generation without increasing costs to individual users. This can be achieved through increased demand from more residents and businesses within the city, increased employment income in the city, and better property market conditions. The land use planning and investment approaches must therefore support the right type of investments in the right areas to promote stabilization and future growth in city revenues.

> "City services provided to less dense communities should not be subsidized by more dense ones. Communities should pay the real cost of receiving those services."
>
> Pablo, Central/Near East Community Conversation 2, 5/5/2012

IMPLEMENTATION ACTIONS

1   Use the framework plan to create certainty around residential and employment density in each area of the city.

2   Right-size systems so that network capacity matches residential and employment demand for each area in the medium term.

3   Balance investment in areas of greatest need with investment in areas of greatest potential.

4   Address equity: ensure that a good standard of core services are provided to all groups in all areas including high-vacancy areas.

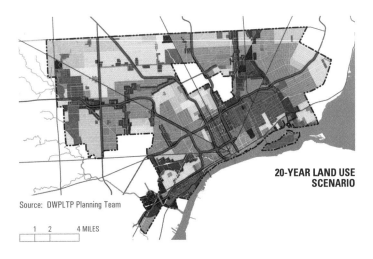

20-YEAR LAND USE SCENARIO

Source: DWPLTP Planning Team

1   2   4 MILES

The 20-Year Land Use scenario is the primary tool for coordinating the transition of the city from its current state to a more sustainable future

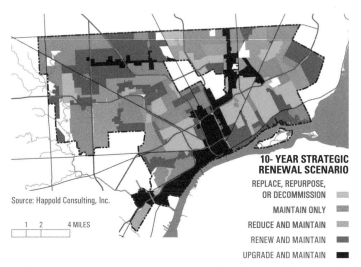

10- YEAR STRATEGIC RENEWAL SCENARIO

REPLACE, REPURPOSE, OR DECOMMISSION
MAINTAIN ONLY
REDUCE AND MAINTAIN
RENEW AND MAINTAIN
UPGRADE AND MAINTAIN

Source: Happold Consulting, Inc.

1   2   4 MILES

In 10 years, the future of some areas of the city remains undecided. As a result of this the systems in these areas are maintained but not renewed. When a decision has been made about the future use of these areas the systems can be renewed or decommissioned.

SYSTEMS FOR A CHANGING CITY

Four types of change may be required to achieve a better quality of life and business in Detroit, as well as to provide adequate services for all residents and businesses while adjusting to real demands and a changing city form:

- In almost all cases, physical systems must be transformed to reflect the changing scale and pattern of residential, commercial, and business activity in Detroit now and in the future.

- In many cases, the regulatory basis on which services are mandated or charged for will also need transformation to permit changes that are necessary but currently not permitted under current legislation.

- In most cases there are likely to be benefits available from individual utility agencies reviewing their internal processes and reconsidering whether their organizational structure is still suited to the services they will be delivering.

- Lastly, there may be further cases where end users will be better served if the number and type of agencies delivering a given service was varied (either to introduce competition where there is currently none, or to benefit from specialization and exploitation of regional / national economies of scale).

Years of constrained budgets and scrutiny by regulators have led many agencies to be more efficiently run. However, excessively lean running of systems that are inherently oversized will not deliver optimum performance for city or agencies. It is a vital role of the plan to now help systems agencies to understand the changing future structure of the city in order to reshape the location and capacity of systems accordingly.

UNDERSTANDING RENEWAL CYCLES. Reform of the delivery of city systems will be underpinned by how the individual systems are renewed and replaced as they start to reach the end of their design lives. Decisions about what to do with each system in each part of the city need to be made carefully around the time of a major renewal in order to avoid over-investing in an area that is running below capacity and likely to remain so, or under-investing in capacity in an area that is likely to see an increase in activity in the near future. The strategic aspect of the proposed approach lies in ensuring that, for each system, these decisions are not only right for the individual system in question but are also coordinated with the other systems in the city and, in turn, with long-term land use planning for the city. The Strategic Framework is intended to be a tool that enables greater coordination than has previously been possible among city systems providers.

Providing a clear land use plan for Year 20 will enable the providers of city systems to implement a coordinated program for transition that aligns with future land use. Providers will be able to avoid expensive renewals and maintenance of aging infrastructure systems where this is not necessary (such as in Innovation Ecological and Innovation Productive areas) while maintaining and upgrading systems to support the employment centers and residential neighborhoods.

PROLONGATION OF RENEWAL DECISIONS IN SOME AREAS. A phased approach will also enable areas of lower vacancy to be stabilized as their future role becomes clear and to review and respond to how the city is changing over the next decade. The maps above show the recommended investment approaches to be applied in the city up to Year 20. As time passes, the areas with a Maintain Only approach will require decisions to be made because the age of the infrastructure will not permit indefinite prolongation of a full renewal. By Year 10, the level of service applied to all areas of the city will be determined, enabling long-term cost savings.

LIFE IN THE CITY AS THE TRANSITION TAKES PLACE. Detroit's infrastructure for utilities and transportation is linked to the location of its other important community services, including schools, health clinics, policing, and other public services. The process used to determine the investment approach for city systems in each neighborhood may also be used to locate and invest in social services there. Because these community-supportive services are critical to maintain, improve, and provide in the near term as well as over the long term, decisions about their placement and investment will necessarily involve the insight and collaboration of the communities they serve.

The matrix on the following pages describes in greater detail what the different investment approaches will feel like in different parts of the city. The capacity and ways of delivering service will change, but not the level of service, which will remain at least at its current levels.

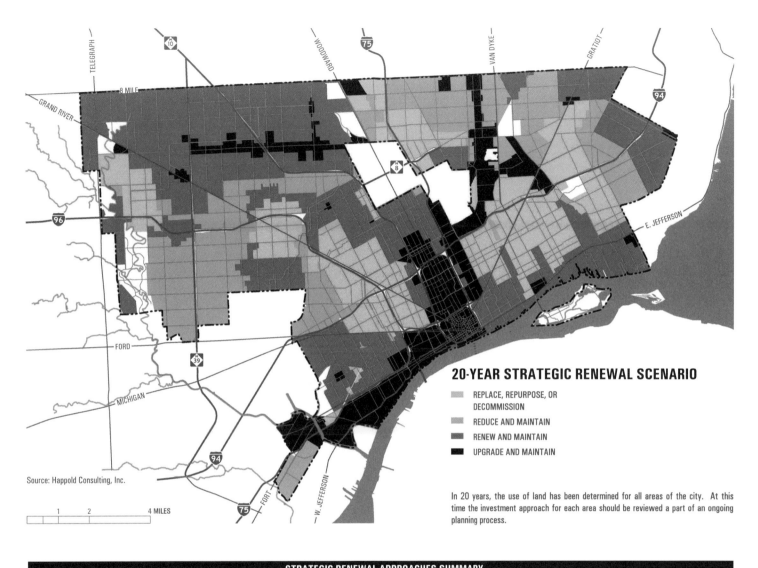

20-YEAR STRATEGIC RENEWAL SCENARIO

- REPLACE, REPURPOSE, OR DECOMMISSION
- REDUCE AND MAINTAIN
- RENEW AND MAINTAIN
- UPGRADE AND MAINTAIN

Source: Happold Consulting, Inc.

1 2 4 MILES

In 20 years, the use of land has been determined for all areas of the city. At this time the investment approach for each area should be reviewed a part of an ongoing planning process.

THE CITY SYSTEMS ELEMENT : THE SUSTAINABLE CITY

STRATEGIC RENEWAL APPROACHES SUMMARY				
UPGRADE AND MAINTAIN	**RENEW AND MAINTAIN**	**REDUCE AND MAINTAIN**	**MAINTAIN ONLY**	**REPLACE, REPURPOSE, OR DECOMMISSION**
▪ Service Level: Improved service level maintained at better quality ▪ Actions: Fully maintain and undertake renewal or upgrade as required ▪ Outcomes: Improved neighborhood with increase capacity and resilience	▪ Service Level: Core service level at the same or better quality ▪ Actions: Fully maintain and renew at current level or upgrade if required ▪ Outcomes: Viable neighborhood with same or increased capacity	▪ Service Level: Core service level but for a smaller number of residents as these areas are unlikely to regain residents to historic population levels ▪ Actions: Maintain and undertake scheduled renewal at lower capacity ▪ Outcomes: Area continues as viable neighborhood with lower capacity	▪ Service Level: Basic service level but quality declining over time ▪ Actions: Planned maintenance extending current systems life ▪ Outcomes: By 20-year horizon, systems are either renewed at full or reduced capacity	▪ Service Level: Basic service level but quality declining over time ▪ Actions: Planned maintenance to extend current systems life ▪ Outcomes: Area transitions from current use in 20-25 years. Systems eventually retired.

10-YEAR STRATEGIC RENEWAL APPROACHES

	UPGRADE AND MAINTAIN	**RENEW AND MAINTAIN**
WHERE	These areas are projected to stabilize at a level above current capacity. These areas include: City Center, District Centers, Neighborhood Centers, and Primary Employment Districts.	These areas are projected to stabilize at a level that is near current capacity. These areas include: Traditional Medium Density, Traditional Low Density, Green Mixed Rise, and Secondary Employment Districts.
WATER	The water mains in these areas are likely to be comprehensively renewed and capacity added. For that reason the areas are likely, after an initial period of interruption for installment, to benefit from fewer service interruptions or changes in water pressure. This may be accompanied by measures to reduce demand at the point of consumption (e.g. dual flush toilets, recycling of rain water, etc.).	The water mains in these areas are likely to be comprehensively renewed although they may not be targeted for the first wave of change since they are neither running massively below capacity, nor do they need additional capacity installed to allow for future development. On this basis they will ultimately enjoy a more reliable service between 5 and 10 years from now, although further decline in service quality should be halted as soon as possible.
ENERGY	Areas with limited substation capacity will be prioritized for capacity upgrade. In some new industrial areas it may be necessary to assemble parcels to provide new businesses room to locate and expand, fully utilizing the upgraded energy infrastructure. Networks will be placed underground to allow for higher volumes of development and reduce the visual impact of the power grid.	These areas will see the benefits of full replacement of aging systems in line with normal replacement cycles. Since these areas are not faced with significant capacity issues there is little need to accelerate replacement. A change to below ground power lines may not be necessary in some of these areas, and as a result, many of the power lines are likely to remain above ground.
WASTE	Waste disposal and treatment in these areas will be characterized by high frequency collection combined with splitting of waste into multiple streams and land-fill diversion.	Disposal and treatment of waste in these areas will occur at the same frequency of collection but, over time, programs will be introduced to provide curbside recycling for all areas.
ROAD & TRANSPORT	All areas designated for upgrade will see ongoing renewal of the road network. Additionally, there may be changes made to road layout and intersections as part of the implementation of a more efficient public transit network, including BRT. The focus will be on increasing the capacity and frequency of transit service to these areas while reducing the cost of delivering this service through greater efficiency. It remains possible that these areas will still have excess road capacity.	All roads in these areas will be schedule for regular ongoing maintenance and renewal. Public transit service will increase in effectiveness as services from these areas will focus on providing connections to high speed, high frequency BRT routes. Residents will enjoy access to a wider range of employment, education, and services.

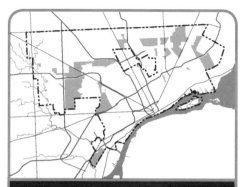

REDUCE AND MAINTAIN

These areas are projected to stabilize at a level significantly below the current system capacity. These areas include: Live+Make and Green Residential.

In these areas, investment in reducing capacity of the system should take place relatively early because of the daily costs of running the system significantly below capacity. Areas where the occupancy is already significantly below capacity but has stabilized will be prioritized over areas where population levels continue to fall. Residents in these areas will experience an improvement in quality of service and supply levels after system has been renewed at a lower capacity.

These areas may see a reduction in system capacity, and these reductions should be made as early as possible. One example of a reduction in capacity is currently being undertaken by MichCon in High-Vacancy residential areas. Under this pilot program MichCon is retiring every second gas supply pipe to reduce the length of supply pipes in use. Any properties that would be left stranded by this process will be re-connected to the system from the opposite side of the lot.

Efficiencies can be found through sorting of waste into different streams. It may be that some of the more inert streams can be collected less frequently than the core waste streams.

In areas that have experienced substantial population loss, it is difficult to offer regular public transportation service because potential ridership is too low and heavily subsidized services do not make financial sense. However, digital mobile technology offers the possibility of introducing 'on demand' transit systems that allow users to message the next mini-bus, which then adjusts its route accordingly.

MAINTAIN ONLY

The population projections of these areas remain uncertain, but the infrastructure system could be made viable if the population levels should increase.

In a small number of areas, it is not yet clear what the future land use will be in 10 years and beyond. These areas have been given the land use Green Residential Transitional but will be reviewed at or before Horizon 2. At this point, the land use will change to a final designation, and the appropriate investment approach will be applied (upgrade and maintain, renew and maintain, reduce and maintain).

Importantly, the Maintain Only approach retains the existing systems capacity in place and keeps open all potential options for the future of the neighborhood to which it is applied. However, until such time as the decision on the final status of a neighborhood is taken, it makes little sense to invest any more than necessary in the systems. This 'wait and see' strategy should only be adopted sparingly as it is the direction given by the plan that gives public and private investors the certainty required to make the long-term decisions that are in the city's best interest. Furthermore, in some areas, the infrastructure is so old that a regime of general maintenance without a significant system renewal is no longer viable. As the systems move towards the very end of their design lives, it is inevitable that system outages and failures will become more frequent. For these areas, a clear decision to renew or decommission must be made in a timely fashion.

REPLACE, REPURPOSE OR DECOMMISSION

This approach is taken in areas where the land designation is expected to transition to an entirely different land use and the existing system will either be of no material use or may serve a different purpose than the one for which it was installed.

In the areas where vacancy has reached a very high level and where the land use plan designates a change of land use, it will make little sense to invest in renewing the systems. Instead, the systems within these newly designated areas will either be replaced in their entirety, repurposed and refashioned for a different function – or, in some cases, simply decommissioned. In these areas, the process of retiring the non-essential services (eg roads with 100% vacancy that are not required for through-traffic) may start before residential use is phased out completely. Thus, there will also be some pre-transition investment. For example, new green spaces may be created as former streets are converted to stormwater catchments or future amenities.

In order to provide core services to the remaining residents in these areas, it will still be necessary to maintain the systems for some time (up to 10 years). However, it should be noted that areas specifically designated as Land Use Change coincide strongly with the areas that not only have the oldest infrastructure (meaning that indefinite maintenance is infeasible) but have also experienced the highest levels of abandonment and vacancy. Where residents do choose to remain for the long term, future infrastructure service provisions will be incorporated into the systems serving the main new land use in the area.

THE CITY SYSTEMS ELEMENT : THE SUSTAINABLE CITY

BLUE AND GREEN INFRASTRUCTURE CAN HELP ADDRESS THESE ISSUES:

TOPOGRAPHY

FLOOD PRONE AREAS

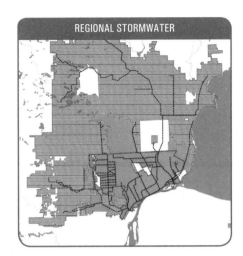

REGIONAL STORMWATER

WATER SYSTEM CONFIGURATION

WIDE ROADS

AIR EMISSIONS SOURCES

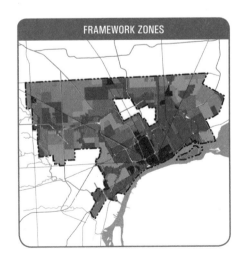

FRAMEWORK ZONES

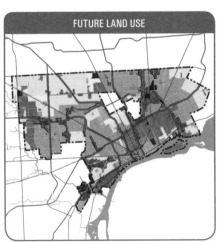

FUTURE LAND USE

PUBLICLY OWNED LAND

CREATE LANDSCAPES THAT WORK
RETHINKING APPROACHES TO 20TH CENTURY INFRASTRUCTURES

A NEW INFRASTRUCTURE SYSTEM SHAPED BY URBAN CONTEXT, TOPOGRAPHY, AND OTHER FACTORS. Blue and green infrastructure can help address water and air quality issues. The specific types of systems proposed, and their proposed locations within the City takes into account a wide range of factors, including:

- topography, especially low-lying, flood-prone areas along the Rouge and Detroit Rivers;
- availability of vacant land;
- existing stormwater system configuration, locally and regionally;
- future land use;
- air pollution sources, including facilities with air emission permits and interstates;
- soil types, which tend to be highly impervious; and
- wide roads plus traffic volume.

When it rains, the amount of stormwater that becomes runoff in an area depends on how pervious (porous) the ground is. When rain flows over grass, some of it is absorbed into the ground; when it flows over pavement, virtually all of it becomes runoff that currently enters the sewer system. Areas with more buildings and parking lots or driveways have higher amounts of runoff. During heavy rainstorms, too much runoff enters the system too quickly and exceeds the capacity of the wastewater treatment plant. The idea of the blue infrastructure network is to reduce the overall amount of runoff that enters the system and to slow down the runoff that does, so that all runoff can be fully treated by the treatment plant.

The blue infrastructure network is comprised of a series of independent systems, which vary in scale. Each system includes at minimum a place to collect stormwater. Two main types of collection area exist: retention ponds and detention basins. A retention pond is a type of collection area designed to hold stormwater until the water is either absorbed into the ground or evaporates into the air. Retention ponds are usually wet. In Detroit, retention will work most effectively at smaller scales (for example, as rain gardens or small retention ponds no larger than a few contiguous lots). Detroit's soils are largely clay, which acts like a barrier and does not absorb much stormwater. Stormwater that enters the pond can only evaporate very slowly in a pond with a clay bottom, and if the pond is always full, it will not be able to absorb water during rain storms.

Detention basins, on the other hand, can be viable options for larger types. Detention basins are usually dry and focus on holding stormwater only temporarily. They focus on changing the rate of stormwater that enters the system. Because they will slowly release water back into the combined system, they will require infrastructure connections back to the system. The additional expense of the system connection makes detention most viable at larger scales (not worth investing in cost of reconnecting to system unless significant capacity can be achieved). By contrast, retention basins do not require connections back into the system (although they can be designed to include check dams, a feature that that redirects any overflow back into the system to prevent flooding).

Although denser areas have the most runoff, they unfortunately have the fewest opportunities for blue infrastructure. Stormwater from denser areas must be directed to other areas of the city which have available space to store stormwater. As a result, conveyance types of stormwater management complement collection types. Conveyance types carry stormwater from areas with less opportunity for collection to other areas that have more opportunities. The most common conveyance type is a swale, a grassy channel along a road that directs the flow of stormwater along the surface, instead of through pipes underground. Surface flow has two key advantages over pipes: slowed by grass and other vegetation, water flows more slowly through swales, and the vegetation also acts a filter that cleans stormwater as it passes by trapping sediment or other particles in the stormwater. Directing stormwater with gravity only, swales always run from higher elevation areas to lower elevation areas. Lower elevation areas are the most effectively locations for either retention or detention types.

Different combinations of conveyance, retention, and detention types comprise the different stormwater systems. Stormwater boulevards are citywide roads that focus primarily on conveyance. Their long length allows them to transport stormwater effectively from one area of the city to another. Because they tend to have a variety of conditions along their length, they can collect stormwater from lower vacancy areas and transport it downhill to higher vacancy areas, where large detention ponds can temporarily hold it before slowly releasing it back into the stormwater system. Stormwater boulevards function most effectively when topography changes gradually over long distances. Most of Detroit is shaped like this; a central ridge along Woodward slopes generally down towards the eastern and western city borders. The northern end of this ridge is higher, and it gradually slopes down towards the Detroit River. Southwest Detroit, however, is

PRECEDENT

DECENTRALIZED INFRASTRUCTURE

Philadelphia's updated stormwater regulations encourage urban infill through exemptions for redevelopment projects. On-site stormwater management with vegetated systems provide a range of benefits.

Image Source: Philadelphia Water Dept.

PRECEDENT

INTEGRATED SYSTEM

Wilsonville protects functional open space at the community scale and introduces green infrastructure at smaller site scales. The City directs development charge revenues toward projects that protect healthy waterways and restore degraded streams.

Image Source: US Geological Survey

characterized with a different kind of topography. It has a more mounded topography, with may different high and low points in close proximity to one another. Here, a distributed network of smaller, independent systems is more appropriate. Each smaller system includes a collection area in one of the downhill locations, which collects stormwater that runs off surrounding higher areas.

Lower vacancy areas have fewer opportunities for blue infrastructure, so in these areas, swales and small retention types are important. Small retention types retain some stormwater, and the remaining runoff can flow into swales, which will transport it to other areas with more opportunities for blue infrastructure. Higher vacancy areas can have many, larger detention basins.

Transitions between areas of higher and lower vacancy offer important opportunities for blue infrastructure. Here, the adjacency between an area of high runoff and an area of high opportunity for collection reduces the need to transport stormwater long distances. In these cases, the edge of high-vacancy can have a high prevalence of collection areas. These "wet buffers" work most effectively if the high-vacancy area lies downhill from the denser area. However, if the opportunities for collection are up-hill, they can still collect any runoff that has flowed across the high-vacancy area. In this case, it is important to catch the stormwater before it enters the lower vacancy area with fewer opportunities to collect it. In a similar way, wet buffers can also help collect stormwater at abrupt changes in topography. For instance, most interstates in Detroit are sunken, so any stormwater that flows down one slope of an interstate will become trapped. Here, a high concentration of ponds on the upper edge of an interstate can collect runoff before it flows into the interstate.

IMPLEMENTATION ACTIONS

1   Deploy surplus land as multifunctional infrastructure landscapes, primarily addressing flood water mitigation and air quality.

2   Bring health and social benefits associated with landscapes and green facilities to lower income groups with poor access to transportation.

PILOT PROJECT

1   Blue Infrastructure — see Land Use chapter

PRECEDENTS

1   Decentralized Infrastructure : Philadelphia, PA

2   Integrated System : Wilsonville, OR

"Any new initiatives should strive to reduce pollution. Detroit is one of the most polluted cities in America. 48209-48217 being the worst. Clean, green, healthier environment /no more emissions or smoke stacks!!!"

Rolando, Town Hall Meetings 9/2010

"You can smell gases from factories and see all of the smoke these factories are producing. It's sick because they are harming the environment and also causing health problems to the citizens living here."

Adreanna, Detroit 24/7, 5/2012

"I could really see this infrastructure setting Detroit apart from other cities. Communities could participate in maintaining this infrastructure, and I can foresee it providing jobs."

John, City Systems Open House, 8/21/2012

1.

2.

3.

4.

20TH CENTURY INFRASTRUCTURE → **21ST CENTURY INFRASTRUCTURE**

STORMWATER MANAGEMENT **OR** ALLOW FAST CAR TRAVEL

MONO-FUNCTIONAL

ALLOW MULTIMODAL TRANSPORT — CAPTURE AND CLEAN STORMWATER — REDUCE MAINTENANCE COSTS — CREATE HABITAT — PROMOTE RECREATION — CLEAN AIR

MULTI-FUNCTIONAL

WATER **OR** VEHICLES

SINGLE USER

WATER — PEDESTRIANS — VEHICLES — WILDLIFE — BICYCLISTS

MULTIPLE USERS

PULL COMMUNITIES APART

DIVIDE COMMUNITY

BRING COMMUNITIES TOGETHER

COMMUNITY ASSET

COMMUNITIES NOT CONSULTED

TOP-DOWN DECISION MAKING

INCLUSIVE PROCESS

INCLUSIVE APPROACH TO DECISION MAKING

Image Sources: 1) Sean Marshall, Wikimedia Commons; 2) Marvin Shaouni; 3) Lamiot, Wikimedia Commons; 4) US Environmental Protection Agency

THE CITY SYSTEMS ELEMENT : THE SUSTAINABLE CITY

BLUE / GREEN INFRASTRUCTURE TYPES

	CARBON FOREST	INDUSTRIAL BUFFER	STORMWATER BOULEVARD	SURFACE LAKE	DISTRIBUTED NETWORK
DESCRIPTION	Forests that repurpose vacant land around expressways and abandoned rail corridors.	Forested areas that repurpose vacant land around industrial uses.	Citywide, broad, retrofitted streets that include swales along their length and intermittent roadside detention ponds (primarily in high-vacancy areas). Character of blvd adapts to different urban conditions along their length.	Large, low-lying vacant areas allow for flooding to create lakes, which provide significant retention capacity for storms; swales and other surface conveyance mechanisms direct stormwater into these areas.	Multiple independent networks of swales and other surface conveyance elements that direct stormwater to small and medium-scale retention/detention ponds in lower lying areas.
FUNCTION	Absorb carbon dioxide, particulate matter, and other pollutants in vehicular exhaust emitted into the air by car and truck traffic.	Reduce the impacts of industrial uses on nearby residential neighborhoods, by absorbing air-borne pollutants, reducing sound, blocking light/glare, and providing a visual barrier. Buffers also act as an amenity to firms by creating a more attractive, healthy business environment.	CONVEYANCE AND DETENTION Collect stormwater from many areas of city and transport to areas with road-side detention ponds for holding and slow release back into the combined system.	HIGH CAPACITY DETENTION /RETENTION Topography naturally directs surface runoff to these areas, making them suitable for capturing stormwater.	CONVEYANCE AND DETENTION The topography of these areas calls for multiple independent systems to collect stormwater from higher areas and direct it towards lower areas.
LOCATION	Extend 500 feet from the edges of expressways.	Buffer widths vary depending on the scale, intensity, and type of industrial use as well as the character of the adjacent land. General buffer widths are 200 feet.	Primary corridors: Radial arterials (Woodward, Jefferson, Gratiot, Grand River) and proposed Ring Road connecting employment districts. Secondary corridors: McNichols west of Woodward and 7 mile east of Woodward .	Internal depressions in city's topography in high-vacancy areas, and potentially moderate-vacancy areas.	Areas with greater internal variation in topography, like Southwest Detroit. These areas have many high points and low areas in close proximity to one another.

    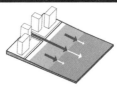

INFILTRATION PARK	DISPERSED PONDS	CONCENTRATED PONDS	WET BUFFER	RIVER MARSHLAND
Parks that combine stormwater management with recreation.	Small ponds, rain gardens, or other small-scale blue infrastructure within neighborhoods or employment districts that can fit within 1-2 average-sized residential lots.	Many small to medium ponds in close proximity to one another in higher-vacancy areas.	High concentration of ponds at significant edges between framework zones or along interstates.	Treatment wetlands and vegetated buffer strips in parks and vacant lots.
DETENTION/RETENTION Reduce maintenance costs, repurpose limited maintenance parks and provide additional sources of funding/maintenance for parks (potential for partnerships between DRD and DWSD).	**SMALL-SCALE RETENTION AND NEIGHBORHOOD** Stability / Visual Amenity	**HIGH CAPACITY RETENTION**	**DETENTION AND NEIGHBORHOOD STABILITY** Wet buffers catch runoff before it enters an area of lower vacancy with fewer opportunities for blue infrastructure, or immediately after runoff leaves an area of lower vacancy.	**RETENTION AND TREATMENT** Treat stormwater before it flows into the Detroit or Rouge Rivers; these components are a last chance to capture and clean stormwater before it enters the rivers. Wetlands and buffer strips also create additional aquatic habitats.
Limited maintenance parks are good candidates to be retrofitted as infiltration parks, but parks in high-vacancy areas, low-lying areas, or river-front parks may be considered as well.	Low- or moderate-vacancy areas; should especially be prioritized in land depressions that are not candidates for surface lakes because there is not enough residential vacancy.	High-vacancy areas, especially areas near the Rouge or Detroit Rivers, land situated to capture runoff from many low-vacancy areas that do not have many opportunities for retention within them, and along downhill edges of high-vacancy areas.	On up-hill interstate edges and the high-vacancy sides of edges between framework zones.	Parks and vacant lots along or near the Detroit or Rouge Rivers.

BLUE AND GREEN INFRASTRUCTURE BY FRAMEWORK ZONE

INDUSTRIAL STRENGTH

LOW-VACANCY AREAS

HIGH-VACANCY AREAS

MODERATE-VACANCY AREAS

RIVERFRONT

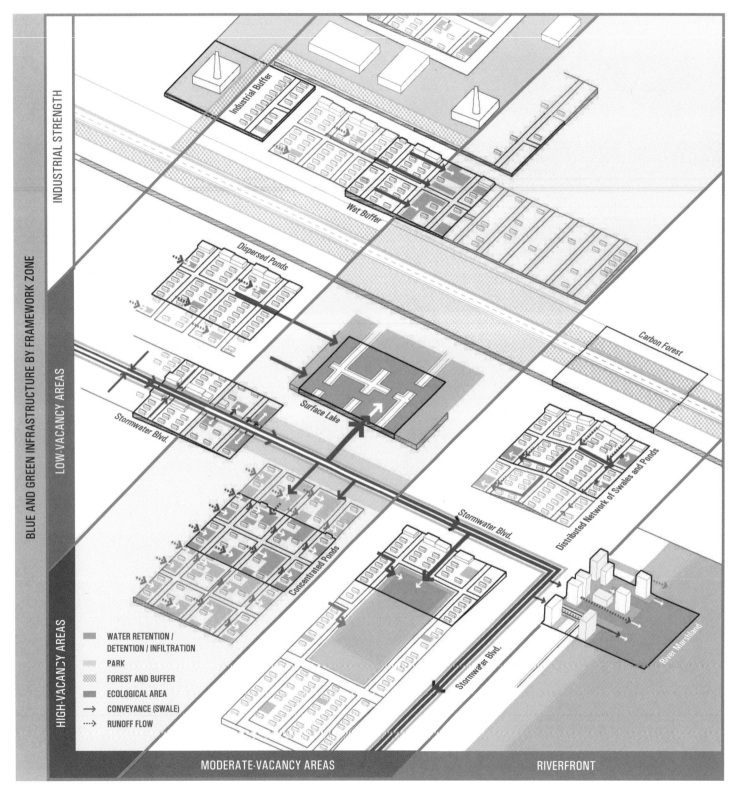

Industrial Buffer

Wet Buffer

Dispersed Ponds

Carbon Forest

Surface Lake

Stormwater Blvd.

Distributed Network of Swales and Ponds

Concentrated Ponds

Stormwater Blvd.

Stormwater Blvd.

River Marshland

WATER RETENTION /
DETENTION / INFILTRATION

PARK

FOREST AND BUFFER

ECOLOGICAL AREA

CONVEYANCE (SWALE)

RUNOFF FLOW

As the conditions in the city vary from area to area so will the appropriate elements of a blue infrastructure system. However, these elements must link together to form a larger network to capture and clean stormwater.

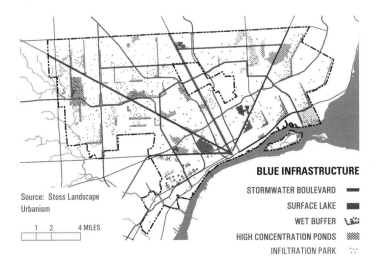

BLUE INFRASTRUCTURE

Source: Stoss Landscape
Urbanism

1   2   4 MILES

STORMWATER BOULEVARD	▬
SURFACE LAKE	■
WET BUFFER	
HIGH CONCENTRATION PONDS	▨
INFILTRATION PARK	

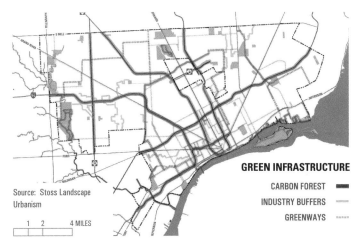

GREEN INFRASTRUCTURE

Source: Stoss Landscape
Urbanism

1   2   4 MILES

CARBON FOREST	▬
INDUSTRY BUFFERS	
GREENWAYS	

BLUE INFRASTRUCTURE

Blue infrastructure networks capture and clean stormwater runoff from all areas of the city and reduce the frequency and magnitude of combined stormwater/ sewage discharges. Each system type works in a different way that is appropriate for different kinds of topographic and urban conditions. Downhill, higher vacancy areas function as major collection areas, detaining stormwater from uphill areas of the city with lower vacancy (and higher runoff). Swales connect major runoff-producing areas to collection areas.

Blue infrastructure has the potential to reduce runoff that enters the system, but other challenges must be addressed as well, including:

EXISTING, LENGTHY PURCHASING AND PROCUREMENT PROCESS: slows repair process when malfunctions occur;

STAFFING: personnel shortages / training deficiencies (too few people, especially in management positions, and this problem will only worsen as many in department retire in near future); and

LEGAL CONSTRAINTS: currently, state policy does not allow cities to use blue infrastructure to meet long-term control requirements; only hard infrastructure is seen as acceptable way to reduce overflows.

Procurement processes and staffing shortages impact "hard" infrastructure today, and blue infrastructure will likely face similar challenges. Training and education will be important components of implementing blue infrastructure to ensure DWSD staff are comfortable and familiar with maintaining blue infrastructure. State-level advocacy will be needed to overcome legal constraints.

GREEN INFRASTRUCTURE

Green infrastructure networks improve resident health. Carbon forests are the primary example, because they repurpose vacant land around highways and rail corridors to absorb carbon dioxide, particulate matter, and other pollutants in vehicular exhaust, emitted into the air by car and truck traffic and trains. The recommended minimum width for carbon forests is 500 feet. Beyond this distance, the negative health impacts of pollutants in vehicle exhaust drop off sharply. The carbon forest can begin within the right-of-way of the existing interstate (set back from the edge of the interstate as required by state law for vehicle safety) and extend beyond the right-of-way as land is available, ideally creating a 500 ft forested band. Actual width will vary based on the availability of vacant land.

Some green infrastructure can be integrated within neighborhoods, just as blue infrastructure can. Landscape can be a new basis for creating new kinds of urban lifestyles in areas rich with recreational and other outdoor opportunities. Other areas need industrial buffers that repurpose vacant land to created protective, forested zones around industrial uses. Green landscapes can also be economic assets, offering job opportunities related mostly to their construction and maintenance.

The scale and type of landscaping depends on the scale and intensity of neighborhoods or industries. Specific buffer widths will vary according to available land, but general suggested buffer widths are

- Live+Make: No Buffer
- Light Industry: 200 ft buffer
- General Industry: 1,320 ft buffer
- Heavy Industry: 2,640 ft buffer

Innovative uses of land in Detroit do face technical and legal barriers. Just as conventional infrastructures in Detroit are outdated and inefficient, traditional forms of green space and water features need upgrading and updating. Individual lot and block structures are restrictive and must be met with a range of proposed landscapes adaptable to multiple scales and to overlay existing traditional city grid patterns.

EXISTING: CURRENT WATER SYSTEM CONFIGURATION

| 1 | 2 | 3 | 4 | 5 | 6 | 7 | 8 | 9 | 10 | 11 | 12 | 13 | 14 | 15 | 16 | 17 | 18 | 19 | 20 | 21 | 22 | 23 | 24 | 25 | 26 | 27 | 28 | 29 | 30 | 31 | 32 | 33 | 34 | 35 | 36 |

There were 36 combined sewer overflow discharges into the Detroit River in 2011.[1]

(COMBINED STORMWATER/SEWER SYSTEM)

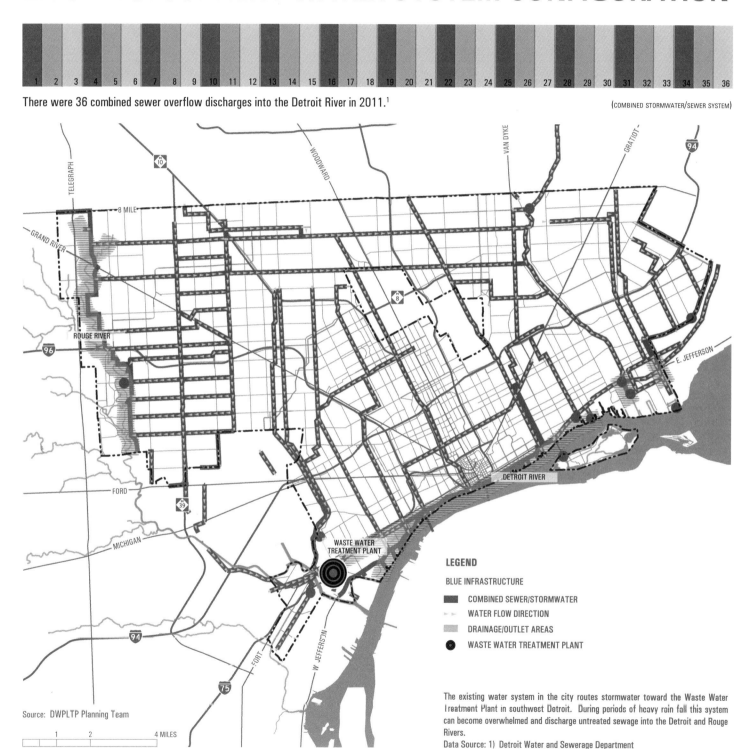

LEGEND

BLUE INFRASTRUCTURE

- COMBINED SEWER/STORMWATER
- WATER FLOW DIRECTION
- DRAINAGE/OUTLET AREAS
- WASTE WATER TREATMENT PLANT

Source: DWPLTP Planning Team

The existing water system in the city routes stormwater toward the Waste Water Treatment Plant in southwest Detroit. During periods of heavy rain fall this system can become overwhelmed and discharge untreated sewage into the Detroit and Rouge Rivers.
Data Source: 1) Detroit Water and Sewerage Department

PROPOSED: 2030 BLUE INFRASTRUCTURE SYSTEM

A comprehensive citywide blue infrastructure system could have prevented all but 5 of these discharges.[1]

(COMBINED STORMWATER/SEWER SYSTEM)

LEGEND

BLUE INFRASTRUCTURE

▬ STORMWATER BLVD

■ SURFACE LAKE

WET BUFFER

DISTRIBUTED NETWORK

HIGH CONCENTRATION PONDS

DISPERSED PONDS

INFILTRATION PARK

A reimagined infrastructure system will contain a range of blue infrastructure elements that can clean our water and air and help to improve quality of life for residents.
Data Source: 1) Stoss Landscape Urbanism

Source: DWPLTP Planning Team

1   2   4 MILES

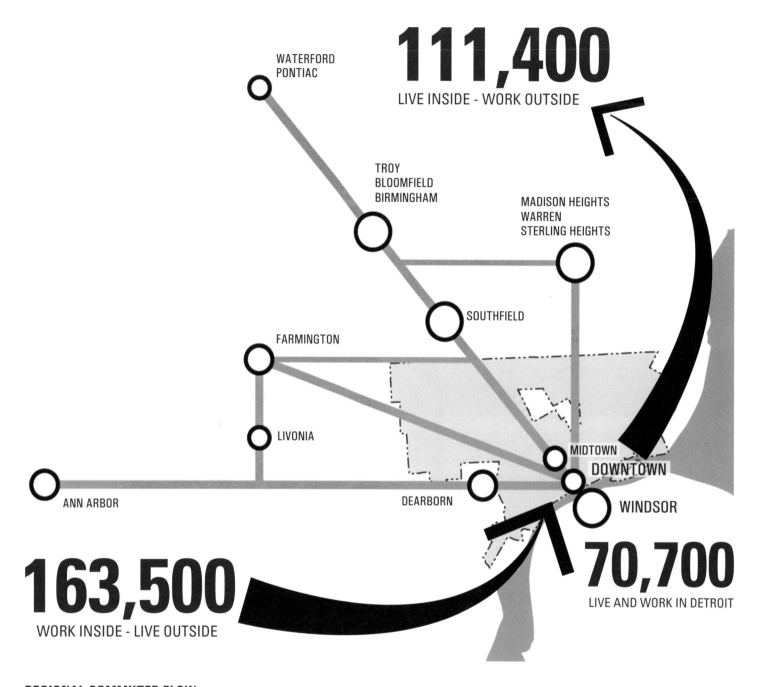

111,400
LIVE INSIDE - WORK OUTSIDE

WATERFORD
PONTIAC

TROY
BLOOMFIELD
BIRMINGHAM

MADISON HEIGHTS
WARREN
STERLING HEIGHTS

SOUTHFIELD

FARMINGTON

LIVONIA

MIDTOWN
DOWNTOWN

ANN ARBOR

DEARBORN

WINDSOR

70,700
LIVE AND WORK IN DETROIT

163,500
WORK INSIDE - LIVE OUTSIDE

REGIONAL COMMUTER FLOW

 TRANSIT CONNECTIONS
○ EMPLOYMENT CENTERS

As well as travel within the city, today's Detroiters require good access to employment
centers outside of the city, in neighboring counties.

Data Source: 2010 Longitudinal Employer-Household Dynamics

RECONFIGURE TRANSPORTATION C

REALIGNMENT WITH THE CITY. The highest priority for systemwide change is transportation or mobility. Detroit is heavily car-dependent (over 85% of trips are taken by car) and while the Motor City legacy may persist for several decades to come, real change is happening now. Rising fuel prices and environmental issues are starting to bite. Dispersed job centers limit access and choice of employment for working and low-income families without cars. This means that diversifying the transportation options (for both people and freight) is fundamental.

One of the best ways to reduce transportation-related pollution and increase quality of life (as well as business attractiveness) is for more people to live near to where they work and thus make shorter commutes. Detroit faces a challenge in this respect because 62% of Detroiters are currently employed outside of the city, with average commute times of over 40 minutes. Only when there are greater levels of employment within the city can this be addressed. Therefore the transformation of the transportation network should not only respond to the largely unplanned restructuring of the city that has taken place in recent decades but should also be used to promote and support a planned economic restructuring that can bring more employment into the city in the future. The improved system needs to be provided in a way that is affordable in the short term and in a way that is flexible in the medium term in order to respond to change further down the line.

CONNECTIVITY AND QUALITY OF LIFE. Transportation connects city residents to jobs, and also to public services (health and education) as well as places of recreation and entertainment—all of which contribute strongly to their quality of life. Changing the role and speed of routes in the city will be vital to enhancing access across a wider range of transport modes. Detroit's movement systems for people are primarily road based. These roads must accommodate not only cars but also public transit, freight, and non-motorized movement.

Detroit has a very large road capacity but does not provide optimal connections. Although highways take traffic efficiently through the city or from downtown to points in the suburbs, these highways sever the city internally, disconnecting neighborhoods and undermining social connections as well as connections to jobs. As the population lessens in the foreseeable future, it will be more important than ever to "right-size" the road network and integrate it with other modes and design changes that to allow faster access and a more coherent, connected feeling throughout the city.

Freight movement, logistics, and waste processing have important direct consequences for quality of life in the city (such as environmental impact) as well as indirect consequences (such as an improved and therefore healthier business environment). As Detroit moves to a more multi-centered urban pattern, the hierarchy of routes for freight and waste processing must be examined and defined to best serve traffic into and through the new city as the hub of a regional network.

"[We] need a regional transit authority that is well funded to cover operational cost."

City Systems Open House, 8/21/2012

"Will the system realistically link inner-city workers to suburban job markets? There are not enough jobs in the city."

David, City Systems Open House, 8/21/2012

THE CITY SYSTEMS ELEMENT : THE SUSTAINABLE CITY

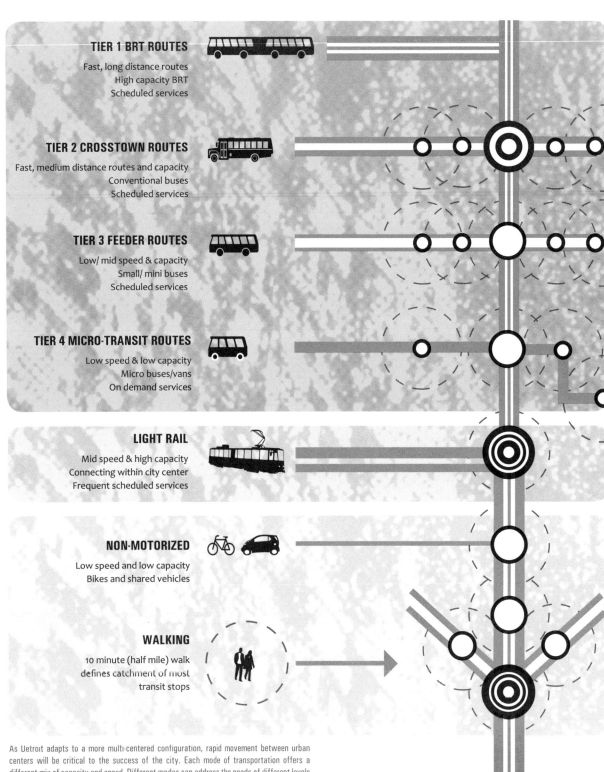

BUS

TIER 1 BRT ROUTES

Fast, long distance routes
High capacity BRT
Scheduled services

TIER 2 CROSSTOWN ROUTES

Fast, medium distance routes and capacity
Conventional buses
Scheduled services

TIER 3 FEEDER ROUTES

Low/ mid speed & capacity
Small/ mini buses
Scheduled services

TIER 4 MICRO-TRANSIT ROUTES

Low speed & low capacity
Micro buses/vans
On demand services

RAIL

LIGHT RAIL

Mid speed & high capacity
Connecting within city center
Frequent scheduled services

NON-MOTORIZED

NON-MOTORIZED

Low speed and low capacity
Bikes and shared vehicles

WALKING

10 minute (half mile) walk
defines catchment of most
transit stops

As Detroit adapts to a more multi-centered configuration, rapid movement between urban
centers will be critical to the success of the city. Each mode of transportation offers a
different mix of capacity and speed. Different modes can address the needs of different levels
of density and proximity to employment or service centers.

"Have you considered the possibility of converting roads to half capacity - so as to be only used non-motorized vehicles? Maybe they would be only half a lane, instead of closed?"

Transportation & Infrastructure Working Session, 6/7/2012

"As we put down more bike lanes, people are starting to use more alternative transit."

Transportation Working Session, 2/10/2012

NETWORK ADJUSTMENTS. The following changes proposed to the system can all be commenced incrementally and without large investments. Local impacts will be felt immediately but the greatest change will be felt once the networks reach a maturity that allows simple, reliable multimodal transport for all residents at a reduced cost.

Insert an intermediate layer in the road hierarchy and introduce a ring-road — providing faster connections across the city. This should be reflected in both the road network and the transit system that runs on it. The current inefficient pattern of mid-scale transit routes serving all areas of the city at similar speed and occasionally in parallel should be replaced by a clear, tiered system of rapid transit routes linking the major employment centers in and beyond Detroit, supported by smaller feeder routes.

- Make space available for other modes, particularly dedicated lanes for faster transit services, and bicycle lanes.

- Support the development of non-motorized modes for shorter journeys or as the start and end portions of longer ones. This will require focused development of enhanced sidewalk provision in key activity centers as well as the development of an integrated network of greenways and cycling routes linking centers to one another and to residential areas.

- Decommission surplus capacity so that it no longer imposes a maintenance burden. This may mean closing minor roads in areas which have fallen vacant or reducing lane capacity on major roads—allocating surplus to green space or landscape infrastructures.

PLANNING FOR INTERCHANGES. For both transit and freight, the development of a multimodal and hierarchical system presents challenges and opportunities at the interchange locations. These crossing points can stimulate economic activity as a result of the increased traffic or the emergence of transit oriented development although the emphasis must always be upon easy interchange between transport modes. In some cases the logistical and spatial requirements for an effective interchange may require a significant investment. As a result, while the system generally should anticipate change the interchange points are likely to be more long-lived and should seek a loose-fit relationship to any future changes.

191

THE CITY SYSTEMS ELEMENT : THE SUSTAINABLE CITY

EXISTING: CURRENT PUBLIC TRANSIT ROUTES

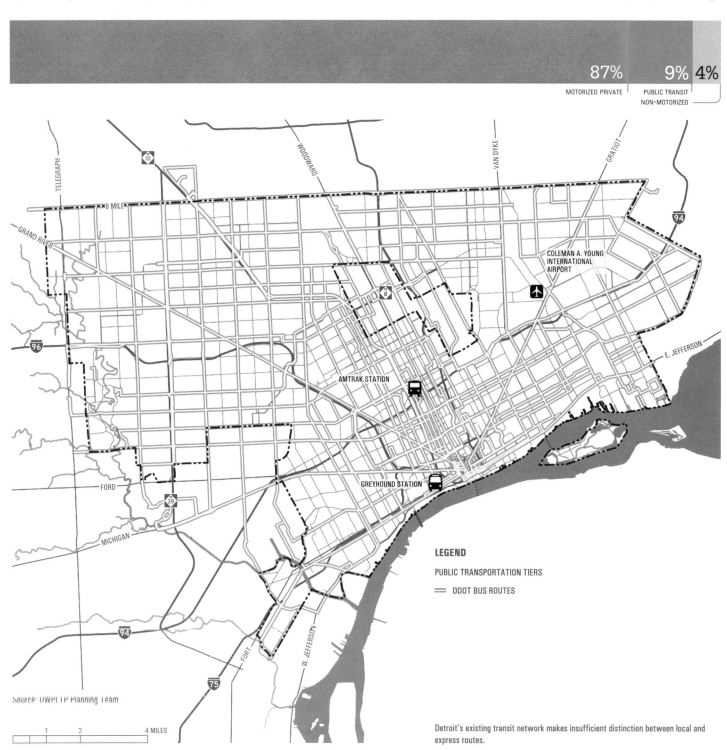

87% 9% 4%

MOTORIZED PRIVATE | PUBLIC TRANSIT
NON-MOTORIZED

COLEMAN A. YOUNG
INTERNATIONAL
AIRPORT

AMTRAK STATION

GREYHOUND STATION

LEGEND

PUBLIC TRANSPORTATION TIERS

=== DDOT BUS ROUTES

Source: DWPLTP Planning Team

1 2 4 MILES

Detroit's existing transit network makes insufficient distinction between local and
express routes.

PROPOSED: 2030 PUBLIC TRANSIT ROUTES

60%	30%	10%
MOTORIZED PRIVATE	PUBLIC TRANSIT	NON-MOTORIZED

LEGEND

PROPOSED PUBLIC TRANSIT BY TIER

- LIGHT RAIL
- TIER 1 BRT ROUTES
- TIER 2 CROSSTOWN ROUTES
- EMPLOYMENT DISTRICTS
- ○ TRANSIT NODES

PROJECTED 2030 POPULATION DENSITY

- 0–2 PEOPLE PER ACRE
- 3–6
- 7–10
- 11–14
- 15–18
- > 19

Source: DWPLTP Planning Team

A simpler and more reliable transit system creates space for alternative modes of transportation and provides for faster transfer between those modes.

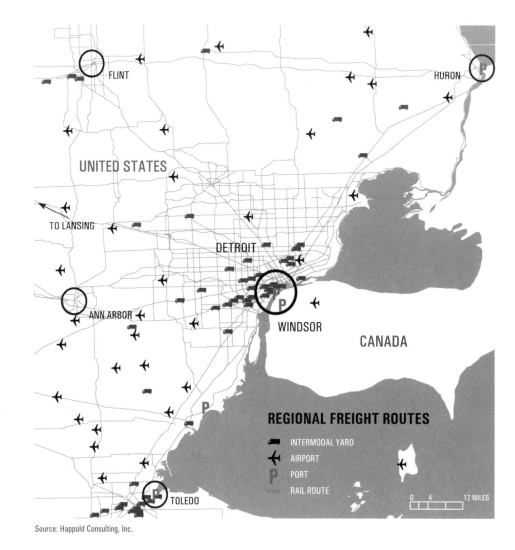

"What are plans to expand the airport? We are missing an opportunity to generate funds from a more fully operational facility. Point-to-point flights and international trade should be explored."

Beverly, Town Hall Meetings, 9/2010

Detroit's strategic position makes it an important freight hub for North America. Links to Windsor and five adjacent cities offer potential for Detroit to enhance facilities in the Transportation, Distribution, and Logistics sector and increase employment.

Source: Happold Consulting, Inc.

FREIGHT. Efficient freight movement to and within the city is essential to Detroit's economic performance. Beyond this, Detroit has the strategic position and legacy networks to be a freight hub of continental significance. Building, or renewing, the world class freight movement hubs in Detroit has the capacity not only to serve Detroit industry but to become a major source of employment and wealth creator in its own right. To achieve this, Detroit must reorganize its freight networks at city level.

- Reinforcing the main freight routes and facilities, particularly the upgrade of key road and rail routes (such as I-94 upgrade and upgrade of the main rail interlockers). In addition, it will be important to expand the capacity of international crossings as well as Detroit's air and water gateways.

- Creating interchanges, which allow the efficient transhipment, breakdown, and repacking of freight between different routes and different modes. Projects such as the Detroit Intermodal Freight Terminal (DIFT) will be essential to support this.

- Connecting Detroit businesses to the primary freight network, ensuring that the city road network and railroad spur system is sufficient for Detroit businesses to seamlessly access main freight routes or key interchanges—reinforcing Detroit's image as an attractive business location.

- Support the consolidation of DTW (Detroit Metro Airport) as a major international hub or 'aerotropolis' and ensure that the links between the airport and Detroit are sufficient to ensure that city businesses and jobs benefit. Additionally, Coleman A. Young Municipal Airport should be optimized to ensure maximum connectivity between the city and the surrounding region for local freight and package movements.

- Reinforce the capacity of the port facilities to service the industrial clusters in the southwest of the city and ensure transport connections between the facilities and the clusters are integrated with the wider networks.

Achieving these projects will require coordinated action among transportation system agencies, logistics operators, and city and regional authorities in order to identify key routes and interchange points, acquire the required land for system upgrade and to develop combined funding approaches.

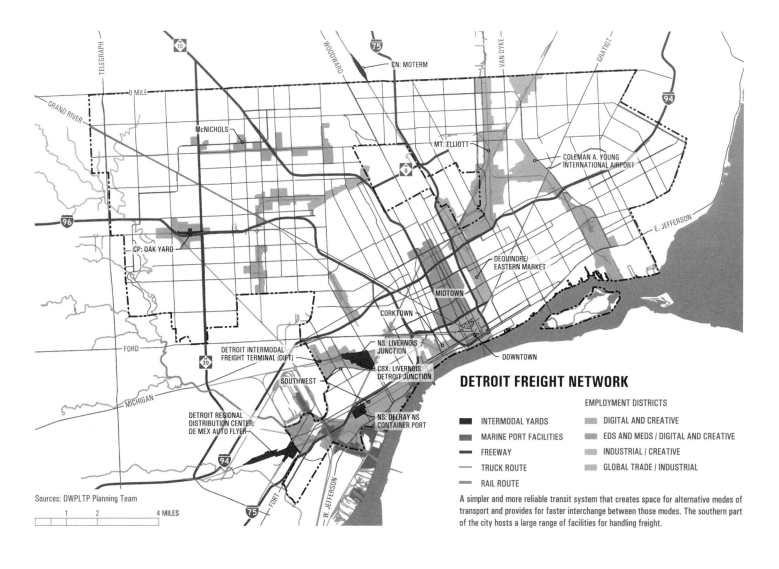

DETROIT FREIGHT NETWORK

EMPLOYMENT DISTRICTS

■ INTERMODAL YARDS	▨ DIGITAL AND CREATIVE
▨ MARINE PORT FACILITIES	▨ EDS AND MEDS / DIGITAL AND CREATIVE
▬ FREEWAY	▨ INDUSTRIAL / CREATIVE
— TRUCK ROUTE	▨ GLOBAL TRADE / INDUSTRIAL
▬ RAIL ROUTE	

A simpler and more reliable transit system that creates space for alternative modes of transport and provides for faster interchange between those modes. The southern part of the city hosts a large range of facilities for handling freight.

Sources: DWPLTP Planning Team

1   2   4 MILES

THE CITY SYSTEMS ELEMENT : THE SUSTAINABLE CITY

IMPLEMENTATION ACTIONS

1   Realign city road hierarchy to provide faster connections between employment, district, and neighborhood centers.

2   Enhance transit service and increased ridership by realigning transit system to provide integrated network based on fast connections between regional employment centers, supported by feeder services from residential areas.

3   For higher-vacancy areas, provide smaller-scale, flexible on-demand services.

4   Align pattern of development in centers and neighborhoods to support greater number of walking and cycle trips, including promotion of greenways.

5   Support freight and logistics industries through upgrade of key routes and provision of enhanced connections across the border to Canada.

6   Provide large-scale multimodal freight interchange facilities to support local industry and overall city logistics role.

PILOT PROJECT

1   Route Hierarchy

ENHANCE COMMUNICATIONS ACCESS
HARNESSING NEW CONNECTIVITY

D

PRECEDENT

SUSTAINABLE DUBUQUE

The City of Dubuque launched Sustainable Dubuque in 2009. The program brings together IBM Research, utilities providers, smart-meter suppliers and community groups to provide residents with real-time feedback on energy and water consumption.

Image Source: http://www.sustainablecitynetwork.com

PILOT PROJECT

TRANSIT PHONE APP

Development of a multi-modal integrated transportation mobile application that facilitates trip planning within and beyond the city. This can pre-date the establishment of a Regional Transport Authority (RTA) and should also accommodate non-motorized transportation.

Image Source: http://www.play.google.com

Detroit currently has good levels of coverage by communications and data services. Unlike other city systems, the rise in demand for data has been so great that growth in systems has been possible even as the population has declined. This underlying situation allows the national regional service providers involved to justify continued investment in the network. However, Detroit must aim high. In future, a constantly upgraded, high quality base communications network will be essential to underpin the transformation of Detroit in order to enable smarter delivery of services, smarter use of infrastructure and the development of new economies.

In the future Detroit will have limited budgets while retaining a significant number of vulnerable residents within the city. Excellent communications will be essential to delivering life quality improving services within financial constraints. Examples of this include development of e-enabled service delivery for transportation systems including real-time transit information and facilitation of low cost on-demand services for those living in high-vacancy areas or vulnerable groups as well as development of e-government to include a wide range of public services.

The use of new technologies can also improve utilization and resilience of physical networks enabling them to be reduced in size. Examples of this include development of smart grids for utility systems which enhance utilization and reduced resource use or development of transportation management systems which allow greater efficiency from smaller infrastructures, such as integrated traffic signal control.

Lastly, many of the future economic growth sectors on which the resurgence in Detroit's employment levels depend, are underpinned by very high speed, high volume data and communications links. This will require investment in additional capacity to ensure that key employment and academic centers within Detroit have access to world class data ICT connections in terms of speed and capacity.

IMPLEMENTATION ACTIONS

1 Ensure high-speed data networks are in place to serve existing and new economic sectors and wider community.

2 Develop e-government platform to maximize efficiency of social service delivery.

3 Utilize improved data network to develop smart infrastructure systems which deliver improved service with smaller capacity infrastructure.

PRECEDENT

1 Sustainable Dubuque: Dubuque, IA

PILOT PROJECT

1 Transit Phone App

"In many areas on the East side of Detroit, the street lights are not working. We need to investigate the light poles and make sure there is not structural damage to the lights. Having all of the lights working at night will decrease the chance of robberies and car jackings."

Alvera, Detroit 24/7, 5/2012

IMPROVE LIGHTING EFFICIENCY
FLEXIBLE SOURCING FOR IMPROVED PERFORMANCE

Detroit's public lighting network has been particularly affected by the loss of population and tax base in the city Plans for its reform are important in and of themselves, but also to demonstrate progress and change in the city's systems management approach. Until recently, the city-owned network provided power via its own generation stations to the city's public lighting and public buildings. Rising costs, falling revenues, and aging infrastructure forced the PLD to draw back from generation and did not provide sufficient funds to maintain the network. By 2012, only 35,000 of 85,000 light fittings were in working order. In response to this, the city government has proposed a comprehensive plan incorporating physical transformations and organizational changes.

The proposed reduction in number of light fittings from 85,000 to approximately 45,000 includes the removal of lights in alleyways and removal of extra light poles on residential streets. More efficient light fittings (including LEDs) will replace the remaining ones, supplemented by "off the grid" technologies such as solar-powered lights for sparsely inhabited areas. The city government plans to selectively upgrade and enhance lighting provision along main thoroughfares and within key city and district centers. An upgrade program has already been partially implemented within the Downtown and Midtown areas.

Continued support should be given to the transfer of ownership of the public lighting network to a private body able to outsource operations and maintenance, and with independent financial powers.

These proposed transformations will make a major contribution to creating a network that aligns physically with the city's current needs and fiscal capacity. This plan can be built on to serve the needs of the future city by providing targeted upgrades in neighborhood and district centers, while further reducing lighting provision in transition areas of high-vacancy as they are vacated.

IMPLEMENTATION ACTIONS

1   Reduce number of lights and upgrade all remaining lights to low-energy LED type.

2   In high-vacancy areas, take some parts of the network off-grid, using solar power for generation.

3   Transfer ownership of the network to a new Public Lighting Authority which can procure services from the private sector competitively.

PILOT PROJECT

1   Weatherization and Energy

PRECEDENT

1   Public Lighting Outsourcing

PILOT PROJECT

WEATHERIZATION AND ENERGY

The district-level weatherization and energy demand reduction program is delivered by a joint venture Energy Services Company (ESCo) formed by public authority and private providers. Results are measured, monitored, and evaluated in a citywide program.

Image Source: http://images.fastcompany.com/

WASTE STREAMING AND INCENTIVE PROGRAM

A district-level waste streaming and incentive program is delivered by a joint ventured formed by public authority and waste collection companies, including demolition and construction waste firms.

Image Source: http://www.designswan.com/

REDUCE WASTE AND INCREASE RECYCLING
TOTAL WASTE MANAGEMENT

F

Detroit currently operates a centralized approach to waste management. Regular collection services, provided by the City of Detroit Department of Public Works (DPW), particularly for residential customers and public buildings and by private collection services for commercial enterprises, bring the majority of nonindustrial waste generated in Detroit to the City's incinerator, operated by Greater Detroit Resource Recovery Authority (GDRRA). The GDRRA recovers some materials, such as metals, for recycling and generates electricity as well as steam, which is fed to the Detroit Thermal network. For the next ten years, the City of Detroit has secured a lowest-price-match guarantee for processing City-collected waste whereby the incinerator will match the lowest price offered by any alternative provider (currently $25/ton).

In recognition of the environmental imperative to recover a greater proportion of the materials within Detroit's waste streams, DPW has piloted curbside recycling programs to deliver waste to the advanced materials recovery facility north of 8 Mile. The emerging changes in Detroit's population, economy, and land use will lead to reducing overall volumes of waste and changing composition of the waste stream. Reducing waste volumes potentially means reduced efficiency for collection routes and reduced levels of locally sourced fuel for the incinerator, prompting the need for greater waste streams from outside Detroit.

The Strategic Framework recognizes that Detroit's waste management approach will evolve over time to meet the changing structure of the city and emerging environmental requirements. Key initiatives will be as follows:

- Mitigate environmental impact of existing waste streams, ensuring that planned upgrades to the incinerators' emission control systems are implemented to be compliant with rising U.S. EPA and international best-practice requirements.

- Minimize waste generators: Engaging with residents, businesses, and packaging producers to identify pathways to reduce total waste levels;

- Constantly review waste collection routing in order to achieve greatest possible efficiency in context of changing city population and economic activity patterns; and

- Increase coverage of targeted curbside recycling programs to cover all future residential neighborhoods in the city. Recycling programs should continue to utilize metro Detroit's existing high standard materials recovery facilities.

1   Reduce total levels of waste through citizen education and work with packaging industry.

2   Develop targeted and citywide curbside recycling program.

3   Ensure that incinerator emissions remain at or below US EPA standards and international best practice.

1   Waste Streaming and Incentive Program

WASTE PRODUCED & RECYCLED IN DETROIT

DETROIT

WASTE RECYCLED   WASTE NOT RECYCLED

WASTE PRODUCED + RECYCLED IN OTHER U.S. CITIES

SAN FRANCISCO

NEW YORK

CHICAGO

BOSTON

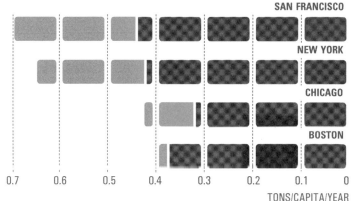

0.7   0.6   0.5   0.4   0.3   0.2   0.1   0

TONS/CAPITA/YEAR

WASTE RECYCLED   WASTE NOT RECYCLED

"The most effective strategies that I think are happening in the city are introducing recycling to students in public schools. . . . It teaches kids like us how to treat the environment and keep it healthy and well looked after."

- Zarin, Detroit 24/7, 5/2012

ACTIVELY MANAGE CHANGE G
ORGANIZATIONAL SUPPORT FOR PHYSICAL CHANGE

ORGANIZING FOR LONG-TERM CHANGE. Detroit's systems will be transformed gradually over time. There is no affordable model for the instantaneous remodeling of all of the systems of a large city. Transforming the systems will require smart thinking that identifies the optimal rate of change. Compared to the typical lifespan of social and economic trends, infrastructure systems have a very long service life extending up to 50 years. Nevertheless, long-term decisions for different parts of the network are taken every year as rolling programs of investment are directed to particular areas and system elements. In this context, long-term change must start now. This will require effective and transparent management and, in some cases, organizational change in order to drive through the totality of changes described.

The systems transformations set out in the plan are likely to require organizational change on two fronts: Making changes to the laws, regulation and mandated levels of service that govern the jurisdiction, service provision and financing of systems in Detroit on the one hand, and reconsidering investment priorities to directly impact the maintenance, upgrade or decommissioning approach of each network on the other. An example of the first type of regulatory change would be to take legal steps to permit the creation of a Regional Transportation Authority, while an example of the second type of change would to push for changes to the way in which construction and maintenance of roads is funded by the state and by the national government.

RESPONSIBILITY FOR AND IMPACT OF INDIVIDUAL SYSTEM CHANGES. The Strategic Framework provides the basis for reaching a coordinated approach between all stakeholders, residents, businesses and system providers. This will cover changes to the physical infrastructure or operational approach of individual systems to place them on a more efficient and sustainable basis and coordination of investment decisions and service delivery between agencies so that they can undertake the long-term planning and delivery of major investments with the necessary level of certainty.

Although the responsibility for implementing each individual change is unlikely to be shared between system providers, it should be acknowledged that the results of each change will be felt by other systems. There are three different types of interaction: Inter-dependencies (streamlining one system facilitates operational efficiencies for another), Indirect benefits (improving quality of life and environmental justice through more efficient use of space and resources) and Interagency operation (using the by-products of one system in another).

199

IMPLEMENTATION ACTIONS

1   Adopt Strategic Framework Plan as basis for systems transformation and put in place rolling review program.

2   Create an interagency platform to coordinate change across public and private sector bodies.

3   Communicate with affected communities and monitor processes for emerging success and unforeseen adverse impacts.

PRECEDENT

1   GIS Database: Cleveland, OH

EARLY ACTION

1   Regional Transit Authority

Sources: Strategic Operating Alternatives Report to the Greater Detroit Resource Recovery Authority, 2009 Lalonde, Suzanne, "Big City Recycling," Proceedings - 2003 Solid Waste/Recycling Conference of the Federation of New York Solid Waste Associations.

THE CITY SYSTEMS ELEMENT : THE SUSTAINABLE CITY

MANAGING CHANGE OVER TIME

	5 YEARS	10 YEARS	20 YEARS
CITY PLAN	• Adoption of Detroit Strategic Framework • Create interagency platform for key infrastructures	• Review of Detroit Strategic Framework • Review and update systems coordination plan	• Second review of Detroit Strategic Framework • Review and update systems coordination plan
ORGANIZATIONS	• Internal agency reforms (rationalization of operations and outsourcing where appropriate) • Establish Regional Transit Authority (RTA)	• Legislative reforms for agency mandates and / or funding structures • Development of formal interagency coordination mechanisms	• Consolidation of interagency coordination mechanisms
NEIGHBORHOODS	• Apply differentiated investment approaches according to Strategic Framework Plan	• Review impact of differentiated investment approaches • Apply final investment approaches to areas where decision has, until now, been left open temporarily	• Second review of impact of differentiated investment approaches
PHYSICAL NETWORKS	• Reconfiguration of service patterns where this can be achieved inside existing agency mandates and using existing hardware /vehicle fleets etc. • Implementation of pilot projects	• Review of impact of reconfigured networks • Delivery of major priority projects	• Second review of impact of reconfigured networks and development of plans for consolidation with upgraded hardware and more permanent networks

Managing change should take place at four key levels and be phased realistically over time. Different periods of time will be busiest for different types of activity.

GIS DATABASE

Cleveland's Geographical Information Systems (GIS) database is the City's foundation for managing system assets. It can also can serve as the platform for a comprehensive strategy combining age of infrastructure and maintenance costs with projected population and block capacity.

REGIONAL TRANSIT AUTHORITY

Establish a regional transit authority (RTA) for the main parts of the metropolitan area, including Detroit. The RTA will take responsibility for planning, integration, strategic operation, and investment decisions for all types of transit services across the metro area.

Image Source: http://www.riderta.com

SERVICE	PROVIDER
ELECTRICITY	Detroit Edison (part of DTE) Public Lighting Department (PLD)
GAS	Michcon (part of DTE)
HEAT	Detroit Thermal (part of Thermal Ventures)
POTABLE WATER	Detroit Water and Sewerage Department (DWSD)
DRAINAGE	Detroit Water and Sewerage Department (DWSD)
STORMWATER DRAINAGE	Detroit Water and Sewerage Department (DWSD)
WASTE COLLECTION	Department of Public Works (DPW)
TELECOMS AND DATA	AT&T and other private providers
STREET LIGHTING	Public Lighting Department (PLD)
INTRA CITY PUBLIC TRANSPORT	Detroit Department of Transport (DDOT)
SUBURBAN PUBLIC TRANSIT	Suburban Mobility for Regional Transportation (SMART)
ROADS	Michigan Department of Transportation (MDOT), Department of Public Services (Wayne County) and Department of Public Works (City of Detroit)

The chart lists the current public and private service providers found within the city of Detroit.

CREATE AN INTERAGENCY PLATFORM. Overall success will depend heavily on effective coordination among service providers, both public and private, to enhance efficiency, integrate systems, allocate resources wisely, and reduce costs. The Strategic Framework recommends that an interagency platform be created to serve as a forum for coordinating the reform of systems that serve Detroit, and as a single point of contact for engagement with the many groups engaged with the transformation of the city, including public and private system agencies, civic groups, municipal planning organizations, and the nonprofit sector. The platform will allow all of the service agencies, public and private, to come together on a regular basis to:

- assess detailed changes and trends within the city in terms of economy, population, and changing land use and system demand;

- agree on common plans for future system development and investment;

- coordinate operation and management;

- coordinate maintenance and renewal work; and

- evaluate the impacts of change on individual communities, as well as review opportunities for mitigation.

PHASING AND HANDLING CHANGE OVER TIME. There are many reasons why the physical changes to the systems should be phased over time. Service providers should ensure provision of alternative approaches to service provision ahead of any system withdrawal or reconfiguration. Operators should prioritize areas where upgrade or land use change is most urgent and support longer-term approaches in areas where the development strategy or land use opportunities are not fully clarified. Innovative development concepts can be explored through small-scale pilot projects in the short term to test the viability of larger-scale deployment in the medium to long term.

The chart on the opposite page shows a general approach to the phasing of the systems transformations at four different levels: The implementation of the Strategic Framework, organizational change, neighborhood change, and the physical changes to the networks or city systems.

CIVIC ENGAGEMENT. Communicating the important details of the system change and the rationale behind it to the city residents is of paramount importance. Detroiters should know what is going to happen and why. They should also have the opportunity to place their points of view in a process that effectively and equitably responds to the sometimes conflicting demands that underlie the need for systems to support economic growth, quality of life, environmental justice, and fiscal sustainability in as balanced a way as possible.

201

THE CITY SYSTEMS ELEMENT : THE SUSTAINABLE CITY

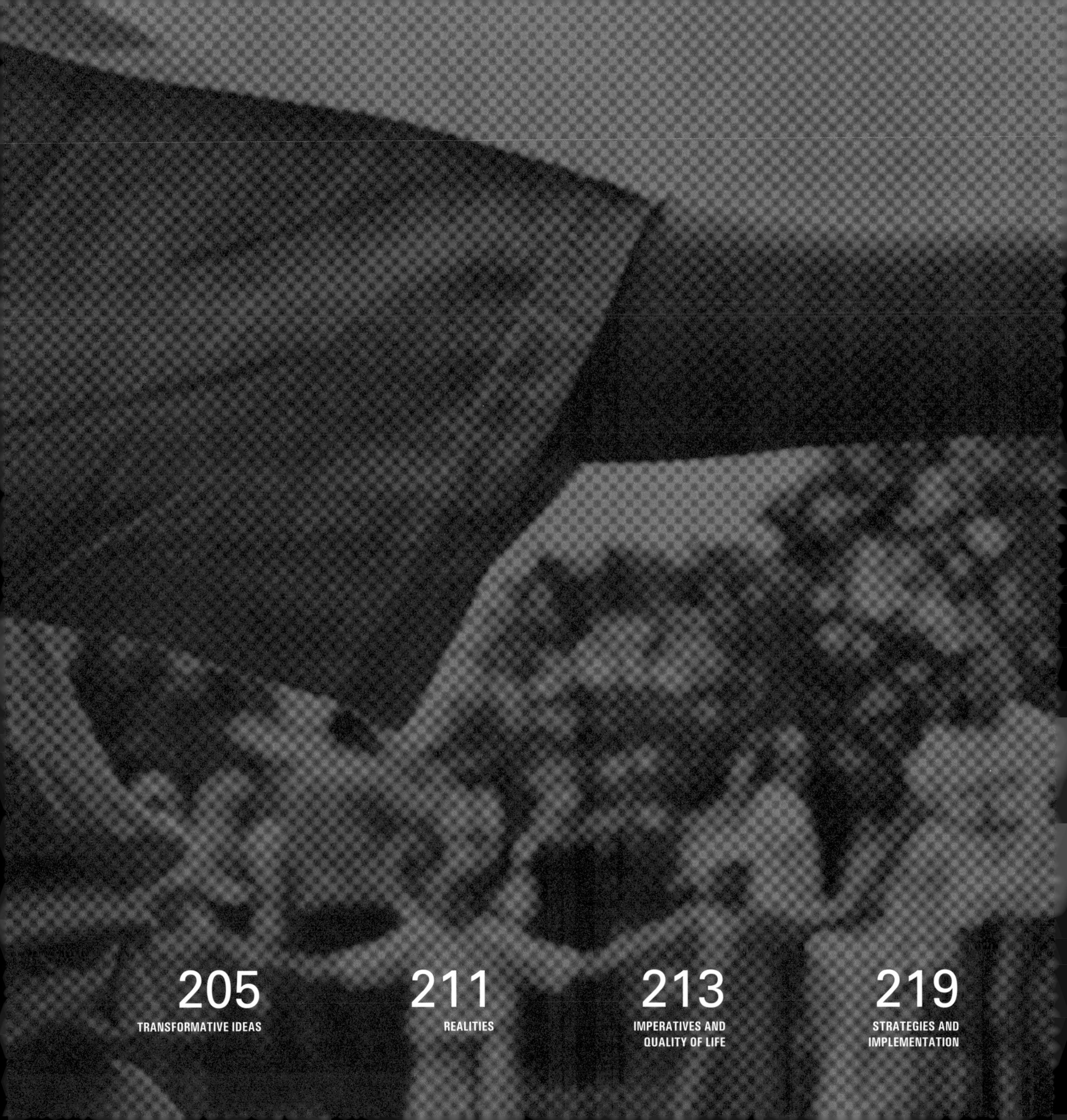

THE NEIGHBORHOOD ELEMENT

THE CITY OF DISTINCT AND REGIONALLY COMPETITIVE NEIGHBORHOODS

A Day in the Life *Improving the Qualities of Life*

Irma, Bill, and Aisha's neighborhood is having its first block party in 30 years today. That's because the Neighborhood Watch organization that Aisha started six years ago has gone from arson-busting and crime reports to moonbounces and cake walks. It hardly seems possible that the pleasant green space where neighborhood kids are playing and grown-ups are cooking out and talking was once a notorious vacant lot that neighbors used to call "The Blob."

It started when Bill, a bank teller, went to an open brainstorming session the CDC co-sponsored with the local church to gather "small but beautiful" ideas for making the neighborhood more healthy. He asked the CDC to talk to his bank's vice president about a small donation or micro-loan for a community garden. Then Irma—a neighbor Bill had seen but never really talked to—asked if her grandson's Boy Scout troop could volunteer. Aisha offered her group's watchful eye for clean-and-green efforts. With a grant for seeds and supplies from a local family foundation, the project was underway. "Take Back the Blob," became the neighborhood's rallying cry.

No one quite expected or foresaw the real bonus of that meeting: When the Detroit Strategic Framework was launched and the City called for transformative ideas for neighborhoods, Irma, Bill, and Aisha were ready with a vision. Their relationships with the CDC, bank, and the foundation helped them take their idea to reality.

Guiding their thinking is a technical facilitator who shows them how their plans for the neighborhood can fit into a bigger vision for the city and the region. It quickly becomes apparent that there are many possibilities, but not in every location. Irma is interested in creating a food co-op next to the new garden to increase access to healthy food. Both Aisha and Irma want to build in a strong youth component, and maybe even a new community center for kids to learn about food cultivation and sales, plus have a place to do arts projects and maybe even a "Study on the Green" space with plenty of natural light for after-school activities. Bill wants to make sure that seniors can stay in their homes as the neighborhood property values stabilize or even rise. All are interested in finding out how transportation can connect them—and their fresh produce—to the flourishing Eastern Market district.

That's tomorrow, though. Today is the day Aisha lands on the number chosen for the ultimate prize: The Chocolate Blob cake Irma made with her grandson, complete with Blobberry filling (raspberries from the bushes in the garden). The future is bright, all right. But today is pretty sweet, too.

TRANSFORMATIVE IDEAS
NEIGHBORHOOD RECOMMENDATIONS

FUTURE OPPORTUNITY. For Detroit's neighborhoods, challenge reveals opportunity. Many of Detroit's neighborhoods today are defined by the innumerable challenges to quality of life, including public safety, education, health and employment, rather than their capacity to realize a thriving place in which to live. Yet within these challenges exist strengths in the city's historic neighborhoods, such as Grandmont Rosedale and Indian Village; striking mid-century hallmarks of urban design, such as Lafayette Park; and emerging Live+Work environments in Corktown and Eastern Market. The breadth of these types of neighborhood provides the starting point for Detroit's neighborhood transformation.

The Detroit Strategic Framework recommends a variety of ways to strengthen Detroit's neighborhoods by leveraging existing assets and strengths while addressing specific challenges. The result will be more sustainable and attractive places to live; better quality of life; and inviting, affordable living options for a diverse range of households. Whether low- or high-income; single or married; with or without children; retired, working, or in school; longtime residents or newcomers, Detroit residents need options that connect them to work opportunities, services, recreation—and each other. **Detroit must be welcoming to all, including those moving in from neighboring cities, those who are originally from other countries, and those with limited means.**

A series of framework zones can define a range of existing conditions shared by parts of the city, focusing specific strategies to address the real conditions of different neighborhoods, using a wide array of ideas for design ("typologies").

More than two years of neighborhood engagement and information sharing has led to the creation of these strategies. The important feedback provided by this dialogue has been woven into a series of tactics, tuned to the existing physical and market conditions within the framework zones, broken into implementation horizons, and targeted to achieve overall objectives for neighborhoods of all types. In each case, the strategies themselves are built to fulfill important quality-of-life objectives that have been defined through community feedback.

The overarching goal of the Neighborhood Element of the Strategic Framework Plan is to create a diversity of regionally competitive neighborhoods for Detroit. These diverse neighborhoods should provide many options to residents for all stages of their lives, from infancy to aging in place. Although Detroit has attempted land use strategies before, the Detroit Strategic Framework Plan has conducted a broad-scale consideration of the many and diverse possibilities for neighborhoods, engaging residents in an ongoing discussion of their vision for neighborhoods of all kinds. The challenges to neighborhoods are urgent and demand flexible, practical solutions that can grow and change with the city.

5

NEIGHBORHOODS
TRANSFORMATIVE
IDEAS

Images Source: Marvin Shaouni

1 A CITY OF MANY KEY ASSETS

Neighborhood parks, educational institutions, centers for medical innovation, an iconic skyline, historic neighborhoods, and an unmatched international riverfront: Detroit has the foundational assets that make cities attractive. At the center of this are the assets woven within the city's neighborhoods, where families come together, communities are fostered, and dynamic life thrives. These include majestic trees, inherent civic capacity, neighborhood organizations, retail, churches, parks, recreation centers, schools, and cultural centers. Detroit must find a way to support these important places and qualities while cultivating an environment in which many more can be established through the capacity of Detroiters. To get there, resources must be strategically focused so that the investments will benefit all residents. In creating and sustaining such assets, the quality of life for Detroiters can improve as the city's attractiveness to potential new residents grows.

Proportional representation of the number of times a location was mentioned as an assetin open-ended feedback between September 2010 and June 2012.

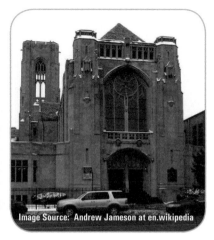

Image Source: Andrew Jameson at en.wikipedia

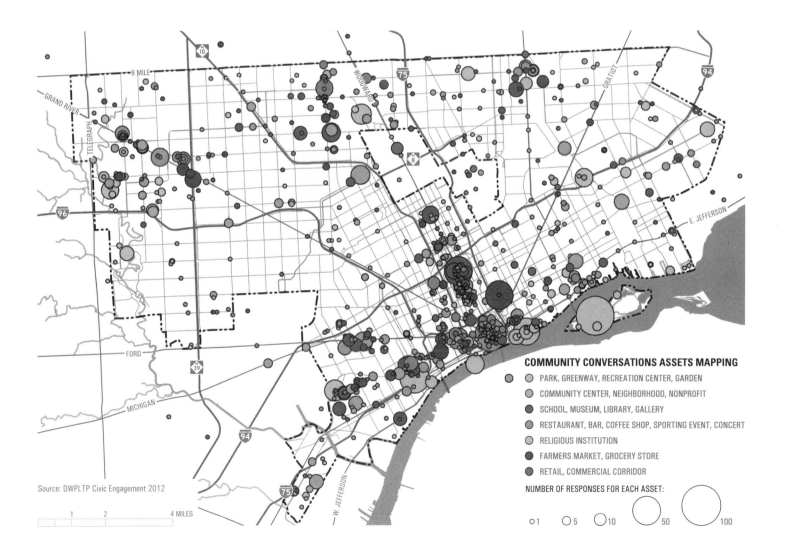

COMMUNITY CONVERSATIONS ASSETS MAPPING

- PARK, GREENWAY, RECREATION CENTER, GARDEN
- COMMUNITY CENTER, NEIGHBORHOOD, NONPROFIT
- SCHOOL, MUSEUM, LIBRARY, GALLERY
- RESTAURANT, BAR, COFFEE SHOP, SPORTING EVENT, CONCERT
- RELIGIOUS INSTITUTION
- FARMERS MARKET, GROCERY STORE
- RETAIL, COMMERCIAL CORRIDOR

NUMBER OF RESPONSES FOR EACH ASSET:

1   5   10   50   100

Source: DWPLTP Civic Engagement 2012

1   2   4 MILES

THE NEIGHBORHOOD ELEMENT : THE CITY OF DISTINCT AND REGIONALLY COMPETITIVE NEIGHBORHOODS

2 A CITY OF NEIGHBORHOOD CHOICES

Smaller cities may be defined by one prevailing neighborhood type, or a center within which the majority of the population lives. Large-scale cities such as Detroit can provide a wider array of neighborhood choices. Unfortunately, today, Detroit has not fulfilled that opportunity. Although each neighborhood choice may not appeal to every household, each household should be able to find a neighborhood choice that suits it. **One of Detroit's most unique and powerful potential strengths is its potential to provide a range of regionally competitive neighborhoods to attract and retain a greater number of residents.** This is important because Detroit continues to lose residents to other nearby cities.

The strategies put forth in this element of the Strategic Framework show how to address specific existing challenges and leverage inherent strengths to create a range of neighborhood choices. These include traditional neighborhoods (low and medium density), neighborhoods of mixed use and higher density (neighborhood center, district center, and city center), new neighborhoods for urban living and making (art and artisanal, clean-industry innovation, and live+work entrepreneurship), and new neighborhoods for urban green living (green residential and green mixed-rise). While stabilizing and strengthening a number of Detroit's existing neighborhoods and mixed-use areas will contribute to a collection of attractive, well-known neighborhood types, it is within the new neighborhood typologies that Detroit may transform existing liabilities of vacancy, abandonment, and disinvestment into new dynamic urban areas for living that reinvigorate unused or overlooked assets to create completely new neighborhood models, establishing Detroit as a leader in urban revitalization and design.

3 A CITY OF DIFFERENT STRATEGIES FOR DIFFERENT NEIGHBORHOODS

Strategies used to strengthen and reinforce existing neighborhoods, and new neighborhoods for urban living, must be as diverse as the quality-of-life elements they seek to improve. To achieve this, each strategy must be defined by specific existing conditions, the range of possible future neighborhood typologies associated with those conditions, and the overall quality of the objectives being given priority. Beyond that, each potential strategy must be effectively coordinated to ensure its broad viability and impact across the city. Detroit can no longer withstand well-intentioned investments that may benefit one neighborhood, while ultimately undermining the viability of others.

Within this model, the range of potential implementers, from residents to institutions, can customize specific tactics to achieve their goals, operating within a common framework for decision making, linking overall objectives for land use, economic growth, and city systems with strategies tailored to achieve specific results. **This allows each strategy to address the unique needs, capacity, and assets of each neighborhood to maximize the impact of investment and effort.**

Images Source: Marvin Shaouni

 ## 4 — A CITY OF DIVERSE HOUSING TYPES FOR DIVERSE POPULATIONS

 ## 5 — A CITY OF RESIDENTS WHO ENGAGE IN THEIR OWN FUTURES

Thriving contemporary cities are hallmarks of diversity, including employment options, income, ethnicity, social interests, and individual expertise. Within this context, Detroit must provide a diverse array of housing types to appeal to a range of people and households. At the height of the automotive boom within Detroit and its region, the single-family home came to dominate the city's housing spectrum, creating housing stock that has limited the city's ability to meet current market demand for greater multi-family housing.

To be viable and sustainable, Detroit's neighborhoods now need to provide a wider choice of housing types. The Detroit Strategic Framework coordinates neighborhood strategies with existing conditions and future typology objectives to create strategic, targeted housing rehabilitation, renovation, and new construction across multiple neighborhood types, including traditional neighborhoods; mixed-use centers; and new, innovative neighborhood types such green mixed-rise, green residential, and live+make. The breadth of these neighborhood typologies provides a platform for creating a variety of housing options.

Many Detroit residents are recognized, active participants in their future. They have long done for themselves what others could not, and they have been an integrated part of the planning process for the Detroit Strategic Framework. The process has capitalized on the insight, capacity, and commitment of all Detroiters to realize a comprehensive decision-making framework. **The means and methods for achieving the substantial transformative strategies identified within the process will require no less integration and engagement with all Detroiters— residents and civic leaders—ensuring a voice for everyone.** Residents bring with them a localized expertise that adds unmatched value to integrated strategies for investment. To ensure residents have the opportunity to participate in their future, the Detroit Strategic Framework provides a comprehensive framework for decision making that will facilitate better, more informed coordination for all residents. This includes continuing to facilitate neighborhood dialogue regarding how neighborhoods can use the Framework and its strategies, making sure that important strategies being used in one neighborhood can create a better-performing city at large.

RETAIL & SERVICES

$1.5B $200M

32%

$1.5 BILLION OF DETROIT RESIDENT EXPENDITURES ARE MADE OUTSIDE THE CITY EACH YEAR[1]

$200 MILLION OF DETROIT RESIDENT GROCERY EXPENDITURES ARE MADE OUTSIDE THE CITY EACH YEAR[2]

32% OF DETROITERS' ANNUAL INCOME IS SPENT ON TRANSPORTATION[3]

COMMUNITY

DETROIT HAS THE 2ND HIGHEST VIOLENT CRIME RATE IN THE U.S.

FOR UNITED STATES CITIES WITH OVER 100,000 POPULATION[4]

21% OF DETROIT'S PARKS ARE IN GOOD CONDITION

DETROIT RANKS LAST IN ACRES OF PARK SPACE PER RESIDENT

33K 1.6K 25% LOSS 66% LOSS

33,000 DANGEROUS BUILDINGS IN DETROIT[5]

1,600 CHURCHES, BLOCK CLUBS, AND COMMUNITY ORGANIZATIONS IN DETROIT[6]

25% LOSS IN TOTAL NUMBER OF DETROIT HOMEOWNERS BETWEEN 2000-2010[7]

66% LOSS IN DETROIT'S MEDIAN HOUSING SALES PRICE (2006-2010). MEDIAN SALES PRICE IN 2010: $23,591[8]

ONLY 21% OF DETROIT'S PARKS ARE IN GOOD CONDITION[9]

DETROIT IS RANKED LAST IN ACRES OF PARK SPACE PER RESIDENT[10]

HEALTH & EDUCATION

50% HIGHER RISK OF DEATH FROM HEART DISEASE

29% 29% OF CHILDREN IN DETROIT SUFFER FROM ASTHMA[11]

3x

69.1% OBESE OR OVERWEIGHT DETROITERS

21% OVERWEIGHT YOUTH

82% 82% OF DETROITERS HAVE A HIGH SCHOOL DIPLOMA OR LESS[15]

ONLY **32%** 32% OF DETROITERS WITHOUT A HIGH SCHOOL DIPLOMA ARE EMPLOYED[16]

60% DECLINE

DETROIT'S CHILDHOOD ASTHMA RATE IS THREE TIMES HIGHER THAN THE NATIONAL AVERAGE[11]

69.1% OF DETROITERS ARE OBESE OR OVERWEIGHT[12]

DEATHS RESULTING FROM HEART DISEASE IN DETROIT ARE 50% HIGHER THAN THE NATIONAL AVERAGE[13]

21% OF DETROIT'S YOUTH ARE OVERWEIGHT[14]

IN DETROIT PUBLIC SCHOOLS ENROLLMENT FROM 2001-2010[17]

REALITIES
THE STATE OF DETROIT'S NEIGHBORHOODS

Although Detroit's long and increasingly public decline has been documented as a monolithic event, population decline, disinvestment, and poor employment opportunities have specifically devastated the city's neighborhoods and residents. Over the last 10 years, the pace of this decline has increased, with another quarter of the population leaving, and the total number of vacant housing units doubling to 79,725 out of 349,170 overall. Resulting financial crises and market conditions reveal similar struggles, where tens of thousands of homes fall to tax foreclosure each year and 33,000 of the city's vacant housing units have become abandoned and declared open and dangerous buildings, contributing to localized blight and public safety challenges. **While some signs of resurgence are being measured, including notable market demand for multi-family housing, Detroit's abundance of unused single-family properties continue to create tremendous burdens.**

Ultimately, each of these conditions further constrains resources by limiting the financial capacity to support important services and systems, while stretching them to cover vast areas of the city with diminished populations that can no longer sufficiently support them. At the same time, residents within the city are faced with an increasingly poor quality of life, including high rates of violent crime and property crime, remarkably low workforce participation, low educational attainment, and significant health issues. The amenities and services that many residents want are unavailable, leaving some without options for basic necessities, and contributing to over $1.5B in lost spending each year as residents must seek goods and services outside of the city.

The intersection of such constrained resources and poor quality of life is illustrated within neighborhoods and across the city each day. Where a family cannot afford a car, they must rely on inadequately funded public transportation and endure such long commutes that getting and keeping a job is continually compromised. Or, where the same family has only a convenience stores within walking distance for food shopping, while unmaintained city parks and unsafe streets limit physical activity, family members are at higher-than-average risk for obesity, diabetes, high blood pressure, and heart problems.

In every way, the challenges facing the Detroit are rendered in the lives of its residents. The Detroit Strategic Framework recognizes that this reality is unacceptable, and proposes a comprehensive, coordinated approach to improve quality of life in neighborhoods while creating a more sustainable city overall. Business as usual will not work, and important actions can be taken today to the lay the groundwork for long-term transformation.

1) Social Compact 2010; 2) Social Compact 2010; 3) American Community Survey 2010 5-Year, Happold Consulting, Inc., 4) Federal Bureau of Investigation 2011, 5) Buildings, Safety Engineering, and Environmental Department; 6) City Planning Commission; 7) US Census 2000, 2010; 8) PolicyMap; 9) Detroit Recreation Department 2006; 10) Trust for Public Land 2010; 11) Detroit Alliance for Asthma Awareness; 12) Michigan Department of Community Health 2009; 13) Michigan Department of Community Health 2007; 14) Michigan Department of Community Health 2009; 15) American Community Survey 2010 5-Year; 16) American Community Survey 2010 5-Year; 17) Detroit Public Schools

We must promote a range of sustainable residential densities.

We must promote stewardship for all areas of the city by implementing short- and long-term strategies.

IMPERATIVES
NEIGHBORHOOD ACTIONS AND IMPACT

Nowhere is the need for Detroit's quality of life to improve more evident than in its neighborhoods, where people live their lives, and plan for their futures. Two very important and interwoven objectives for neighborhoods must be achieved.

First, the quality of life for every Detroiter must be dramatically improved. Detroit's neighborhoods must again be able to offer residents the basic and important components to flourish: excellent schools, connections to jobs for a range of skills and backgrounds, safety on the street and in the home, and important retail services and amenities. The coordinated and organized strategies in the Neighborhoods Element are directed toward supporting and enabling this objective, suiting solutions to different types of neighborhoods and engaging residents as the authors of their future.

Second, we must promote a range of sustainable densities across the city. The traditional neighborhood densities in a vast area of the city are unsupportable and cannot properly contribute the necessary revenues to provide the basic services that form the foundation for a higher quality of life. The Strategic Framework offers several types of neighborhoods to achieve sustainable densities. The Framework also recognizes that not all neighborhoods can go everywhere—and in particular, areas with continually diminishing populations where quality of life is overwhelmingly compromised, will no longer be designated for future residential development. Even so, all Detroiters—regardless of where they may live—must have an improved quality of life, including in areas of land use change (that is, the Alternative Use neighborhoods; see page 257).

Achieving these objectives establishes a more efficient, sustainable, and equitable city with a collection of neighborhoods that will be significantly more attractive to potential future residents.

WHAT WE LEARNED FROM CIVIC ENGAGEMENT FEEDBACK

- Comments about NEIGHBORHOODS were the most frequent type of comment out of approximately 180 topics

- Over 1/2 of the survey respondents stated "getting together with a group of neighbors and fellow citizens" was an EFFECTIVE WAY OF IMPROVING THEIR NEIGHBORHOODS

- Over 1/3 of neighborhood assets mentioned by participants fell into the category including NEIGHBORHOODS, COMMUNITY CENTERS, AND NEIGHBORHOOD NON-PROFITS

- Top neighborhood strategies recorded from DWP participants included:

    - REDUCE BLIGHT by making properties cleaner and safer

    - ENCOURAGE INDIVIDUALS AND FAMILIES TO STAY IN DETROIT, contribute to community, be neighborly, MAINTAIN PROPERTY, and convince others to move to or stay in Detroit

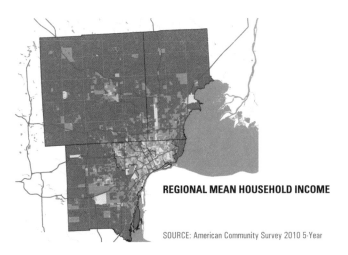

REGIONAL MEAN HOUSEHOLD INCOME

SOURCE: American Community Survey 2010 5-Year

QUALITY-OF-LIFE elements are a tracking mechanism for positive change within Detroit's neighborhoods. There are 13 total Quality-of-Life elements. Each Quality-of-Life element has a definition and a metric or set of metrics that can be mapped across the city's neighborhoods. Each Quality-of-Life element is also measured and mapped across the region to establish a regional benchmark for success. The goal is to ensure that Detroit's neighborhoods are both locally and regionally competitive places to live.

The composite quality-of-life scores across all 14 elements also provide a tool with which communities can prioritize resources to best serve the quality-of-life needs of its residents. For example, if a neighborhood is scoring poorly across the health metrics, resources could be prioritized to buffer neighborhoods against pollutants, provide additional healthy food options, remediate contaminated sites or provide recreational opportunities. Similarly, if an area has very high unemployment, resources could be deployed to provide additional jobs training opportunities. The metrics allow communities to evaluate their own opportunities and challenges and take action to improve quality of life.

When assessing quality of life within the city, it is important to set Detroit in context as part of a greater region. In the example of prosperity and income there are only a few areas within the City of Detroit that are regionally competitive in terms of household income.

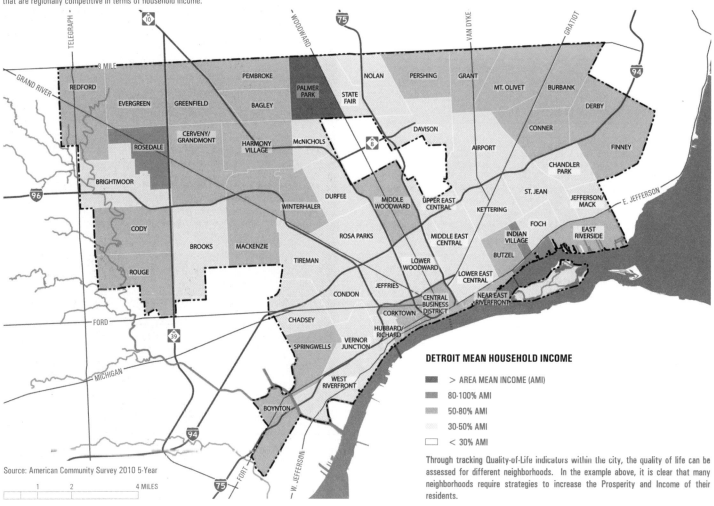

DETROIT MEAN HOUSEHOLD INCOME

- ▇ > AREA MEAN INCOME (AMI)
- ▇ 80-100% AMI
- ▇ 50-80% AMI
- ▒ 30-50% AMI
- ☐ < 30% AMI

Source: American Community Survey 2010 5-Year

1   2   4 MILES

Through tracking Quality-of-Life indicators within the city, the quality of life can be assessed for different neighborhoods. In the example above, it is clear that many neighborhoods require strategies to increase the Prosperity and Income of their residents.

DEFINITIONS

The quality-of-life definitions have been defined through the civic engagement process

METRICS

Standards of measurement by which efficiency, performance, progress, or quality of a plan, process, or product can be assessed

QUALITY OF LIFE

QUALITY-OF-LIFE ELEMENTS

 SAFETY

The sense of physical and emotional security, primarily focused on the individual or family, but also extending to surroundings

Total crime/population

 HEALTH

The physical and mental well-being for all Detroiters

Health indices: obesity, asthma, heart disease, childhood lead rates

 EDUCATION

The opportunity to gain a quality education for all ages, incomes and abilities

Percent of population over 25 with Bachelor's degree or higher

 PROSPERITY AND INCOME

The opportunity for long-term, fulfilling employment that allows for personal growth, self-sufficiency, and wealth creation

Average household income

 COMMUNITY

The inherent sense of belonging with neighbors, sharing common interests and working together to achieve common goals

Number of active community organizations, including places of worship

 PHYSICAL CONDITION

The state of constructed and natural surroundings

Number of vacant, open and dangerous buildings, vacant housing units not for sale or rent (nonseasonal)

 HOUSING

Quality dwelling options that provide shelter and safety for all residents

Percent of occupied housing units

 PUBLIC SERVICES

Core services provided by the city government and allied providers, ranging from utilities to maintenance and sanitation

Road quality index

 MOBILITY

The ability to effectively and efficiently access employment, housing and services

Average travel time to work

 ENVIRONMENT

The physical, chemical, and biotic factors that affect the surroundings and conditions in which a person, animal, or plant lives

Pounds of toxic materials released

 RECREATION

Places to accommodate physical activity and social interaction

Percent of population within 1/4 mile of park in good or fair condition, percent of population with convenient access to regional park

 CULTURE

Numerous events and cultural activities that define the social composition of daily life

Number of community assets

 RETAIL SERVICES AND AMENITIES

Places to facilitate material, service, and entertainment needs

Retail leakage to surrounding communities, locations and sizes of regional shopping centers

DETROIT'S HOUSEHOLD POPULATION COMPOSITION

"Partner with the faith-based community in effecting change in the community and city, and allowing the faith-based community to play a major/important role in the process."

Eleazar, Faith-Based Summit, 3/29/2011

"I want to move to Detroit but I must feel safe and have safe greenways to ride my bike. I like a more populated neighborhood and trust among neighbors are important to me."

Kendra, Website, 2010-2011

FAMILIES WITH CHILDREN	SINGLE PARENT FAMILIES	SENIORS	COUPLES	NEW AMERICANS	COLLEGE STUDENTS	YOUNG ADULTS
10%[1]	24%[1]	11%[1]	12%[1]	5%[2]	7%[2]	18%[1]

LEAVING

The population leaving the city is primarily made up of skilled workers and families with school-aged children. One in four people leaving the city leaves the state altogether.

-7%

THE AVERAGE HOUSEHOLD SIZE IN DETROIT IS PROJECTED TO DROP 7% [3]

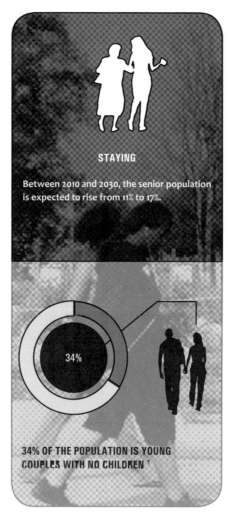

STAYING

Between 2010 and 2030, the senior population is expected to rise from 11% to 17%.

34%

34% OF THE POPULATION IS YOUNG COUPLES WITH NO CHILDREN [1]

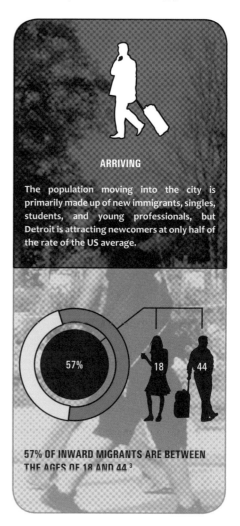

ARRIVING

The population moving into the city is primarily made up of new immigrants, singles, students, and young professionals, but Detroit is attracting newcomers at only half of the rate of the US average.

57%

18   44

57% OF INWARD MIGRANTS ARE BETWEEN THE AGES OF 18 AND 44 [3]

WHAT ARE CURRENT AND FUTURE RESIDENTS LOOKING FOR IN DETROIT?

Recognizing that Detroit must be welcoming to all, the city's neighborhoods must provide attractive choices for all types of people and families. At the start of the planning process we asked: Who will live in Detroit and where will they live?

VALUE PROPOSITION. Attracting new residents and retaining those who currently live in the city requires an effective "value proposition." For Detroit, this proposition is firmly based on offering a high quality of life that is well within each resident's grasp. This is arguably a proposition the city has not been able to effectively make. People make decisions about cities based on what their neighborhoods offer, including access to employment opportunities, quality schools, efficient and effective public services, housing options, safety and security, and affordability. Detroit must deliver on these to make itself truly regionally competitive—where area residents, city residents, and those coming to the region for the first time can truly see themselves, and in many cases their families, living in Detroit.

Achieving this objective has been elusive for Detroit, and it will continue to be so until Detroit can make a viable value proposition. The city must do this while also confronting an inherent challenge faced by such a large minority-majority city: the cultural distances and misconceptions that fuel isolationist perspectives and neither work to improve the city's outlook, nor embrace the dynamism and change experienced by all cities. **Detroit should work to attract and retain all residents, regardless of race, gender, lifestyle, or household need.**

POPULATION DYNAMICS. All major American cities have population changes each year, representing people arriving and leaving. For those with stable populations, the number of people arriving and leaving remain in balance, and in many cases more people actually arrive than leave, contributing to net population gain. Today, Detroit attracts new residents, but its arriving population is smaller than those choosing to leave, resulting in a net population loss of over 25 percent in the last 10 years. The Detroit Strategic Framework proposes to maximize those elements that attract residents (and compel others to stay), while directly confronting the obstacles that cause continual population loss or limit the attraction to newcomers.

LEVERAGING STRENGTH AND IDENTIFYING NEW OPPORTUNITIES. Developing and reinforcing a variety of neighborhood types to suit current residents and attract new ones calls for identifying and building upon the important attributes that have allowed Detroit's most successful neighborhoods to rise. In many cases, it is important to note, these attributes represent the intersection of civic stewardship, political advocacy, and assets such as important services and amenities.

Together, Detroit's neighborhoods must also contribute to a residential network that supports a wide range of lifestyles and households, improves overall quality of life, competes regionally and nationally, retains and attracts residents to the city, makes Detroit a more sustainable and efficient city, raises real estate market values, and accommodates a cultural shift — easing the tension between "insiders" and "outsiders."

1) US Census 2010; 2) American Community Survey 2010 5-Year; 3) Happold Consulting, 2000-2010

DEVELOPMENT TYPES

FLEX

F

WAREHOUSE

W

ARTISANAL

A

SAMPLE LIFESTYLE ILLUSTRATIONS FOR LIVE+MAKE NEIGHBORHOODS

NEIGHBORHOOD ILLUSTRATION

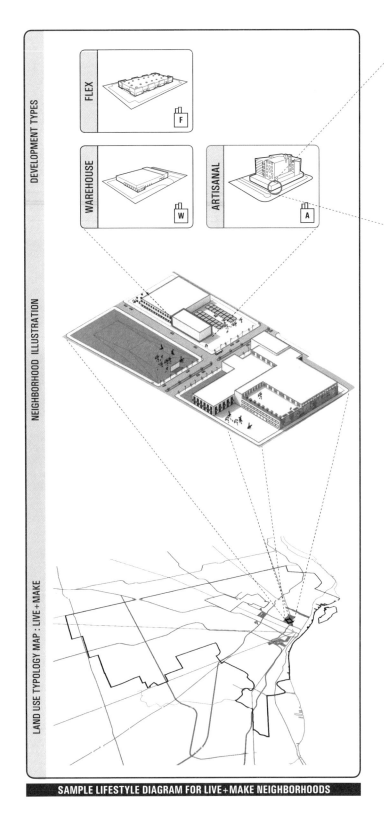

LAND USE TYPOLOGY MAP : LIVE+MAKE

SAMPLE LIFESTYLE DIAGRAM FOR LIVE+MAKE NEIGHBORHOODS

The adjacent illustration explains how each neighborhood type lays out a series of implementation actions necessary to achieve its land use vision. The implementation actions are organized around quality of elements prioritized for that typology. A range of appropriate development types for each neighborhood type is also included to ensure that new development supports the larger neighborhood vision.

"Make unique neighborhoods. Some of the world's best cities are known for their unique, walkable neighborhoods/ districts that connect to each other via rail, bus, bike etc."

Antonio, Planning Cluster Meetings, 1/27/2011

"I imagine [the] Detroit that amazed me when I was a child in the '70s! The well-kept neighborhoods and businesses. The Downtown area full of shopping and tourists."

Eva, Town Hall Meeting, 1/29/2011

STRATEGIES AND IMPLEMENTATION
MOVING FROM CONDITIONS TODAY TO MORE DESIRABLE NEIGHBORHOODS FOR ALL

HOW TO USE THIS CHAPTER. The Neighborhoods Element of the Detroit Strategic Framework draws from and supports the Land Use Element. Like the Land Use Element, the Neighborhoods Element articulates a range of options for existing and new types of land uses (focused, in this case, on residential neighborhoods). The Neighborhoods Element extends the discussion toward quality-of-life measures and the performance of neighborhoods, in recognition that community and technical experts will need to engage in participatory planning and ongoing, fine-grained evaluation to strengthen, create, and sustain Detroit's neighborhoods in ways unique to each and every one. Such collaborative work will require patience, time, and significant investment resources from many sectors, including government, nonprofit groups, neighborhood organizations, philanthropic organizations, business leaders, social support systems such as schools and service providers, and cultural groups.

The following pages describe citywide and neighborhood-based strategies to address the quality-of-life issues Detroit residents face. There are five major neighborhood types: Urban Mixed Use, Urban Live+Make, Urban Green, Traditional Neighborhoods, and Alternative Use. Within each neighborhood type, a map shows where these neighborhoods will be located in the 50-year land use horizon. Associated with each neighborhood type is a series of strategies organized around addressing the quality-of-life issues specific to that neighborhood, and also intended to help neighborhoods achieve their vision for a vibrant and more sustainable future. The prioritized quality-of-life elements for each neighborhood type were developed through a combination of the civic engagement outreach and the planning expertise of the technical planning team. The strategies reflect public comments collected from a vast array of civic engagement tactics as well as precedents, best practices, and current initiatives within the community. Creating priorities for each neighborhood type helps focus limited resources to best address the quality-of-life issues specific to each type of neighborhood. Through the civic engagement process, it also became evident that certain quality-of-life issues are universal to all parts of the city. These issues—including public safety, education, prosperity/income, and physical condition, among others—are addressed under a full list of strategic interventions in the citywide strategies.

For each neighborhood type, a two-part illustration depicts (1) the necessary steps to stabilize that neighborhood, and (2) the strategies that can transform that neighborhood to achieve a vision for a better future. Stabilization strategies are geared towards stemming the tide of population loss and degradation of a neighborhood's physical condition. Stabilization strategies within a specific neighborhood should be used in combination with citywide strategies that address public safety and improve education to have the greatest immediate impact. Strategies that transform neighborhoods are geared toward improving quality of life by building on the unique assets, resources, and community capacity associated with a particular neighborhood. The strategies for both stabilization and transformation are supplemented with current initiatives and proposed pilot projects that are well aligned with the overarching quality-of-life goals of the neighborhood. Many of the tactics necessary to improve quality of life in the city are already being tried and tested, but the Detroit Strategic Framework seeks to leverage these initiatives and expand their application to other neighborhoods when they are proven successful. Each neighborhood type has a Development Types Table that lays out which framework zones and development types are most compatible with that neighborhood. For instance, in a Live+Make neighborhood, the most appropriate form of residential development is limited to the adaptive reuse of industrial buildings for new multi-family residential uses; new single-family housing development would not be in keeping with the vision for the neighborhood typology. However, within a Live+Make neighborhood, there is a wider array of industrial and landscape uses possible in order to encourage innovation, entrepreneurship, and economic growth. This development prioritization can help community development organizations, public leadership, and private developers steer resources to the most appropriate areas of the city to improve quality of life.

FIVE TRANSFORMATIVE IDEAS : SIX IMPLEMENTATION STRATEGIES

| **A** | **ADDRESS QUALITY-OF-LIFE CHALLENGES THAT AFFECT ALL DETROITERS** |

Certain challenges facing Detroit's neighborhoods cut across all parts of the city. They include public safety, education, health, and city services. While there may be place-based strategies to address these issues in specific neighborhoods, a larger set of coordinated strategies must be developed to address these challenges on a citywide scale. Similarly, effective strategies developed in one neighborhood hold the potential to benefit neighborhoods across the city. **The citywide strategies represent recommendations that can be applied within all of Detroit's neighborhoods.** Many of these recommendations came directly from Detroit residents and neighborhood organizations who witness the challenges to their neighborhoods on a daily basis. This set of strategies contains the seeds of change to improve quality of life across all neighborhoods that will need further development as the Detroit Strategic Framework moves into implementation.

| **B** | **CREATE DENSE, WALKABLE, MIXED-USE NEIGHBORHOODS** |

URBAN MIXED USE NEIGHBORHOODS seek to leverage employment districts to create higher-density, mixed-use residential communities. Growth in these areas builds on the economic engine of medical centers, universities, industry, and corporations to catalyze future residential, retail, and economic development. These areas include the Central Business District, Midtown, New Center, and the McNichols corridor. **The character of these districts is shaped by the major cultural and institutional assets within them, including high-quality parks and public spaces, museums, theaters, stadiums, and schools.** Urban Mixed Use districts are the hubs of a regional transit network that can connect the city to the larger region, state, and Detroit Metropolitan airport.

| **C** | **REGENERATE NEIGHBORHOODS THROUGH FUSION OF ART AND INDUSTRY** |

URBAN LIVE+MAKE NEIGHBORHOODS are built from functionally obsolete industrial areas within the city. The spaces afforded by former industrial buildings allow for their creative reuse for a wide range of entrepreneurial and artistic uses. Residential lofts may be incorporated into the redevelopment, but **the focus of the district is on entrepreneurship, creativity, and innovation, leading to new forms of business, production, art, and lifestyle.** Open space on the fringes of these districts provides opportunity for research or artistic exploration and events. These areas reinvent entrepreneurship for the 21st century within the space of discarded 20th century industry.

COMPOSITE LAND USE MAP: 50 YEAR HORIZON

1 2   4 MILES

URBAN MIXED USE LAND USE TYPOLOGIES

CITY CENTER
DISTRICT CENTER

URBAN LIVE+MAKE LAND USE TYPOLOGIES

LIVE+MAKE

D REPURPOSE VACANT LAND TO CREATE GREEN NEIGHBORHOODS

E RENEW TRADITIONAL NEIGHBORHOODS

F UTILIZE PRODUCTIVE LANDSCAPES AS THE BASIS FOR A SUSTAINABLE CITY

URBAN GREEN NEIGHBORHOODS take landscape as the predominant transformational development. **These neighborhoods transform a perceived liability (vacant land) at multiple scales, from the individual side lot to interconnected greenways, integrating it with the residential fabric of the neighborhood.** Central to these neighborhoods is the creation of a unified, neighborhood-scale vision for repurposing its land and rebuilding community.

TRADITIONAL NEIGHBORHOODS. Today a large percentage of the city consists of traditional neighborhoods made up of detached single-family homes on tree-lined streets, and ringed by commercial corridors. However, many of these neighborhoods have lost some of their luster as residents have left, foreclosures have occurred, and the cost of maintaining the physical environment has placed a major burden on residents. Traditional Neighborhoods need improvements to their city systems and infrastructure to make them competitive with peer neighborhoods in the region. **When transformation is achieved in these neighborhoods, by all appearances they will be competitive with their regional peers, but the means and methods to have achieved their transformation will be different.**

ALTERNATIVE USE AREAS are areas that are anticipated to see declining population and the expansion of vacant land. Given the challenges associated with very high-vacancy, many people living in these areas would move to a safer, amenity-rich neighborhood if provided the opportunity. At the same time, many residents have a loyal devotion to their properties and larger communities. While the opportunity to rebuild these neighborhoods into what they were is no longer a possibility, action must be taken to improve the quality of life for residents who will continue to live in these areas. **These areas hold the potential for reinvention through new productive land uses, and the rights of existing residents must be upheld by integrally involving residents in the reinvention process.**

URBAN GREEN
LAND USE TYPOLOGIES

GREEN MIXED-RISE
GREEN RESIDENTIAL

TRADITIONAL
RESIDENTIAL
LAND USE TYPOLOGIES

TRAD. LOW-DENSITY
TRAD. MEDIUM-DENSITY
NEIGHBORHOOD CENTER

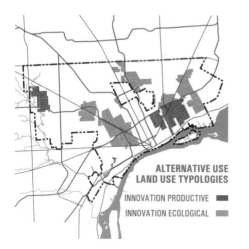

ALTERNATIVE USE
LAND USE TYPOLOGIES

INNOVATION PRODUCTIVE
INNOVATION ECOLOGICAL

"Help create a plan for building new, viable, self-sustaining communities of the future with an emphasis on changing the culture of our youth... by promoting the development of a community workforce that will help improve the quality of life for city residents within their neighborhoods and communities. The goal is to build healthy, strong, vibrant, self-sustaining neighborhoods and communities in Detroit."

Ann, Planning Cluster Meeting, 2/5/2011

CITYWIDE STRATEGIES may be applied within any or all neighborhood types. Many citywide strategies should be deployed in conjunction with more specific neighborhood-based strategies. For example, safety strategies are fundamental to the long-term stabilization and transformation of all neighborhood types. They should be given priority in all neighborhoods, and used in conjunction with more place-based, neighborhood-specific strategies (such as neighborhood stabilization around public and charter schools). Many of the citywide strategies were collected directly from the recommendations of city residents. They reflect the community's collective response to the issues that most directly affect residents on a daily basis.

PRIORITIZED CITYWIDE STRATEGIES

SAFETY

1. Institute citywide, neighborhood-based CompStat program.[1]
2. Realign police districts and station locations with current population densities.
3. Incorporate Crime Prevention Through Environmental Design (CPTED) standards.
4. Establish dedicated police liaison for each neighborhood.
5. Create systems to coordinate community-based, institutional and public safety networks.

EDUCATION

1. Co-locate community learning centers within existing successful public and charter schools.
2. Develop comprehensive community-based schools program and implement corresponding pilot projects.
3. Develop continuing education programs to focus job training around emerging local economies.[2]

PROSPERITY AND INCOME

1. Develop programs that prioritize hiring of Detroit residents.
2. Leverage capabilities of local immigrant workforce by expediting naturalization process for permanent residents.
3. Train prisoner reentry work force to participate in the implementation of citywide DFC pilot projects.
4. Provide mentorship to steer informal economies towards business-to-business (B2B) opportunities.
5. Incentivize neighborhood-based entrepreneurial businesses.

HEALTH

1. Assess citywide ground conditions and feasibility of urban agriculture.
2. Empower nonprofits to coordinate citywide urban food systems initiatives.[3]
3. Leverage local food system economies through expanded institutional Buy Local programs.
4. Prioritize establishment of connected citywide greenway systems.

COMMUNITY AND IDENTITY

1. Establish policy and funding to organize block clubs, neighborhood organizations, and community development organizations (CDOs) to implement the Strategic Framework.[4]
2. Create neighborhood-based, publicly accessible database of land ownership, vacancy, and building conditions to hold private owners responsible to communities for maintenance of properties.[5]
3. Create a neighborhood resource kit that provides financial, legal, real estate, and economic development resources tailored to each community.
4. Utilize co-located community learn center space to centralize all components of the neighborhood resource kit.
5. Provide support to neighborhood-based events and festivals.

PHYSICAL CONDITION

1. Prioritize code enforcement programs targeting absentee property owners and landlords.
2. Prioritize neighborhood stabilization programs within ⅓ mile of community-based schools.
3. Coordinate large-scale deconstruction pilot projects.
4. Develop expedited side lot and adopt-a-lot disposition programs.
5. Develop coordinated citywide, neighborhood-based vacancy management program addressing preservation of historic structures and maintenance of vacant land.

ADDRESS QUALITY-OF-LIFE CHALLENGES THAT AFFECT ALL DETROITERS

PRIORITIZED CITYWIDE STRATEGIES

MOBILITY

1   Develop tiered transit hierarchy to improve overall service delivery.

2   Incentivize development of on-demand, non-fixed route feeder services including mini- and micro-bus services.

3   Improve bus stops and facilities for bus riders.

4   Expand use of information apps providing real time service information.

5   Create transit lane network with priority signalization.

6   Prioritize development of Complete Streets as part of all right-of-way improvements.

HOUSING

1   Implement home ownership programs focused on incentivizing market demand.

2   Extend demand benefits to ensure retention of existing residents.[6]

3   Assess and address the city's current property tax system.

4   Provide online tools to streamline review and payment plans for tax foreclosed properties.

RETAIL SERVICES AND AMENITIES

1   Incentivize strategic nodal development of retail services and amenities.

2   Develop corridor design standards to improve visual appearance and walkability.

3   Create policy constraints that restrict the number of liquor and lotto stores that do not offer affordable fresh food or healthy options.

ENVIRONMENT

1   Prioritize reuse of vacant land for blue infrastructure.

2   Prioritize reuse of vacant land as industrial buffers and carbon forests.

3   Prioritize the strategic remediation of contaminated sites.

RECREATION

1   Complete additional phases of existing greenway systems to create a connected, citywide network.[7]

2   Promote alternative park maintenance strategies such as adopt-a-park where community capacity exists.

PUBLIC SERVICES

1   Implement infrastructure strategies recommended by the Strategic Framework.

2   Facilitate establishment of business improvement districts and special assessment districts where neighborhood interest exists.

3   Implement a citywide recycling program.

CULTURE

1   Establish long-term, dedicated funding sources to cultural institutions.

2   Support neighborhood-based public art.

Precedents and Examples: 1) Detroit Police Department, Wayne State University, Detroit Medical Center, Henry Ford Hospital System; 2) Deconstruction, agriculture, advanced manufacturing, etc.; 3) Detroit Food Policy Council; 4) Community Development Advocates of Detroit, Black Family Development; 5) Data Driven Detroit Neighborhood Parcel Tool; 5) Data Driven Detroit Neighborhood Parcel Tool; 6) Greater mortgage availability, marketing, homeowner equity insurance, etc. 7) Detroit RiverWalk, Dequindre Cut greenway, Southwest bike lanes

THE NEIGHBORHOOD ELEMENT : : THE CITY OF DISTINCT AND REGIONALLY COMPETITIVE NEIGHBORHOODS

CREATE DENSE, WALKABLE, MIXED-USE NEIGHBORHOODS

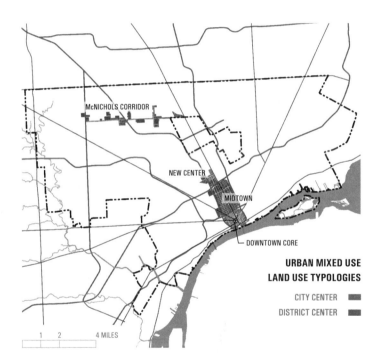

**URBAN MIXED USE
LAND USE TYPOLOGIES**

CITY CENTER
DISTRICT CENTER

URBAN MIXED USE NEIGHBORHOODS include the City Center and District Center land use typologies. These neighborhoods strive to achieve the highest densities of residential population in the city within active commercial environments. Employment opportunities around retail, office, medical, and education abound and should be leveraged to increase the residential population and create a 24/7 mixed-use environment. A wide variety of incubator space is available for small-business start-ups. These neighborhood types offer high-quality retail services and amenities in a walkable environment that is well connected to bus and rail transit networks, as well as bikeways and pedestrian routes. Public space improvements to parks and along streets will include sidewalk cafes, public art, and pocket parks, providing the catalyst for more active streets and future residential and commercial development opportunities.

In addition to the active street life associated with dense urban living and vibrant retail districts, Urban Mixed Use supports a wide range of cultural and recreational amenities to attract residents and visitors. Support for existing and future artistic, cultural, and historic institutions is critical to fostering community identity and achieving long-term goals for quality of life. Creative, innovative, and artistic uses should be encouraged in addition to preservation and adaptive reuse of historic structures to celebrate the authentic and unique assets of each district. Equitable development ensures that each district will support a diverse population of existing residents and new residents within a wide range of racial, ethnic, age, and income levels.

225

THE NEIGHBORHOOD ELEMENT : THE CITY OF DISTINCT AND REGIONALLY COMPETITIVE NEIGHBORHOODS

URBAN MIXED USE NEIGHBORHOOD STRATEGIES

PRIORITIZED QUALITY-OF-LIFE ELEMENTS AND STRATEGIES FOR URBAN MIXED–USE NEIGHBORHOODS

HOUSING

1   Establish density targets and focus development in high-density areas.

2   Leverage major employers and anchor institutions to create residential market demand incentives in geographies targeted for population growth.[1]

3   Implement tax abatement and other buyer incentives to incentivize demand in target development areas.

4   Create and utilize gap financing mechanisms to enable development of mixed income/mixed-use multi-family developments and build market strength.[2]

5   Incentivize adaptive reuse of historic structures to preserve authenticity of districts.

6   Target 20% low to moderate income units in key new development to ensure mixed-income communities.

7   Leverage federal and state programs[3] to develop mixed-income communities around public housing and adjacent neighborhoods.[4]

8   Develop and incentivize green building standards for new construction and retrofit development.

RETAIL SERVICES AND AMENITIES

1   Incentivize retail nodes to create walkable retail districts.[5]

2   Create mixed-use design guidelines to ensure retail design that reinforces walkable districts.

3   Develop, fund, and sustain programs that support entrepreneurship and small business start-ups.[6]

4   Support pop-up retail initiatives as catalysts to permanent future retail districts.

5   Work with CDOs to establish retail recruitment programs to ensure mix of high quality retail services and amenities.

6   Establish and fund comprehensive retail development packages that include recruitment, site selection/acquisition, employee training, interior/exterior renovations, infrastructure improvements, and start-up costs in identified retail districts.

RECREATION

1   Incorporate public space improvements to catalyze areas targeted for new development.[7]

2   Establish programming and park improvements around prioritized city parks.[8]

3   Design, construct, and connect network of bike paths and greenways within the public right-of-way.[9]

CULTURE

1   Secure long-term funding for major city/regional cultural attractions.[10]

2   Develop, market, and fund local ecosystem of arts organizations.[11]

3   Develop and support events that promote creative culture and unique Detroit assets.[12]

PUBLIC SERVICES

1   "Upgrade and Maintain" city systems infrastructure per City Systems Element to accommodate increased future residential capacity and expanded employment districts.

2   Prioritized renewal of public lighting grid around high-density residential areas, employment centers, and major event locations.

MOBILITY

1   Prioritize completion of the M-1 Rail streetcar project.

2   Establish downtown as hub of the regional transit system.

3   Tie in multimodal connections at the New Center commuter rail station.

4   Prioritize frequent, dependable crosstown bus service along the McNichols corridor.

"Increase the attractiveness for young professionals and businesses to locate Downtown by promoting a strong retail environment for locally-owned businesses, in addition to cultural and sports amenities.

Kristin, Planning Cluster-based Meetings, 1/2011-3/2011

Precedents and Examples: 1) Live Midtown/Downtown; 2) Tax credits, grants, low interest loans and other subsidies; 3) U.S. Department of Housing and Urban Development's Choice Neighborhoods program; 4) Potential locations: Brush Park, Brewster Douglass; 5) Potential locations: Woodward, Cass Corridor, Livernois, Vernor 6) D-hive. HATCH Detroit; 7) Capitol Park, RiverWalk, Livernois Streetscape; 8) Think Detroit PAL (Police Athletic League), Detroit Futbol League, New Center Park events, Friends of Palmer Park, Clark Park Coalition; 9) City of Detroit Non-Motorized Transportation Plan, Dequindre Cut Greenway, Midtown Loop; 10) Tri-County Detroit Institute of Art millage, Tri-County Detroit Zoo millage; 11) Detroit Creative Corridor Center; 12) Detroit Design Festival, Movement, Dally in the Alley

PRECEDENTS

1 Live Downtown / Live Midtown: Detroit

2 DLECTRICITY: Detroit

The tables below describe the range of appropriate Framework Zones, neighborhood typologies, and development types for Urban Mixed Use neighborhoods. They are intended to focus development to the appropriate locations within the city to achieve the overall land use vision for these neighborhoods.

EARLY ACTION

1 M-1 Rail Streetcar Project

FRAMEWORK ZONES

Greater Downtown

Low-Vacancy 1

PILOT PROJECT

1 Comprehensive Retail District Program

TYPOLOGIES

City Center Only

District Center Only

Appropriate for both Typologies

APPROPRIATE DEVELOPMENT TYPES

RESIDENTIAL

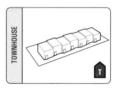 TOWNHOUSE — T

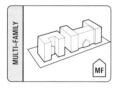 MULTI-FAMILY — MF

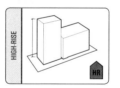 HIGH-RISE — HR

RETAIL

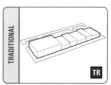 TRADITIONAL — TR

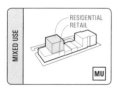 MIXED USE — MU (RESIDENTIAL, RETAIL)

BLUE AND GREEN INFRASTRUCTURE

 SMALL RETENTION — BG

 STORMWATER BLVD. — BG

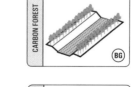 CARBON FOREST — BG

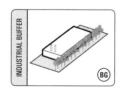 INDUSTRIAL BUFFER — BG

COMMUNITY OPEN SPACES

PARKS — CO

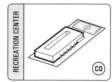 PLAZA — CO

RECREATION CENTER — CO

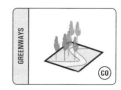 GREENWAYS — CO

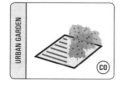 URBAN GARDEN — CO

CURRENT: URBAN MIXED USE NEIGHBORHOODS TODAY

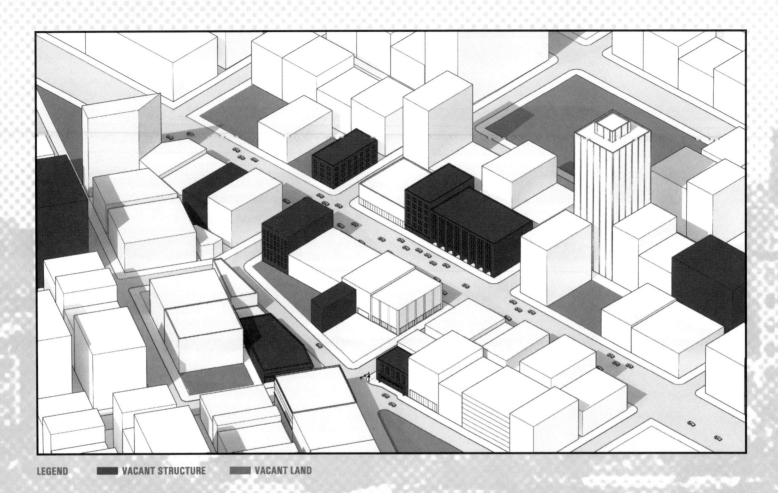

LEGEND ■ VACANT STRUCTURE ■ VACANT LAND

URBAN MIXED USE CURRENT CONDITIONS

Urban Mixed Use neighborhoods are characterized by their adjacency to major commercial, educational, and medical employment anchors. These employment anchors act as catalysts to future mixed-use growth, including residential and retail development. While these areas frequently have many of the ingredients necessary for a mixed-use environment, including some existing multi-family housing, pedestrian-scaled retail, and proximity to transit, these areas still lack the commercial and residential densities to support a more vibrant urban environment.

Short-term efforts will focus on greatly increasing the number of residents in these specific areas. The use of specific financing tools will be critical first steps to establishing market-rate development. Preserving and adapting existing structures should be a priority so that each neighborhood can retain its authentic character. Strategic investment in parks and public spaces can spark new commercial and residential development. City systems would be upgraded to support the establishment of the employment districts and accommodate increased residential

density. Light rail and Bus Rapid Transit would serve major connections between these neighborhoods and others. Connectivity would be supported by major crosstown bus routes, connections to a citywide system of bicycle routes, and opportunities to walk places.

PROPOSED: URBAN MIXED USE NEIGHBORHOODS IN 50 YEARS

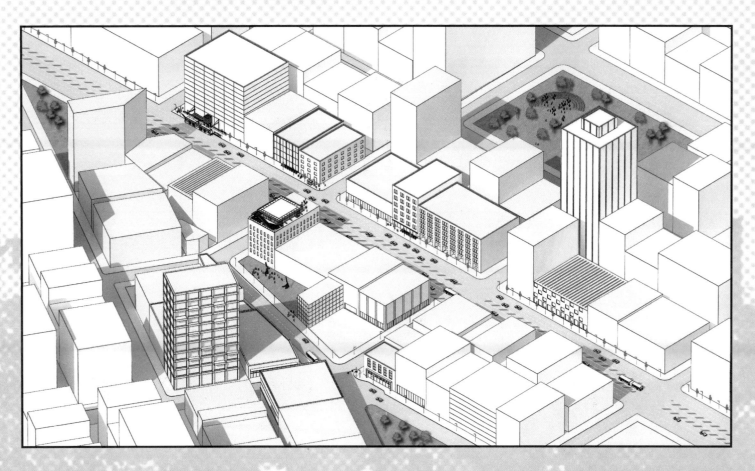

URBAN MIXED USE LONG-TERM VISION

Once unsubsidized market-rate development is established, the focus will be on using development to reinforce the specific identity of each mixed-use district. Eds and Meds serve as anchor institutions to vibrant walkable communities in Midtown and throughout the McNichols corridor. Private-sector investment around the Digital/Creative firms catalyzes growth in the downtown. New green building standards or design guidelines establish Detroit at the cutting edge of energy and environmental design issues. Similarly long-term funding sources for both major cultural institutions and small, independent arts organizations should be secured to solidify Detroit's place as a cultural center both nationally and internationally. As residents return and visitors discover these destinations, retail districts in these neighborhoods will serve residents and attract shoppers from the city, region, and state. To attract high-quality stores, a comprehensive retail start-up package will need to be assembled that focuses on the most appropriate retail types for each such district. A combination of access to bus rapid transit, conventional buses, zip cars, and in some cases light rail, will be offered in Mixed Use districts to provide efficient connections within the city, as well as to the region and Detroit Metro Airport.

1. Incorporate multi-modal transportation options including light rail, bus rapid transit, bike lanes, and car sharing to better connect residents to jobs and amenities.

2. Provide incentives to create density through new infill construction or adaptive reuse of historic structures for residential and commercial uses.

3. Develop walkable retail nodes with services and amenities to support neighborhood residents and attract citywide and regional visitors.

4. Incorporate high-quality public spaces to act as civic gathering spaces and catalyze new development.

THE NEIGHBORHOOD ELEMENT : THE CITY OF DISTINCT AND REGIONALLY COMPETITIVE NEIGHBORHOODS

"Our architectural heritage is our least appreciated asset."

William, Planning Cluster-based Meeting, 1/27/2011

"I love that Detroit has a world-class art museum that engages with the community. Art is vital to the health and growth of strong communities...having a solid foundation in the arts is one of the strengths of Detroit."

Ashley, Detroit 24/7 "Beautiful Detroit," 5/2012

PILOT PROJECT

COMPREHENSIVE RETAIL DISTRICT PROGRAM

Establish and fund comprehensive retail development packages that include site selection/acquisition, employee training, interior/exterior renovations, infrastructure improvements, and start-up costs in identified retail districts.

Image Source: Hamilton Anderson Associates

URBAN MIXED-USE NEIGHBORHOODS PROVIDE NEW BUSINESS AND ENTREPRENEURSHIP OPPORTUNITIES FOR ALL DETROITERS

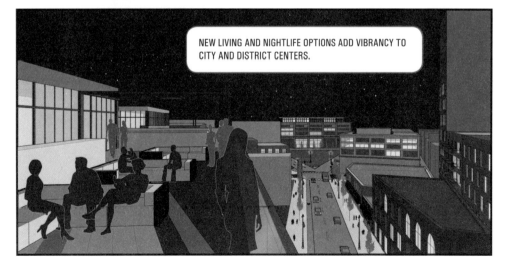

NEW LIVING AND NIGHTLIFE OPTIONS ADD VIBRANCY TO CITY AND DISTRICT CENTERS.

PRECEDENT

DLECTRICITY

DLECTRICITY is Detroit's new contemporary light festival that debuted in 2012. Receiving 200+ entries from around the world, DLECTRICITY sponsors selected 35 artists and designers to illuminate the historic architecture of Midtown for this weekend event.

Image Source: Marvin Shaouni

STRATEGIES AND IMPLEMENTATION

M-1 RAIL STREETCAR PROJECT

The M-1 rail streetcar project is an opportunity to invest in the future of Detroit with an efficient and modern transit alternative that reestablishes key linkages among downtown, cultural destinations, health and educational facilities, and stadia. It will complement and support intercity passenger rail services and future envisioned bus rapid transit within the region.

Image Source: M-1 Rail

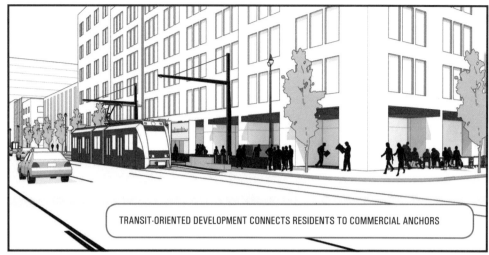

TRANSIT-ORIENTED DEVELOPMENT CONNECTS RESIDENTS TO COMMERCIAL ANCHORS

"Having nodes of commercial areas are great for place-making."
Neighborhoods Working Session, 6/6/2012

A MIXTURE OF USES AND GREATER DENSITY CAN SUPPORT INNOVATIVE TRANSIT ALTERNATIVES SUCH AS BIKE-SHARE AND CAR-SHARE PROGRAMS LIKE "ZIP CAR"

LIVE MIDTOWN/DOWNTOWN

In effort to repopulate and improve quality of life in Midtown and Downtown Detroit, several anchor institutions have offered their employees incentives to relocate to these districts. These programs have been wildly successful, with not enough supply of multifamily housing to meet demand.

Text Source: Joann Muller, www.forbes.com
Image Source: Hamilton Anderson Associates

MIXED-USE DEVELOPMENT INTEGRATES RESIDENTIAL LIVING WITH IMPORTANT FUNCTIONS, INCLUDING RETAIL SERVICES AND CULTURAL DESTINATIONS

Image Source: Hamilton Anderson Associates

231

THE NEIGHBORHOOD ELEMENT : THE CITY OF DISTINCT AND REGIONALLY COMPETITIVE NEIGHBORHOODS

REGENERATE NEIGHBORHOODS THROUGH FUSION OF ART AND INDUSTRY

LIVE+MAKE LAND USE TYPOLOGY

LIVE+MAKE ▬

1 2   4 MILES

EASTERN MARKET

CORKTOWN

LIVE+MAKE NEIGHBORHOODS occur within or next to formerly industrial areas. Vacant industrial buildings, at times historic in character, provide space for economic, creative, or productive reinvention. Entrepreneurship and artistic expression are celebrated as integral components of district identity. Residential uses are mixed with productive uses, providing the opportunity for either residential loft conversion or flex space within new development. Research, small-scale production, and commercial activities stimulate economic growth and entrepreneurship. These districts also provide opportunity for jobs and skills training around emerging economies such as computer numeric control (CNC) fabrication and advanced manufacturing. While limited, commercial activities and production/artisanal retail are integrated to create a greater mix of uses and stimulate more active streets and public spaces. Tax and regulatory structures should be modified to give incentives for entrepreneurship in these areas.

In less dense areas of Live+Make, where there is greater availability of vacant land, landscape-based productive uses such as agriculture, research plots, aquaculture, and energy fields are encouraged. To address environmental issues associated with former industrial areas, environmental remediation of brownfield sites and integration of green technologies associated with the growth of new industries within the district are highly encouraged. These districts are also suitable for establishment of university-sponsored research programs or extension locations.

URBAN LIVE+MAKE NEIGHBORHOOD STRATEGIES

PROSPERITY AND INCOME

1   Establish programs that provide resources and skills development training around unique local economies such as deconstruction, urban agriculture, CNC manufacturing, etc.[1]

2   Incentivize adaptive reuse of obsolete or historic industrial buildings to develop new productive uses.[2]

3   Offer comprehensive support system for new business start-ups.

4   Provide incentives for new business start-up including, but not limited to tax abatement.

5   Relax business start-up and use regulations to allow a greater array of commercial activity and promote informal economy.

ENVIRONMENT

1   Incentivize brownfield remediation as part of redevelopment costs.

2   Prioritize open space uses that remediate contaminated soils.

3   Prioritize locations for blue infrastructure pilot projects.

4   Prioritize locations for experimental green technology and research pilot projects.

CULTURE

2   Promote arts and events spaces and landscapes.[3]

3   Identify and organize arts or gallery districts.

4   Curate and fund the creation of public art.[4]

COMMUNITY

1   Establish / empower CDOs and public and private stakeholders to oversee district vision and implementation.

2   Promote unique district identity based on existing assets.

3   Incorporate public space/community gathering space as part of district visions.

PUBLIC SERVICES

1   "Upgrade and Maintain" city systems infrastructure per City Systems chapter to meet demands of new productive uses and increased residential capacity.

HOUSING

1   Prioritize gap financing for adaptive reuse of industrial structures as multi-use spaces, including residential lofts.

"I think it's great when artists are able to harness their visions and engage community in meaningful ways. You can see that in the Power House neighborhood, in the North End, and in the Artist Village in Brightmoor."

George, Detroit 24/7 "Strengthening Community," 5/2012

Precedents and Examples: 1) Focus: HOPE; 2) Russell Industrial Center; 3) Detroit Design Festival, Art Basel Miami Beach; 4) Lincoln Street Sculpture Park, Wynwood Arts District Miami

PRECEDENTS

1 Ponyride: Detroit
2 Roosevelt Park: Detroit
3 Red Bull House of Art: Detroit

EARLY ACTIONS

1 Recovery Park
2 Bloody Run Creek

PILOT PROJECT

1 Live+Make co-housing development

The tables below describe the range of appropriate Framework Zones, neighborhood typologies, and development types for Live+Make neighborhoods. They are intended to focus development to the appropriate locations within the city to achieve the overall land use vision for these neighborhoods.

FRAMEWORK ZONES

Industrial Land Use Change

High-Vacancy

TYPOLOGIES

☐ Live+Make

APPROPRIATE DEVELOPMENT TYPES

RESIDENTIAL

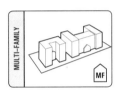 MULTI-FAMILY — MF

RETAIL

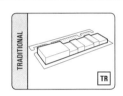 TRADITIONAL — TR

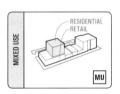 MIXED USE — MU (RESIDENTIAL RETAIL)

INDUSTRIAL

 ARTISANAL — A

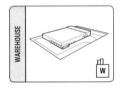 WAREHOUSE — W

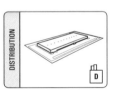 DISTRIBUTION — D

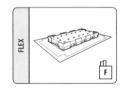 FLEX — F

BLUE AND GREEN INFRASTRUCTURE

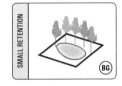 SMALL RETENTION — BG

 STORMWATER BLVD. — BG

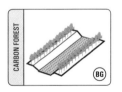 CARBON FOREST — BG

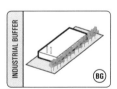 INDUSTRIAL BUFFER — BG

COMMUNITY OPEN SPACES

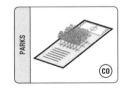 PARKS — CO

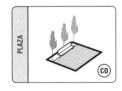 PLAZA — CO

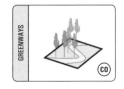 GREENWAYS — CO

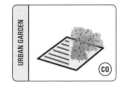 URBAN GARDEN — CO

TRANSITIONAL LANDSCAPES

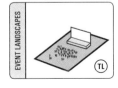 EVENT LANDSCAPES — TL

 ARTSCAPES — TL

 PHYTOREMEDIATION — TL

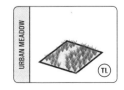 URBAN MEADOW — TL

235

THE NEIGHBORHOOD ELEMENT : THE CITY OF DISTINCT AND REGIONALLY COMPETITIVE NEIGHBORHOODS

CURRENT: LIVE+MAKE NEIGHBORHOODS TODAY

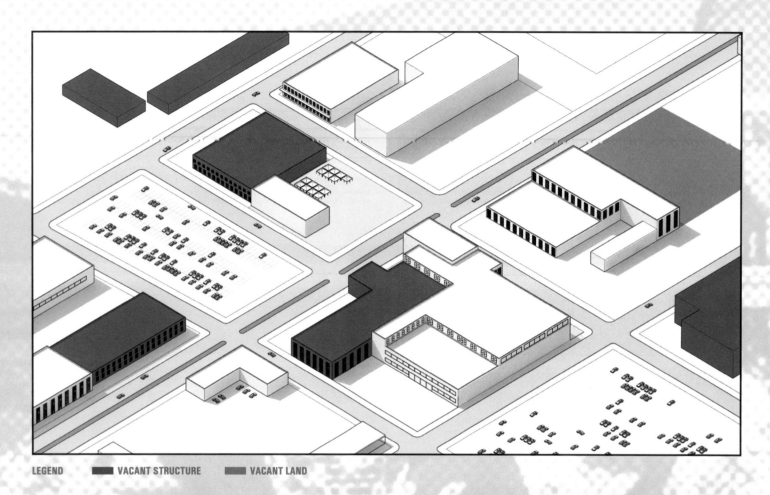

LEGEND ▬ VACANT STRUCTURE ▬ VACANT LAND

LIVE+MAKE CURRENT CONDITIONS

Places designated as potential Live+Make neighborhoods are characterized by vacant and functionally obsolete industrial buildings, interspersed among vacant land and surface parking. Few, if any, residents live in these areas now. Existing businesses within Live+Make neighborhoods tend to be open during set business hours, but upon closing, leave these areas feeling desolate and abandoned. Street infrastructure has largely been left unmaintained, and there are few pedestrian-scaled public spaces.

Initial strategies should focus on creating the environment for entrepreneurship, small modern production and creative expression. Priority should be placed on public infrastructure improvements, including streets, sidewalks, and lighting to promote safety and walkability within the district. Development financing should be identified for the adaptive reuse of industrial buildings for new productive uses. Where environmental conditions impede future redevelopment of the district, brownfield and environmental remediation will be needed. Arts-related events should be actively programmed to promote the identity and culture of the district.

PROPOSED: LIVE+MAKE NEIGHBORHOODS IN 50 YEARS

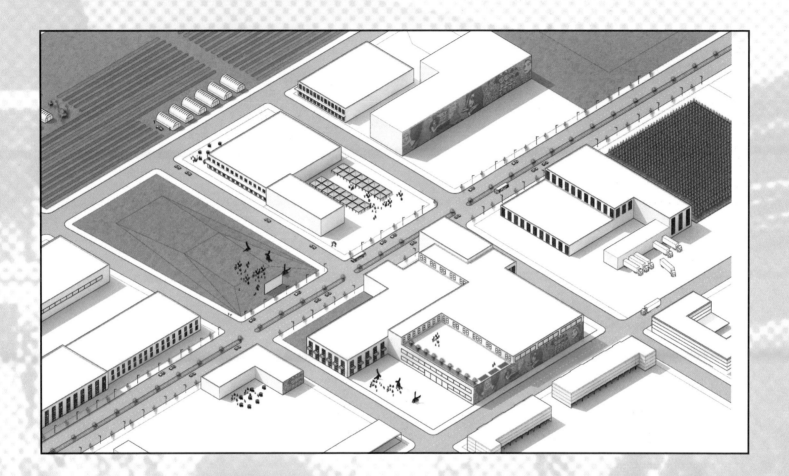

LIVE+MAKE LONG-TERM VISION

The transformation of Live+Make neighborhoods is primarily focused on giving people ample opportunity to imagine, invent, and create new forms of industry and art. Incentives packages, including development of support networks and start-up funding/financing, should be developed to lure artists, small businesses and entrepreneurs to the district. Regulatory frameworks should be put in place to allow a wide range of uses while still protecting public health, safety, and well-being. To support the innovative and entrepreneurial endeavors within these districts, skills and jobs training could be integrated in some Live+Make districts to allow employment creation at all levels of education and experience. As with the Innovation areas, the public space of Live+Make districts also has the potential to act as research incubators for experimentation around new green technologies or blue and green infrastructure. Outside of employment districts or areas where residential use is already growing, Live+Make neighborhoods should renew city systems at a reduced capacity to meet lower industrial and residential demands from its former intensive industrial uses.

1. Adaptive reuse of obsolete vacant or underutilized industrial buildings for entrepreneurial activity, artisanal production or residential dwelling.

2. Repurpose large-scale vacant land for Live+Grow opportunities that tie into adjacent networked entrepreneurial activities: warehousing, distribution, and commercial uses.

3. Remediate contaminated former industrial land by integrating phytoremediation and other landscape-based uses.

4. Define and program outdoor event spaces to establish neighborhood identity.

237

THE NEIGHBORHOOD ELEMENT : THE CITY OF DISTINCT AND REGIONALLY COMPETITIVE NEIGHBORHOODS

THE ADAPTIVE REUSE OF VACANT INDUSTRIAL BUILDINGS INTO WORKFORCE TRAINING SPACES SUPPORTS SMALL BUSINESS BY PROVIDING OPPORTUNITIES FOR BOTH YOUTHS AND ADULTS

NEW TRAINING FACILITIES FOR MODERN INDUSTRIES, INCLUDING DIGITAL DESIGN FABRICATION

PONYRIDE

"Ponyride nurtures collaboration using shared resources, knowledge, and ideas to cultivate opportunities created by the strengths and crises of Detroit. They engage a diverse group of creative socially conscious entrepreneurs giving them the opportunity for production, community outreach, and education."

Image and Text Source: Ponyride

ROOSEVELT PARK

Renovations to the park adjacent to the Michigan Central Depot provide a shared public open space amenity for the local community and visitors alike. The Park provides a venue for various organized arts, music, food, and athletic events throughout the year.

Image Source: UrbanDetail

CREATE OUTDOOR PUBLIC EVENT SPACE FOR FESTIVALS, DIY FAIRS, AND THE ARTS

CONVERSION OF FORMER INDUSTRIAL BUILDING INTO CONDO UNITS FOR BOTH LIVING AND WORKING

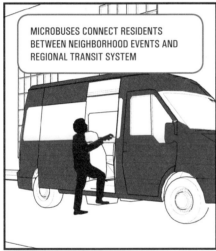

MICROBUSES CONNECT RESIDENTS BETWEEN NEIGHBORHOOD EVENTS AND REGIONAL TRANSIT SYSTEM

LIVE-MAKE NEIGHBORHOODS FOSTER INNOVATION, CREATIVITY AND COLLABORATION

Image Source: Ponyride

239

PRECEDENT

RED BULL HOUSE OF ART

This artist residency program provides Detroit-area artists with studio space, supplies, and support to expand their personal work. Red Bull intends to provide an authentic platform for the local artist community to grow through exposure and interaction in a professional gallery venue.

Image Source: Tadd Heidgerken, Architect

THE LIVE+GROW AREAS PRODUCE COMMUNITY JOBS

EARLY ACTION

RECOVERY PARK

Recovery Park aims to revitalize Detroit through innovative job creation projects benefiting those persons and communities in recovery. Within five years, the nonprofit expects to incubate numerous businesses that will provide hundreds of jobs for Detroit residents.

Image Source: Detroit Collaborative Design Center

THE NEIGHBORHOOD ELEMENT : THE CITY OF DISTINCT AND REGIONALLY COMPETITIVE NEIGHBORHOODS

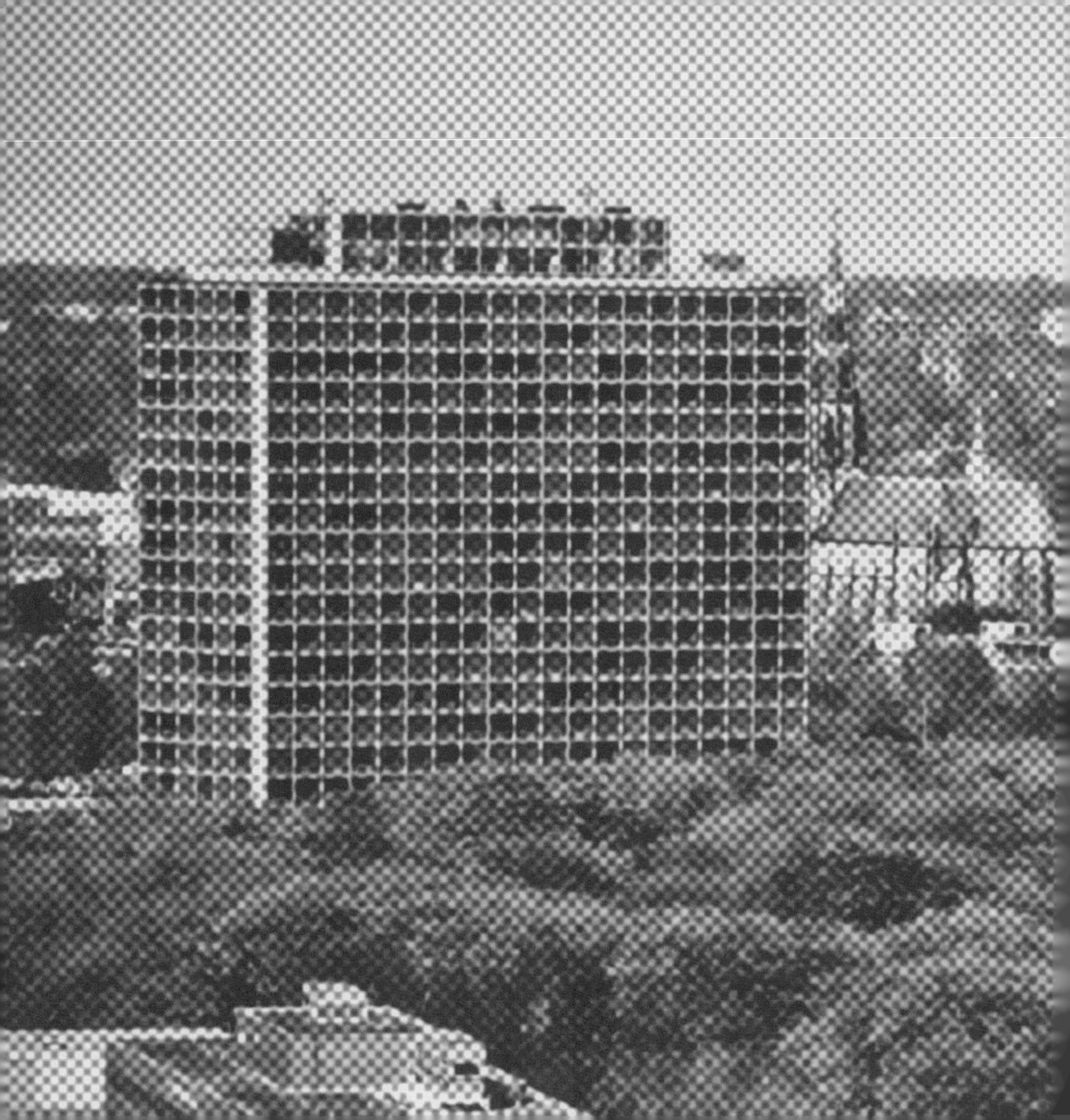

REPURPOSE VACANT LAND TO CREATE GREEN NEIGHBORHOODS

URBAN GREEN
LAND USE TYPOLOGIES

GREEN MIXED-RISE
GREEN RESIDENTIAL

1 2   4 MILES

URBAN GREEN NEIGHBORHOODS include the Green Residential and Green Mixed-Rise land use typologies. These neighborhoods occur in areas of moderate land vacancy. Here the creative repurposing of vacant land provides the greatest opportunity to improve quality of life for residents. New residential development is only targeted for Green Mixed-Rise neighborhoods where dense multi-family and townhouse residential development types mix with commercial uses and are integrated with the landscape in a park-like setting. Three variations of Green Mixed-Rise exist, depending on location in city. One variation is water-based and occurs along the riverfronts. An ecological variation provides habitat/recreation (Lafayette Park is closest to this form). Finally, a productive version includes community gardens or other types of productive open space.

Although no new residential development should occur in Green Residential neighborhoods, neighborhood improvements should be focused on the repurposing of open space and maintenance of the existing housing stock. Residents would be encouraged to take possession of vacant side lots and use them for gardens or a wide range of small-scale agricultural or artisanal uses. Larger areas may be assembled for greenway projects or blue infrastructure. New commercial development in Green Residential neighborhoods should be consistent with productive use of open space. For instance, garden-to-table cafes and fresh food markets associated with local food production should be encouraged to improve access to healthy foods. Artisanal uses and small-scale production should have a means of commercial sale to the communities in which they are located.

While repurposing of open space provides the freedom for greater experimentation with land uses, the development of community is also a critical component to these neighborhoods. Public amenities such as community gardens and public art create distinct and unique neighborhood identities. **Neighborhood planning around vacant land helps to unite communities and provide direction to guide neighborhood improvements.** Such efforts catalyze neighborhood and grassroots efforts to repurpose vacant land, clean neighborhoods and eliminate blight. In specific neighborhoods where strong civic organizations have galvanized efforts to clean, program, and improve neighborhood parks and schools, the ability to organize and improve their communities will continue to be an important support for the transition to Green Neighborhoods.

241

THE NEIGHBORHOOD ELEMENT : THE CITY OF DISTINCT AND REGIONALLY COMPETITIVE NEIGHBORHOODS

URBAN GREEN NEIGHBORHOOD STRATEGIES

PRIORITIZED QUALITY-OF-LIFE ELEMENTS AND STRATEGIES FOR URBAN GREEN NEIGHBORHOODS

PHYSICAL CONDITION

1. Prioritize boarding, code enforcement, and removal of vacant and dangerous structures within ½ mile of public schools and along Safe Routes to community-based schools.[1]
2. Leverage public funding for demolitions to establish jobs-creating, skills-development programs around deconstruction of vacant structures.[2]
3. Create new economies around deconstruction of vacant properties.[3]
4. Prioritize disposition of publicly owned land to responsible private land ownership.[4]
5. Target code enforcement programs on absentee property owners and landlords.
6. Identify and assemble large, contiguous tracts of land for public greenways, blue/green infrastructure projects, and alternative land uses.

COMMUNITY

1. Develop community-based neighborhood plans to address repurposing of vacant land.[5]
2. Organize grassroots and community-based vacant land and building maintenance program.[6]
3. Encourage a wider range of artistic uses for vacant land and buildings within neighborhoods.[7]

HEALTH

1. Prioritize locations for U.S. Department of Housing and Urban Development's *Healthy Homes Initiative* to assess health risks inside and outside of older homes.
2. Prioritize locations for carbon forest pilot projects along major highways.
3. Target disposition of public land for urban agriculture and community gardens.
4. Incentivize purchase of locally produced foods.[8]
5. Incentivize commercial uses that leverage neighborhood-based food economy.[9]
6. Incentivize institutional/commercial buying of locally produced food.[10]
7. Support efforts to establish local food networks.[11]

RECREATION

1. Assemble land for trails and greenway connections inside and outside of the public right-of-way.[12]
2. Prioritize sites along rivers and major parks for development of public recreational amenities that serve the city at large.
3. Promote alternative park maintenance strategy where community capacity exists.
4. Reuse / reinvent vacant land for recreational uses.[13]

HOUSING

1. Identify historic and key assets for renovation and reuse.
2. Assemble large tracts of land adjacent to parks and natural assets for Green Mixed-Rise development.

> "I think I would use residential vacant land for communal purposes. Have bonfires, rent swim-mobiles in the summer, market area, meeting space, picnics, sack races and of course, farming. Having such a place that adults and young people alike shared would improve safety while promoting and teaching a long-term blue print for civic engagement."
>
> Detroit 24/7

Precedents and Examples: 1) Neighborhood Stabilization Program, City-funded demolitions, State-run foreclosure settlements; 2) Detroit GreenWorks Solutions; 3) Architectural Salvage Warehouse, latent energy production in non-reusable building materials; 4) Genesee County Land Bank Adopt-A-Lot Program, Detroit side lot disposition program; 5) Lower Eastside Action Plan, Urban Neighborhood Initiatives; 6) Motor City Blight Busters, Detroit Mower Gang, Philadelphia Vacant Lot Program, Genesee County Clean and Green Program; 7) Power House, Squash House, Yellow House; 8) Fair Food Network Double Up Food Bucks program; 9) Central Detroit Christian CDC's Peaches and Greens program, Café Sunshine; 10) Anchor Strategies Buy Local program; 11) Detroit Black Community Food Security Network, Eastern Market Corporation; 12) Conner Creek Greenway; 13) Ride It Sculpture (Skate Park)

PRECEDENTS

1 Lower Eastside Action Plan (LEAP): Detroit

2 Conner Creek Greenway: Detroit

3 Peaches and Greens: Detroit

EARLY ACTION

1 Extended Side-lot disposition program

PILOT PROJECT

1 Large-scale demolition/deconstruction

The tables below describe the range of appropriate Framework Zones, neighborhood typologies, and development types for Urban Green neighborhoods. They are intended to focus development to the appropriate locations within the city to achieve the overall land use vision for these neighborhoods.

FRAMEWORK ZONES

Low-Vacancy 2

Moderate-Vacancy 1

Moderate-Vacancy 2

TYPOLOGIES

Green Mixed-Rise Only

Green Residential Only

Appropriate for both Typologies

APPROPRIATE DEVELOPMENT TYPES

RESIDENTIAL

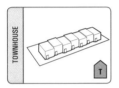 TOWNHOUSE — T

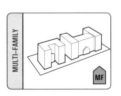 MULTI-FAMILY — MF

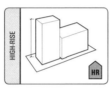 HIGH-RISE — HR

RETAIL

 AUTO–ORIENTED STRIP — AS

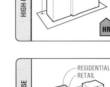 TRADITIONAL — TR

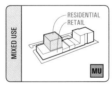 MIXED USE — MU
RESIDENTIAL RETAIL

 BIG BOX — BB

 LIFESTYLE — L

BLUE AND GREEN INFRASTRUCTURE

 LOW–LYING LAKE — BG

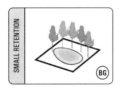 SMALL RETENTION — BG

 STORMWATER BLVD. — BG

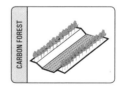 CARBON FOREST — BG

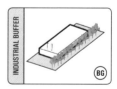 INDUSTRIAL BUFFER — BG

COMMUNITY OPEN SPACES

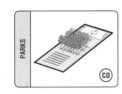 PARKS — CO

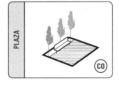 PLAZA — CO

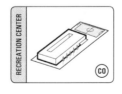 RECREATION CENTER — CO

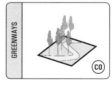 GREENWAYS — CO

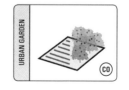 URBAN GARDEN — CO

TRANSITIONAL LANDSCAPES

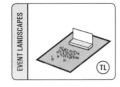 EVENT LANDSCAPES — TL

 ARTSCAPES — TL

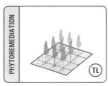 PHYTOREMEDIATION — TL

 URBAN MEADOW — TL

243

CURRENT: URBAN GREEN NEIGHBORHOODS TODAY

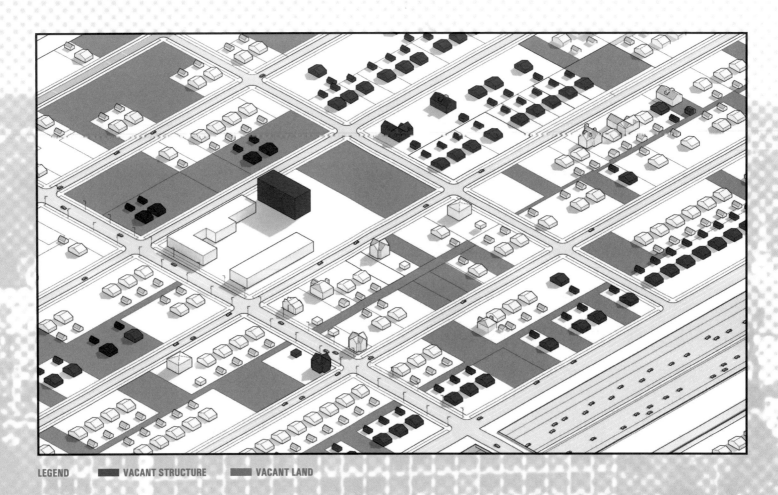

LEGEND ███ **VACANT STRUCTURE** ███ **VACANT LAND**

URBAN GREEN CURRENT CONDITIONS

Neighborhoods best suited to become Urban Green (Green Residential and Green Mixed Use) are characterized by widely varying degrees of land and building vacancy. Some areas appear nearly completely intact, while others have few, if any, occupied houses on a block. Frequently, vacant land and buildings are not maintained, challenging the neighborhood environment for remaining residents. Areas adjacent to major highways or industry further pose major health hazards to residents, leading to even greater land and building vacancy.

The first priority for Green Residential Neighborhoods should be stabilization of the physical environment. It will be critical to evaluate the condition of homes, both interior and exterior, to ensure the safety and health of residents. Community and neighborhood organizations must be closely engaged in developing vacant land management plans to ensure that a community-based vision for the repurposing of vacant land is achieved, and that demolitions and other efforts to eliminate blight are integrated with each neighborhood's overall objectives. With such engagement

and collaboration, a focused and responsive demolitions program should be instituted to remove vacant and dangerous structures from neighborhoods. If the opportunity can be developed, philanthropic investment should be leveraged against public funds to create a new economy around deconstruction of vacant structures and provide needed jobs and skills training in economically distressed communities. Cleared land should then be promptly returned to responsible private ownership within the neighborhood or assembled for medium-to-large-scale blue infrastructure or greenways projects. City systems in these neighborhoods are renewed at a reduced capacity to reflect a smaller and more dispersed residential population from its original capacity. There will be no changes in the level of service delivery to properties, however.

PROPOSED: URBAN GREEN NEIGHBORHOODS IN 50 YEARS

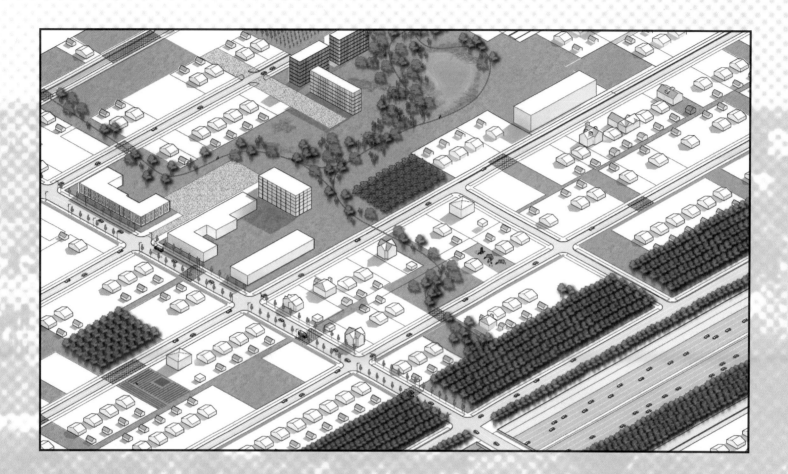

URBAN GREEN LONG-TERM VISION

Open space is the greatest asset of Urban Green neighborhoods and provides the opportunity for small-scale economic development, environmental remediation, and neighborhood amenities. Land should be returned to productive use, including urban agriculture that could create new commercial opportunities around fresh foods markets or restaurants; as well as multiple scales of blue and green infrastructure. In some particular neighborhoods where larger-scale blue infrastructure projects might make sense, coordination with public landholding entities would provide the opportunity to "think big." Given the large amounts of vacant land, Urban Green neighborhoods are appropriate locations to integrate industrial buffering and carbon forest projects. Land adjacent to large parks, natural assets, or transit networks should be assembled and disposed for new Green Mixed-Rise development. Neighborhood identity should be cultivated through public art integration. Urban Green neighborhoods also offer the greatest opportunity for greenway development.

1 Eliminate blight to stabilize neighborhoods, prioritizing areas around schools, through demolition or deconstruction of vacant structures.

2 Engage in neighborhood-based planning to strategize reuse of vacant land around a comprehensive, community-endorsed planning process.

3 Identify and assemble land in areas suitable for long-term green mixed-rise development.

4 Integrate blue and green infrastructure into vacant land strategies.

THE NEIGHBORHOOD ELEMENT : THE CITY OF DISTINCT AND REGIONALLY COMPETITIVE NEIGHBORHOODS

A DAY IN THE LIFE OF AN URBAN GREEN NEIGHBORHOOD...

"Recycle the materials from demolished buildings - there is such a huge amount of housing stock - mostly beautiful buildings - that it would be stupid not to save at least the material from most of them for rehab on the rest."

Sam, Planning Cluster-based Meeting, 1/27/2011

"The most crime is where the majority of condemned houses are located...I wouldn't walk out the door by myself, and it's still not all that safe during the day. If we started demolishing these houses, we wouldn't have to worry as much about the crime. I can't walk to the store because of the crime.."

Seniors Working Session, 2/15/2012

PILOT PROJECT

LARGE-SCALE DEMOLITION / DECONSTRUCTION

Large-scale deconstruction programs are designed to change Detroit's urban blight from a liability into an asset by using the materials and resources obtained from decaying buildings as an economic stimulant for deprived neighborhoods.

Image Source: WARM Training Center

DECONSTRUCTION REMOVES BLIGHT AND PROVIDES A SYSTEM OF NEW JOB OPPORTUNITIES TO NEIGHBORHOOD RESIDENTS AROUND SUSTAINABLE INDUSTRY

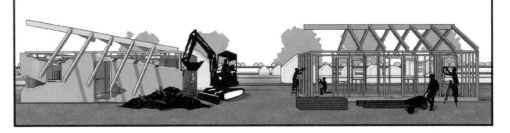

GREEN MIXED-RISE IS ATTRACTIVE RESIDENTIAL LIVING WITHIN A MATURE LANDSCAPE SETTING

PRECEDENT

LOWER EASTSIDE ACTION PLAN (LEAP)

LEAP is a community-driven project designed to engage people in a process to transform vacant land and property into uses that improve the quality of life in Detroit's neighborhoods and surrounding areas.

Text and Image Source: LEAP

CONNER CREEK GREENWAY

Conner Creek Greenway is nine miles of cycling infrastructure that traces the original Conner Creek and links people, parks, green spaces, neighborhoods, schools and shops. The Greenway is sponsored by the Detroit Eastside Community Collaborative (DECC).

Image Source: Hamilton Anderson Associates

NEW GREEN INFRASTRUCTURE SUCH AS CARBON FORESTS AND INDUSTRIAL BUFFERS IMPROVE THE HEALTH OF RESIDENTS BY REDUCING POLLUTANTS AND PROVIDING RECREATIONAL OPPORTUNITIES

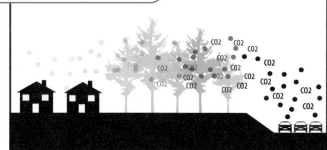

DEQUINDRE CUT BEFORE: OBSOLETE INFRASTRUCTURE LIES UNSAFE, UNMAINTAINED AND OVERGROWN

Image Source: Detroit Riverfront Conservancy

DEQUINDRE CUT AFTER: TURNING LIABILITY INTO COMMUNITY ASSET

Image Source: Detroit Riverfront Conservancy

BETWEEN REHABILITATED HISTORIC PROPERTIES, SIDE LOT DISPOSITION, AND BLOTTING STRATEGIES, RETURN VACANT LAND TO PRIVATE OWNERSHIP AND PROVIDE SPACES FOR PLAY-LOTS, GARDENS, AND SMALL RETENTION PONDS.

PEACHES AND GREENS

In response to the lack of access to fresh foods in the city, this program provides residents with access to fresh fruits and vegetables via a mobile produce truck and produce market. Peaches and Greens is a program of Central Detroit Christian Community Development Corporation.

Image Source: Central Detroit Christian CDC

247

THE NEIGHBORHOOD ELEMENT : THE CITY OF DISTINCT AND REGIONALLY COMPETITIVE NEIGHBORHOODS

RENEW TRADITIONAL NEIGHBORHOODS

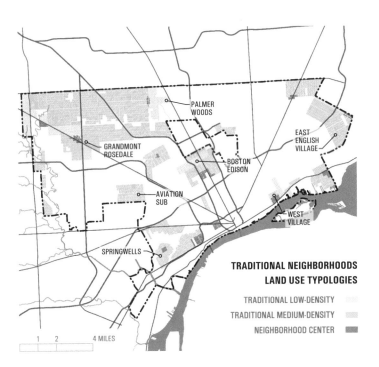

PALMER WOODS

EAST ENGLISH VILLAGE

GRANDMONT ROSEDALE

BOSTON EDISON

AVIATION SUB

WEST VILLAGE

SPRINGWELLS

**TRADITIONAL NEIGHBORHOODS
LAND USE TYPOLOGIES**

TRADITIONAL LOW-DENSITY

TRADITIONAL MEDIUM-DENSITY

NEIGHBORHOOD CENTER

1 2   4 MILES

TRADITIONAL NEIGHBORHOODS include Traditional Low-Density, Traditional Medium-Density, and Neighborhood Center land use typologies. Traditional Low-Density consists primarily of Detroit's existing neighborhoods, some of which are historic, where lot widths exceed 45'. Traditional Medium-Density consists of primarily detached single-family houses on lots ranging from 30' to 45' in width and is the predominant historical neighborhood form of the city. These neighborhoods will maintain their existing character as primarily residentially-focused neighborhoods and attempt to improve city services and infrastructure to make them regionally competitive with peer neighborhoods. As in all Detroit neighborhoods, decisive and immediate action must be taken to ensure Traditional Neighborhoods have safe, well-lit streets, and that overall public and residential safety is enforced. Again, as in all Detroit neighborhoods, other essential services will need to achieve higher levels of reliability. Well-maintained sidewalks and roads are part of this vision. Over time, where additional residential growth capacity and demand exist, infill housing that complements the character of the neighborhoods should be encouraged to increase density.

Clustering commercial and social activities will help to reinforce symbiotic uses and improve walkability within commercial areas. In keeping with aspirations for all neighborhoods in Detroit, schools should function as neighborhood hubs and provide space for both learning and recreational opportunities for the greater community. Retail services and amenities should be clustered to create nodes that serve adjacent neighborhoods. The road and transit network serving Traditional Neighborhoods should be designed with complete streets to accommodate all modes of transit including pedestrians and bikes as well as blue infrastructure to manage stormwater. Innovative improvements to bus and transit service should be implemented to improve service efficiencies and travel time for residents.

TRADITIONAL NEIGHBORHOOD STRATEGIES

 SAFETY

1   Implement CompStat program in cooperation with neighborhood stakeholders and CDOs.[1]

2   Coordinate network of block clubs and neighborhood organizations to secure public safety funding, share strategies, and facilitate communication with the Detroit Police Department to address neighborhood safety issues.

3   Coordinate neighborhood CB patrols with public safety officers to improve response times.[2]

4   Create partnerships between the City and neighborhood CDOs to secure vacant homes, clear titles, and quickly return homes to responsible private ownership.

 PHYSICAL CONDITION

1   Target code enforcement programs on absentee property owners and landlords.

2   Prioritize neighborhood stabilization within 1/2 mile of community-based schools by demolishing vacant structures in poor condition.

 HOUSING

1   Secure and rehabilitate homes in good condition and return to private ownership.

 EDUCATION

1   Implement community-based schools pilot project(s) where community capacity exists:

- Redefine the school's attendance area to a walkable neighborhood geography (1/2 mile radius around the school); eliminate overlapping geographies and open enrollment at pilot school.

- Outreach to students and parents within the neighborhood to build community capacity.

- Coordinate with Safe Routes to Schools to maximize walking and reduce busing costs.

2   Co-locate Community Learning Centers, community services, and amenities in strong community-based schools during non-classroom hours.[3]

 PUBLIC SERVICES

1   Create CDO-organized Special Assessment Districts to supplement city services for safety, snow removal, and mosquito abatement where community interest and capacity exist.

2   Advocate for Special Assessment District legislation to permit neighborhood special districts for infrastructure, public space, and service improvements similar to existing Business Improvement District (BID) legislation.

 RETAIL SERVICES AND AMENITIES

1   Prioritize development of retail nodes per Land Use chapter corridor recommendations.

2   Partner with CDOs, neighborhood organizations, building owners and retailers to identify neighborhood-compatible retail mix.

3   Develop pop-up retail pilot projects to assess market demand for new retail services and amenities.

Precedents and Examples: 1) Midtown Wayne State University Police CompStat Program; 2) Detroit 300, AmeriCorps Urban Safety Project; 3) Playfields, playgrounds, gymnasiums, kitchen facilities, libraries, theaters, music rooms, art rooms;

PRECEDENT

1   Community Learning Centers: Cincinnati, OH

EARLY ACTION

1   Neighborhood pop-up retail

PILOT PROJECTS

1   Code enforcement and landlord strategies
2   Neighborhood-based CompStat program
3   Community-based schools

The tables below describe the range of appropriate Framework Zones, neighborhood typologies, and development types for Traditional Neighborhoods. They are intended to focus development to the appropriate locations within the city to achieve the overall land use vision for these neighborhoods.

FRAMEWORK ZONES

Low-Vacancy 1
Low-Vacancy 2
Moderate-Vacancy 1

TYPOLOGIES

Traditional Low-density
Traditional Medium-density
Neighborhood Center
Appropriate for all Typologies

APPROPRIATE DEVELOPMENT TYPES

RESIDENTIAL

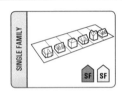 SINGLE FAMILY — SF SF

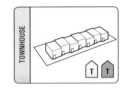 TOWNHOUSE — T T

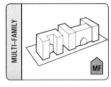 MULTI-FAMILY — MF

RETAIL

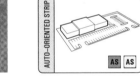 AUTO-ORIENTED STRIP — AS AS

TRADITIONAL — TR

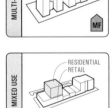 MIXED USE — RESIDENTIAL RETAIL — MU

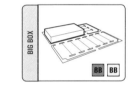 BIG BOX — BB BB

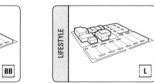 LIFESTYLE — L

BLUE AND GREEN INFRASTRUCTURE

SMALL RETENTION — BG

 STORMWATER BLVD. — BG

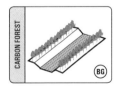 CARBON FOREST — BG

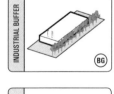 INDUSTRIAL BUFFER — BG

COMMUNITY OPEN SPACES

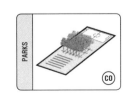 PARKS — CO

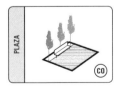 PLAZA — CO

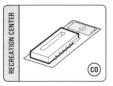 RECREATION CENTER — CO

 GREENWAYS — CO

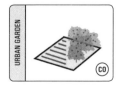 URBAN GARDEN — CO

TRANSITIONAL LANDSCAPES

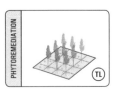 PHYTOREMEDIATION — TL

CURRENT: TRADITIONAL NEIGHBORHOODS TODAY

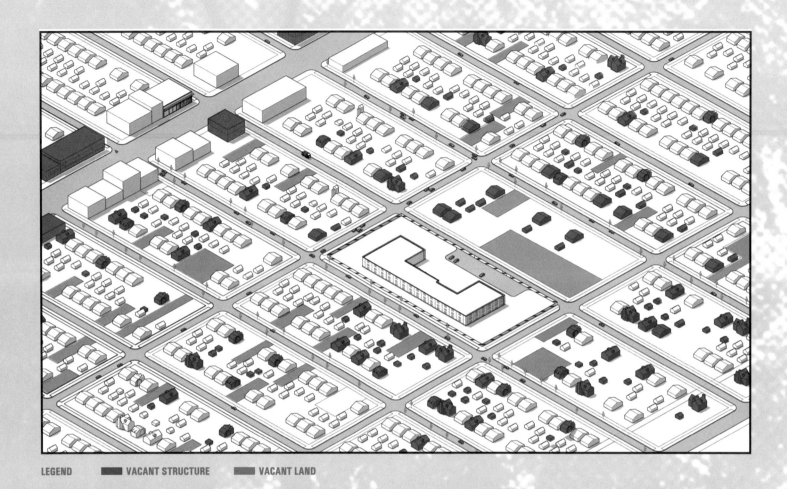

LEGEND   ■ VACANT STRUCTURE   ■ VACANT LAND

TRADITIONAL NEIGHBORHOODS CURRENT CONDITIONS

Traditional neighborhoods, often anchored by neighborhood schools, largely maintain their original historical appearance as blocks of occupied detached single-family homes. However, particularly in light of challenges such as the mortgage and property tax foreclosure crisis and a declining overall citywide population, these areas have begun to see increasing building vacancy and more absentee landlords. Commercial corridors, both traditional and auto-oriented, have similarly experienced significant vacancy and no longer provide goods and services to meet residents' needs.

Initiatives to address safety and crime should be the highest priority to stabilize Traditional Neighborhoods. Development of a comprehensive, fully funded, and staffed public safety strategy is critical to Traditional Neighborhoods' long-term viability. In order to address actual and perceived issues of safety, the physical condition of the Traditional Neighborhoods should be improved by an upgraded and well-maintained public lighting grid and demolition of vacant and dangerous structures. Vacant houses in good condition should be quickly rehabilitated and returned to private ownership where market demand exists. Code enforcement, particularly targeting absent and negligent landlords, must be well funded and staffed. As part of the safety strategy, areas immediately around public and charter schools, bus stops, and Safe Routes to Schools must be prioritized to ensure the safety of children.

PROPOSED: TRADITIONAL NEIGHBORHOODS IN 50 YEARS

TRADITIONAL NEIGHBORHOODS LONG-TERM VISION

After safety, improving the quality of education to attract and retain families is the next-highest priority for Traditional Neighborhoods. Schools should be seen as neighborhood hubs and should open their facilities to a wide range of community uses and services, including community learning centers, gathering spaces, and recreational opportunities. City services should be renewed at full capacity with the introduction of recycling services and right-of-way improvements, including sidewalk and street maintenance and street tree planting. New street and roadway design should support complete streets with bicycling and walking, blue infrastructure, and a larger system of bike and greenway connections. Utility maintenance and renewal should be prioritized in Traditional Neighborhoods. Infill housing should be encouraged to increase densities where demand exists. Similarly, where demand exists, a comprehensive strategy should be developed to attract and support small business retail start-ups in walkable nodes that serve adjacent neighborhoods. Traditional neighborhoods are connected to employment centers and retail services and amenities through proximity to rapid bus transit and crosstown bus routes, and supplemented by non-fixed route, on-demand mini-bus service.

1. Renew city systems including street lighting with coordinated public safety initiatives and revised tiered transit hierarchy.

2. Prioritize stabilization and code enforcement in areas within a 1/2 mile of public and charter schools.

3. Establish public and charter schools as community learning centers to provide neighborhood gathering space, jobs and skills training, lifetime learning, and recreational opportunities.

4. Develop retail nodes around transit stops to provide services and amenities to neighborhood residents.

THE NEIGHBORHOOD ELEMENT : THE CITY OF DISTINCT AND REGIONALLY COMPETITIVE NEIGHBORHOODS

A DAY IN THE LIFE OF A TRADITIONAL NEIGHBORHOOD...

"Existing, strong neighborhoods of single family homes should also be reinforced with focus on cleaning up commercial corridors and neighborhood amenities."

Margaret, Planning Cluster-based Meetings, 1/2011-3/2011

"Safety at a school is the number one thing that determines whether or not a parent will send their child to that school - is my child safe and do you care about my child?"

Education Session, 6/20/2012

Image Source: Marvin Shaouni

PILOT PROJECT

SCHOOLS AS COMMUNITY ANCHORS

The aim of this pilot project is to reestablish schools as community anchors by redefining schools' attendance areas to only include their surrounding neighborhoods. Schools and partnering organizations may hold outreach activities for students and families to reinforce the importance of education in the community.

SCHOOL FACILITIES CAN ACCOMMODATE LEARNING OPPORTUNITIES AND PROVIDE RESOURCES FOR THE ENTIRE COMMUNITY BEYOND THE TYPICAL SCHOOL DAY

Image Source: Doug Coombe

NEIGHBORHOOD STABILIZATION AND CODE ENFORCEMENT EFFORTS PRIORITIZED WITHIN A 1/2 MILE OF SCHOOLS

PILOT PROJECT

CODE ENFORCEMENT AND LANDLORD STRATEGIES

Build a code enforcement partnership between the City, CDOs, and neighborhood association in a single neighborhood target area focusing on strategies to deal with problem absentee landlords.

Image Source: Hamilton Anderson Associates

EVERY NEIGHBORHOOD SHOULD HAVE ADEQUATE CITY SERVICES

NEIGHBORHOOD-BASED COMPSTAT PROGRAM

CompStat is an interactive mapping systems that monitors crime rate within Detroit. The goal of the program is to reduce crime and enhance Detroit's quality of life by making neighborhood's aware of the crime-rate within their area.

Image Source: CompStat

EARLY ACTION

NEIGHBORHOOD POP-UP RETAIL

In the pop-up retail model, businesses set up temporary sales locations to gain exposure, quickly sell limited merchandise, test market potential in a new location, and/ or build interest in a specific neighborhood commercial area.

Image Source: Margarita Barry, huffingtonpost.com

"Please make neighborhoods safe to walk and bike in. Link these safe, walkable neighborhoods to compelling destinations: transit, stores, schools, etc."

Brian, Detroit 24/7, 5/2012

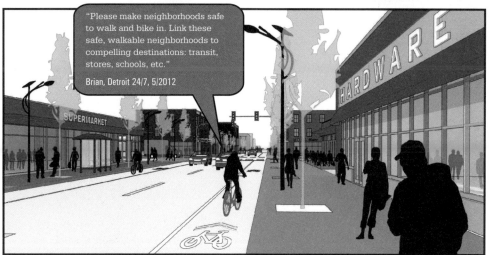

255

TRADITIONAL NEIGHBORHOODS SUPPORT A RANGE OF TRANSIT OPTIONS, INCLUDING STANDARD BUS SERVICE

PRECEDENT

COMMUNITY LEARNING CENTERS

The Community Learning Center Institute leads the development of schools as community learning centers, each with a set of financially self-sustaining, co-located community partnerships responsive to the vision and needs of each school and its neighborhood.

Image Source: Marvin Shaouni
Text Source: http://clcinstitute.org/

UTILIZE PRODUCTIVE LANDSCAPES AS THE BASIS FOR A SUSTAINABLE CITY

**ALTERNATIVE USE
LAND USE TYPOLOGIES**

INNOVATION PRODUCTIVE

INNOVATION ECOLOGICAL

ALTERNATIVE USE AREAS consist of Innovation Productive and Innovation Ecological land use typologies. The Detroit Strategic Framework recommends a gradual depopulation of these areas, but recognizes that there will be residents still living in these areas for years, if not decades, to come. These areas are comprised of both residents who feel strongly attached to their neighborhoods and do not want to leave, and others who would gladly relocate to a more traditional neighborhood if they had the means or opportunity. For those who would choose to relocate, programs should be developed to allow them to do so. For those who choose to stay, it is imperative to ensure that their basic levels of service are met, including provisions for safety and security. New alternative land uses provide jobs opportunities for residents around agriculture, aquaculture, energy fields/ forests and research plots. Pilot projects around alternative city services such as waste collection, recycling, and non-fixed route transit ("transit on demand," available to residents by appointment or by diverting nearby routes on request) should be developed in these areas while vacant commercial corridors should be repurposed for blue infrastructure. While the long-term identity of these neighborhoods should not be residential in character, they still must sustain and support the people who live within them.

257

ALTERNATIVE USE AREAS STRATEGIES

PRIORITIZED QUALITY-OF-LIFE ELEMENTS AND STRATEGIES FOR ALTERNATIVE USE AREAS

 HOUSING

1. Establish voluntary House-to-House programs to assist residents in the High-Vacancy areas to move to more densely populated areas.

 PHYSICAL CONDITION

1. Assemble large contiguous areas of vacant land under public ownership for economic uses or alternative productive land uses.
2. Develop large-scale blue infrastructure projects such as low-lying lakes.
3. Transition underutilized commercial land to blue infrastructure.[1]
4. Organize neighborhood-based removal of vacant housing units and clean-up program.[2]
5. Create pilot program to test low-cost means to prevent illegal dumping.

 COMMUNITY

1. Create neighborhood-based vacant land utilization and management plans.[3]
2. Work with community organizations to align mission / goals with Strategic Framework land use recommendations and improve service delivery to existing residents.

 PROSPERITY AND INCOME

1. Incentivize new economies and job creation around productive land uses that leverage vacant land, such as agriculture, aquaculture, energy fields/forests, and research plots.[4]
2. Revise zoning and regulatory framework to allow greater range of alternative uses and informal business opportunities.

 ENVIRONMENT

1. Rubbelize underutilized secondary roads.
2. Retire secondary gas and water at trunk lines on 100% vacated blocks.
3. Create incubators for innovative waste collection and recycling program.
4. Partner with universities and research institutions to create innovation centers focused on agriculture, brownfield remediation, energy production, and land research.
5. Establish low maintenance ecological landscapes.[5]

 MOBILITY

1. Develop pilot projects for Tier 4 micro-transit routes.

 PUBLIC SERVICES

1. "Replace, Repurpose, or Decommission" city systems infrastructure per City Systems Element, based on existing and anticipated population.
2. Maintain core services for remaining residents.

"Low density will not work. Sadly for the people who won't or can't leave their homes when they're the last remaining 2 or 3 houses on the block - they might just have to. How can the city afford to maintain all of that green space?"

Janet, Facebook, 5/2012

Precedents and Examples: 1) Mack Avenue Green Thoroughfare Project; 2) Motor City Blight Busters, Detroit Mower Gang; 3) Lower Eastside Action Plan; 4) D-Town Farms; 5) "Green Zone" Saginaw, MI

PRECEDENTS

1. Motor City Blight Busters: Detroit
2. D-Town Farm: Detroit

EARLY ACTIONS

1. Hantz Farms
2. MSU Innoversity: MetroFoodPlus Innovation Cluster @ Detroit
3. Urban agriculture zoning ordinance revision

PILOT PROJECTS

1. Voluntary house-for-house swap program
2. Large-scale blue infrastructure

The tables below describe the range of appropriate Framework Zones, neighborhood typologies, and development types for Alternative Use Areas. They are intended to focus development to the appropriate locations within the city to achieve the overall land use vision for these neighborhoods.

FRAMEWORK ZONES

Moderate-Vacancy 2

High-Vacancy

TYPOLOGIES

☐ Appropriate for both Typologies

APPROPRIATE DEVELOPMENT TYPES

 WORKING/PRODUCTIVE
 RESEARCH PLOT (WP)
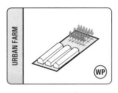 URBAN FARM (WP)
 ENERGY FIELD / FOREST (WP)
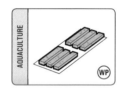 AQUACULTURE (WP)

ECOLOGICAL LANDSCAPES
 NATURE PARK (EL)
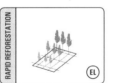 RAPID REFORESTATION (EL)
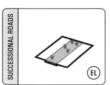 SUCCESSIONAL ROADS (EL)
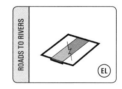 ROADS TO RIVERS (EL)

BLUE AND GREEN INFRASTRUCTURE
 LOW-LYING LAKE (BG)
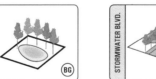 SMALL RETENTION (BG)
STORMWATER BLVD. (BG)
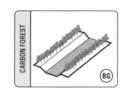 CARBON FOREST (BG)
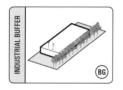 INDUSTRIAL BUFFER (BG)

COMMUNITY OPEN SPACES
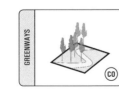 GREENWAYS (CO)

TRANSITIONAL LANDSCAPES
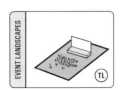 EVENT LANDSCAPES (TL)
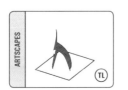 ARTSCAPES (TL)
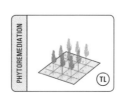 PHYTOREMEDIATION (TL)
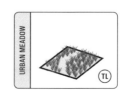 URBAN MEADOW (TL)

CURRENT: ALTERNATIVE USE AREAS TODAY

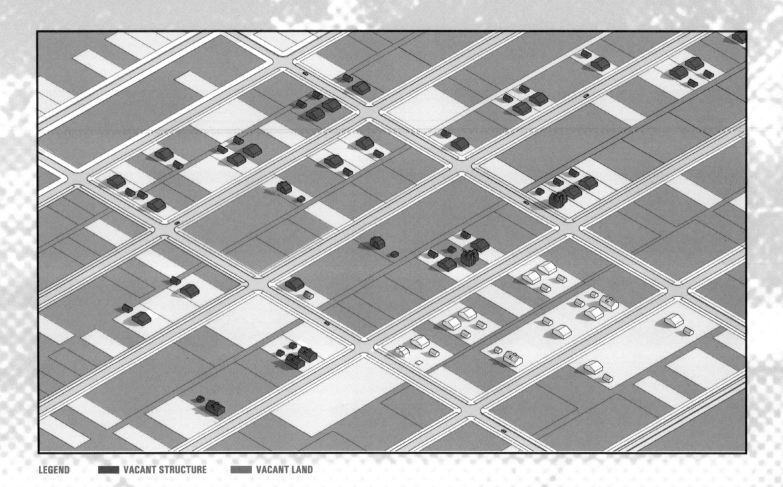

LEGEND ▬ VACANT STRUCTURE ▬ VACANT LAND

ALTERNATIVE USE AREAS CURRENT CONDITIONS

Alternative Use neighborhoods in their current state are characterized by a high degree of land vacancy. While there still remain pockets of residential homes, many areas are nearly completely vacant or, if houses do still remain, they are no longer occupied. Vacant land and houses are frequently unmaintained, leaving them vulnerable to illegal activities, such as scrapping, squatting, arson, or dumping. Commercial areas similarly reflect very high degrees of land and building vacancy. Street and sidewalk infrastructure have largely been poorly maintained.

In order to stabilize Alternative Use neighborhoods, two major tactics should be employed. For residents who wish to move to other, more densely populated neighborhoods in the city, public- and private-sector entities might develop modest incentive programs that allow residents to find and secure their own options for new housing choices. City systems should be replaced, repurposed, or decommissioned. However, core systems such as gas, electricity, and water will remain in place until residential areas are 100% vacated. Due to very low population densities,

transit services could be provided by on-demand micro-buses and vans that feed major bus rapid transit and crosstown bus routes—although it is important to be realistic about the costs and capacity of the regional transportation system, as well as residents' ability to pay. For residents who wish to stay, neighborhood-based planning would clearly support the transition to new land uses but would mitigate impacts on existing residents and improve quality of life during the transition. Opportunities should be identified to ensure that local residents are offered employment opportunities associated with new land uses.

PROPOSED: ALTERNATIVE USE AREAS IN 50 YEARS

ALTERNATIVE USE AREAS LONG-TERM VISION

The long-term transformation of Alternative Use neighborhoods hinges on the re-imagination and reuse of vacant land for productive uses or, where there is excess vacant land, returning it to an ecologically and environmentally sustainable state. Large contiguous areas should be assembled under public control for future disposition and productive reuse. Where former residential areas are completely vacated, roads can be rubbelized and infrastructure decommissioned to diminish the cost and maintenance burden on city systems. A few of these areas are suitable for university research extensions. As part of these facilities, programs should be developed that benefit Detroit residents with educational and skills-training opportunities. In all new development for productive land uses, Detroit residents should be prioritized for hiring and employment opportunities.

1. Revise zoning to allow expanded range of landscape-based reuse options.

2. Assemble public land for large-scale reuse for blue infrastructure, ecological or productive landscape development types.

3. Prioritize job opportunities associated with productive reuse for neighborhood residents.

4. Replace, repurpose, or decommission city systems infrastructure and develop alternative systems delivery such as on-demand micro-bus bus connections to regional transit system.

A DAY IN THE LIFE OF AN ALTERNATIVE USE AREA...

"Motor City Blight Busters works to improve the neighborhood around Grand River/ Lahser. [They] have been instrumental in reviving the business strip with groups like Artists Village."

Colleen, Detroit 24/7, 5/2012

"If the current residents were provided housing swaps into planned and safe communities - it would enable the city to enact some eminent domain and demolish urban blight. Giving current residents the opportunity to move to better housing, improved services and a safe environment for their families."

Craig, DWP Website

PRECEDENT

MOTOR CITY BLIGHT BUSTERS

Motor City Blight Busters cleans dump sites and neighborhoods, tears down blighted houses, builds new homes, and paints homes; using over 21,000 gallons of paint, 15,500 pounds of nails and 15,470 sheets of plywood, and demolishing 113 houses in a 23-year period. MCBB also founded Angel's Night to counteract Halloween arson.

Image Source: detroitmoxie.com

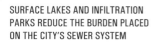

SURFACE LAKES AND INFILTRATION PARKS REDUCE THE BURDEN PLACED ON THE CITY'S SEWER SYSTEM

PILOT PROJECT

VOLUNTARY HOUSE-FOR-HOUSE SWAP PROGRAM

A trial house-for-house swap program would allow residents in High-Vacancy areas to move to higher-density, safer areas of the city with better services. This pilot project must be preceded by an in-depth civic engagement program to ensure residents' confidence in the program.

Image Source: Marvin Shaouni

PILOT PROJECT

LARGE-SCALE BLUE INFRASTRUCTURE

Large areas of vacant land can be assembled for large-scale blue infrastructure projects, like surface lakes and infiltration parks. Blue infrastructure projects will help alleviate the burden of stormwater on the city's combined sewer system to decrease sewer discharges into the Detroit and Rouge Rivers.

Image Source: Hamilton Anderson Associates

MSU INNOVERSITY

Partner with universities and research institutions, such as Michigan State University, to create innovation centers focused on agriculture, brownfield remediation, energy production, and land research.

Image Source: ceres.net

AQUACULTURE INCLUDES THE FARMING OF FISH. SUCH FARMS CAN HELP TO SUPPLEMENT THE FRESH FOOD SUPPLY IN THE CITY. ENCLOSED FACILITIES CAN FUNCTION YEAR ROUND.

EXTENDED GROWING SEASONS CAN BE ACCOMMODATED IN TRANSLUCENT, SEMICIRCULAR STRUCTURES, KNOWN AS "HOOP HOUSES." LONGER GROWING SEASONS MEAN GREATER PRODUCTION OF FOOD.

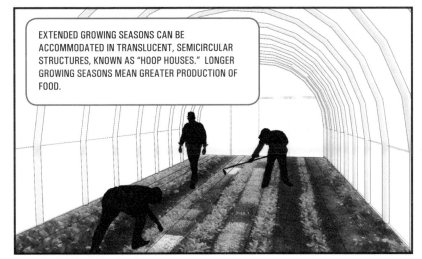

LANDSCAPE FOR ENVIRONMENTAL REMEDIATION AND AS A VISUAL AMENITY

D-TOWN FARM

In operation for six years and recently acquiring a 10-year lease from the City of Detroit, D-Town Farm has expanded from a 2-acre plot to a 6-acre production, growing chemical-free, organic vegetables.

Image Source: dtownfarm.blogspot.com

RAPID REFORESTATION CAN BE USED TO QUICKLY ESTABLISH FORESTS. FAST-GROWING TREE SPECIES CAN ACT AS FILTERS TO CLEAN POLLUTANTS FROM AIR AND AS SPONGES TO ABSORB STORMWATER RUN-OFF

263

THE NEIGHBORHOOD ELEMENT : THE CITY OF DISTINCT AND REGIONALLY COMPETITIVE NEIGHBORHOODS

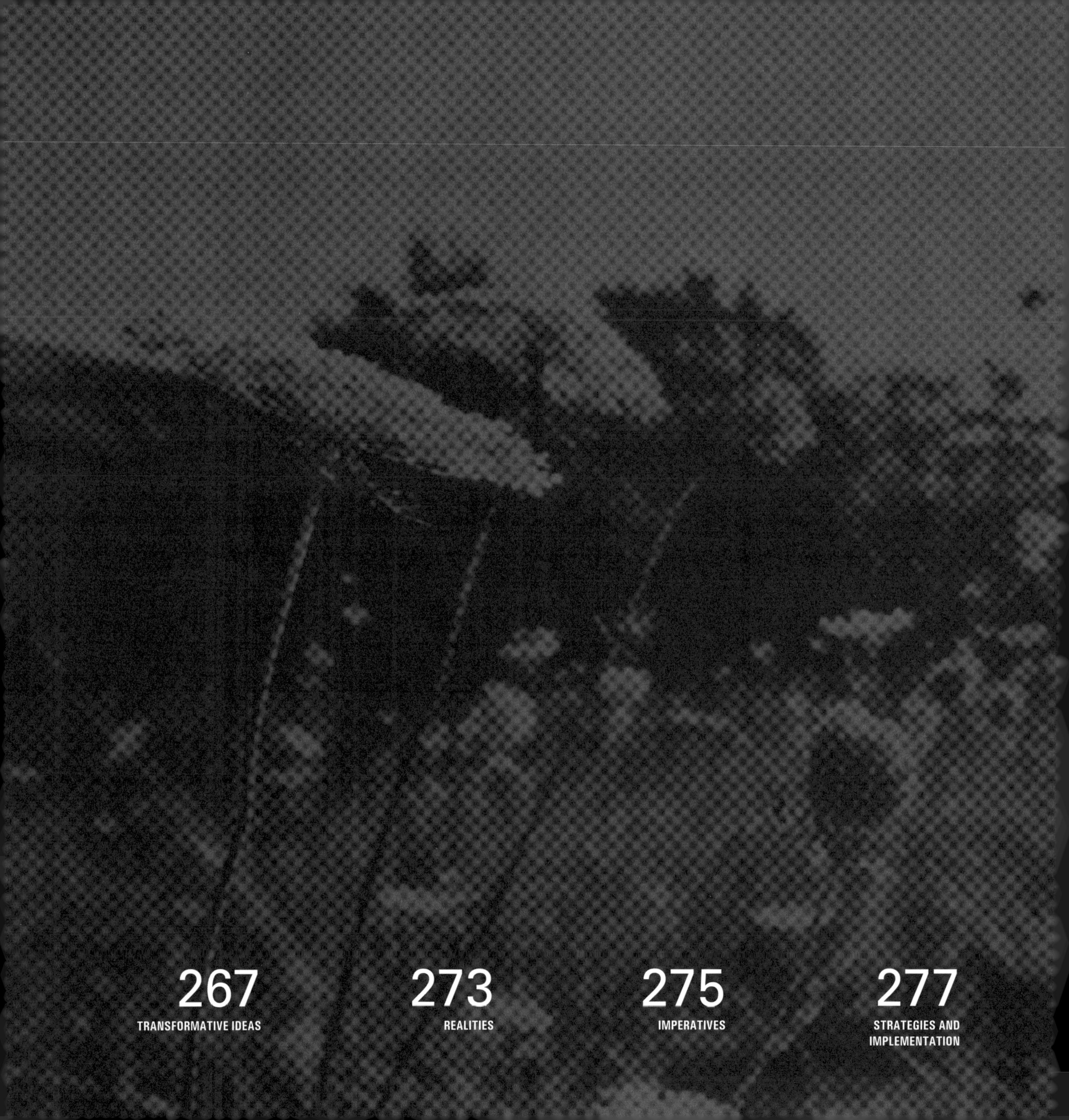

THE LAND AND BUILDINGS ASSETS ELEMENT

A STRATEGIC APPROACH TO PUBLIC ASSETS

DETROIT FUTURE CITY
A Day in the Life *Putting the Land Back to Work*

Back when Chandra was getting her degree at MSU, she never dreamed she'd live in Detroit. But when her sister relocated to Detroit with her husband, and then a job opened up at the Recreation Department the summer after Chandra got her master's degree, she saw it as a sign.

Through her job, Chandra is getting to know her new home in ways she never anticipated. She meets with community groups to discuss neighborhood visions for green space, talks with church groups and local schools to help them align their own decisions about reinvestment with those of the public agencies, and participates in discussion with the other public agencies in charge of Detroit's land to help mesh their overlapping missions and policies. When she needs a break—and needs to be reminded what it's all for—she takes a brief bike ride along the greenway she cut her teeth on when she arrived six years ago.

After back-to-back meetings all day, that bike ride is looking pretty good. Luckily, she has the perfect excuse to leave work right at 5 p.m. today: her sister's baby shower is tonight, and she has to stop off in Corktown on her way to pick up a gift for the celebration. At her last meeting of the day at 4 p.m., Chandra can't tell what energizes her most: the Strategic Framework working group's progress on a zoning overlay proposal for a new Live + Make residential community, or the thought of a relaxing bike ride to a great dinner with family and friends, and the celebration of a new Detroiter-to-be.

TRANSFORMATIVE IDEAS
LAND AND BUILDING ASSETS

Vacant land and buildings are among Detroit's most valuable assets for its future. While in the abstract this may seem reasonable, to those dealing with these properties it is difficult to internalize. The sheer magnitude of the inventory, the difficulties of maintaining it, the obstacles to reuse, and the limited resources affecting every public agency in the city are all barriers to recognizing the untapped potential of the city's public land inventory. The challenge does not stop at public land: In fact, far more vacant and underutilized properties remain in private ownership.

Turning vacant land from burdens to assets will take more than changes in specific policies and practices. **All public agencies—whether city, county, or state—will need to change how they think about land, and make equally fundamental changes to the way they acquire, manage, and dispose of land and buildings, and the way other public agencies regulate them.** Without such a change in thinking and practice, the inventory of vacant land and buildings in its current condition will not only fail to become an asset, it will continue to act as a roadblock to the implementation of creative strategies for land use, environmental restoration, economic growth, and neighborhood revitalization.

If public land is to become an asset, all of the different public agencies that hold land need to align their missions around a single shared vision—not only a vision for "better land management," but a vision that reflects the aspirations for the city as a whole, as expressed in its land use and environmental plans, economic growth strategies, and neighborhood revitalization efforts. Within these plans and strategies, public land plays a critical role. Indeed, without a coordinated, strategic approach to the acquisition, disposition and reuse of public land, none of those strategies can come to fruition.

A transformative strategy is about more than the parcels in public ownership themselves. It also must provide an integrated approach to land and buildings across the entire city. A truly transformative strategy for land repurposing, redevelopment, and management will demand that the City look at its regulations governing vacant land and problem properties in private ownership, and how those regulations and their enforcement help or hinder the achievement of Detroit's revitalization goals. It calls for rethinking the county's tax foreclosure practices, to better link them to strategies of acquisition and disposition of public land; and for aligning decisions about public facility siting, reuse, or closures with public land decisions, as well as with the larger land use, environmental, and economic growth strategies being pursued by the City of Detroit.

267

PUBLIC LAND WORKING GROUP AGENCIES:

- Detroit Land Bank Authority
- City of Detroit – Planning and Development
- City of Detroit – City Planning Commission
- City of Detroit – General Services
- Wayne County Treasurer
- Wayne County Land Bank
- Michigan Land Bank Fast Track Authority
- Detroit Economic Growth Corporation
- Michigan State Housing Development Authority
- Detroit Housing Commission
- Detroit Public Schools
- Detroit Water & Sewerage Department

Each of these 12 agencies has a different mission and goal related to the use and reuse of public land. These agencies continue to meet to create a strategic and coordinated approach to the use and reuse of publicly held land.

5 LAND AND BUILDINGS ASSETS TRANSFORMATIVE IDEAS

1 A CITY THAT SHARES A VISION: COORDINATING THE MANAGEMENT OF VACANT LAND

Public land and facility strategies must be aligned with the City's strategies for neighborhood revitalization, economic growth, and creation of blue/green infrastructure, while the activities of all public landholding entities and other public agencies must be grounded in a single, coordinated, strategic framework.

We need to begin thinking of properties in public ownership and those in private ownership as part of a single system. **All land, whatever its legal ownership, is public in the sense that how it is used and maintained affects its neighbors and the community as a whole, and affects the city's ability to preserve its neighborhoods and build its economy.** More important than who actually owns the inventory is how it fits into the vision for the city. Detroit needs to develop a coordinated system in which all entities operate consistently across all aspects of public land management and private land regulation, making decisions based on clear policy goals and principles, and utilizing available legal and financial tools as efficiently as possible. Wherever title to any single parcel resides, that parcel should be seen as being part of single inventory, guided by a single set of policies and goals.

Such a profound change in thinking and procedures will not be easy. The transformation of Detroit's approach to its land will require many separate agencies, with separate missions and priorities, to subordinate their differences to a common direction and purpose, and to foster unprecedented connections among landholding, regulatory, and user agencies. In the long run, public landholding agencies and those leading the city's regeneration should explore realignment of responsibilities, including reducing the number of separate entities holding title to public parcels, to increase the system's efficiency and take better advantage of the legal and technical capacities of particular agencies.

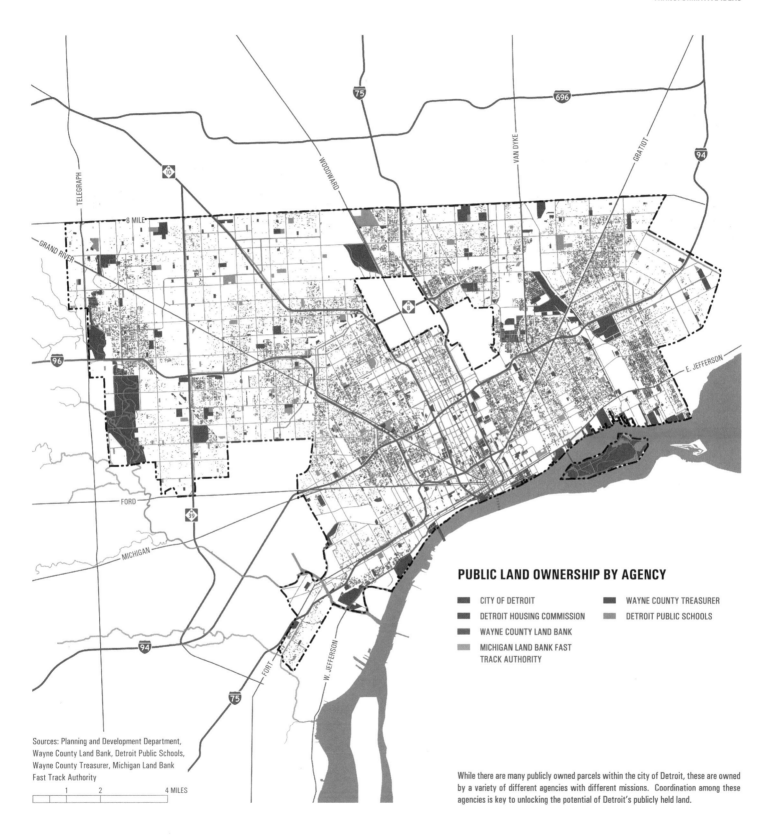

PUBLIC LAND OWNERSHIP BY AGENCY

- CITY OF DETROIT
- DETROIT HOUSING COMMISSION
- WAYNE COUNTY LAND BANK
- MICHIGAN LAND BANK FAST TRACK AUTHORITY
- WAYNE COUNTY TREASURER
- DETROIT PUBLIC SCHOOLS

Sources: Planning and Development Department, Wayne County Land Bank, Detroit Public Schools, Wayne County Treasurer, Michigan Land Bank Fast Track Authority

1 2 4 MILES

While there are many publicly owned parcels within the city of Detroit, these are owned by a variety of different agencies with different missions. Coordination among these agencies is key to unlocking the potential of Detroit's publicly held land.

1.

2.

2   A CITY WHERE EVERYTHING IS CONNECTED: VIEWING VACANT AND PROBLEM PROPERTIES WITHIN ONE INTERRELATED SYSTEM

Detroit contains an estimated 150,000 vacant properties, roughly 2/3 vacant land parcels and the rest vacant buildings. Of these, the eight public landholding entities control about 66,000, or well under half. In addition, the city contains an unknown number of problem properties that are still occupied, including underutilized, poorly maintained industrial buildings and many absentee-owned houses and small apartment buildings suffering from neglect.

Historically, the respective systems designed to deal with publicly owned and privately owned properties have not been integrated. The latter is managed as a regulatory function, and has regrettably suffered from the lack of resources that burdens several of Detroit's systems. Many ordinances are on the books, but are poorly or intermittently enforced, with too few personnel to keep up with the volume of properties.

Decisions about vacant land and problem properties, whether in public or private ownership, need to be made through a single lens: How will these properties be treated, so their outcomes will benefit the city by stabilizing neighborhoods, fostering economic growth, and creating opportunities for new infrastructure and innovation, rather than continuing to act as a drag on the city's future?

3   A CITY OF STRATEGIC APPROACHES: RECOGNIZING THE UNIQUENESS OF EACH PROPERTY'S VALUE AND CHALLENGES

A coordinated approach to addressing Detroit's vacant land must begin with a strategic approach to addressing the land in public ownership to maximize the city's ability to create long-term value and enhance community amenities and quality of life through its use and reuse. **This approach must be grounded in a basic principle: Vacant land is not fungible—each property has its own problems, and its own potentials.** Every decision a public agency makes about land has strategic implications, this applies to the following areas:

- Property acquisition, including establishing policies about which properties should be added to the public inventory;

- Property disposition, including determining the most appropriate reuse, identifying suitable buyers, and selecting the most appropriate disposition methods;

- Property holding strategies, including when properties should be held for long-term public purposes, for assembly into more buildable or marketable sites, or for future reuse potential;

- Maintenance of public land; and

- Demolition of vacant structures

All decisions about public land should be made on the basis of strategic principles designed to lead to the betterment of the city.

3.

4.

4 **A NEW URBAN LANDSCAPE: USING LAND FOR INFRASTRUCTURE AND INNOVATION**

5 **A CITY WHERE PUBLIC FACILITY INVESTMENTS COUNT: ALIGNING PUBLIC FACILITIES WITH LAND USE TRANSFORMATION**

Many people in Detroit, as elsewhere, still think of reuse of vacant land as equivalent to redevelopment of new buildings to replace the ones that have been torn down. Yet the reality is that, outside certain key locations, continuing demographic and economic trends project that little new development will take place in Detroit for many years. **This is a challenge, but also a great opportunity. It means that Detroit's vast inventory of vacant land can be used for a variety of new purposes, to foster innovations in public open space, urban agriculture, clean energy, and more; and to build a new network of blue/green infrastructure to divert stormwater from the city's overtaxed sewer system and clean the city's air.**

Pursuing this idea also demands a change in attitude toward the large areas of vacant land that cover many parts of the city. Rather than seeing this land as largely worthless, and being eager to unload it to any willing private party, the public sector should see this land as being of value, and of creating large, contiguous tracts where current holdings may be substantial but fragmented. This, in turn, calls for greater emphasis on holding rather than selling public land, and on making it more costly for private entities—often speculators—to hold onto vacant parcels instead of using them productively or relinquishing them.

It also requires us to think about the smaller lots in traditional neighborhoods not as necessarily future infill sites, but as long-term open spaces in those neighborhoods, and to ensure that they are used in ways that strengthen, rather than undermine, the fabric of those areas.

Finally, it calls for an open-minded, creative approach to innovation and experimentation. The sheer scale of the vacant land available creates the opportunity to try out different reuse alternatives, some of which may be new and largely untried. Both through its land use regulations and its disposition policies, the City should encourage the full range of ideas for reuse of vacant land in ways that hold promise to further the city's revitalization and enhance its quality of life.

Much of the public land inventory in Detroit is made up of public facilities, including public schools, parks, recreation facilities and community centers, police substations, and more. Those facilities are an important part of the 'glue' holding the city's neighborhoods together, and define the quality of life in those neighborhoods. Today, as a result of declining population and financial resources, many of those facilities, particularly school buildings, have been closed, and many others, including many of the city's parks, fall short of their promise. Population and fiscal constraints are realities that cannot be wished away, but a different approach can be taken within those constraints to integrate decisions about public facilities into larger decisions about Detroit's future land use.

Decisions about public facilities are being made in Detroit every year—whether to close a facility or invest money in upgrading it, whether to close a park or reduce its ongoing maintenance, where to consolidate public facilities and services, how to reuse vacant facilities, and more. Each of these decisions affects far more than the facility itself. **Going forward, all such decisions should be aligned with the larger strategies governing the future of the neighborhoods and other areas in which they are located. Outcomes should enhance the stability of neighborhoods slated for revitalization, or help further the conversion of other areas into blue/green infrastructure or other non-development reuses.**

Image Sources: 1) Hamilton Anderson Associates; 2) Andrew Jameson—Wikimedia Commons; 3) Delaware Center for the Inland Bays; 4) Detroit Public Schools

271

AGENCY MISALIGNMENT

OCTOBER 2011 PROPERTY AUCTION

13K

13,000 DETROIT PROPERTIES WERE LISTED IN WAYNE COUNTY'S OCTOBER 2011 AUCTION[1]

$500

MINIMUM BID PRICE AT OCTOBER 2011 AUCTION[2]

6K

PROPERTIES UNSOLD AT OCTOBER 2011 AUCTION

50%
PUBLIC OWNERSHIP

HALF OF ALL PROPERTIES FROM OCTOBER 2011 AUCTION REVERTED BACK TO PUBLIC OWNERSHIP[4]

8

EIGHT SEPARATE PUBLIC AGENCIES MANAGE DETROIT'S PUBLIC LAND

EXCESSIVE ABANDONMENT

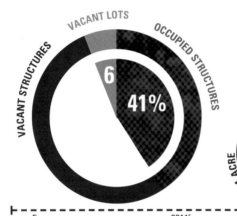

VACANT LOTS
VACANT STRUCTURES
OCCUPIED STRUCTURES
6
41%

>1 ACRE
<1 ACRE
2%

80K 104K 66K

FORECLOSED PROPERTIES IN DETROIT BY TYPE, 2011[5]

45,000 PARCELS HAVE BEEN TAX FORECLOSED SINCE 2010

98% OF ALL CONTIGUOUS PUBLICLY OWNED PARCELS IN DETROIT ARE LESS THAN ONE ACRE IN TOTAL SIZE[7]

79,725 OF DETROIT'S 349,170 HOUSING UNITS ARE VACANT[8]

104,000 OF DETROIT'S 385,390 PARCELS ARE VACANT[9]

66,000 PROPERTIES IN DETROIT ARE PUBLICLY OWNED[10]

PUBLIC EXPENDITURE BURDENS

46%

130

30%
PARKS IN POOR CONDITION

120
LIMITED MAINTENANCE

83%

14 OF THE DETROIT'S 30 RECREATION CENTERS HAVE BEEN CLOSED SINCE 2005[11]

130 PUBLIC SCHOOLS HAVE BEEN CLOSED OR CONVERTED TO CHARTER SCHOOLS IN DETROIT SINCE 2005[12]

30% OF DETROIT'S PARKS ARE IN POOR CONDITION[13]

120 DETROIT PARKS ARE CATEGORIZED AS LIMITED MAINTENANCE:[14] GRASS IS MOWED ONCE A YEAR AND TRASH IS NOT COLLECTED

83% OF DETROIT'S VACANT PARCELS ARE ZONED RESIDENTIAL[15]

REALITIES

THE STATE OF DETROIT'S PUBLIC LAND

While many American cities also have large public land inventories, and are affected by market constraints that limit their ability to reuse their vacant land and buildings, no other city in the United States faces that reality to the extent of Detroit. As public officials and policy-makers begin to frame a strategic response to the public and vacant land inventories, they are faced with three daunting challenges:

THE SCALE OF VACANCY. The scale of the vacant property inventory, both in total and in public ownership, is far greater in Detroit than in any other American city. The number of vacant properties, as well as the number of houses acquired by speculators and rented out, continues to grow and destabilize neighborhoods. The number of properties going to tax foreclosure auction has been rising steadily, and in the fall of 2012 exceeded 20,000, an increase of two-thirds over the preceding year. Turning these vacant properties into an asset, in the face of limited resources and market demand constraints, is a major challenge.

WEAK MARKET CONDITIONS. Detroit is tasked with finding uses for vacant land that are not only achievable within the constraints of the current market, but which can plant the seeds for future market recovery. The growth of the vacant property inventory to its current proportions is more than anything else a reflection of extremely weak real estate market conditions, which—in conjunction with the limited public resources available—impose severe constraints on what can be done with vacant land. Since 2000, the number of vacant units has skyrocketed, while since peaking in 2005-2006, real estate sales and house values have plummeted. The median sales price for houses in Detroit in 2011 was only $17,500.

Demographic and market trends show a continuing loss of population, and a continuing loss of demand for home ownership in many of the city's neighborhoods that have been stable up to this point. With a large surplus of predominantly single-family housing units in Detroit, there are only a few locations in the city where it still makes sense to build new houses. Meanwhile, the cost of rehabilitating a long-empty older house or apartment building usually vastly exceeds the resulting market value. Even in Downtown and Midtown, where market demand appears to be stronger, making the numbers work for new development or major rehabilitation is challenging.

MULTIPLE PUBLIC LANDHOLDING AGENCIES. Public land in Detroit is held by many separate agencies, including city, county, and state agencies, as well as autonomous or quasi-governmental entities such as the Detroit Public Schools, the Detroit Housing Commission, and the Detroit Economic Growth Corporation. Few other cities have such fragmented holding of their public land inventory. There is no consistency of policy, procedure, or mission among these agencies, while many are hamstrung by burdensome legal requirements and complex procedures. The Department of Planning and Development controls the largest number of properties, yet its ability to do strategic disposition is constrained by procedural obstacles, including the need to obtain City Council approval for all transactions, however small and insignificant from a citywide perspective.

Public landholding agencies also must act in a context wherein well over half of the vacant buildings and land parcels in the city are owned not by the public sector, but by private owners. With the cost of holding vacant land in Detroit negligible, and regulation minimal, landowners can sit on properties, destabilizing neighborhoods or blocking the assembly of vacant land into buildable parcels. The Wayne County tax foreclosure process, meanwhile, continues to funnel an ever-growing number of properties into a revolving door of real estate speculation, further destabilizing the city's neighborhoods.

Building a coordinated, strategic system for land management cutting across organizational and institutional boundaries, including maintaining the growing inventory of public properties and public facilities, is the challenge faced by the agencies holding public land in Detroit.

BREAKING THE VICIOUS CYCLE OF SPIRALING VACANCY. Detroit's public land inventory can become a powerful asset in building a better future for the city. Current practices, however, do little more than maintain the status quo, while failing to take advantage of this valuable resource; indeed, they perpetuate a vicious cycle in which vacancy triggers more vacancy, and in which properties move through a revolving door of speculation until they are stripped of value and end up abandoned. The sheer scale of the problem, though, coupled with the complex realities of market weakness and institutional/ organizational fragmentation, demand bold new approaches, capable of breaking away from prior practices, overcoming these challenges and turning public land into an asset for Detroit's regeneration.

1-4) Wayne County Treasurer (WCT) 2011; 5) Data Driven Detroit; 6) WCT; 7) Planning and Development Department (P&DD), Detroit Public Schools (DPS), WCT, Michigan Land Bank Fast Track Authority, & Hamilton Anderson Associates; 8) US Census 2010; 9) Pⅅ 10) P&DD, DPS, Wayne County Assessor; 11) Detroit Recreation Department (DRD); 12) The American Prospect; 13) DRD 2006; 14) DRD; 15) P&DD

We must be strategic and coordinated in our use of land.

IMPERATIVES
PUBLIC LAND ACTIONS AND IMPACT

The use and maintenance of vacant and problem properties affect the quality of life in the city's neighborhoods more profoundly than almost any other single element in the urban environment. Vacant buildings contribute to crime, have an impact on public health, undermine neighbors' property values, and above all foster a sense of decay and decline that in turn leads to loss of confidence among residents and businesses— in their neighborhoods and in the city as a whole.

Detroit's ability to address its problem property issues is impeded by its severe fiscal and market constraints, but it is equally impeded by the absence of a systematic, coordinated approach to the problem, in which all public and private stakeholders are fully engaged. Such engagement is not an easy goal to achieve; it means creating a coordinated system in which all entities operate consistently, making decisions based on clear policy goals and principles, and utilizing each entity's legal and financial tools as efficiently as possible, while fully engaging non-governmental partners in making decisions and tackling problems. Having such a system is more important than who actually owns the inventory. Whoever holds title to individual parcels, however, the whole should be thought of as a single inventory, guided by a single set of policies and goals, and integrated with parallel strategies to address the larger part of the vacant property inventory that remains in private hands. It will require many separate agencies, with separate missions and priorities, to subordinate many of their differences to a common direction and purpose.

WHAT WE LEARNED FROM CIVIC ENGAGEMENT FEEDBACK

- 40% of survey respondents chose INCREASE IN BLIGHT as the most damaging impact of population loss in their neighborhood.

- Survey respondents ranked imperative #5, WE MUST BE STRATEGIC AND COORDINATED IN OUR USE OF LAND, as the third most important out of all 12 imperatives.

- Comments about VACANCY & ABANDONMENT were the fourth most frequent type of comment out of approximately 180 topics.

- Participants mentioned over 200 parks, greenways, recreation centers, and gardens as top assets in their communities citywide.

- Top public land strategies recorded from DWP participants included:

  - ENFORCE CODES on privately owned land and structures.

  - IMPROVE AND STREAMLINE METHODS OF SELLING PUBLIC LAND.

CREATING A COORDINATED, STRATEGIC SYSTEM FOR MANAGING PUBLIC ASSETS. A coordinated, strategic system for managing Detroit's public land assets must cut across and integrate five areas of responsibility with respect to publicly owned land: acquisition and assembly, disposition, holding, maintenance, and demolition. Each poses distinct challenges. This system should also include a public role in dealing with privately owned problem properties.

STRATEGIC PROPERTY ACQUISITION AND ASSEMBLY. Public agencies are reluctant to add to the public land inventory because of the difficulties of maintaining and reusing the existing inventory. Many city residents are painfully aware of the city's problems maintaining the existing inventory. Moving toward a strategic approach for making public land an asset will require both public officials and residents to rethink that position, yet refrain from adding properties wholesale or without careful thought.

Multiple public landholding agencies should agree on the priorities for strategic acquisition, and develop an ongoing joint process with the Wayne County Treasurer's Office to identify and target properties for public acquisition through the tax foreclosure process. This means not only knowing which properties should be prioritized for acquisition, but which public entity is the most appropriate one to take the properties in each case.

An important goal of strategic property acquisition is the assembly of larger publicly owned sites. The vast majority of publicly owned properties are small parcels, unsuitable for many potentially valuable uses; even where public agencies hold larger parcels, they are often broken by privately owned out-parcels that impede their reuse. Systematic assembly of individual parcels into larger sites can create shovel-ready sites for future industries or other businesses in employment growth areas. Other large sites in high-vacancy areas can be converted to blue/green infrastructure. As public landholding entities identify their priority areas for acquisition, they should perform fine-grained, block-by-block analysis to identify and prioritize specific parcels that contribute to assembly of larger sites in key locations.

Property acquisition cannot be divorced from the rest of the system. It would be premature to acquire too many properties before practices for disposition and reuse have been improved to the point where properties are targeted for the most appropriate disposition and reuse as they are acquired. Similarly, maintenance systems must be improved to handle demand from the properties being added to the inventory. Failure to do so could make matters worse, and reinforce widespread community concerns about the City's ability to deal with its property assets.

PROPERTY DISPOSITION AND REUSE. Disposition is the single most important element in the strategy for public land. Each property disposition involves three separate but closely interwoven decisions:

- WHAT REUSE should the property be put to?
- WHAT ENTITY should most appropriately carry out the reuse?
- WHAT DISPOSITION METHOD is the best way to get property into the hands of the most appropriate user?

The first decision flows from the Strategic Framework's goals for land use, economic growth, city systems, and neighborhood stabilization and revitalization. The second clearly follows from the first: Whatever the reuse, each property should be conveyed to an entity with a compatible mission for that reuse, as well as the capacity to carry it out. These will be different for each reuse, dictating a different pool of potential buyers in each case. In some cases, the best strategy will be not to dispose of the property at all, but to hold it in inventory.

Finally, the method of disposition must be selected to ensure that the property ends up in the right hands. An auction is unlikely to be the best way to get a property to a community-serving organization for long-term greening, for example. Where the entity currently holding the property lacks the legal authority to dispose of it appropriately, a procedure should be established to convey the property to an entity that has the necessary authority, which then disposes of the property.

The shared disposition system should include the following features:

- a common property database, including a user-friendly and accessible web presence for all public land information;
- formal policies and procedures for disposition that all of the public landholding entities follow and that are readily available to the public in written form;
- a single 'front door' for receiving and processing applications for public land;
- an efficient and goal-oriented disposition process, with transparent guidelines and procedures; and
- ongoing coordination and integration with public and private agencies pursuing the city's land use, economic growth, and environmental goals.

In the final analysis, the disposition of public assets is a process designed to serve the larger goals of the community, and must be carried out in that spirit.

STRATEGIES AND IMPLEMENTATION
PLANS FOR ACTION

PROPERTY HOLDING. Not all properties should be sold off, even when a willing buyer is present. Selling an individual small parcel in an area where public entities hold multiple parcels, and where assembly of those properties, along with strategic acquisition, can create a significantly more marketable or buildable property, is counterproductive. The value the City realizes is likely to be small compared to the future value that could be created, while by selling individual parcels, the opportunity for assembly may be lost. Properties should be held in the public land inventory for three different reasons:

- LONG-TERM PUBLIC BENEFIT: properties that are best used for stormwater management or public open space should be retained indefinitely in public ownership;
- ASSEMBLY: properties in areas—particularly those identified as economic growth target areas—that can be assembled into larger and more buildable parcels; and
- MARKET CHANGE: properties that should be held by the City because they are in areas that are likely to experience market improvement within the next 10 years or sooner, at which time the City can promote significantly higher-quality redevelopment or reuse.

Although in the latter two cases, the ultimate goal is to convey the properties out of the public inventory, holding the property until the most appropriate time for reuse will significantly enhance its reuse potential and the fiscal benefits to the city.

MAINTENANCE. Maintaining the thousands of vacant properties under public control is a massive challenge. Despite valiant efforts, limited resources and other constraints leave many vacant lots inadequately maintained, and many vacant buildings inadequately secured. The City can enhance its maintenance of vacant land and reduce blight by targeting maintenance resources to key areas, using creative strategies to reduce maintenance costs, holding private owners accountable for their properties, and enlisting civic organizations and residents as partners.

Specific strategies that can achieve these objectives include targeting maintenance resources more carefully to threatened residential neighborhoods, using creative landscape interventions to reduce maintenance costs, and shifting some maintenance responsibilities to other entities. Individual lots in low-vacancy areas should be sold or leased where possible to private entities, whether sold to homeowners as side lots, used as community open space, or maintained by neighborhood associations or block groups. Enforcing maintenance requirements for privately owned properties will motivate them to take responsibility for their properties or pay the City of Detroit to maintain them.

DEMOLITION. 40,000 to 50,000 vacant buildings stand in Detroit today. Realistically, perhaps no more than 10 percent of them are likely to be reused or mothballed for future reuse, while additional buildings continue to be vacated and abandoned every day. With the population continuing to decline, neither the financial resources nor the market demand exist to save these thousands of buildings all over the city, nor are such resources likely to exist in the short term. The magnitude of the problem calls for resources to be targeted where it will have the greatest positive impact on the surrounding area.

To make sure that we save buildings that can and should be saved, demolition decisions should be made on the basis of: (1) how they affect the stability and viability of residential neighborhoods and economic growth target areas; and (2) how they affect realization of long-term goals for land use, economic growth, neighborhood stabilization and the environment. While room must be made for buildings that would need to be taken down because of urgent health and safety concerns despite overall neighborhood and planning objectives, those should be exceptions. Priority criteria for demolition may include:

- Buildings in vital but at-risk neighborhoods, where the abandoned building is a blighting influence on the surrounding properties;
- Buildings in economic growth target areas, where demolition will remove a blighting influence or further land assembly for reuse; and
- Buildings in areas slated for blue infrastructure, where the building location and footprint affects the utility of larger areas for stormwater management.

A procedure should be put in place to engage the Detroit Economic Growth Corporation, Detroit Planning and Development Department, Detroit Water and Sewerage Department, and other relevant public agencies, as well as key neighborhood associations and community development organizations (CDOs), to ensure the effective use of limited resources.

Post-demolition site treatment also deserves greater attention, particularly for properties in low-vacancy residential neighborhoods, where the risk of the vacant lot becoming a blighting factor in itself is significant. Wherever possible, the most appropriate landscape intervention for the lot should be identified in advance—in consultation with neighborhood organizations and CDOs—and incorporated into the demolition specification. This will reduce the overall cost of treating the property and ensure that the lot becomes a community asset rather than a problem.

PILOT PROJECT

RESTRUCTURED DISPOSITION PROCESS

Develop a coordinated strategy for strategic disposition of properties in public ownership through the partnership of multiple land-holding agencies.

Image Source: Hamilton Anderson Associates

USING A DECISION-MAKING MATRIX

No plan can prescribe the ideal future outcomes for a community, particularly in a city the size and complexity of Detroit. The future is uncertain, and is likely to both present challenges and offer opportunities that cannot be predicted in advance. For that reason, the focus of the Detroit Strategic Framework is not to lay down prescriptive uses and outcomes, but—as reflected in its title—to provide a strategic framework for local decision making. Nowhere is that reflected more clearly than in the area of land assets, where decisions about thousands of properties must be made over the coming years, within a constantly changing economic, social, and political environment. The purpose of this section is to provide a framework within which public officials, business and community leaders, and residents can make informed, strategic decisions designed to lead to the best outcomes for the city and its residents. In that process, the decision matrix can be a valuable tool.

A decision matrix is a tool that public officials and others use to solve a problem, by posing a series of either/or questions that gradually lead the user to the best solution or solutions from the wider range of theoretical options. The decision matrices in this chapter can be used by planners, public officials, community groups, and residents to identify the most appropriate disposition strategies or outcomes for those parcels.

To illustrate how a decision-making matrix is used, an example is presented on the facing page. In order to reach a conclusion about the most appropriate disposition strategy, a series of questions is asked about the parcel. The answers to the questions for a hypothetical property are highlighted in the matrix. In the illustration, the questions are

- **STEP 1: CATEGORY.** What type of property is it? This matrix is to be used to evaluate alternatives for parcels of publicly owned vacant land larger than 1 acre in predominantly residential neighborhoods. Other decision matrices, presented later, will do the same for small vacant land parcels, for vacant houses, and for parcels in economic growth target areas.

- **STEP 2: FRAMEWORK ZONE.** What framework zone is the parcel located in? Since development strategies vary on the basis of the framework zone, this is a key piece of information for planning the disposition of the parcel. In the hypothetical case shown here, the parcel is in a Moderate-Vacancy zone.

- **STEP 3: PROPERTY FEATURE.** Is the parcel suitable for assembly? Whether a parcel is suitable for assembly, in the sense that it may be surrounded by other vacant land or vacant buildings, is an important consideration for determining its reuse potential. In the hypothetical case, the parcel is not suitable for assembly, at least in the near term—it may be surrounded by occupied buildings, or land clearly slated for some other purpose.

- **STEP 4: AREA CHARACTERISTICS.** What is the level of market demand in the area? The near-term redevelopment potential of the property is most powerfully driven by the level of market demand in the immediate area; only limited market demand for new development exists in the vicinity of the hypothetical parcel.

These four questions allow the user to answer the fifth, critical question:

- **STEP 5: REUSE/DISPOSITION OPTIONS.** What are the most appropriate reuse or disposition options for the property? Since the user knows from the first four questions that the property is in a Low-Vacancy 1 zone, but one where the market at present is weak, it is likely that the most appropriate solution may be to find an interim green use for the property, while holding it for future redevelopment as market conditions improve. This is not, however, the only possible disposition option—if there are other parcels in the area that are more market-suitable, or if suggested by the particular features of the parcel, it may be appropriate to cycle the property into long-term green reuse, whether for open space, agriculture, or blue/green infrastructure. To try to package the parcel in the short run for redevelopment, however, appears clearly inappropriate.

This exercise points out the limitations as well as the value of a decision matrix—it can help the user zoom in on an appropriate decision, but cannot substitute for additional, more detailed information the user may have, nor for the user's exercise of judgment.

KEY TO THE MATRIX

1 CATEGORY

The category refers to the basic type of property under consideration—in this case, a vacant parcel larger than 1 acre within a residential area.

2 FRAMEWORK ZONE

The Framework Zone in which the parcel is located—in this case, the parcel is located in a Moderate-Vacancy zone.

3 PROPERTY FEATURE

The key feature on the parcel with respect to its redevelopment potential—in this case, by virtue of its location or adjacent uses, it is deemed "not suitable" for near-term assembly into a larger parcel.

4 AREA CHARACTERISTICS

The key features of the area with respect to its redevelopment potential—in this case, the area has limited market demand.

5 REUSE/DISPOSITION OPTIONS

The alternative reuse options available for a property—in this case, the preferred option is to use the parcel for an interim green use while holding for redevelopment. Selling or leasing for long-term green reuse is an alternative, while selling for near term redevelopment is not presently a realistic option.

DECISION-MAKING MATRIX FOR REUSE OF NEIGHBORHOOD PARCELS

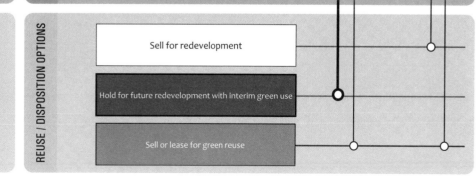

1 CATEGORY
Neighborhood parcel (>1 acre)

2 FRAMEWORK ZONE
Low-Vacancy 1 | Low-Vacancy 2 | Moderate-Vacancy | High-Vacancy

3 KEY PROPERTIES
Suitable for assembly
Not suitable for assembly

4 AREA CHARACTERISTICS
Strong market demand
Limited market demand

5 REUSE / DISPOSITION OPTIONS
Sell for redevelopment
Hold for future redevelopment with interim green use
Sell or lease for green reuse

I-75

I-696

VAN DYKE

GRATIOT

I-94

WOODWARD

M-10

8 MILE

GRAND RIVER

I-96

M-8

E. JEFFERSON

FORD

M-39

MICHIGAN

I-94

FORT

W. JEFFERSON

I-75

PUBLICLY OWNED VACANT PROPERTY

█ PUBLICLY OWNED VACANT PROPERTY

Sources: Planning and Development Department,
Wayne County Land Bank, Detroit Public Schools,
Wayne County Treasurer, Michigan Land Bank
Fast Track Authority

1   2   4 MILES

While the 66,000 publicly owned parcels in the city of Detroit have traditionally been
seen as a liability, through a strategic and coordinated approach, this land can be turned
into a valuable asset to help move the city forward.

FIVE TRANSFORMATIVE IDEAS : SIX IMPLEMENTATION STRATEGIES

THE LAND AND BUILDINGS ASSETS ELEMENT : A STRATEGIC APPROACH TO PUBLIC ASSETS

281

A | TARGET VACANT PUBLIC LAND AND BUILDINGS IN EMPLOYMENT DISTRICTS FOR ECONOMIC GROWTH

Detroit has strong assets for economic growth, yet is held back by the shortage of 'move-in' buildings and shovel-ready buildable sites into which local firms can expand, and new firms from outside Detroit can locate. The strategic reuse of public land holdings—coupled with an aggressive strategy to make private land speculation more costly—may be the critical element in Detroit's ability to realize its economic growth potential. By positioning publicly and privately owned vacant land in and around economic growth employment districts for assembly and reuse, Detroit can level the playing field to compete with suburban greenfield development opportunities.

Detroit needs a series of highly focused strategies to create sites that can be marketed on short notice to potential users, as well as to create opportunities for existing firms to grow their businesses. These strategies fall into three broad categories:

- strategic acquisition and assembly of properties to create desirable and buildable sites;
- targeted disposition of properties to developers and end users around specific economic development goals, while holding properties for further assembly; and
- strategies to increase the cost of holding vacant land and buildings by private owners, while fostering the greater use of underused industrial and commercial buildings.

These strategies are detailed in the next section on using land assets for economic growth.

B | USE VACANT PUBLIC LAND AS A TOOL FOR NEIGHBORHOOD STABILIZATION

While not the only factor threatening the stability of Detroit's vital yet at-risk residential neighborhoods, the proliferation of vacant lots and empty buildings scattered around those areas are a significant force blighting these neighborhoods and accelerating their decline. Factors contributing to blight include the inadequate maintenance that many lots receive, difficulty in putting them back into neighborhood-enhancing reuse, housing vacancy and abandonment, and the continued proliferation of privately owned vacant lots and problem buildings. Targeted strategies for these sites can minimize their blighting effect and turn them into neighborhood assets.

High priority must be given to actions to remove existing blighting elements in at-risk neighborhoods, and to the extent possible, prevent future blighting elements from appearing. Specific strategies that should be pursued include

- systematically reusing vacant lots in ways that contribute to neighborhood stability, such as community gardens, side lots, and other landscape treatments to create attractive low-maintenance environments;
- expeditiously recycling vacant and abandoned houses for reoccupancy where feasible, or demolition where reoccupancy is not feasible;
- adopting regulatory programs and incentives to motivate more responsible ownership by absentee landlords; and
- increasing the cost of holding vacant land and buildings by private owners.

All of these actions should be planned and implemented through partnerships among city agencies, neighborhood associations and community development corporations, to leverage the energy and human resources that these organizations are willing and ready to bring to stabilize and rebuild their neighborhoods.

These activities should be coordinated closely with other neighborhood stabilization activities, including steps to increase public safety, foster greater home ownership, and build stronger neighborhood organizations.

IMPLEMENTATION ACTIONS

1   Identify strategic targets for acquisition of properties by public entities.
2   Adopt policies for targeted disposition and holding of properties in economic growth areas.
3   Increase the cost of holding vacant property.
4   Adopt program to foster greater use of underused buildings.

IMPLEMENTATION ACTIONS

1   Reuse vacant lots to enhance neighborhood stability.
2   Adopt targeted demolition strategy based on stabilization priorities.
3   Address problem landlords.
4   Increase the cost of holding vacant property.
5   Pursue targeted neighborhood stabilization strategies.

C — TRANSFORM LARGELY VACANT AREAS THROUGH BLUE AND GREEN INFRASTRUCTURE

Large parts of Detroit are dominated by vacant land and buildings with little or no short-term or medium-term development potential, but with the ability to be turned into valuable assets for the city through a variety of green reuse alternatives. Today's largely unmanaged, chaotic vacant land environment in these areas contributes to the sense of neglect felt in many parts of the city, undermining the quality of life not only for the residents of these areas, but for the city as a whole.

Perhaps the most dramatic potential for transformation lies in the use of public land for blue/green infrastructure; that is, reuse of land to absorb stormwater and divert it from the city's sewer system, or to clean the air and improve community health. Reusing vacant land in these ways can save the city hundreds of millions or billions of dollars in sewer upgrading costs while creating landscaped and maintained marshes, lakes, greenways, and forests that will remove blight, enhance their surroundings while linking them to the rest of the city, and potentially create future market value and redevelopment opportunities.

D — LINK PUBLIC FACILITY AND PROPERTY DECISIONS TO LARGER STRATEGIES

In recent years, many schools, parks, recreation centers, police substations, and other public facilities have been closed as Detroit adjusts to new fiscal and demographic realities. Some have been used for other purposes, while many sit vacant. At the same time, Detroit Public Schools has built, expanded, or upgraded other school facilities. Decisions about which facilities should be closed, or where services or maintenance should be reduced or enhanced, as well as the reuse of vacant facilities, should be guided by the City's land use and neighborhood stabilization goals, in order to maximize the value of existing facilities and reduce the blighting effect of vacant buildings and the potential destabilizing effect of future closings. At the same time, the presence of a number of new or significantly upgraded school facilities represents an important opportunity for neighborhood stabilization. Targeted neighborhood strategies around new or significantly upgraded schools, along with co-location of other community-serving activities can maximize their value as neighborhood assets while enhancing the quality of life in the surrounding area.

IMPLEMENTATION ACTIONS

1 Hold land between interstates/industrial areas and neighborhoods for green infrastructure (do not release for future residential development).
2 Acquire available land for blue infrastructure in key locations.

IMPLEMENTATION ACTIONS

1 Create priority system for public land and parks acquisition.
2 Create joint policies and systems for disposition of public property.
3 Adopt coordinated maintenance strategy for public land.
4 Adopt targeted demolition strategy based on stabilization priorities.
5 Use new and upgraded schools as community anchors for stabilization.
6 Review criteria for school closing to reflect neighborhood stability factors.
7 Update parks and recreation facilities planning to reflect current and future populations and budgets (update aspects of 2006 Strategic Master Plan by the DRD).
8 Parks and recreation planning at neighborhood scales: refine citywide strategy of Detroit Strategic Framework through smaller-scaled analysis.

283

E — INCORPORATE MORE INNOVATIVE VACANT LAND MAINTENANCE APPROACHES

Only a handful of the thousands of vacant sites in Detroit are likely to see redevelopment—in the sense of new buildings—over the next decade or more. As demolitions continue to take place, the number of vacant parcels is likely to grow. If there is one central question that must drive the entire discussion of public land, it is this: how can one transform these thousands of parcels from their current status, where they blight neighborhoods and form barriers between communities, to a new status in which they become assets, enhancing rather than blighting their surroundings, and linking rather than separating the different parts of the city?

While vacant land today fragments the city, isolating neighborhoods from one another, it can become a vehicle for re-knitting the city's fabric. The secret lies in giving a central role to the use of landscape in its many forms and variations, as laid out elsewhere in this Framework as the vehicle for transforming vacant land into a productive part of the urban environment, whether with respect to ongoing maintenance, short-term holding uses, or long-term reuse for purposes such as stormwater management, urban agriculture, carbon forests, and more. Landscape needs to become a central rather than a peripheral element in Detroit's toolkit of urban land uses. This is as true in neighborhoods—where many scattered vacant parcels need to be integrated into the community fabric through sensitive landscape treatments—as in high-vacancy areas, where large-scale uses for vacant land are needed.

IMPLEMENTATION ACTIONS

1. Adjust city maintenance standards, strategies, and practices to vary by framework zone and future land use (do not mow all vacant lots in city regardless of location, but instead adopt different lower-cost maintenance strategies in different areas); look for partnerships to help with land maintenance.

2. Form partnerships with community groups and other organizations, businesses, and individuals to help maintain land.

3. Refine set of landscape maintenance typologies and develop cost estimates to implement.

F — USE MORE AGGRESSIVE REGULATORY TOOLS

Well over half of the vacant properties in Detroit are privately owned, including the great majority of the city's vacant buildings. No vacant property strategy that focuses entirely on the publicly owned inventory, yet fails to address the private inventory, can hope to be transformative for the city's future. In addition to vacant properties, large numbers of occupied but poorly maintained properties, often owned by short-term speculators, are destabilizing the city's neighborhoods, while rising numbers of properties—vacant and occupied—are appearing on the county's annual tax auctions. More aggressive, targeted strategies to address these challenges need to be an integral part of the public land strategy.

The City needs to establish clear standards for maintenance of vacant properties by private owners, and use its regulatory authority aggressively to increase the cost of doing business for those owners who do not maintain their properties to the full required standards. Restructuring and effectively enforcing existing vacant property ordinances is an important first step. A second priority should be strategies to motivate responsible landlord behavior and penalize speculators who do not maintain their properties, a critical issue in many neighborhoods where more and more formerly owner-occupied houses are falling into the hands of absentee owners. Finally, the tax foreclosure process, through which thousands of properties move through a revolving door of speculation, foreclosure, and ultimate abandonment, needs to be addressed.

Neighborhood associations and CDOs need to be full partners with the public land agencies in designing and carrying out these strategies. Not only do these agencies lack the resources to tackle the problem on their own, but many of Detroit's neighborhood associations and CDOs are actively seeking opportunities to take responsibility for the future of their neighborhoods. Only by tapping their energy—not merely in carrying out City initiatives, but by playing a strong role in framing and designing those initiatives—will Detroit have a realistic chance to succeed in finding new purposes for its vacant land.

IMPLEMENTATION ACTIONS

1. Increase the cost of holding vacant property.

2. Address problem landlords.

3. Create formal partnership with Wayne County Treasurer for tax foreclosure auctions.

DECISION-MAKING MATRIX: INDUSTRIAL LAND ACQUISITION & DISPOSITION

1 PROPERTY

Industrial Land

2 PROPERTY TYPE

Identifying Industrial Area Priorities for Acquisition

Identifying Industrial Area Priorities for Disposition

3 PROPERTY SUB-TYPE

Site in Economic Growth Employment District

Site not in Economic Growth Employment District

Small parcel (<1 acre): assembly feasible

Small parcel (<1 acre): assembly not feasible

Medium parcel (1-10 acres)

Large parcel (>10 acres)

4 REUSE ALTERNATIVES

Do not acquire

Prioritize large sites

Prioritize sites closer to existing public land

Prioritize sites that are either (1) vacant land or (2) buildings in usable conditions

Bundle with other parcels for infill industrial or compatible development

Sell to adjacent property owner

Use for non-development purpose in area compatible with existing industrial fabric

Use for non-development purpose in area without intact industrial fabric

Sell to adjacent property owner

Sell individually for infill industrial or compatible development

Bundle with other parcels for infill industrial or compatible development

Sell to adjacent property owner

Sell individually for infill industrial or compatible development

Bundle/create assemblage with other parcels for infill industrial or compatible development

Hold with interim use for future redevelopment

Use for non-development purpose in area compatible with existing industrial fabric

5 PREFERRED SELL HOLD OPTIONS

Hold for assembly

(1) Sell to adjacent viable industrial user, or (2) Use for non-development purpose

(1) Sell to adjacent viable industrial user or if viable development parcel, (2) Sell to developer for industrial development, or (3) Hold where substantial assembly opportunity exists

(1) Sell to developer to build industrial (or compatible mixed-use) building or buildings, or (2) Hold where substantial assembly opportunity exists

TARGET VACANT PUBLIC LAND AND BUILDINGS IN EMPLOYMENT DISTRICTS FOR ECONOMIC GROWTH

Detroit has strong economic growth potential: many Detroit firms want to grow, while other firms want to move to Detroit, adding jobs and strengthening the local tax base. Three broad strategies should be used to put vacant land and buildings in the service of economic growth:

STRATEGICALLY ACQUIRE AND ASSEMBLE LAND FOR DESIRABLE/BUILDABLE SITES. One of the biggest constraints on Detroit's economic growth is the shortage of good quality 'move-in' buildings and shovel-ready buildable sites. Few of the many vacant industrial and commercial buildings in Detroit are in move-in condition; most require major rehabilitation in order to be usable. Similarly, while public agencies hold large amounts of vacant land in employment districts, most of it is fragmented—often broken up by parcels held by speculators—and not suitable for redevelopment.

Public land can become a critical asset in efforts to address this problem. While adopting a strategic approach to disposition, public agencies must also acquire properties in economic growth districts where these properties clearly further the goal of creating buildable sites for economic development and job creation. This should be a top priority for vacant land acquisition by public agencies, along with acquisition of industrial buildings that can be rendered move-in at reasonable cost. Objectives for property acquisition can include developing sites that can be marketed to businesses coming into the city or that need new/expanded facilities. In addition, they can be sites identified close to existing major industrial or other job-generating facilities, to be used to further the expansion of those facilities in place.

COMBINE TARGETED DISPOSITION TO DEVELOPERS AND END USERS WITH STRATEGIC HOLDING FOR FUTURE ASSEMBLY. While creating a pool of buildable sites and usable buildings is a necessary step toward fostering an effective economic growth strategy, it must be matched with a parallel systematic approach to the disposition of land and buildings in employment districts. The fundamental principle is that no public land should be sold except for uses that clearly further creating jobs, or strengthening the vitality of the employment district; furthermore, that small parcels should not be sold at all, if by so doing the opportunity for significantly greater impact through assembly is lost. These parcels should be held in inventory while the process of acquisition and assembly takes place.

Priority should go to sales to an end user, either an adjacent existing business or institution already in place, or a firm locating or relocating in the city. Where land is sold to a non-user, such as a developer or investor, the public agency should not only be as certain as possible that the development will actually take place, but should build in provisions for the property to revert back to the City or other public agency in the event that the developer fails to perform within a reasonable time. While some land in employment districts can be used for non-development uses, such as blue/green infrastructure, those uses should be limited to those which also enhance the attractiveness or marketability of the employment district.

INCREASE THE COST OF HOLDING VACANT PROPERTY. The fragmentation of ownership in Detroit's employment districts makes it all but impossible for an effective land reuse strategy to take place without aggressively tackling the privately owned vacant and underutilized properties interspersed throughout these areas, often held by speculators who anticipate potential public interest in these properties. Under current conditions, the cost to a private landowner to hold a vacant property, neglect it, and allow it to become a nuisance, while impeding economic development efforts, is all but zero. The City should immediately increase the cost of holding vacant land by establishing a vacant land registration fee, imposing clear maintenance requirements for privately owned vacant land, and aggressively enforcing both fee payment and maintenance requirements.

In addition, many occupied buildings in employment districts are severely underutilized, often occupied by a firm that may use as little as 10 percent of the building's floor area, or using buildings that can support labor-intensive activities for storage. Voluntary approaches, including facilitating owners' leasing space in their buildings, should be used to address this concern.

IMPLEMENTATION ACTIONS

1   Identify strategic targets for acquisition of properties by public entities.
2   Adopt policies for targeted disposition and holding of properties in economic growth areas.
3   Increase the cost of holding vacant property.
4   Adopt program to foster greater utilization of underutilized buildings.

PILOT PROJECT

1   Target acquisition and assemblage in employment districts

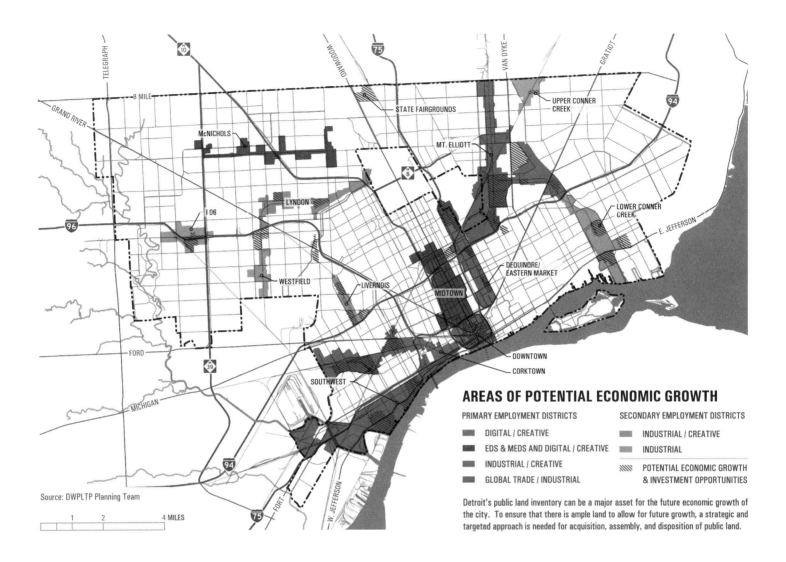

AREAS OF POTENTIAL ECONOMIC GROWTH

PRIMARY EMPLOYMENT DISTRICTS

- DIGITAL / CREATIVE
- EDS & MEDS AND DIGITAL / CREATIVE
- INDUSTRIAL / CREATIVE
- GLOBAL TRADE / INDUSTRIAL

SECONDARY EMPLOYMENT DISTRICTS

- INDUSTRIAL / CREATIVE
- INDUSTRIAL
- POTENTIAL ECONOMIC GROWTH & INVESTMENT OPPORTUNITIES

Detroit's public land inventory can be a major asset for the future economic growth of the city. To ensure that there is ample land to allow for future growth, a strategic and targeted approach is needed for acquisition, assembly, and disposition of public land.

Source: DWPLTP Planning Team

1   2   4 MILES

TARGET PUBLIC LAND STRATEGIES TO SPECIFIC DISTRICTS. Every economic growth district presents different opportunities stemming from the existing patterns of land ownership, the concentration of potentially developable land and the needs of the economic clusters best suited to each district. These factors directly influence the approach to assembly, disposition, and management of publicly owned land. The needs of specific economic clusters, in particular, dictate three distinct approaches for publicly owned land in economic districts.

INDUSTRIAL USE DISTRICTS. The market for industrial real estate is different from the market and needs of other economic activities. Industrial users are looking for land in large, easy-to-develop sites that are close to infrastructure and generally near other industrial activity. With the exception of adaptive reuse of former industrial structures, it is difficult to attract new industrial development to sites of less than 5 acres, as space—either in a building or on the grounds—is required for different combinations of truck staging, material storage, warehousing, fabrication, packaging and parking. Large, market-ready sites for industrial development are rare in established cities, including Detroit. Proactive and sustained approaches to

land assembly are needed to transform small, scattered vacant parcels into large, marketable development sites.

To support modern industrial development in Detroit, publicly owned land should be held and expanded through targeted acquisition strategies to create large, marketable sites for private investment within the core industrially based employment districts. These districts include Southwest, Mt. Elliott, and Dequindre-Eastern Market.

NON-INDUSTRIAL USES. Unlike industrial uses, where the availability of large development sites drives the market, the size of available parcels is often not the primary challenge faced by businesses in non-industrial clusters. Firms within the information technology, creative, and Eds & Meds clusters can utilize a wide range of sites and structures of different sizes, depending upon the needs of each individual business. Within economic growth districts that target non-industrial employment like McNichols, Midtown, and Downtown, the primary approach is to adopt disposition policies to ensure that properties are sold for the most

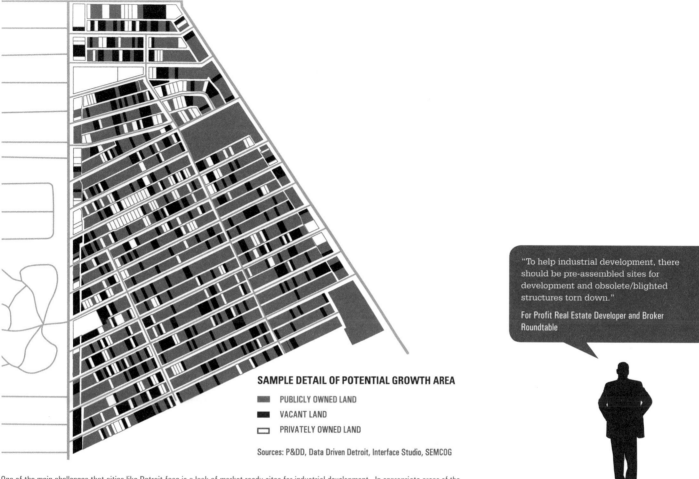

SAMPLE DETAIL OF POTENTIAL GROWTH AREA

■ PUBLICLY OWNED LAND

■ VACANT LAND

□ PRIVATELY OWNED LAND

Sources: P&DD, Data Driven Detroit, Interface Studio, SEMCOG

> "To help industrial development, there should be pre-assembled sites for development and obsolete/blighted structures torn down."
>
> For Profit Real Estate Developer and Broker Roundtable

One of the main challenges that cities like Detroit face is a lack of market-ready sites for industrial development. In appropriate areas of the city, public agencies can build off of the current public land portfolio and begin to create market-ready sites for development.

appropriate reuse and to individuals and firms that are best qualified to redevelop the property, and that have a clear, sensible plan for its redevelopment. Public agencies should consider offering established institutions, such as medical centers or other major employers, in these areas the right of first-refusal to acquire public land and buildings, in order to enable these institutions to assemble land to meet their facility needs.

RETAIL ACTIVITY. The land use framework plan calls for focusing retail in a series of established nodes designated as neighborhood centers and district centers. Public land within these centers should be assembled into marketable sites. Where market demand exists, these properties should be released to investors and developers through a competitive request for proposals; in some areas, however, they will have to be held in public ownership for some period in order to avoid creating an oversupply. It is preferable to hold valuable parcels, even for many years, rather than sell them in the short run for development that, by virtue of inadequate scale or quality, will hinder achievement of the district's economic potential in the long run.

POTENTIAL GROWTH AREAS. Given Detroit's long-term economic development potential, the inventory of land and buildings inside the areas currently designated as employment districts may not be adequate to accommodate potential long-term growth in jobs and economic activity. In order to provide the opportunity for orderly expansion of these districts in the future, and to forestall pressures for expansion into inappropriate areas such as sound, well-established residential districts, the Strategic Framework identifies a number of high-vacancy areas with substantial public land holdings adjacent to employment districts. These areas, called priority hold areas, are designated as land reserves for future employment district expansion. Public land acquisition activities should be pursued in these areas in order to advance long-term assembly of large buildable parcels. While interim green uses may be appropriate, land in these areas should not be committed for long-term use incompatible with future economic development and job-generating reuses.

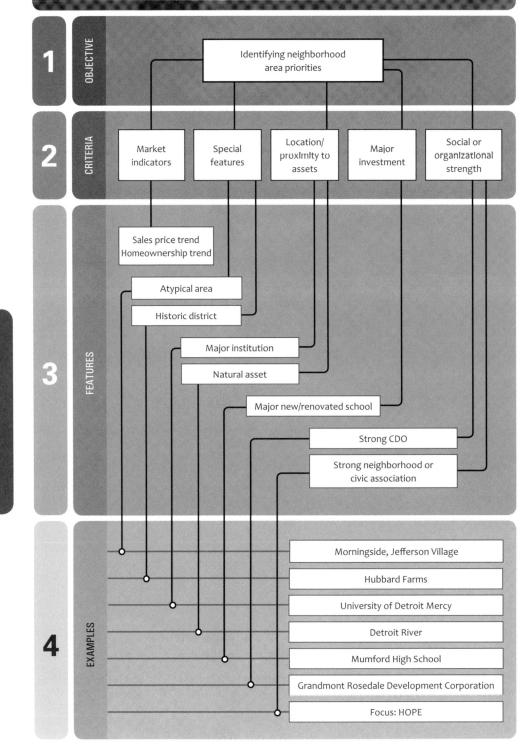

DECISION-MAKING MATRIX: NEIGHBORHOOD AREA PRIORITIES

1 OBJECTIVE

Identifying neighborhood area priorities

2 CRITERIA

- Market indicators
- Special features
- Location/proximity to assets
- Major investment
- Social or organizational strength

3 FEATURES

- Sales price trend / Homeownership trend
- Atypical area
- Historic district
- Major institution
- Natural asset
- Major new/renovated school
- Strong CDO
- Strong neighborhood or civic association

4 EXAMPLES

- Morningside, Jefferson Village
- Hubbard Farms
- University of Detroit Mercy
- Detroit River
- Mumford High School
- Grandmont Rosedale Development Corporation
- Focus: HOPE

"Sitting on my front porch the other day with my daughter, we were just talking about the number of homes in the city that are vacant (a strange conversation to have with an 8 year old). The ironic part to this problem is that there are so many families living in a home far too small for them, are homeless, or are in the process of losing their home. Detroit has an obscene amount of houses that could be repurposed for families to use – but with all the bureaucracy the homes are left to sit, be vandalized, rot, and then burned down. Irony."

Tim, Detroit 24/7, 5/2012

USE VACANT PUBLIC LAND AS A TOOL FOR NEIGHBORHOOD STABILIZATION B

Detroit contains a continuum of neighborhoods and residential areas, varying by vacancy, market activity, physical condition, social and economic dynamics, organizational strength, and other factors. At one end, we find areas that are largely vacant, with scattered occupied houses surrounded by vacant land and abandoned buildings; at the other, sound, well-maintained residential neighborhoods with high rates of homeownership. Even many of Detroit's strongest neighborhoods, however, are dotted with vacant land and buildings, often neglected and inadequately maintained, while in many of Detroit's highest-vacancy, most heavily disinvested areas, one finds intact streets or blocks, and dedicated homeowners and civic associations.

The different conditions of different neighborhoods, particularly with respect to their physical characteristics and market activity reflected in the framework zones, dictate different public land strategies. Most of the city's vital neighborhoods are in the Low-Vacancy framework zone. At the same time, while there are vital neighborhoods in the other framework zones, the proliferation of vacant land and buildings in higher-vacancy areas has undermined the fabric of many once-vital neighborhoods, leading to the need for different approaches to public land management and disposition in many of these areas. Within each framework zone, moreover, we find certain areas that by virtue of location or physical characteristics stand out from the rest of the areas in the framework zone and call for public land strategies that may be significantly different from those generally recommended for the zone. These areas are identified as atypical areas.

LOW-VACANCY. As noted, most of Detroit's stronger neighborhoods are in the low-vacancy framework zone, with the strongest (outside the Greater Downtown area) characterized as Low-Vacancy 1. These areas are one of the city's most important assets and critically important for its future, yet threatened by the growing presence of vacant land and abandoned buildings. This presence, coupled with declines in homeownership and market values, places even the strongest areas at risk of destabilization and deterioration. These areas need strategic policies to treat vacant and abandoned properties in ways that minimize their blighting effect, and ultimately begin to contribute to the stability of the neighborhood. These neighborhoods also have many of the strongest neighborhood associations, which can become effective partners with respect to carrying out many of the public land initiatives.

These strategies need to focus on minimizing the destabilizing impact of vacant land and buildings, as well as poorly maintained, deteriorating housing, and transform these properties into neighborhood assets. Where vacant buildings cannot realistically be restored to productive use, they must be demolished. While infill development may take place on some key vacant lots within low-vacancy areas, most will remain vacant, and must be maintained and reused—using the varied treatments described in the Land Use Element to make them attractive parts of the neighborhood landscape.

IMPLEMENTATION ACTIONS

1. Reuse vacant lots to enhance neighborhood stability.

2. Adopt targeted demolition strategy based on stabilization priorities.

3. Address problem landlords.

4. Increase the cost of holding vacant property.

5. Pursue targeted neighborhood stabilization strategies.

PILOT PROJECTS

1. Target property disposition only in low-vacancy and other areas of strength

2. Create restructured process to facilitate strategic disposition of inventory

CIVIC ENGAGEMENT FEEDBACK

- Creatively use and maintain unsold municipally owned land and structures that are currently not serving as public spaces

- Lease City-owned property for public art installations and events

- Create small parks in (City-owned and privately owned) vacant lots

- Use closed schools as community centers

- Create one collective agency to manage publicly owned homes

"Start a 'keep it dry' campaign for vacant buildings. If a vacant building is dry, it can sit there for 200 years."

Creative Cluster - Working Session

"We have devalued property in the city of Detroit, but for seniors, their home is the only value they have to pass along to the other generations. But if you have abandoned homes on your street, then your house has no value in the market. How can we engage the seniors to find how to bring value back into their home?"

Seniors Round Table, 2/15/2012

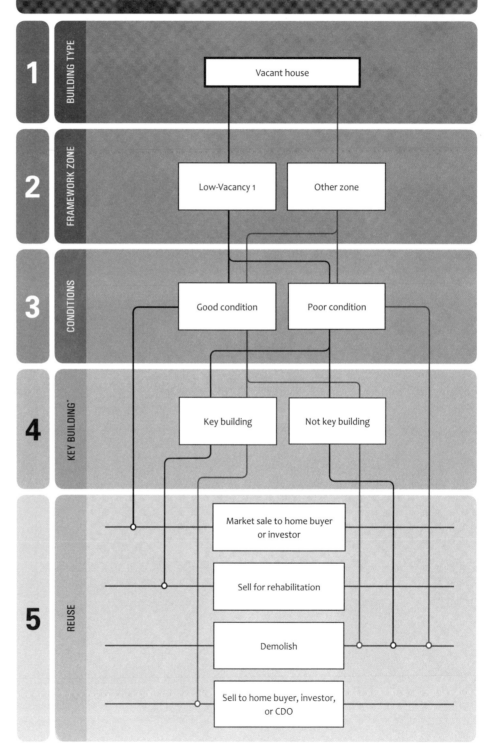

DECISION-MAKING MATRIX: VACANT HOUSE

1 BUILDING TYPE
- Vacant house

2 FRAMEWORK ZONE
- Low-Vacancy 1
- Other zone

3 CONDITIONS
- Good condition
- Poor condition

4 KEY BUILDING
- Key building
- Not key building

5 REUSE
- Market sale to home buyer or investor
- Sell for rehabilitation
- Demolish
- Sell to home buyer, investor, or CDO

One of the major problems facing many neighborhoods is the decline in homeownership, and the growing number of houses owned by absentee landlords, many of whom are short-term speculators with little concern for the neighborhood's future. In tandem with strategies that focus on vacant properties, the city—in partnership with CDOs and neighborhood organizations—should mount a concerted strategy to establish and enforce standards for responsible absentee ownership, prioritizing strong neighborhoods being destabilized by absentee buying. At the same time, strategies to encourage more people to buy houses in these neighborhoods for owner-occupancy should be actively pursued by the City and its neighborhood partners. These areas generally fall into the category of traditional neighborhoods in the typology presented earlier in the Framework, and as a rule, the public land strategies are designed to enable these areas to maintain their current character, while strengthening them so that they can continue to contribute to the city's vitality.

MODERATE-VACANCY. Moderate-vacancy areas are in some respects the most widely varying residential areas in Detroit, ranging from areas that have the potential to remain vital—although they are plagued by higher levels of vacancy than the low-vacancy areas—to areas that are clearly trending toward greater disinvestment and abandonment. As a result, future planning efforts need to be based on a finer-grain assessment of these areas, in order to identify which areas should be targeted for strategies largely similar to those proposed for low-vacancy areas, which may include areas located in close proximity to major assets or to strong neighborhoods; and which should be addressed in ways similar to those proposed for high-vacancy areas.

While the low-vacancy areas are likely to retain their current character in the typology, the higher level of vacancy in the Moderate-Vacancy framework zone suggests the possibility of some areas transitioning over the coming years from traditional neighborhoods to other forms of neighborhood, most probably the Green Mixed-Rise or Green Residential areas in the typologies. Over the next few years, the City should closely monitor trends in housing market activity, investment, and disinvestment in these areas, in order to identify which are on a clear trajectory toward lower densities, and potential future changes in character. As these trends are identified, strategies should be put in place to use vacant properties for longer-term green reuses, and to foster land use transitions in ways that maintain the quality of life for remaining neighborhood residents.

HIGH-VACANCY. The High-Vacancy framework zone contains some key areas that should be prioritized for neighborhood stabilization and revitalization, but also contains many other areas where the neighborhood fabric has largely been lost through abandonment and disinvestment. Over the coming years, strategies must be pursued to further an orderly transition of these areas into green residential areas or landscape areas. While strategies in the stabilization priority areas are likely to be similar to those in low-vacancy areas, those areas are likely to make up only a small part of the land area in the High-Vacancy framework zone. The strategies in most other areas within this zone are designed to focus more on facilitating reuse for blue/green infrastructure or similar landscape treatments, and may include initiatives to help ease the burden of moving for those families who want to relocate to other parts of the city.

Each parcel in public ownership has a different set of characteristics that can be used to determine the most appropriate action to improve the area around that parcel. These include whether the parcel is completely vacant or contains a building, the condition of the building, and the condition of the surrounding neighborhood.

*Building that is architecturally or historically valuable, or which contributes to maintaining the texture of the block or neighborhood

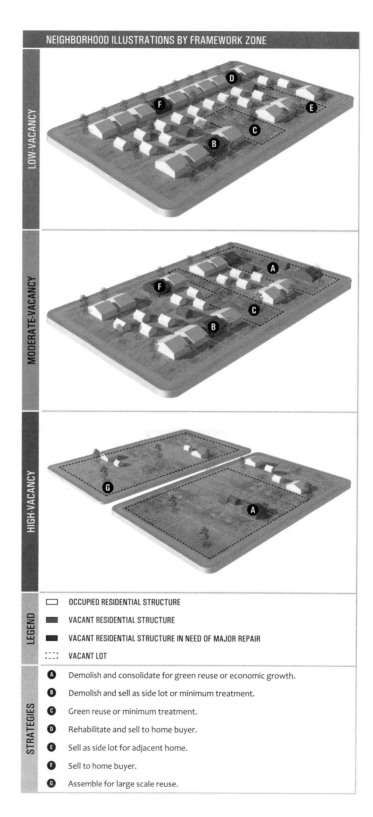

NEIGHBORHOOD ILLUSTRATIONS BY FRAMEWORK ZONE

LOW-VACANCY

MODERATE-VACANCY

HIGH-VACANCY

LEGEND

☐ OCCUPIED RESIDENTIAL STRUCTURE

▬ VACANT RESIDENTIAL STRUCTURE

▬ VACANT RESIDENTIAL STRUCTURE IN NEED OF MAJOR REPAIR

⫶⫶⫶ VACANT LOT

STRATEGIES

Ⓐ Demolish and consolidate for green reuse or economic growth.

Ⓑ Demolish and sell as side lot or minimum treatment.

Ⓒ Green reuse or minimum treatment.

Ⓓ Rehabilitate and sell to home buyer.

Ⓔ Sell as side lot for adjacent home.

Ⓕ Sell to home buyer.

Ⓖ Assemble for large scale reuse.

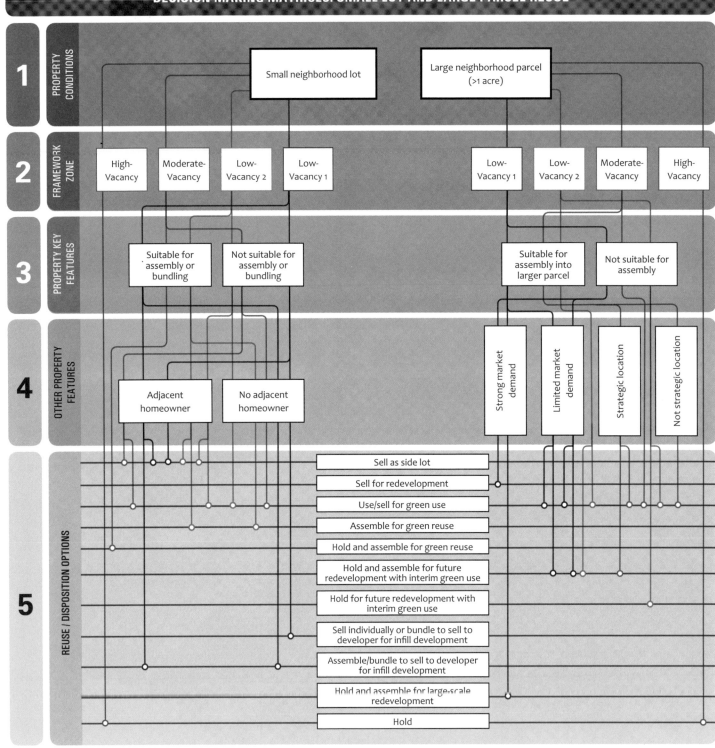

DECISION-MAKING MATRICES: SMALL LOT AND LARGE PARCEL REUSE

1 — PROPERTY CONDITIONS

- Small neighborhood lot
- Large neighborhood parcel (>1 acre)

2 — FRAMEWORK ZONE

- High-Vacancy
- Moderate-Vacancy
- Low-Vacancy 2
- Low-Vacancy 1
- Low-Vacancy 1
- Low-Vacancy 2
- Moderate-Vacancy
- High-Vacancy

3 — PROPERTY KEY FEATURES

- Suitable for assembly or bundling
- Not suitable for assembly or bundling
- Suitable for assembly into larger parcel
- Not suitable for assembly

4 — OTHER PROPERTY FEATURES

- Adjacent homeowner
- No adjacent homeowner
- Strong market demand
- Limited market demand
- Strategic location
- Not strategic location

5 — REUSE / DISPOSITION OPTIONS

- Sell as side lot
- Sell for redevelopment
- Use/sell for green use
- Assemble for green reuse
- Hold and assemble for green reuse
- Hold and assemble for future redevelopment with interim green use
- Hold for future redevelopment with interim green use
- Sell individually or bundle to sell to developer for infill development
- Assemble/bundle to sell to developer for infill development
- Hold and assemble for large-scale redevelopment
- Hold

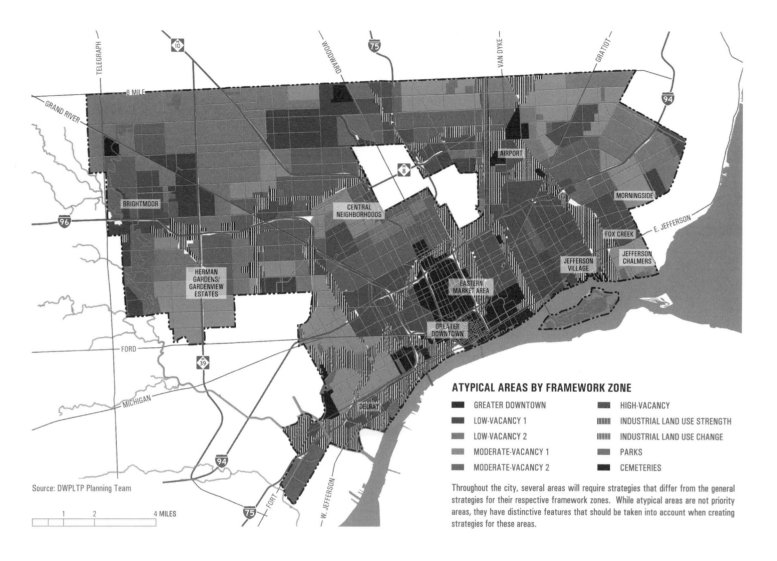

ATYPICAL AREAS BY FRAMEWORK ZONE

■ GREATER DOWNTOWN	■ HIGH-VACANCY
■ LOW-VACANCY 1	▨ INDUSTRIAL LAND USE STRENGTH
■ LOW-VACANCY 2	▨ INDUSTRIAL LAND USE CHANGE
■ MODERATE-VACANCY 1	■ PARKS
■ MODERATE-VACANCY 2	■ CEMETERIES

Source: DWPLTP Planning Team

Throughout the city, several areas will require strategies that differ from the general strategies for their respective framework zones. While atypical areas are not priority areas, they have distinctive features that should be taken into account when creating strategies for these areas.

ATYPICAL AREAS. Atypical areas are smaller geographic areas within a particular framework zone that have distinctive features that make them stand out from the rest of the framework zone, and which call for public land strategies that are likely to be significantly different from those generally recommended for the zone. Those distinctive features typically include one or more of the following:

- location, such as being situated on the Detroit River waterfront;
- concentrations of public land that may make an area suitable for a particular reuse strategy;
- large-scale public investment in infrastructure or area improvement; or
- strong neighborhood or civic infrastructure, such as civic associations or a strong CDO.

The identification of these areas as atypical does not imply that they should be given priority over other areas in the same framework zone. Whether they should also be treated as priority areas will depend on how they fit into the city's land use and economic growth strategies.

NEIGHBORHOOD IMPROVEMENT ACTIONS

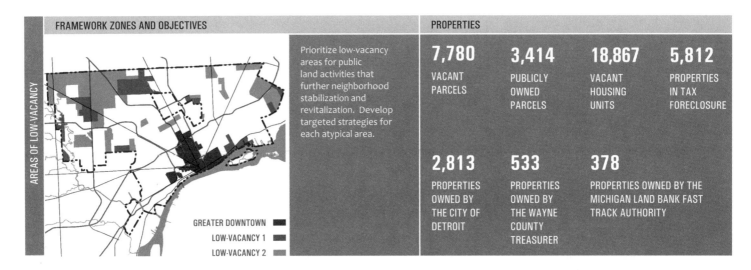

FRAMEWORK ZONES AND OBJECTIVES		PROPERTIES			

AREAS OF LOW-VACANCY

Prioritize low-vacancy areas for public land activities that further neighborhood stabilization and revitalization. Develop targeted strategies for each atypical area.

GREATER DOWNTOWN
LOW-VACANCY 1
LOW-VACANCY 2

7,780 VACANT PARCELS	**3,414** PUBLICLY OWNED PARCELS	**18,867** VACANT HOUSING UNITS	**5,812** PROPERTIES IN TAX FORECLOSURE
2,813 PROPERTIES OWNED BY THE CITY OF DETROIT	**533** PROPERTIES OWNED BY THE WAYNE COUNTY TREASURER	**378** PROPERTIES OWNED BY THE MICHIGAN LAND BANK FAST TRACK AUTHORITY	

AREAS OF MODERATE-VACANCY

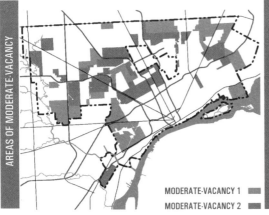

Identify key moderate-vacancy areas, based on criteria such as proximity to low-vacancy areas or particular physical, civic or locational assets, where public land activities should be prioritized to further neighborhood stabilization and revitalization. Facilitate transition in other areas to Green Residential or other typologies. Develop targeted strategies for each atypical area.

MODERATE-VACANCY 1
MODERATE-VACANCY 2

36,403 VACANT PARCELS	**24,339** PUBLICLY OWNED PARCELS	**39,717** VACANT HOUSING UNITS	**11,199** PROPERTIES IN TAX FORECLOSURE
20,651 PROPERTIES OWNED BY THE CITY OF DETROIT	**4,094** PROPERTIES OWNED BY THE WAYNE COUNTY TREASURER	**2,969** PROPERTIES OWNED BY THE MICHIGAN LAND BANK FAST TRACK AUTHORITY	

AREAS OF HIGH-VACANCY

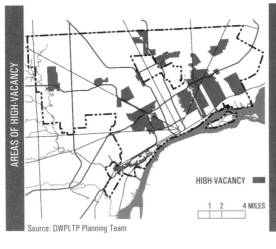

Identify key high-vacancy areas, based on criteria such as proximity to low-vacancy areas or particular physical, civic or locational assets, where public land activities should be prioritized to further neighborhood stabilization and revitalization. Develop targeted strategies for each atypical area.

HIGH-VACANCY

1 2   4 MILES

Source: DWPLTP Planning Team

49,160 VACANT PARCELS	**36,499** PUBLICLY OWNED PARCELS	**13,908** VACANT HOUSING UNITS	**2,856** PROPERTIES IN TAX FORECLOSURE
32,244 PROPERTIES OWNED BY THE CITY OF DETROIT	**1,826** PROPERTIES OWNED BY THE WAYNE COUNTY TREASURER	**3,482** PROPERTIES OWNED BY THE MICHIGAN LAND BANK FAST TRACK AUTHORITY	

ACQUISITION AND ASSEMBLY	DISPOSITION AND REUSE	PRIVATE PROPERTIES	MAINTENANCE	DEMOLITION
Acquire properties in key locations, such as areas around new/expanded school projects or high visibility sites.	Dispose of individual or bundled parcels to qualified users, including side lots to adjacent homeowners and properties to neighborhood organizations for green uses. Dispose of properties to developers for infill development only in key locations and Low-Vacancy 1 areas. Do not hold properties for assembly except in special cases.	Implement strategies to increase maintenance standards and accountability of owners of vacant land. Implement targeted strategies to address problems of absentee landlords. Enlist neighborhood organizations and CDOs as partners to increase enforcement capacity.	Provide higher level of property maintenance. Enlist neighborhood organizations and CDOs as partners. Use alternative site treatments to reduce maintenance costs and stabilize neighborhoods.	Prioritize demolition of blighting vacant structures where they are likely to affect neighborhood stability.
Acquire properties only in key locations within priority and atypical areas.	Dispose of individual parcels to qualified users, including side lots to adjacent homeowners in stabilization priority areas and properties to neighborhood organizations and other users for green uses. Do not hold properties for assembly except in special cases.	Implement strategies to increase maintenance standards and accountability of owners of vacant land in stabilization priority areas, including targeted strategies to address problems of absentee landlords. Enlist neighborhood organizations and CDOs in those areas as partners to increase enforcement capacity.	Provide higher level of property maintenance in stabilization priority areas, including enlisting neighborhood organizations and CDOs as partners. Use alternative site treatments to reduce maintenance costs and stabilize neighborhoods in stabilization priority areas.	Prioritize demolition of key blighting vacant structures where they are likely to affect neighborhood stability in stabilization priority areas.
Acquire selected properties only in key locations within priority and atypical areas, or where needed to further blue/green infrastructure strategies.	Dispose of individual parcels in stabilization priority areas to qualified users, including properties to neighborhood organizations and other end users for green uses. Retain public ownership of land to be used for blue/green infrastructure.	Implement strategies to increase maintenance standards and accountability of owners of vacant land in stabilization priority areas, including targeted strategies to address problems of absentee landlords. Enlist neighborhood organizations and CDOs as partners in those areas where available to increase enforcement capacity.	Maintain properties in stabilization priority areas where neighborhood organizations and CDOs are available to enlist as partners. Use alternative site treatments to reduce maintenance costs and stabilize neighborhoods in stabilization priority areas.	Prioritize demolition only of key blighting vacant structures where they are likely to affect neighborhood stability in stabilization priority areas.

295

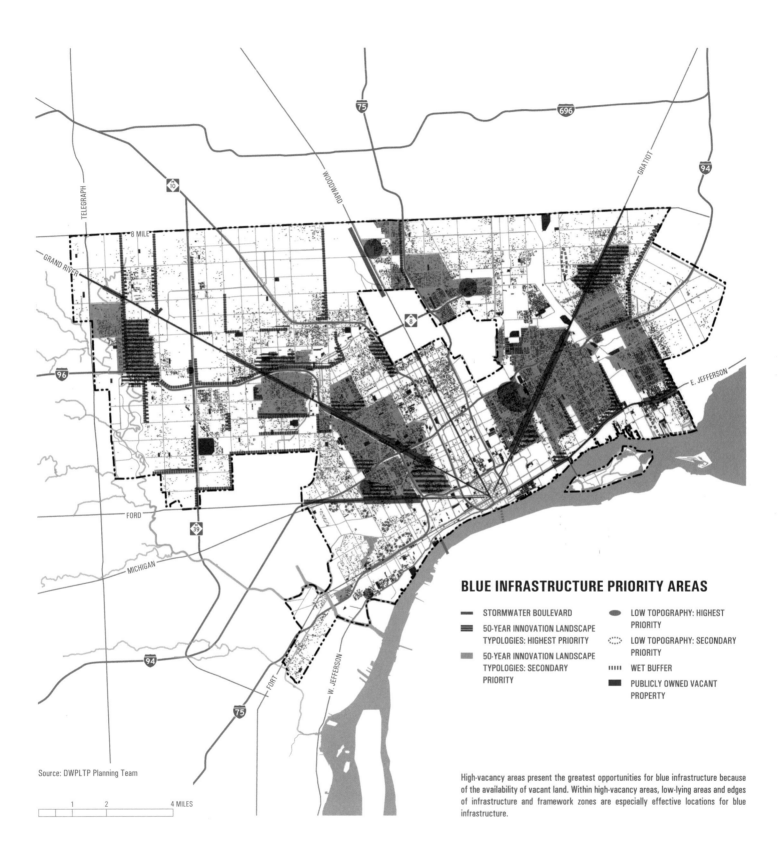

TELEGRAPH

8 MILE

GRAND RIVER

WOODWARD

GRATIOT

FORD

MICHIGAN

W. JEFFERSON

FORT

E. JEFFERSON

BLUE INFRASTRUCTURE PRIORITY AREAS

STORMWATER BOULEVARD

50-YEAR INNOVATION LANDSCAPE
TYPOLOGIES: HIGHEST PRIORITY

50-YEAR INNOVATION LANDSCAPE
TYPOLOGIES: SECONDARY
PRIORITY

LOW TOPOGRAPHY: HIGHEST
PRIORITY

LOW TOPOGRAPHY: SECONDARY
PRIORITY

WET BUFFER

PUBLICLY OWNED VACANT
PROPERTY

Source: DWPLTP Planning Team

1   2   4 MILES

High-vacancy areas present the greatest opportunities for blue infrastructure because
of the availability of vacant land. Within high-vacancy areas, low-lying areas and edges
of infrastructure and framework zones are especially effective locations for blue
infrastructure.

TRANSFORM LARGELY VACANT AREAS THROUGH BLUE AND GREEN INFRASTRUCTURE C

Detroit contains thousands of acres of vacant land largely in public ownership for which no substantial redevelopment potential—in the sense of new buildings—exists within the time frame of this plan. At the same time, Detroit faces significant challenges to quality of life and air and water quality, particularly with respect to stormwater management and pollution from interstate highways and heavy industry. By reusing large amounts of the public land inventory for blue and green infrastructure—to address air quality and stormwater management issues—the City can improve its quality of life, transform blighting expanses of vacant land into productive public assets, and realize significant fiscal benefits with respect to future sewerage system expenditures.

BLUE INFRASTRUCTURE. In addition to the fiscal benefits it offers, creation of blue infrastructure can help further two major citywide goals: maximizing stormwater runoff reductions and stabilizing neighborhoods. These goals can be advanced in different parts of the city through different strategies. In high-vacancy areas, large parcels can be used to retain large amounts of stormwater, while in lower-vacancy areas, smaller-scale approaches such as creating rain gardens and small retention ponds capture smaller amounts of stormwater but provide attractive assets for neighborhoods, helping to stabilize or increase property values. Land currently in public ownership can be used for all of these purposes, and additional public acquisition is encouraged in areas where selective acquisition can help assemble larger or better-configured sites capable of yielding particularly high runoff reductions. Once placed into service for blue infrastructure, these uses should be seen as permanent ones. Future land use changes should only be considered where carried out in close consultation with the Detroit Water and Sewerage Department (DWSD) to ensure that the land use change does not affect the capacity of the system.

The Rouge River watershed is currently being pursued by DWSD as a priority area for runoff reduction, while downtown Detroit should be seen as a future priority area.

MAXIMIZING RUNOFF REDUCTION. High-vacancy areas will be the priority locations for designating existing public land and targeting future acquisition for blue infrastructure for maximum runoff reduction, with the possible addition of selected Moderate-Vacancy 2 areas trending toward significant population decline. In addition to the priority areas noted above, priority parcel criteria include

- frontage on or close proximity to stormwater boulevard;
- location in advantageous topographic areas;
- location within relatively low points in city topography;
- location along Rouge or Detroit Rivers;
- location along wet buffers (these can include edges between framework zones or along interstate highways, where particularly well-suited for stormwater collection due to runoff direction/topography); and
- size greater than a half-acre or feasibility of assembly into larger parcels through consolidation of public holdings or selective public acquisition.

Sites with strong potential for blue infrastructure should be retained in public ownership in order to ensure that they can be incorporated into the emerging system. DWSD would be responsible for maintenance of properties designated for blue infrastructure.

IMPLEMENTATION ACTIONS

1. Hold land between interstates/industrial areas and neighborhoods for green infrastructure (do not release for future residential development).
2. Acquire available land for blue infrastructure in key locations.

EARLY ACTION

1. DWSD Blue Infrastructure Project

PILOT PROJECTS

1. Stormwater Boulevard
2. Blue Infrastructure Master Plan

STORMWATER BOULEVARD

In partnership with DWSD and SEMCOG, convert short segment of arterial road to stormwater boulevard. Narrow the road, install swales and bicycle lanes, and construct retention ponds on adjacent vacant, publicly owned land.

Image Source: Delaware Center for the Inland Bays

DWSD BLUE INFRASTRUCTURE PROJECTS

DWSD is implementing small-scale blue infrastructure pilot projects in coordination with SEMCOG and Greening of Detroit in northwestern Detroit. Additional blue infrastructure projects should be aligned with their efforts.

Image Source: SEMCOG Low Impact Development Manual

INFRASTRUCTURE MASTER PLAN

In partnership with DWSD and SEMCOG, undertake a citywide master planning process for blue infrastructure. Use more detailed data (LiDAR, etc.) to refine DFC vision.

Image Source: DWPLTP Planning Team

SITES FOR NEIGHBORHOOD STABILIZATION. Since the plan recognizes that demolition in low-vacancy areas over the coming years is likely to substantially exceed the amount of infill construction likely to take place, a substantial number of additional vacant lots are likely to be created in these areas. Blue infrastructure is a highly appropriate use for these properties, because it offers the opportunity to create attractive, productive uses for these sites, many of which can be maintained by neighborhood organizations, block groups, or individual homeowners. Blue infrastructure can also be added to the grounds of closed schools or to limited maintenance parks, which can include recreation elements like paths and sitting areas. For larger sites like these, DWSD may need to be involved in maintenance. While larger parcels (> ½ acre) or parcels which can be assembled into larger sites are most desirable, small parcels can also be used for blue infrastructure in low-vacancy areas.

NEAR-TERM PRIORITIES FOCUS ON HIGH-IMPACT, LOW-COST SOLUTIONS. Near-term top priorities for blue infrastructure are two-fold:

- Use blue infrastructure as a neighborhood stabilization approach (in Low-Vacancy areas);
- Implement inexpensive techniques that are highly effective in reducing stormwater runoff, and that do not require any additional land acquisition (in High- or Moderate-Vacancy 2 areas).

These are generally smaller-scale strategies that can begin right away on suitable land that is already in public ownership. Small to moderate-scale projects in high-vacancy areas provide the opportunity to test new ideas at relatively low costs. For instance, curb cuts and minimal regrading of site topography is a simple, low-cost option for converting vacant lots along major roads to retention/detention sites, which can capture stormwater runoff. Following construction, impact of these projects should be measured to quantify the benefits (gallons of runoff diverted, treatment costs avoided, maintenance costs reductions, etc.). The focus of this kind of project is to deliver high results for reducing stormwater runoff with low costs.

Smaller-scale projects should also be tested in lower-vacancy areas, to measure the impact of these uses on neighborhood stability. These uses might take the form of rain gardens or small retention ponds on vacant, publicly owned residential lots, slightly larger blue infrastructures on the grounds of a closed school, or the conversion of a limited maintenance park to an infiltration park that combines stormwater management with recreational features. Here, measuring runoff avoided is still valuable, but feedback from residents and metrics of property values and changes in vacancy rates will be even more important.

Near-term priorities should also include planning necessary for future projects. An Infrastructural Master Plan should be undertaken right away, and targeted acquisition of key parcels for blue infrastructure should begin (for example, purchasing suitable vacant lots at auction).

Statewide, environmental policy does not fully recognize the benefits of blue infrastructure, requiring investments in expensive conventional ("hard") infrastructure for long-term control plans. Advocacy is needed to change state policies and allow value of blue infrastructure to be counted in these plans, so that additional investments in conventional infrastructure are reduced. Instead, future infrastructure investments should be in more multi-functional systems that clean stormwater and provide other environmental benefits and can include recreational components.

In the longer term, projects like large lakes that have high detention/retention capacities should be prioritized. These are the projects with the greatest impact on reducing runoff that enters the combined system, but will require land acquisition first. Interim maintenance strategies can be implemented on acquired sites while additional acquisition is ongoing. Construction of the systems should proceed as soon as sufficient land is available.

DECISION-MAKING MATRIX: IMPLEMENTING BLUE / GREEN INFRASTRUCTURE

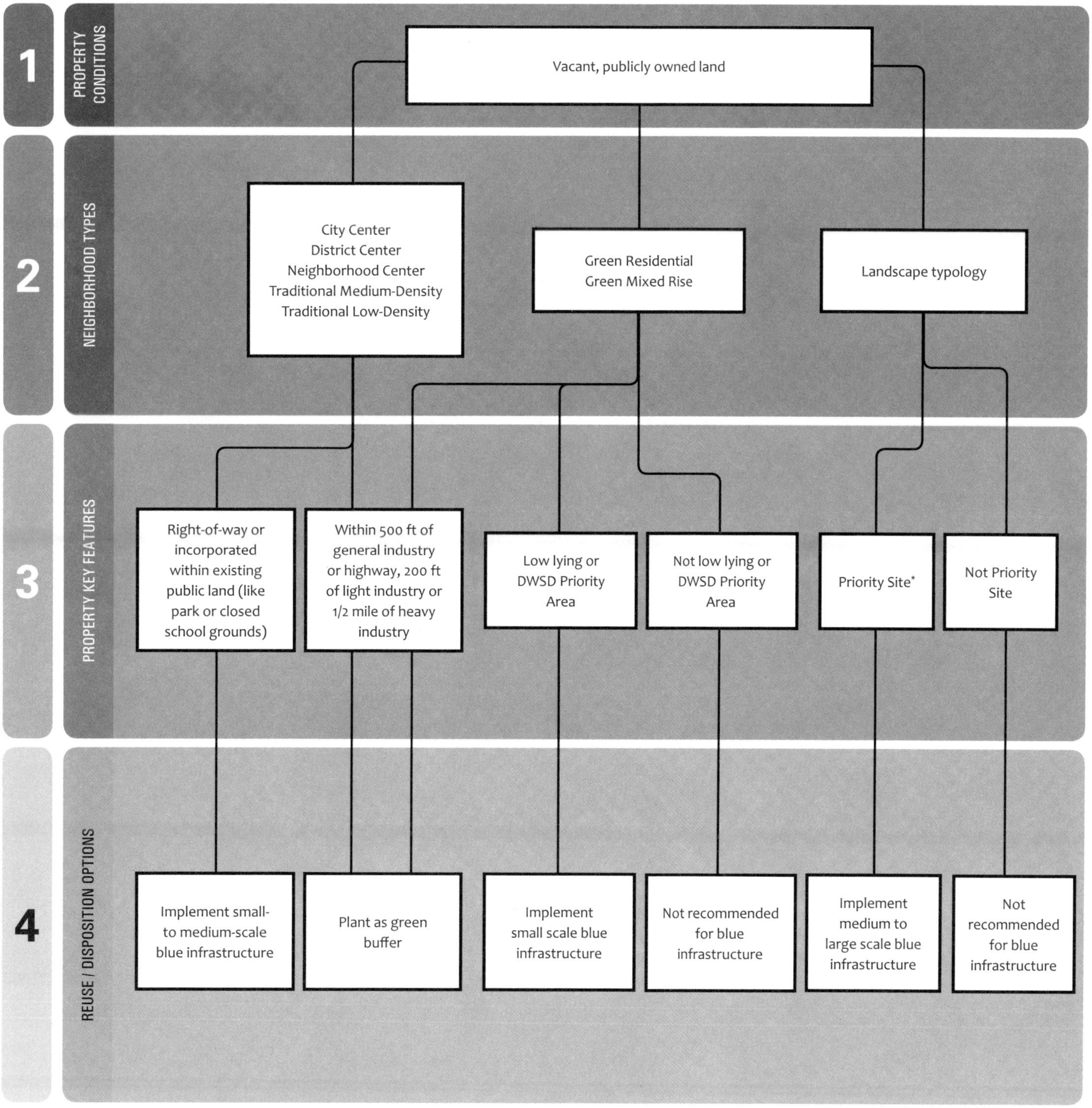

1 PROPERTY CONDITIONS

Vacant, publicly owned land

2 NEIGHBORHOOD TYPES

City Center
District Center
Neighborhood Center
Traditional Medium-Density
Traditional Low-Density

Green Residential
Green Mixed Rise

Landscape typology

3 PROPERTY KEY FEATURES

Right-of-way or incorporated within existing public land (like park or closed school grounds)

Within 500 ft of general industry or highway, 200 ft of light industry or 1/2 mile of heavy industry

Low lying or DWSD Priority Area

Not low lying or DWSD Priority Area

Priority Site*

Not Priority Site

4 REUSE / DISPOSITION OPTIONS

Implement small- to medium-scale blue infrastructure

Plant as green buffer

Implement small scale blue infrastructure

Not recommended for blue infrastructure

Implement medium to large scale blue infrastructure

Not recommended for blue infrastructure

*Site that is architecturally or historically valuable, or which contributes to maintaining the texture of the block or neighborhood

GREEN INFRASTRUCTURE PRIORITY AREAS

- CARBON FOREST
- INDUSTRIAL BUFFER
- INDUSTRIAL LAND USE STRENGTH
- PUBLICLY OWNED VACANT PROPERTY
- SECONDARY EMPLOYMENT DISTRICT

Source: DWPLTP Planning Team

1   2   4 MILES

Vacant land in public ownership that lies between neighborhoods and major sources of air pollution (industry corridors and interstates) should not be released for future residential development. Instead, it should be planted as a forested buffer to absorb pollutants.

GREEN INFRASTRUCTURE

Green infrastructure uses include carbon forests and industry buffers that can improve air quality and enhance the quality of life and attractiveness of the city. Priority parcels for green infrastructure are those located within 500 feet of an interstate or major arterial highway, and parcels located between major industrial (or polluting infrastructure facility) areas and residential neighborhoods.

As with blue infrastructure, these uses should be seen as permanent ones, with future land use changes limited to those that do not affect the capacity of the system.

Implementing these new uses may take time, especially in areas where suitable vacant land is scarce. Parcels in public ownership that meet these criteria should not be released for new development (with the exception of some areas, which may be suitable for industrial use where demand exists), and should be planted densely with seedlings.

CONSTRUCTION COSTS AND MAINTENANCE REQUIREMENTS. Planting a forest like this is very inexpensive. Seedlings typically cost around $1 each, and if planted using a 10' x 10' grid spacing, so that the cost per acre is less than $450. Maintenance efforts required will include the following.

- Biomass maintenance (take care of fallen trees, etc.)
- Succession maintenance (thin out/remove trees as needed; seed later species)
- Trash removal
- Maintain visual access/ sightlines for safety
- Maintenance of any trails incorporated into forests

Neighborhood residents, other volunteers, researchers, or students could undertake these tasks. Research activities could be incorporated with maintenance, as these forests provide opportunities for measuring urban air quality, carbon sequestration, and other related topics.

Tree selection can also reduce maintenance needs. Initially, fast-growing trees should be planted. These trees will help shade out grasses, improving visibility through the forest floor for improved safety. Later, interplant with slow-growing dominant forest-type species that will ultimately grow and out-shade the fast-growing species. Finally, the forest floor can be seeded with diverse forest floor species, creating a rich ecological experience for residents and habitat for local wildlife and migrating birds.

COOPERATION NEEDED FOR IMPLEMENTATION. Carbon forests will require cooperation from many different local, regional, and state agencies. Many different landowners will need to be involved, especially for carbon forests. Within 500 feet of an interstate, land is typically owned by at least three different parties:

- Interstate right-of-way owned by Michigan Department of Transportation
- Adjacent local road owned by Wayne County
- Adjacent lots may be privately or publicly owned, by any number of agencies

Industry buffers too may combine vegetation planted on the same lot as the industrial use as well as forests beyond the site border.

Outside of industry parcels or road rights-of-way, these forests could be owned by the City, Land Bank, Trust, DOT, DWSD, or institution and could incorporate recreational features like trails.

301

"Projects like the RiverWalk's wetland filter clean the water and bring back animals. More of those would be helpful, especially around River Rouge. You can see the dirty water from Google Earth. :("

Detroit 24/7, 5/2012

"I appreciate adding the green aspects to the city for true sustainability, especially buffering the industrial areas."

Karen, DWP email comment, 9/2012

ENVIRONMENTAL MITIGATION STRATEGIES

	ILLUSTRATION	DESCRIPTION	APPLICABLE AREAS	MITIGATION/BUFFERING OPPORTUNITIES
NO BUFFER NEEDED		No buffer is needed.	<ul><li>Industrial land use change adjacent to any land use.</li><li>Industrial land use strength adjacent to high-vacancy area.</li><li>Areas where existing adjacencies between industrial and residential land uses will likely dissipate.</li></ul>	Not applicable.
ZONING REGULATION CHANGES		Some buffer needs can be addressed through changes to zoning regulations: adjust setback distances and landscape requirements.	<ul><li>Current industrial areas that are likely to undergo substantial renovation or construction in the future.</li><li>Land that is not currently industrial, but which is targeted for potential conversion to industrial in future.</li></ul>	Buffering opportunities:<ul><li>Required setback distance needs additional consideration</li></ul>
USE OF ADJACENT PARCELS		In the near term, zoning changes will have limited impact on many existing industrial uses. In these cases, look for opportunities outside of industrial parcels for short-term impacts.	Existing industrial areas where current businesses are unlikely to change in near- to mid-term (zoning changes would not impact these businesses, which would likely be grandfathered in until a change in ownership or significant construction triggered compliance with new zoning). For buffering to occur, look for opportunities immediately outside of the industrial parcel on publicly owned land.	Buffering opportunities:<ul><li>Underutilized commercially zoned land lying between industry and residential can be converted to a green buffer</li><li>High vacancy residential blocks adjacent to industry can provide room for a green buffer</li><li>Parks or vacant school sites can be planted to act as buffers</li></ul>
NO CLEAR BUFFERING OPTIONS		In these situations, alternative means of reducing negative impacts on nearby residents should be pursued.	Existing industrial areas where current businesses are unlikely to change in near- to mid-term, and where opportunities for creating physical buffer are minimal. For example, many areas of Southwest Detroit contain low vacancy residential blocks that are adjacent to industry.	Mitigation opportunities:<ul><li>If industry exceeds allowable pollution discharge limits, increase enforcement of standards</li><li>If industry is within allowed discharge limits, but still negatively impacts neighbors, consider raising standard to higher level</li></ul>
NEW INDUSTRIAL LAND		Acquisition plans for new Industrial land should incorporate buffering considerations.	In areas that are not currently industrial, but are identified for future industry, multiple options exist for buffering. Changes to the industrial zoning rules can create buffers on-site for new industrial uses. In addition, any zoning changes or land acquisition can allow sufficient buffering space between future industry and current/future residential neighborhoods.	Buffering opportunities:<ul><li>On-site: change rules of industrial zones to increase set-back distances and create buffers on-site</li><li>Off-site: coordinate land acquisition and zoning changes with current/future adjacent land uses</li></ul>

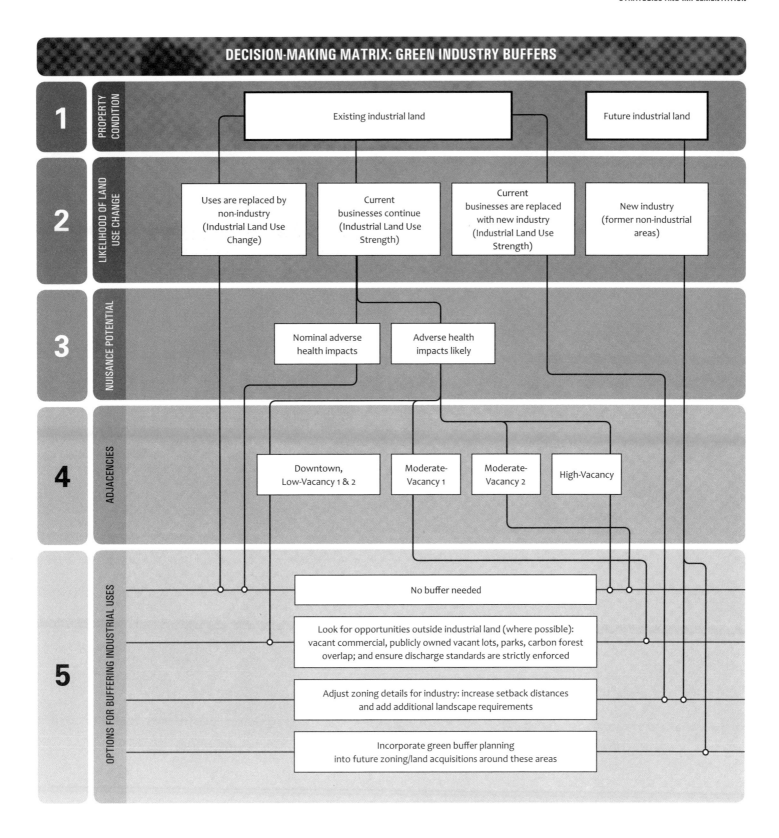

DECISION-MAKING MATRIX: GREEN INDUSTRY BUFFERS

1 PROPERTY CONDITION

Existing industrial land

Future industrial land

2 LIKELIHOOD OF LAND USE CHANGE

Uses are replaced by non-industry (Industrial Land Use Change)

Current businesses continue (Industrial Land Use Strength)

Current businesses are replaced with new industry (Industrial Land Use Strength)

New industry (former non-industrial areas)

3 NUISANCE POTENTIAL

Nominal adverse health impacts

Adverse health impacts likely

4 ADJACENCIES

Downtown, Low-Vacancy 1 & 2

Moderate-Vacancy 1

Moderate-Vacancy 2

High-Vacancy

5 OPTIONS FOR BUFFERING INDUSTRIAL USES

No buffer needed

Look for opportunities outside industrial land (where possible): vacant commercial, publicly owned vacant lots, parks, carbon forest overlap; and ensure discharge standards are strictly enforced

Adjust zoning details for industry: increase setback distances and add additional landscape requirements

Incorporate green buffer planning into future zoning/land acquisitions around these areas

DECISION-MAKING MATRIX: VACANT SCHOOL REUSE OPTIONS

1 BUILDING TYPE

Vacant school building

2 REUSE POTENTIAL

| Facility has significant PRESENT market or adaptive reuse potential | Facility has significant FUTURE market or adaptive reuse potential | Facility has LITTLE OR NO market or adaptive reuse potential |

3 ARCHITECTURAL OR HISTORIC VALUE

Building HAS significant architectural or historic value

Building LACKS significant architectural or historic value

4 POTENTIAL FOR BLUE/GREEN INFRASTRUCTURE

Building HAS potential value for blue/green infrastructure

Building LACKS potential value for blue/green infrastructure

5 NEIGHBORHOOD IMPACT

Reuse WILL impact stable or at-risk neighborhoods

Reuse WILL NOT impact stable or at-risk neighborhoods

6 DECISION OUTCOME

Market for redevelopment

Consider blue/green infrastructure reuse

Evaluate future potential carefully before making decision

Reuse for blue/green infrastructure

Explore other neighborhood-compatible reuse possibilities

Incorporate Into other public holdings for future reuse

Hold and mothball for future redevelopment

PILOT PROJECT

SCHOOL INVESTMENT TARGET AREA

Develop and implement a strategy in partnership with DPS and community stakeholders to maximize the impact of a major school investment, focusing on vacant properties near the facility and building the school's role as a center of community.

Image Source: Detroit Public Schools

Of the many different facilities that government maintains, the future of the city's schools and parks has the most direct impact on residents' quality of life, and is likely to have the greatest impact on Detroit's future. Over the past decades, many schools have been closed, and many parks have been closed or neglected. What to do with closed facilities, and how to make decisions about future school closings and park maintenance issues, are critical decision-making areas for the city's public agencies and residents.

DETROIT PUBLIC SCHOOLS. In recent years, faced with shrinking enrollment, the Detroit Public School District (DPS) has closed many schools around the city, while investing significant resources in building, expanding, and upgrading other schools for the remaining enrollment. In light of the trends, still more schools may be closed in future years. The reuse of vacant school facilities, as well as the selection of which schools may be closed in the future, should take place strategically—in conjunction with the city's land use and neighborhood stabilization goals—in order to reduce the blighting effect of vacant buildings and the potential destabilizing effect of future closings. At the same time, targeted neighborhood strategies around new or significantly upgraded schools along with co-location of other community-serving activities can maximize their value as neighborhood assets. Maximizing the value of schools as community assets, however, may require some rethinking or reworking of the current DPS citywide open enrollment policies.

Closed public schools and their sites can become neighborhood assets. Some closed public schools are already being used for charter schools or for other purposes. Options include adaptive reuse for community benefit facilities such as child care or community centers; secure mothballing of historically or architecturally significant buildings for future reuse; or demolition to facilitate reuse of the site for economic development, open space or large-scale stormwater retention projects.

LINK PUBLIC FACILITY AND PROPERTY DECISIONS TO LARGER STRATEGIES

305

An effective strategy to deal with the future of Detroit's public school facilities should include a number of key elements:

- A decision framework should be developed to guide the use of closed school facilities, which looks at the facility itself, as well as its environs, its location with respect to the framework zones and neighborhood stabilization priority areas, as well as within the blue/green infrastructure strategy.

- Neighborhood stabilization criteria as discussed below should be integrated into and made an explicit part of future school closing decisions.

- Areas in close proximity to major newly constructed or substantially expanded or upgraded schools facilities should be prioritized for stabilization and revitalization activity.

The principle behind the use of neighborhood stabilization criteria is straightforward, and involves three distinct questions:

- How will closing this school affect the stability and vitality of the neighborhood in which it is located?

- Are there alternative ways of using the school that will keep it open (either as a public school or some other community-serving facility) to maintain its benefit to the neighborhood?

- What other activities are underway, by government, CDOs, neighborhood associations or others, to stabilize or revitalize the neighborhood that would be affected by the school closing?

This is particularly important in the Low-Vacancy framework zones and in other areas designed as priority stabilization areas.

Schools can become centers of community. The use of high-quality school facilities as anchors for neighborhood stabilization should be actively promoted, along with other measures to strengthen those schools, including prioritizing demolition of derelict buildings in their vicinity, while fostering rehabilitation of reusable buildings and community-serving vacant lot treatments. These strategies can include conversion of schools into community- or neighborhood-based schools and co-location of other facilities and services that provide community benefits into school facilities.

IMPLEMENTATION ACTIONS

1. Create priority system for public land and parks acquisition.
2. Create joint policies and system for disposition of public property.
3. Adopt coordinated maintenance strategy for public land.
4. Adopt targeted demolition strategy based on stabilization priorities.
5. Use new and upgraded schools as community anchors for stabilization.
6. Review criteria for school closing to reflect neighborhood stability factors.
7. Park management: update parks and recreation facilities planning to reflect current and future populations and budgets (update aspects of 2006 Strategic Master Plan by the DRD).
8. Parks and recreation planning at neighborhood scales: refine citywide strategy of DWP through smaller-scaled analysis.

PRECEDENTS

1. Natur-Park Sudgelande
2. Romanowski Farm Park

EARLY ACTION

1. Priority Greenway Projects

PILOT PROJECTS

1. School Investment Target Area
2. Nature Park

"Detroit Public Library is helping to improve the city by bringing in programs and speakers to help the community feel together and do things that can bring a sense of community to the users."

Kathi, Detroit 24/7, 5/2012

の

DETROIT FUTURE CITY | 2012

306

PARKS, OPEN SPACE, AND RECREATION

- ▬ EXISTING PARK
- ▬ GOLF COURSE
- ▬ CEMETERY
- ● CONVERT TO MULTIUSE PARK
- ● CONVERT TO INFILTRATION PARK IN NEAR TERM
- ● CONVERT TO INFILTRATION PARK IN LONG TERM

- ▦ AREAS TO CONSIDER NEW PARKS
- EXISTING GREENWAY, OFF STREET
- ▪▪▪▪ EXISTING GREENWAY, ON STREET
- ▬ PRIMARY GREENWAY, OFF STREET
- ▪▪▪▪ PRIMARY GREENWAY ON STREET
- ▪▪▪▪ PROPOSED ON STREET BICYCLE PATH
- ▬ PROPOSED ON STREET BICYCLE LANES
- ▪▪▪▪ OTHER PROPOSED GREENWAY
- ▪ RECREATION CENTER

Sources: Detroit Recreation Department, DWPLTP Planning Team

1   2   4 MILES

The future Park System will provide new opportunities for open space in Detroit. While many parks will remain open, some can be converted to multi-use or infiltration parks, which will include elements of blue infrastructure or ecological landscapes.

THE LAND AND BUILDINGS ASSETS ELEMENT : A STRATEGIC APPROACH TO PUBLIC ASSETS

PARKS AND RECREATION

TOWARD PARK REALIGNMENT. All parkland is important, but not all parks should remain traditional parks. Detroit's park system is both too expensive to maintain and is not well-aligned with current population patterns. Since adoption of the strategic master plan for the city park system in 2006, conditions have changed dramatically; both populations and fiscal resources have declined more sharply than anticipated. As a result, it is necessary to:

- find alternative park models that cost less to maintain,

- identify potential future funding and maintenance partners, and

- reposition existing parks based on current and projected future population densities.

Well-maintained, actively used parks in low-vacancy areas play important roles in maintaining property values, stabilizing neighborhoods, and building communities. Parks in these areas should include recreation opportunities, but can also be adapted to include new uses such as blue infrastructure or urban gardens.

In higher-vacancy areas, parks offer key opportunities for blue infrastructure and ecological landscapes or wildlife habitats, representing key nodes in the citywide landscape network.

In addition to traditional, multi-use, and infiltration parks, the proposed landscape networks would broaden the range and availability of recreational open spaces. Blue and green infrastructure could include recreation elements. For example, stormwater boulevards and carbon forests could integrate bike trails and paths, and larger stormwater infrastructure like retention ponds could be engineered to function more like surface lakes to accommodate boating, or could be designed as quickly draining basins that could be used for sports fields during dry weather. Greenways can be created to link neighborhoods across the city, fostering healthy lifestyles and encouraging greater environmental consciousness.

Some areas of the city have inadequate access to local parks. In low-vacancy areas with insufficient park access, parks should be a priority reuse option for vacant land, particularly where alternative maintenance and funding opportunities exist, particularly by engaging neighborhood organizations, CDOs, and local businesses.

307

"I think that all of Detroit is beautiful, but one of my favorite places to go is the river. From the Ambassador Bridge, to Hart Plaza to Chene Part and Belle Isle, the riverfront is one of the most beautiful places in the city limits. It is serene and picturesque and the one place you are guaranteed to see an entirely different country just by standing near a window."

Aria, Detroit 24/7, 5/2012

"The vacant land or buildings should be used to make a park, or something equivalent to that. These buildings are being broken down and used to make houses, which I honestly don't think we need more of. Let's give the kids a reason to get off their butts and go outdoors!"

Samia, Detroit 24/7, 5/2012

"I like the idea of farms and parks, bike trails and flower gardens!"

Evone, Environmental Summit, 5/5/2011

CIVIC ENGAGEMENT FEEDBACK AND PUBLIC PERCEPTIONS

- Hold, maintain, improve, and increase access to city-owned parks
- Keep parks clean and safe, even in the evening
- Increase access to parks
- Empower residents/neighborhood organizations to maintain existing parks
- Diversify types of parks (e.g. add more parks with natural areas)

MAKING MAINTENANCE AFFORDABLE. If Detroit is to have a functioning park system, it must align its maintenance costs with its budget realities. Key steps may include

- reducing the total number of parks;
- adapting existing parks to uses that still benefit communities but are less expensive to operate and maintain, such as stormwater management or wildlife habitats;
- finding potential park maintenance partners, such as neighborhood groups, nonprofit organizations, businesses, and others;
- partnering with other city agencies to adapt and maintain parks to fulfill multiple goals, such as partnering with DWSD to create a blue infrastructure/infiltration park that both captures stormwater and provides recreation opportunities; and
- exploring partnerships with state or regional agencies for maintenance of large parks.

As parks fulfill different roles in Detroit, their maintenance requirements will change in response.

CREATING AN OPEN SPACE NETWORK. The future open space network will provide more diverse recreation opportunities to Detroiters and visitors, and will be better aligned with existing and future residential densities, supplementing traditional parks with a wide range of new park configurations, including nature parks, infiltration parks, and multi-use parks, and linked by a robust network of greenways. Additional recreation features will be incorporated into areas reused for blue and green infrastructure. The new network will be significantly less expensive for the City to maintain, both by changes in its physical configuration and by the opportunities it will provide for a wide range of neighborhood groups, nonprofit organizations, and others to participate in park maintenance.

PRECEDENT

ROMANOWSKI FARM PARK

Residents met for months to discuss, design, and vote on what they wanted to see in their park. In three years, the formerly derelict field was transformed into a recreation park and community resource with a new playground, athletic fields, a pavilion, and several gardens.

Image Source: The Greening of Detroit

EARLY ACTION

PRIORITY GREENWAY PROJECTS

Current Detroit projects underway:

- Kercheval Greenway
- Belt Line Greenway
- Bicycle lanes along Jefferson Ave.
- Extensions to Dequindre Cut and RiverWalk
- Bicycle/pedestrian access on NITC

Image Source: Detroit RiverFront Conservancy

PILOT PROJECT

NATURE PARK

Create a Nature Park in partnership with local non-profit group in a limited maintenance park or on a large vacant lot with mature vegetation. Park construction should incorporate a monitoring/research component in partnership with local universities or high schools on urban ecology topics.

Image Source: Detroit Conservation Leadership Corps

DECISION-MAKING MATRIX: PARK MAINTENANCE OPTIONS

1 PROPERTY TYPE

Existing park

2 CURRENT MAINTENANCE STRATEGY

Maintained

Limited maintenance

3 FRAMEWORK ZONE

Downtown, Low-Vacancy 1 or 2, or Moderate-Vacancy 1

Moderate-Vacancy 2

High-Vacancy

4 FUTURE LAND USE TYPOLOGY

Green Residential or other future land use

Traditional Medium Density and Traditional Low Density

City Center, District Center, Neighborhood Center or Green Mixed Rise

5 ADDITIONAL CONSIDERATIONS

Site is poor candidate for future development

Site is good candidate for future development

Park borders area with lower vacancy that has insufficient park access

Park does not border area with insufficient park access

Area is already well-served by other parks

Area has insufficient park access

6 RECOMMENDED ACTIONS

Keep open

Close in long term

Close in near-term

Convert to non-traditional open space use or blue/green infrastructure

Identify temporary use as holding strategy for future development

Reopen as multi-use park or nature park

Convert to infiltration park

Urban garden

"I would like to see smart uses for vacant land, including partnering with Greening of Detroit for low-maintenance landscaping ([versus] wasteful mowing of parcels)."

Renee, Planning Cluster-based Meeting, 2/15/2011

MAINTENANCE STRATEGIES (TEMPORARY OR PERMANENT)

LOW-VACANCY AREAS	LOW COST PUBLIC MAINTENANCE FOR NEIGHBORHOOD STABILITY AND / OR HOLDING	MAINTAINED LAWN $$$	LOW GROW LAWN $$	PHYTOREMEDIATION $$	MEADOW $-$$
MODERATE-VACANCY AREAS		LOW GROW LAWN $$	PHYTOREMEDIATION $$	MEADOW $-$$	RAPID REFORESTATION $-$$
	SPECIAL CASE: ADJACENT TO LOW / MODERATE-VACANCY	MAINTAINED LOT $$$			
HIGH-VACANCY AREAS	NON-ACTIVE PUBLIC MAINTENANCE	EMERGENT FOREST $0			
	SPECIAL CASE: ADJACENT TO LOW / MODERATE-VACANCY	RAPID REFORESTATION $-$$	ORCHARD $0	LOW GROW LAWN $$	MEADOW $$

LEGEND

$0	NO COST TO CITY
$	VERY LOW COST TO CITY
$$	MINIMAL COST TO CITY
$$$	HIGH COST TO CITY

INCORPORATE MORE INNOVATIVE VACANT LAND MAINTENANCE APPROACHES

How maintenance is handled can determine whether or not the current condition of a vacant parcel degrades residents' quality of life. For example, resident concerns with unmowed vacant lots include safety, perception, and other issues:

- **SAFETY:** Residents have real concerns about personal and property crime associated with unmowed lots; residents often walk in the middle of streets rather than on sidewalks because of concern that someone could be lurking in shadows of tall grass next to the sidewalk.

- **PSYCHOLOGY:** Unmowed lots are perceived as blight, give the impression that no one is looking after them, and invite illegal dumping and other illicit activities.

- **PRACTICALITY:** Some residents use vacant lots for parking, and advocate for mowing so they can continue to do so.

More use should be made of creative landscape interventions that reduce maintenance costs, or shift maintenance responsibilities to other entities. Individual lots in low-vacancy areas should be sold or leased where possible to private entities, whether sold to homeowners as side lots, used as community open space, or maintained by neighborhood associations or block groups. Simultaneously increasing enforcement of maintenance standards on private owners of vacant properties will motivate them to take responsibility for their properties or pay the City to maintain them.

Vacant lots provide opportunities for a wide range of new uses, including interim uses if permanent uses are not anticipated for some time. General maintenance strategies include the following:

- Identifying potential non-development reuse alternatives for vacant parcels.

- Finding opportunities to engage residents, neighborhood organizations, and others in vacant land maintenance.

- Using alternative lot treatments to reduce the cost of maintaining those parcels that need continued public sector maintenance.

- Reducing maintenance of public land in high-vacancy areas except to the extent needed for blue infrastructure purposes.

- Adopting and enforcing minimum maintenance standards for privately owned vacant land, including developing enforcement partnerships with neighborhood associations.

As properties are demolished, particularly in low-vacancy areas, the demolition specification should incorporate the preferred basic landscape treatment for each property, and wherever possible, a maintenance plan developed in partnership with the residents of the neighborhood in which it is located.

The typology of vacant lot strategies presented here is only the beginning. Additional work will be needed to make possible a systematic maintenance strategy for vacant lots, including refining the typology, developing more precise cost estimates, estimating the benefits, and reaching out to potential community partners.

311

IMPLEMENTATION ACTIONS

1. Adjust city maintenance standards, strategies, and practices to vary by framework zone and future land use (do not mow all vacant lots in city regardless of location, but instead adopt different lower cost maintenance strategies in different areas); look for partnerships to help with land maintenance.

2. Form partnerships with community groups and other organizations, businesses, and individuals to help maintain land.

3. Refine set of landscape maintenance typologies and develop cost estimates to implement.

PRECEDENT

1. Vacant Lot Program: Philadelphia

PILOT PROJECT

1. Implement maintenance pilot projects across multiple framework zones

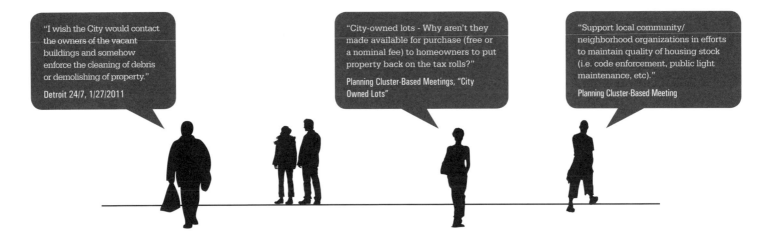

"I wish the City would contact the owners of the vacant buildings and somehow enforce the cleaning of debris or demolishing of property."

Detroit 24/7, 1/27/2011

"City-owned lots - Why aren't they made available for purchase (free or a nominal fee) to homeowners to put property back on the tax rolls?"

Planning Cluster-Based Meetings, "City Owned Lots"

"Support local community/ neighborhood organizations in efforts to maintain quality of housing stock (i.e. code enforcement, public light maintenance, etc)."

Planning Cluster-Based Meeting

CODE ENFORCEMENT

Because even the vast public land inventory represents less than half of the estimated 150,000 vacant land parcels and vacant buildings in Detroit, the condition and ownership of privately owned vacant properties affects the City's neighborhoods, and affecting Detroit's ability to move forward on economic development and other strategies requiring land assembly and reuse. Many of the privately owned vacant lots and buildings in the city are neglected, while in many areas with strong economic development, potential owners sit on key parcels, doing nothing to improve or maintain them, and blocking the city from assembling sites for redevelopment and reuse. On top of that, many occupied buildings are underutilized—particularly in the city's industrial areas—or in the case of absentee rental properties, destabilizing vital but threatened neighborhoods. The problem has been made worse by the City's budget, and the low priority given to code enforcement among the many competing demands faced by the City. In many respects, effective code enforcement is as much a factor in the City's level of public safety as are effective police and fire departments. Public health and safety issues are deeply interwoven with those affecting the public land inventory. Because private owners are responsible for more than half of all vacant properties in Detroit, code enforcement is critical to Detroit's turnaround. If the City does not act aggressively to enforce standards for private ownership, the effectiveness of the public land strategies recommended in this Framework will inevitably be compromised. Reflecting the City's fiscal constraints, it must address these issues in ways that do not unduly overburden the municipal budget, by building strong community code enforcement partnerships with business development groups, neighborhood organizations, and CDOs, and by focusing more aggressively on cost recovery from private property owners.

Two issues come to the forefront for urgent attention to code enforcement:

- addressing privately owned vacant land, and

- addressing the problems associated with absentee landlords.

Each of these priorities demand targeted enforcement strategies.

INCREASING THE COST OF HOLDING VACANT LAND. In Detroit at present, there is virtually no cost associated with holding vacant properties. Property taxes are modest and code enforcement is inadequate. Although the City enacted a vacant property registration ordinance in 2010, it does not apply to vacant lots and is not effectively enforced, while the ordinance itself fails to impose a registration fee on property owners. These issues should be immediately addressed:

- Amend the ordinance to include vacant lots.

- Establish clear minimum standards for vacant lot maintenance.

- Impose a reasonable fee through the registration process on owners of both vacant lots and vacant buildings.

Once these steps have been taken, a major effort should be made to obtain compliance with the ordinance. Fees collected under the ordinance should be dedicated to its enforcement.

In light of its fiscal constraints, the City may want to identify key target areas to initiate enforcement of the registration ordinance and the minimum standards for maintenance. These can include economic development priority areas, as well as areas where strong neighborhood organizations and CDOs are available and willing to work as partners with the City. Engaging neighborhood partnership will not only leverage limited resources, but can support greater overall engagement by residents in their neighborhoods' future. Neighborhood residents are important eyes and ears on the street, identifying problems, resolving many matters before they enter the legal system, and following up to see that owners have indeed carried out their commitments or complied with City orders.

ADDRESSING THE PROBLEM OF ABSENTEE-OWNED RENTAL PROPERTIES. While Detroit's residential neighborhoods have historically been characterized by high levels of homeownership, many neighborhoods today are seeing homeownership rates decline as more and more houses are bought and rented out by absentee owners. Rental housing is not the problem in itself, but can become a problem when the owners are speculators with no long-term commitment to the property or the neighborhood, milking their properties for short-term gain without maintaining them or monitoring their tenants. Widespread anecdotal reports suggest that this is far too often the case. While the long-term strategies for the city's neighborhoods must include steps to increase the number of homebuyers and stabilize homeownership rates, in the short as well as long term, strategies are needed to address absentee landlords directly.

USE MORE AGGRESSIVE REGULATORY TOOLS **F**

As with vacant properties, Detroit requires registration of all rental properties. That requirement is not effectively enforced, however, and in any event is but the first in a series of steps that must be taken to effectively address the challenge posed by absentee landlords. As a first step, the City should actively ensure that all properties are in fact registered. Inexpensive applications of web-based technology, combined with outreach to neighborhood organizations, can significantly increase the level of landlord registration at little cost to the City government. Once a reasonably complete list of absentee owners has been created, the City can create a database of 'bad apples' who can be targeted for enforcement by matching that list with tax payments, code violations, and police calls.

As with vacant properties, the City may want to initiate a landlord strategy in key neighborhoods where this issue is particularly important, and where a strong neighborhood organization or CDO is available and willing to work as a partner to leverage the City's limited resources. Engagement of a neighborhood organization or CDO can make the difference between a strategy that looks good on paper, and one that actually works. In the end, though, an effective rental strategy should provide not only penalties, but incentives. While strictly enforcing the law against problem landlords, the City of Detroit should design a program of incentives for responsible rental property owners. Many landlord incentives can be provided at little or no cost to the public sector.

While the goal of this strategy is not to further additional abandonment but to foster greater maintenance of privately owned properties, some owners may decide, if faced with serious enforcement of minimum standards, to abandon their properties rather than comply with maintenance standards. Other owners may continue to keep their buildings occupied, but fail to comply with orders to make repairs. Where the City government, as a result, must make repairs, maintain vacant lots, or secure or demolish vacant buildings, it should develop an effective process for recovering those costs from the owners. Such a process should not be limited to placing liens on properties, which usually have little or no value, but also include aggressive pursuit of judgments against the owners and their other assets, whatever they may be.

IMPLEMENTATION ACTIONS

1 Increase the cost of holding vacant property.
2 Address problem landlords.
3 Create formal partnership with Wayne County Treasurer for tax foreclosure auctions.

PRECEDENT

1 Cleveland Code Enforcement Partnerships

PILOT PROJECT

1 Code Enforcement / Landlord Strategy

313

CIVIC ENGAGEMENT FEEDBACK AND PUBLIC PERCEPTIONS

- The City is not using its full set of tools to enforce codes that negatively affect residents' surroundings
- Vacant homes that are beyond repair create safety issues.
- No one is properly investigating illegal scrap buyers.
- No one is giving absentee landlords ("slumlords") and businesses fines for blight.
- Developers refuse to demolish or remediate contaminated industrial properties.

LANDLORD STRATEGY ELEMENTS

REGULATORY STRATEGIES				INCENTIVE STRATEGIES	
TRACKING LANDLORDS AND PROPERTIES	ESTABLISHING MINIMUM STANDARDS	ENFORCING MINIMUM STANDARDS	COVERING ENFORCEMENT COSTS	PROVIDING NON-FINANCIAL INCENTIVES	PROVIDING FINANCIAL INCENTIVES
Rental property registration ordinance	Comprehensive code ordinances	Efficient code enforcement operation using effective systems and technology	Establish minimum rental registration fee with penalties for failure to register	Create 'Good Landlord' program with clear standards for designation	Provide fee waivers to qualifying Good Landlords
Absentee landlord registration database	Rental licensing ordinance requiring health and safety inspection as condition of receiving rental license	Targeted deployment of code enforcement resources	Establish schedule of penalties for failure to correct violations and other bad actions	Tie educational and training programs to Good Landlord program	Provide preferential access to housing vouchers for Good Landlords
Systems for finding unregistered properties/ landlords - increasing coverage of registration ordinance (online system, landlord finders)	Point of sale or turnover ordinance requiring certificate of occupancy inspection when property is sold or re-rented	Code enforcement or re-inspection strategy targeting 'bad apples' - landlords/ properties with poor track record	Establish differential fee structure based on landlord track record	Provide better access for Good Landlords to public officials (hot line, regular meetings, etc.)	Provide free or reduced-price goods and services for Good Landlords
Linking registration database to other relevant information - complaints, code violations, health violations, fires, police calls	Adopt responsible landlord guidelines for non-code areas (tenant screening, working with police, etc.)	Community partnerships to leverage municipal code enforcement resources (diversion strategy)	Create efficient *in person* collection procedure for fines, penalties, and nuisance abatement costs	Provide regulatory flexibility and/or fast-track approvals to Good Landlords	Provide low-interest loans for property improvements for Good Landlords
Create 'bad apple picker' - system for classifying landlords based on track record		Create efficient nuisance abatement program focusing on nuisance conditions with significant impact on neighborhood stability			
		Create remedial program for 'bad apples'			
		Offer educational and training programs for landlords			
		Establish efficient administrative violation enforcement process			

As many properties have switched from owner-occupied to renter-occupied, it is importation that the City develops and implements an effective landlord strategy.
This should be a targeted strategy that focuses on enforcement of ordinances for "bad apples" and creates incentives for "good landlords."

PRECEDENT

CLEVELAND CODE ENFORCEMENT PARTNERSHIPS

The City of Cleveland and neighborhood-based community development corporations (CDCs) jointly work with landlords to help them understand their responsibilities for maintaining their properties and help them obtain available resources.

Image Source: Center for Community Progress

EARLY ACTION

TARGETED PROPERTY ACQUISITION

Partner with Wayne County to obtain properties in key target areas at the tax foreclosure auction, including one key economic growth area and one key neighborhood strategy area.

Image Source: Hamilton Anderson Associates

PILOT PROJECT

CODE ENFORCEMENT/LANDLORD STRATEGY

Build a code enforcement partnership between the City, a CDO and a neighborhood association in a single neighborhood target area focusing on strategies to deal with problem absentee landlords.

Image Source: Hamilton Anderson Associates

TAX FORECLOSURE

When a property owner in Detroit fails to pay property taxes for three years, the property is put up for tax auction by Wayne County. The number of properties being auctioned by the county has more than doubled in the last three years, reaching more than 20,000 in the fall of 2012. This number would be far larger if the county brought every eligible property to tax auction. Under the Michigan land bank statute, the county can move these properties to a land bank entity created under state law; otherwise, properties are sold to the highest bidder. In recent years in Detroit, this has created a revolving door of properties being sold to speculators, and ending up back on the foreclosure list a few years later.

While the tax auction process contributes to the problem, it can also contribute to the solution, by being a vehicle through which the city can pursue a targeted, strategic property acquisition effort, by building an ongoing partnership between the public landholding agencies and the Wayne County Treasurer's office. The first step is for the key agencies and decision makers involved with public land to develop priorities for acquisition of properties into the public inventory. These may include key properties needed to create site assemblies for economic development, key properties affecting neighborhood stability, properties needed to consolidate land into suitable parcels for blue infrastructure, or other priorities. Based on those priorities, and working through land bank entities (either at the city, county, or state level), the City of Detroit should develop an ongoing process involving key public and quasi-public agencies such as DPD, DEGC and DSWD to identify specific acquisition priorities in advance of each year's tax foreclosure auction, and work with the Wayne County Treasurer to create a straightforward process to utilize the provisions of the state land bank statute to enable properties to come into public ownership at minimum cost.

This process represents potentially the single most effective way for public agencies to obtain control over key properties that will further the goals of the long-term framework plan at manageable cost. Through partnerships with CDOs and others, it can also be used as a way to help keep homeowners in their homes, and prevent further abandonment in key low-vacancy areas. At the same time, it must be recognized that the sheer scale of tax delinquency in Detroit at present—and the resulting volume of properties coming to tax auction—vastly exceeds the capacity of the public agencies to take control, or to intervene effectively in the outcomes, of all but a small percentage of these properties. The only long-term or sustainable solution to the tax auction revolving door will be found in rebuilding Detroit's economy and its neighborhoods, and restoring its quality of life so that property owners once again have confidence in the city's future, and their place in that future.

IMPLEMENTATION ACTIONS

1   Build community partnerships to leverage limited public resources. Work with the Wayne County Treasurer (WCT) to obtain properties at the tax foreclosure auction, identifying a limited number of properties in key target areas, which should include one key economic growth area and one neighborhood strategy area.

2   Develop an ongoing process involving key public agencies to identify acquisition priorities in advance of each year's tax foreclosure auction.

3   Work with the WCT to create a straightforward process to utilize the provisions of the state land bank statute to enable properties to come into public ownership at minimum cost.

4   Build an ongoing partnership with the WCT to ensure that key properties come into public ownership on an annual basis and to discourage land speculation through the tax foreclosure process.

EARLY ACTION

1   Targeted Property Acquisition

CIVIC
ENGAGEMENT
SUPPORTING LASTING CIVIC
CAPACITY IN DETROIT

**ENGAGEMENTS SITES:
AUGUST 2010 - SEPTEMBER 2012**

✳ ROAMING TABLES (39)

● EXISTING COMMUNITY MEETING (138)

● TECHNICAL WORKING SESSIONS (64)

● COMMUNITY CONVERSATIONS & PREP (20)

○ OTHER DWP MEETINGS (6)

● SUMMITS (7)

● TOWNHALL MEETINGS (11)

● PLANNING CLUSTER-BASED MEETINGS (11)

△ MORE THAN ONE ENGAGEMENT TYPE AT
   LOCATION (13)

⬠ DWPLTP HOME BASE

STREET TEAM DROPS:

● RESIDENTIAL/UNLABELED

● BUSINESS OR ORGANIZATION

Source: DWPLTP Civic Engagement Team

1   2   4 MILES

Mappable engagements from both phases, including the types below. Many
engagements occurred at the DWPLTP Home Base, and many were not mappable (e.g.
electronic engagements like "Detroit 24/7").

CIVIC ENGAGEMENT
SUPPORTING LASTING
CIVIC CAPACITY IN DETROIT

RENEWED WAYS TO LEAD AND COLLABORATE. Detroit is above all a city that makes things, and Detroiters can make things happen. There is no shortage of talented people in Detroit who dedicate their lives to making it a better place. They are neighbors, leaders, dreamers, and doers. You may be one of them: a Neighborhood Watch captain or foot patrol, a troop leader or teen leader, a teacher or police or fire/paramedic, a city employee who sees a practical solution, a shop steward with ideas for daycare at your factory, a deacon with a dream for a civic plaza, an entrepreneur who helps develop a thriving business corridor. You may have knowledge of or access to ideas, data, networks of individuals and institutions, or financial resources. Augmenting and leveraging people's assets, resources, perspectives, and participation is what this section of the Detroit Strategic Framework is all about.

Civic "infrastructure" can be considered an intrinsic system for the city of Detroit. It is an abundant asset that, like Detroit's physical systems, has been stressed and burdened by economic and population losses, deferred or inconsistent maintenance, and a lack of renewal. To put it in more human terms: **Detroiters should be recognized as our most precious asset, and the capacity and vibrancy of individuals and institutions deserve support and renewal.** This civic infrastructure—strong residents, strong leaders, strong organizations, and strong sectors—will enable Detroit to make ongoing, continual progress on pervasive, long-term community issues, such as public safety, equitable job access, education, or health.

WHAT EXACTLY IS CIVIC ENGAGEMENT? Civic engagement is the open and ongoing two-way dialogue among all stakeholders. Essentially, civic engagement is people working together and talking together to move forward together. It entails transparency, accountability, and mutual trust. Civic engagement moves people along a spectrum of support. For some, becoming more engaged means less resistance or fear toward an idea or an initiative. For others, engagement means moving from passive indifference to active involvement or advocacy. Engagement can fuel the passion of still others to be the leaders and outspoken champions for their specific cause or a shared idea, lending their resources and skills as well as bringing others on board. A civic engagement effort is often most successful when it involves a broad range of communities and sectors in conversation, relationship building, idea generation, decision making, and action.

The many valuable definitions and forms of civic engagement prompted the Detroit Works Project Long Term Planning process to adopt a broad understanding of community, including residents, businesses, government, nonprofit, civic, institutional, members of the media, philanthropic, and faith-based groups. The broad concept of 'community' also includes but is not limited to communities based on race, age, culture, ethnicity, and gender.

Engagement is not only something that happens within and for individuals and neighborhoods, and is not only something defined in geographic terms. Engagement exists where there are shared values or a common issue at stake; something that is of deep concern to community stakeholders. Sometimes engaging or organizing around an issue (such as equitable job access or education) is appropriate, while other times engaging particular constituencies (such as the faith community, large corporate employers, health professionals, or the higher education sector) is important. Still other times, engaging by geographic area (such as neighborhood, small business corridor, or multi-county region) is needed. Any given engagement effort should consider these or other groupings at different times in order to be effective and responsive to how people identify themselves within their communities.

DETROIT'S COMMUNITY INCLUDES...

BUSINESSES	PHILANTHROPIC ORGANIZATIONS	NONPROFITS	MEDIA	INSTITUTIONS	GOVERNMENT	FAITH-BASED GROUPS	COMMUNITY DEVELOPMENT GROUPS	RESIDENTS

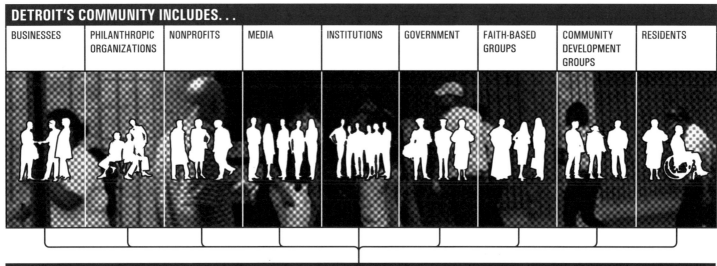

AN ENGAGED COMMUNITY MEMBER...

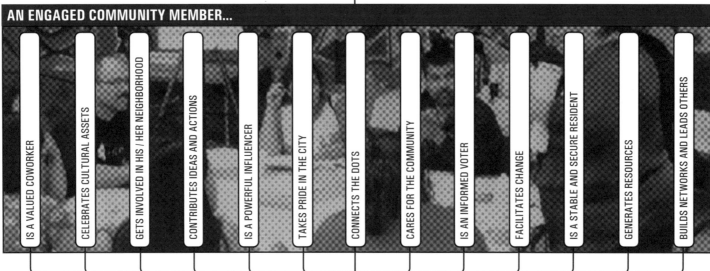

- IS A VALUED COWORKER
- CELEBRATES CULTURAL ASSETS
- GETS INVOLVED IN HIS / HER NEIGHBORHOOD
- CONTRIBUTES IDEAS AND ACTIONS
- IS A POWERFUL INFLUENCER
- TAKES PRIDE IN THE CITY
- CONNECTS THE DOTS
- CARES FOR THE COMMUNITY
- IS AN INFORMED VOTER
- FACILITATES CHANGE
- IS A STABLE AND SECURE RESIDENT
- GENERATES RESOURCES
- BUILDS NETWORKS AND LEADS OTHERS

AN ENGAGED CITY INCLUDES...

- ROBUST DEMOCRATIC PARTICIPATION
- WILLING AND COMMITTED INVESTORS
- AN ATMOSPHERE OF COLLABORATION AMONG SECTORS
- A STRONG SENSE OF PLACE
- ADVOCATES AND IMPLEMENTERS

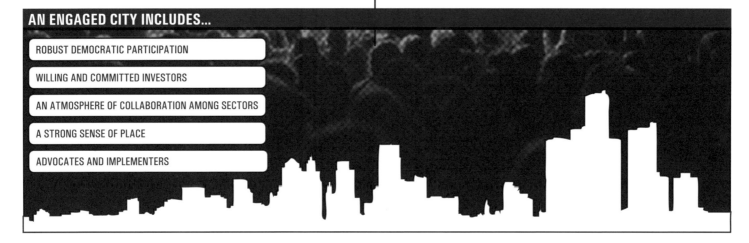

"How can citizens become more involved in planning?"

Street Team, 12/2011

"Community engagement is more than just listening to us rank imperatives. Please be more transparent about how community feedback is actually being incorporated into technical planning."

Northeast Community Conversation #1, 4/17/2012

"There needs to be clarity about what a person can influence in the process."

Community Organizations, Round Table, 1/30/2012

WHY ENGAGE? Civic engagement yields lasting benefits. This is true of any development endeavor or long-term initiative, including the Detroit Strategic Framework. Here's why: first, civic engagement helps strengthen and expand the base of support for a given effort. More people become informed, activated and mobilized through engagement efforts. Opposition is less likely because concerns are addressed within the process. Secondly, engagement creates and empowers leaders who will advocate for and advance an effort. The more champions there are for a plan or an idea, the more likely it is to become a reality. Third, civic engagement strengthens collaboration and connections. It helps pave the way for long-term sustainability of an effort by increasing visibility, credibility, buy-in, accountability, and ownership of solutions and bright ideas. Fourth, civic engagement often nurtures and reinforces a strong connection to place and a sense of identity. Essentially, by engaging in something together, people can witness and feel a shared energy and commitment. Involvement feels rewarding, and the possibility of change and progress excites communities.

Lastly, and perhaps most significantly for the Strategic Framework, civic engagement actually improves the substance or content of an initiative. An effort that has been supported by civic engagement will more accurately reflect the ideas of the people it affects, and helps them raise their voices to influence outcomes. It responds to present-day needs and priorities while incorporating a valuable range of perspectives and expertise.

For all of these reasons, creating a sustained environment of strong civic fabric and a vibrant civic identity will not only enable the Strategic Framework to become a reality, but it also will allow Detroit to incubate and carry out successful efforts and initiatives well into the future.

Such engagement does not just "happen," however. It requires deliberate and targeted investments and efforts by nonprofit organizations, the philanthropic sector, and public and private sectors to learn about it, support it, and initiate it. Engagement also calls for individual leaders to be cultivated and equipped to forge and strengthen connections among constituencies, neighborhoods, organizations, and/or sectors. And finally, it requires all of us to create an atmosphere of trust, respect, shared goals, and mutual responsibility.

Everyone who has dedicated time to the future of Detroit—both within and beyond the city limits—is aware that too many excellent and civic-minded ideas and actions go unrecognized or under-funded because of lack of connections and coordination among all the groups and individuals who are working on solutions for the city. Supporting and investing in a strong civic and cultural fabric creates an enduring asset for Detroit's long-term development and prosperity. When a city's people are strongly connected with each other—active in civic life, focused on shared values, equipped to lead change, and committed to developing healthy and vibrant local institutions and businesses—the city becomes stronger and more sustainable. Engagement is not solely a vehicle to implement and govern change. It is also an outcome and a transformation in and of itself.

CIVIC & POLITICAL ORGANIZATIONS

7 THERE ARE 7 COUNCIL DISTRICTS[1]

96 🔧 THERE ARE 96 LABOR UNIONS IN DETROIT[2]

🌷 **350** THERE ARE 350 COMMUNITY BASED ORGANIZATIONS IN DETROIT[3]

 1.5K THERE ARE 1,496 CHURCHES IN DETROIT[4]

PARTICIPATION & ENGAGEMENT IN DWP

PARTICIPANTS UNDERSTANDING OF DWPLTP INCREASED TO "PRETTY WELL" BY THE END OF THE PROCESS

PARTICIPANTS' UNDERSTANDING OF DWPLTP, ON AVERAGE, INCREASED BETWEEN DECEMBER 2011 AND SEPTEMBER 2012 FROM "SOMEWHAT" TO "PRETTY WELL"[5]

CONNECTING WITH PEOPLE > 163K TIMES

DWPLTP CONNECTED WITH PEOPLE OVER 163,000 TIMES BETWEEN AUGUST 2010 AND SEPTEMBER 2012, AND DWPLTP HAD 30,000 CONVERSATIONS WITH PARTICIPANTS DURING THAT TIME[6]

45% OF PLANNING PROCESS COMMENTS WERE ABOUT HOW TO ENGAGE THE PUBLIC

45% OF COMMENTS ABOUT DWPLTP WERE ABOUT WAYS OF ENGAGING RESIDENTS (EXISTING AND NEW), EXPECTATIONS ABOUT ENGAGEMENTS, AND COMMENTS ABOUT ENGAGEMENT LOGISTICS[7]

INFORMATION OUTLETS

$422M $421,762,000 HAS BEEN INVESTED IN THE CITY OF DETROIT BY 10 FOUNDATIONS* FROM 2008 TO SUMMER OF 2011[8]

✎ **15K** 📋 15,000 ADVOCATES, SIGNERS AND FOLLOWERS OF DECLARE DETROIT[9]

24/7 DETROIT PARTICIPANTS WHO PARTICIPATED IN DETROIT 24/7 SAID THEY FELT MORE POSITIVE ABOUT DWPLTP PROCESS THAN PARTICIPANTS WHO REGISTERED THROUGH OTHER ENGAGEMENTS[10]

100K  THERE ARE APPROXIMATELY 100,000 SOCIAL MEDIA SITES THAT ARE PRO-DETROIT[11]

CONTEXT AND GROUNDING
BUILDING ON STRENGTHS AND SURPASSING BARRIERS

Youth are a particularly critical engagement asset in the Detroit community. First, youth represent a significant proportion of the city's population. There were as many as one in four Detroiters under the age of 17 in 2009[1]. Secondly, many young people hunger for creative ways to engage, and they often initiate innovative actions for developing community. The Detroit Works Project Long Term Planning witnessed this through the robust participation of youth in our Detroit 24/7 online game and engagement platform. And finally, young people make up the civic engagement infrastructure of the future. When youth are civically engaged, they are more likely to graduate from high school. If engagement efforts can capture their energy, imagination, and ideas now, they will not only succeed as adults, but they can continue to invigorate these ideas in Detroit for decades to come.

Many historic challenges affect civic engagement in Detroit. For instance, the history of civic engagement in the city has been plagued with planning fatigue, leaving many residents and leaders with a sense of hopelessness and skepticism. A legacy of corruption in the city has given rise to common attitudes of mistrust. The magnitude of the problems has also engendered feelings of disconnection and immobilization, as well as a sense that the public sector alone cannot adequately meet public needs. "We're tired of talking" has been a common sentiment. On the flip side, there are many in Detroit who have felt far removed from past planning efforts; "No one asked me" is also commonly heard. Linked with these sentiments is a perceived gradual erosion of the sense of belonging and commitment to a place for many in Detroit over the past several decades. Even as many residents continue to express their hometown pride and commitment to Detroit, people leave the city in high numbers. For some, hope and resolve have waned.

Complex and systemic racial dynamics also represent a significant hurdle for civic engagement, as do challenging realities such as high adult illiteracy, pronounced economic disparity, and the complexity and inaccessibility of many public services—the "red tape" often encountered in trying to access or engage with bureaucratic systems. In addition, there are frequently acknowledged capacity challenges within local nonprofit organizations, community-based groups, and public agencies alike for initiating and leading civic engagement efforts, not least of which are fueled by strained financial and staffing resources. While many of these challenges are not unique to Detroit, they underscore the imperative for investment and attention toward reinvigorating civic life, stimulating collective action, and supporting leadership across sectors in the city.

Realities Sources: 1) City Planning Commission (CPC); 2-4) CPC, Michigan Community Resources (MCR); 5-7) MCR; 7-9) DWPLTP Civic Engagement Team; 10) MCR; 11) DWPLTP Civic Engagement Team

*The ten foundations are: 1) Community Foundation for Southeast Michigan; 2) Ford Foundation; 3) John A and Barbara M. Erb Family Foundation; 4) Hudson-Webber Foundation; 5) John S. and James L. Knight Foundation; 6) Max M. and Marjorie S. Fisher Foundation; 7) McGregor Fund; 8) Kresge Foundation; 9) Skillman Foundation; 10) W.K. Kellogg Foundation

Text Source: 1) Data Driven Detroit

"People believe it's just another fad and they already have a plan for the city. And they believe they've been burned by planning efforts before..."

DWPLTP Civic Engagement Audit 2012

"It's an opportunity for me to go in and talk to people about what our role and responsibility is for change. Each Process Leader has made a decision, some type of decision to be at that table, and with that decision comes the responsibility to do something different to make a change."

DWPLTP Civic Engagement Audit 2012

Still, Detroit also clearly has a long history of unique and valuable engagement assets. The city has a legacy of strong union organizing, particularly in the automobile industry. Detroit was once called The City of Churches, and the faith community includes trusted, prominent, and respected leaders that often serve as a galvanizing force. Networks of community development groups advocate for stable and rooted neighborhoods, and a variety of nonprofit organizations provide critical support and outreach to Detroit residents even in the face of constrained resources. Although there is a significant digital divide in the City of Detroit, there is nonetheless a vibrant digital culture that is addressing the divide and leading new ways of civic engagement. Environmental groups, food security advocates, and urban farming projects lead the nation in community organizing around green innovation. Other institutions engage the current and future workforce through their work to strengthen education and provide training opportunities. Vibrant arts organizations and cultural institutions engage communities through a variety of creative means and platforms. The list of people-driven assets in Detroit goes on.

On a business level, many companies and leaders work vigorously to engage their colleagues and develop a vital and energetic entrepreneurial environment in the city. On a governmental level, the new City Charter and the new seven-district Council system suggest fertile ground for establishing a renewed sense of place and belonging, which should also secure stronger and deeper engagement between the community and their local representatives in city government. This in turn holds promise for strong links between neighborhood issues and concerns, along with citywide priorities. Community is calling for stronger alignment and accountability between municipal and other levels of government. And from the philanthropic sector, the city has seen renewed interest and investments in engagement. These are all positive steps forward for building sustainable civic capacity.

In addition to its rich legacy of groups, institutions, and sectors that have pioneered engagement, organizing, and advocacy efforts in past decades that continue to the present day, Detroit is full of important informal engagement entities that knit communities together and create a strong sense of city identity. Detroit block clubs and other informal groups, led by many resourceful residents, drive clean-up and beautification projects, neighborhood-watch efforts, and numerous other examples of neighbor-to-neighbor care and connectivity. Informal civic structures such as small businesses ("the beauty and barber shop,") neighborhood places ("playground, sidewalk, and store"), and emerging digital communities such as Facebook and Twitter (especially important for young people) can be overlooked as models of engagement precisely because they are so natural and informal. This recognition was part of what drove the Strategic Framework process to engage with Detroiters where they already gather, through a series of strategies that mobilized conversations, invited stories, and took the dialogue out of the meeting room and into the streets.

Other informal networks are more interest-based, and may not initially appear to be the strongholds for change that they can be. Throughout Detroit, local heroes have emerged from among car and motorcycle clubs, groups of street artists, and the sometimes serendipitous groups that share values they have not yet realized, such as skateboarders and trail or park-improvement advocates, maternal-child wellness advocates and urban gardeners, or a safety patrol and a mural artist who both have part of the answer to reducing gang "tagging."

"...Their ideas were solicited, recorded, and shared, and I think that was good."

DWPLTP Civic Engagement Audit 2012

"I think it is incredibly important that a group be drawn from some of the most dynamic and powerful leaders that we have in the city and the region...and folks who do have at the same time some more local or neighborhood based connections. I think that so far I've heard conversations exist...in the kind of polarity of both of those...They need to come together. Neither one can do this by themselves."

DWPLTP Civic Engagement Audit 2012

ENGAGING ALL OF DETROIT TO CREATE A NEW FUTURE CITY. Civic engagement once worked to move social mountains in Detroit. In the 20th century, it was Detroit that set the stage for important national conversations about social issues related to job equity, environmental justice, and the fraught relationship between workers and corporate management in the United States.

Over the decades there has been a distinct change in civic participation. In the face of declining city resources and population losses, Detroit residents and community groups have had to fill the gap in quality-of-life needs such as safety, education, and jobs. Now, Detroiters are demanding dramatic improvements in quality of life and quality of business. Real investment of human and financial resources is needed in all sectors to rebuild capacity so that civic engagement is part of the day-to-day infrastructure of how Detroit operates and makes decisions at a citywide level, as well as how it participates in regional and statewide frameworks to address its future.

EMBRACING THE POTENTIAL FOR A MODEL CITY. The Strategic Framework is the vision that results from, is shaped by, and cannot be carried out without expanded and sustained civic engagement. Such an effort calls upon the combined—and enhanced—capacity of Detroit's civic leaders to support and extend their best efforts, not only within specific parts of Detroit nor just in the city itself, but with their peers in the Detroit metropolitan area, the state, and at the national level. This is not only because Detroit needs to connect with the broadest possible support and resources for its ambitious vision, but also because such resources will give Detroit the ability to give back: To show the world how to create a green, prosperous, and equitable city for the future.

The fact is that Detroit is facing head-on what many other cities are on the cusp of: the need to create more sustainable, resilient civic centers for the new millennium. The world needs Detroit's example. The country and the world also need Detroit's success, as a critical American city in the next-century global economy. No single sector can accomplish this alone. Detroit's civic groups and business leaders must collaborate to create the capacity for this important work. This work must balance the short- and medium-term solutions to urgent needs with the equally critical need to maintain a long-term vision and to commit to important, far-reaching priorities for Detroit's future. It necessitates sustaining working relationships that share and seek out knowledge, resources, and best practices within and beyond Detroit's city limits.

CIVIC ENGAGEMENT PROJECT TIMELINE

2010

NUMBER OF PEOPLE ENGAGED TO DATE	AUG	SEP	OCT	NOV	DEC
	10	7,800	9,000	10,200	12,000

CIVIC ENGAGEMENT MILESTONES

AUG
- Soft Launch Meetings began with Citywide Partners to inform about the Detroit Strategic Framework
- Mayor's Advisory Task Force (MATF) formed
- Interagency Working Group formed

SEP
- Detroit Works Project launched
- Website created
- Soft Launch meetings continued
- Detroit Strategic Framework Community Forums (Townhall Meetings)
- Street Team launched to assist with literature drops for the Townhall Meetings
- Community Outreach Partners formed to assist with outreach

OCT
- MATF meetings continued

NOV
- MATF meetings continued

DEC
- MATF meetings continued

2011

JAN	FEB	MAR	APR	MAY	JUN	JUL	AUG	SEP	OCT	NOV	DEC
16,300	20,300	24,200	28,000	31,100	33,100	35,600	38,400	40,400	42,800	45,200	53,700

JAN
- Planning Cluster-Based meetings began

FEB
- Planning Cluster-Based meetings continued
- Summit planning initiated

MAR
- Planning Cluster-Based meetings continued
- Summit planning continued
- Senior Summit

APR
- Summit planning continued
- Hotline launched

MAY
- Faith-based, New Americans, Environmental, Artist, Entrepreneur, and Youth Summits

JUN
- Internally evaluated the project

JUL
- Restructured DWP org chart
- Split DWP into two tracks - short term and long term

AUG
- Assembled DWP Long Term Planning consultant team
- Reviewed community feedback from 1.0 to inform 2.0

SEP
- Continued to review community feedback from 1.0 to inform 2.0
- Recruited Process Leaders to help guide civic engagement
- Hired staff, developed civic engagement plan

OCT
- Continued to review community feedback from 1.0 to inform 2.0
- Continued to recruit Process Leaders to help guide civic engagement

NOV
- Continued to review community feedback from 1.0 to inform 2.0
- Process Leaders' meetings began and continued through rest of the process

DEC
- DWP Long Term Planning launched
- Roaming Table deployed
- Street Team deployed
- Project Goals established
- First DWP 2.0 MATF meeting held

2012

JAN	FEB	MAR	APR	MAY	JUN	JUL	AUG	SEP
65,300	69,000	74,600	81,900	90,000	104,400	108,700	130,500	163,600

JAN
- Home Base opened
- Ambassador Training began and continued through process
- Stakeholder Roundtables launched

FEB
- Detroit Stories began and continued through process
- Introduction of Key Trends
- Introduction of 12 Imperatives

MAR
- Introduction of Directions Phase

APR
- Planning, City Systems, and Environment Toolkits made available
- Community Conversations began
- Introduction of Typologies

MAY
- Introduction of Strategies Phase
- Detroit 24/7 launched

JUN
- Telephone Town Hall
- Roaming Table and Street Team continued

JUL
- Drafting of Strategic Framework plan
- Speakers Bureau deployed

AUG
- Home Base Open Houses
- Introduction of Strategic Framework Plan

SEP
- Traveling Road Show launched
- Community Conversations resumed
- Telephone Townhall

THE CONVERSATION
HOW THE STRATEGIC FRAMEWORK WAS JOINTLY DEVELOPED

Getting people to the table is difficult. Getting people to remain at the table—to stay engaged—can be even more challenging. Communities and community leaders must juggle many urgent priorities that compete for their attention and time. Behind the problem of so-called "disengagement" usually lies a story of interactions that did not help build or sustain trust, efforts that ran aground for lack of resources or because of technical or practical barriers, or the sheer magnitude of a problem overwhelming efforts to address it. Frequently, decisions move forward without the input of many community members whom these decisions most concern.

The Detroit Works Project—a 24-month community effort that led to the development of the Strategic Framework—set out with the ambitious goal of reaching as many Detroit community stakeholders as possible to engage them and help them shape important and timely issues for Detroit's future. As part of this goal, the process aimed to rebuild enthusiasm and trust, create opportunities for community dialogue, and begin to lay the groundwork for future and long-term civic engagement work in Detroit. Using many approaches to extend and deepen the two-way conversation about desired actions and strategies, the process involved, tapped, and partnered with well over 150,000 individuals and organizations in total. This represents one of the most exciting, inventive, and comprehensive public planning processes in the United States and beyond.

HOW THE CONVERSATION STARTED: DETROIT WORKS PROJECT CIVIC ENGAGEMENT PROCESS. The Detroit Works Project publicly began in September 2010 with the desire to rapidly plan and execute a wide array of meetings covering many geographic areas of the city. Since the first step was to introduce the project to the broad Detroit community, initial engagement happened through large "town hall meeting" gatherings. This initial round of engagement aimed to generate momentum and interest, and the volume of participation was inspiring and positive. It was clear that Detroiters were ready to engage in the process of citywide transformation.

These first forums aimed to provide a context for current realities and set the stage for input in plans for the city over the long term. At the same time, the attendance in the hundreds proved logistically challenging, and limited the kind of participation and dialogue that could take place. The DWP team members began to learn how to best prepare participants in advance for what to expect of the discussions, how to participate, and what would happen afterward. These initial engagement activities, which are common to many city engagement processes, were also large-scale, with City officials and technical experts presenting and then inviting input, questions, and comments. Although this helped ground the events in current data and also demonstrated the Mayor's commitment to questions of land use and equitable development, it did not yet allow for interactive dialogue and participant-focused engagement.

The first set of community forums was immensely helpful in defining and shaping the 12 main imperatives of the Strategic Framework. Coming out of these meetings, it became clear that the community needed a space to also address urgent and near-term needs and questions. In response, the Detroit Works Project was reshaped in 2011 to reflect a separate process for addressing very immediate concerns in the community—DWP Short Term Actions, spearheaded by the mayor's office—and a long-range process for arriving at a vision for the city with broad input from residents and business leaders—DWP Long Term Planning. For the reshaping process, three core principles guided how engagement unfolded: 1) incorporating community leadership in engagement decision making; 2) providing transparent information exchange, including valuing and integrating community knowledge; and 3) using communications as a core part of engagement efforts.

ALL REGISTERED PARTICIPANTS WITHIN DETROIT WHO PROVIDED GENDER

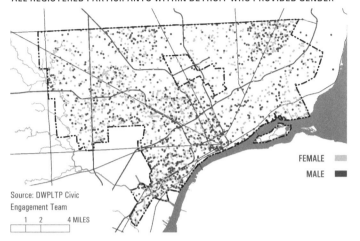

Source: DWPLTP Civic
Engagement Team

1 2 4 MILES

FEMALE
MALE

ALL REGISTERED PARTICIPANTS WHO PROVIDED GENDER, 61.5% FEMALE AND 38.5% MALE.

GENDER

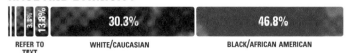

61.5%	38.5%
FEMALE	MALE

ALL REGISTERED PARTICIPANTS WITHIN DETROIT WHO PROVIDED AGE

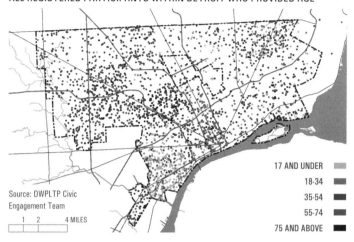

Source: DWPLTP Civic
Engagement Team

1 2 4 MILES

17 AND UNDER
18-34
35-54
55-74
75 AND ABOVE

ALL REGISTERED PARTICIPANTS WHO PROVIDED AGE, 14.1% 17 YEARS AND UNDER, 21.3% EIGHTEEN YEARS AND UNDER, 22.8% 35-54 YEARS, 31.9% 55-74 YEARS, 9.9% 75 YEARS AND OLDER.

AGE

14.1%	21.3%	22.8%	31.9%	9.9%
PEOPLE AGED 17 & UNDER	PEOPLE BETWEEN THE AGES OF 18-34	PEOPLE BETWEEN THE AGES OF 35-54	PEOPLE BETWEEN THE AGES OF 55-74	PEOPLE AGED 75 & OLDER

ALL REGISTERED PARTICIPANTS WITHIN DETROIT WHO PROVIDED RACE & ETHNICITY

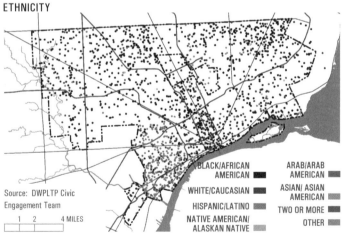

Source: DWPLTP Civic
Engagement Team

1 2 4 MILES

BLACK/AFRICAN AMERICAN
WHITE/CAUCASIAN
HISPANIC/LATINO
NATIVE AMERICAN/ ALASKAN NATIVE
ARAB/ARAB AMERICAN
ASIAN/ ASIAN AMERICAN
TWO OR MORE
OTHER

ALL REGISTERED PARTICIPANTS WHO PROVIDED RACE AND ETHNICITY, 46.8% BLACK/AFRICAN AMERICAN, 30.3% WHITE CAUCASIAN, 13.8% HISPANIC/LATINO, 3.8% OTHER, 2.1% ASIAN/ASIAN AMERICAN, 2.0% TWO OR MORE RACES, 0.8% AMERICAN INDIAN OR ALASKAN NATIVE, 0.4% ARAB AMERICAN

RACE AND ETHNICITY

	3.3%	13.8%	30.3%	46.8%
REFER TO TEXT			WHITE/CAUCASIAN	BLACK/AFRICAN AMERICAN

ALL REGISTERED PARTICIPANTS WITHIN DETROIT WHO PROVIDED GEOGRAPHY

Source: DWPLTP Planning Team

1 2 4 MILES

GREATER DOWNTOWN
LOW-VACANCY 1
LOW-VACANCY 2
MODERATE-VACANCY 1
MODERATE-VACANCY 2
HIGH-VACANCY

ALL REGISTERED PARTICIPANTS WHO PROVIDED GEOGRAPHY, 11.3% HIGH VACANCY, 35.3 MODERATE VACANCY, 26.2% LOW VACANCY, 13.8% GREATER DOWNTOWN, 12.8% NON-DETROIT, 0.6% INDUSTRIAL

GEOGRAPHY

12.8%	13.8%	26.2%	35.3%	11.3%
NON-DETROIT	GREATER DOWNTOWN	LOW-VACANCY	MODERATE-VACANCY	HIGH-VACANCY

0.6% INDUSTRIAL

CIVIC ENGAGEMENT FEEDBACK LOOP

HERE IS WHERE WE ARE.

THIS IS WHAT CHANGED BECAUSE OF WHAT YOU SAID.

THIS IS WHAT WILL HAPPEN NEXT.

HERE IS HOW YOU CAN BE A PART OF IT.

COMMUNITY LEADERSHIP: SHAPED ENGAGEMENT. From the start of the Detroit Works Project, leaders recognized that the work could not be incubated, owned, or shepherded by a select few. As initial engagement activities began in mid-2010, a 55-member Mayor's Advisory Task Force (MATF) was established to help guide the development of the process. Then, as a broader set of engagement, technical, and communications practitioners were brought on board in mid-2011, additional community advisors were recruited to complement the Mayor's Advisory Task Force and broaden the kinds of voices that represented the process. First, a Steering Committee was appointed by the Mayor, with recommendations from philanthropic leaders. This Steering Committee guided the overall effort and was represented by leaders in government, nonprofit, institutional, faith-based, community, and business sectors. The Mayor's Advisory Task Force continued to meet regularly to stay up to date on progress and offer suggestions and recommendations.

In addition, a group of Process Leaders was selected for their expertise in civic engagement among different constituencies and geographic areas in Detroit. They advised the civic engagement process toward blending community and technical expertise. The Process Leaders helped establish a framework for this blended approach and initiated working groups with partners to guide and implement particular engagement activities.

The three groups—Steering Committee, Process Leaders, and the Mayor's Advisory Task Force—represented different and complementary skills, networks, and expertise. They were instrumental in achieving the engagement goals of the Detroit Works Project, and they themselves greatly enriched the development of the Strategic Framework. Finally, trained Ambassadors and Street Team members were also enlisted to facilitate engagement amongst additional communities in Detroit. Altogether, more than one hundred leaders from different aspects of community helped ensure that the process was a far-reaching, authentic, and informed effort. (A full list of the people who helped shape and lead the engagement can be found in the Civic Engagement Appendix and in the Acknowledgements section.)

COMMUNITY KNOWLEDGE: VALUED AND INTEGRATED. From early on, community stakeholders wanted to ensure that their thoughts, priorities, and knowledge would be valued and used in the planning process. In no uncertain terms, the Detroit community wanted an authentic and accountable process. As one person commented, "As a citizen, I'm concerned with, well, what is the plan? You're going to take this information and is it going to make a difference? No one wants to think that they're wasting their time." Community knowledge was viewed as more than anecdotal and secondary. The community members were acknowledged throughout the process as the experts on their own neighborhoods, communities, and fields.

To integrate community expertise, an ongoing working process was established between technical and civic engagement practitioners with various community sectors. Insights, stories, data, and ideas from broad cross-sections of community were shared with the Planning Team, who worked to lay the physical and procedural groundwork that would enact these ideas into a Strategic Framework for support and change. In turn, technical analysis and ideas were blended into this base of community knowledge, which together helped to distill priorities, implications, and recommendations for the future. Although this process was logistically and intellectually challenging (and at times messy), it confirmed how valuable a transparent and accountable mutual exchange of community knowledge and technical knowledge can be, and how far it can go towards achieving credibility, accountability and trust. One stakeholder stated: "…Their ideas were solicited, recorded, and shared, and I think that was good." The end product, the planning elements of the Detroit Strategic Framework, represents integrated viewpoints and expertise from a wide variety of community stakeholders. The process and the product both reflect the strong value placed on community knowledge as an explicit source for recommendations, and it helped to establish a consensus for desired actions.

CIVIC ENGAGEMENT TACTICS

COMMUNITY CONVERSATIONS 1

COMMUNITY CONVERSATIONS 2

DETROIT 24/7 ROAMING iPAD STATION

HOMEBASE

OPEN HOUSES

ROAD SHOW EVENT

ROAMING TABLE

WORKING SESSIONS

YOUTH ENGAGEMENT

"Alternative means of sharing info via social media, email, web presence, etc, as well as for soliciting input."

Katherine, Detroit 24/7, 5/2012

"When these discussions happen, they need to happen neighbor to neighbor."

DWPLTP Civic Engagement Audit 2012

"We can engage residents... by announcing it, putting posters all over the place, and in newspapers."

Rumi, Detroit, 5/2012

COMMUNICATIONS AND ENGAGEMENT: MULTIPLE CHANNELS FOR OUTREACH AND EXCHANGE.

Transparency was a chief concern voiced by residents. The Strategic Framework teams wanted to avoid the "No one talked with me" problem, and community stakeholders wanted to be kept abreast of how the elements of the Strategic Framework were progressing along the way. To complement the knowledge-blending process, the Strategic Framework teams shared information and conducted frequent public updates throughout the process. Direct and simultaneous communication occurred through the Detroit Works HomeBase phone line, web site, the Detroit Stories web site, social media platforms such as Facebook and Twitter, a regular e-newsletter, periodic distribution of flyers, posters, postcards, and other print material. Phone message "blasts" delivered key project updates to thousands of homes. In addition, the HomeBase offices allowed for formal and informal face-to-face communication about the project, and the walls of HomeBase featured exhibits showing how the Strategic Framework began to take shape. Print, radio, and television media partners helped to extend the project's reach still further.

All of these communications strategies, while not distinct from the information exchange process, helped engage a broad cross-section of people and communities in the important and timely questions of the Strategic Framework process. The combination of virtual and digital engagement served as effective ways to engage with a wide range of people.

In addition to the town hall forums, HomeBase, and the use of social media, engagement tactics included, but were not limited to:

- team members' attendance and presentations at existing community meetings and events;

- the Roaming Table, a portable "information booth," staffed and set up in a housing complex, a busy commuter junction, and other locations ideal for engaging in brief one-on-one conversations about Detroit's future;

- an online gaming platform called Detroit 24/7, in which players could earn points for contributing perspectives and ideas related to planning and Detroit's future;

- telephone town hall events, during which high numbers of callers could listen to Detroit community leaders, ask questions, and hear about upcoming events;

- roundtable work sessions, through which sector colleagues convened with technical experts to contribute expertise on relevant parts of the Strategic Framework; and

- two series of district-based Community Conversations, face-to-face interactive events during which people in an area of the city could engage in dialogue with DWP team members and with each other on priorities, hopes, goals related to quality of life, quality of business, and other important aspects of the Strategic Framework.

Although it was challenging to remain transparent and wide-ranging even as the effort was rapid-paced and constantly evolving, the attention to communications linked with engagement proved largely effective for sharing, gathering, and blending information and knowledge. (See the Civic Engagement Appendix for more detail of how this occurred.)

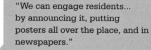

DWPLTP has garnered 136 stories that appeared on the television and radio programs or in the print and online publications of 40 different local and national news organizations, 119,312,772 unpaid print and online media impressions, and nearly five hours of unpaid television and radio coverage.

TOWARD A SHARED VISION
ACTIONS FOR ADVANCING
THE STRATEGIC FRAMEWORK

Simply put, people fuel change. Because of the breadth and depth of community engaged in the original Detroit Works Project, people are now even more prepared and excited to be part of actions to make the Strategic Framework a reality. Out of these initial conversations, a pretty stunning, ambitious, and exuberant vision for Detroit has arisen. Now, to implement the ideas and strategies, the Detroit region needs an engaged constituency of individuals and institutions. We must develop a cadre of capable, organized, and equipped leaders at all levels of community. Informed and motivated community—broadly defined—can transform how an effort unfolds or succeeds.

At the individual level, this translates to cultivating interest and passion, fostering leadership skills and experience, and valuing and paving the way for relationships to flourish. At the broad systems level, it means creating strong cross-issue and cross-disciplinary connections.

Five specific actions are recommended to implement the Strategic Framework, which will sustain and support the vision of a greater future for the city. Each of these five implementation recommendations follow closely from what we have learned throughout the development of the Strategic Framework, and they align under the three broader engagement principles described in the last section.

ESTABLISH A DETROIT STRATEGIC FRAMEWORK CONSORTIUM

ENLIST ADDITIONAL CHAMPIONS FOR IMPLEMENTATION AND POLICY REFORM

INFORM, EDUCATE, AND EQUIP KEY STAKEHOLDERS

STRENGTHEN AND COMPLEMENT THE PUBLIC SECTOR

REPORT BACK FOR TRANSPARENT AND ONGOING PROGRESS

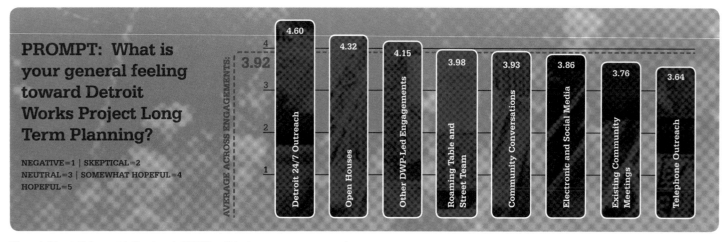

PROMPT: What is your general feeling toward Detroit Works Project Long Term Planning?

NEGATIVE=1 | SKEPTICAL=2
NEUTRAL=3 | SOMEWHAT HOPEFUL=4
HOPEFUL=5

AVERAGE ACROSS ENGAGEMENTS: **3.92**

Detroit 24/7 Outreach	4.60
Open Houses	4.32
Other DWP-Led Engagements	4.15
Roaming Table and Street Team	3.98
Community Conversations	3.93
Electronic and Social Media	3.86
Existing Community Meetings	3.76
Telephone Outreach	3.64

When asked to rate their current feelings towards DWPLTP, participants gave an average answer of 3.92, closest to "Somewhat Hopeful". The bar chart to the right shows the average response to this question for the different engagement techniques employed during DWPLTP.

ESTABLISH A DETROIT STRATEGIC FRAMEWORK CONSORTIUM

The Steering Committee, along with several of the project's other community advisors, are developing an idea for an entity that would be charged with stewarding the implementation and the civic engagement of the Strategic Framework into the future. This consortium, along with its potential partners, members, or advisors, would be a significant stride toward establishing a permanent civic stewardship structure for the City of Detroit that transcends many boundaries: geographic, economic, ethnic, issues, scales (neighborhood, city, regional), and sectors (public and private, nonprofit and government, resident and formal).

The Consortium would be composed of a group of civic-minded leaders who would connect plans to resources and would support, integrate, advance, and monitor efforts to enact and update the Strategic Framework recommendations and strategies, as well as to anticipate new challenges for the city in the coming decades. The Consortium would build from the release of the Strategic Framework to ensure that it remains a relevant "living" resource that informs and/or guides multiple efforts to improve quality of life and quality of business in Detroit, and help them become aligned and sustained over time. The Consortium would also help align or coordinate initiatives across all of the Framework's planning elements. The Consortium could be established in a manner that permits it to evolve into a permanent stewardship structure for the city.

ENLIST ADDITIONAL CHAMPIONS FOR IMPLEMENTATION AND POLICY REFORM

A single group cannot shoulder the responsibility for advancing Detroit's prosperity. In addition to the core Consortium membership, it will be critical to cultivate and align additional champions—both at individual and institutional levels—to become active and passionate advocates for the Strategic Framework. Particularly when they are respected and trusted leaders in their communities or sectors, champions can be a powerful voice to help efforts gain credibility and traction. Such champions will help ensure that the Strategic Framework stays on the public's, policy makers', and decision makers' radar screens. They can also be tapped as influencers to help reduce or remove barriers to the effort's success, can serve as implementers to drive and participate in particular initiatives that align with the Strategic Framework, or carry out comprehensive policy reform relevant to the Framework's aims.

INFORM, EDUCATE, AND EQUIP KEY STAKEHOLDERS

The vision of the Strategic Framework cannot be a static statement. Concerted efforts must continue to really "take the plan to the city" and engage individuals and institutions on what it is about, who shaped it, why it is so critical, and most importantly, how to use it and align it with existing plans. Every sector in Detroit demands this kind of knowledge and dialogue in order to move forward. However, it is important to note that, as always, engagement requires engagers. Professional organizers or engagement specialists often serve as centers of gravity to connect people to action. They can coordinate and drive the effort to introduce the Strategic Framework and build momentum and consensus within and among pockets throughout the city.

District HomeBases can help establish a place and a connection at the neighborhood level. As an interviewed stakeholder stated, "We can continue to use the tools that Detroit Works incorporated, and on a smaller scale in our neighborhood, continue the same process." District HomeBases would provide a physical place where people could come and discuss what can specifically happen in their neighborhood related to the implementation of Detroit Works Project Long Term Planning. Establishing a physical space where people can access information is a key part of involving community in the implementation process and of keeping the process transparent.

STRENGTHEN AND COMPLEMENT THE PUBLIC SECTOR

We must pursue a collaborative regional agenda that recognizes Detroit's strengths and our region's shared destiny. Government cannot provide all of the answers to Detroit's issues, nor can it implement all of them alone. National examples such as New Orleans, Pittsburgh, Cleveland, and Philadelphia illustrate that work like this is a multi-faceted community endeavor of talking and working together to answer complex questions and collaboratively implement the answers. These examples point to civic engagement as a system that underlies Detroit's operations. Cities are a complex overlap of many systems that address needs such as for transportation and energy, but also must address the need for a system of engagement.

This requires that we broaden ownership. Detroit—a city of national and global importance--will need to engage with a sustainable and sustaining web of stakeholders that suit its position in the region and the nation (not only "by Detroit for Detroit," but a collaboration among all levels of government and geography).

Detroit's civic infrastructure must relate through all scales of action: Neighborhood actions collaborating with citywide actions; neighborhood organizing partnering with citywide organizing; citywide efforts relating to the regional context; and all efforts related to and helping shape statewide objectives for economic growth, quality of life, and other important measures of successful communities. Engaging multiple sectors and multiple scales builds the capacity to implement citywide policies through multi-format engagement.

Initially, implementing the Detroit Strategic Framework requires drilling down the citywide strategies to the district and neighborhood levels, enabling residents to use the citywide Strategic Framework as a basis for neighborhood decision making to improve quality of life. As communications and resources become more robust, these localized efforts can in turn help in revisiting and updating citywide objectives and strategies.

REPORT BACK FOR TRANSPARENT AND ONGOING PROGRESS

QUESTIONS, IDEAS, ANSWERS, SOLUTIONS, REPEAT: The cycle of sharing and developing information together is a fundamental engine of civic engagement and community progress. The information-sharing and civic insights that supported the development of the Strategic Framework must continue to support it through its adoption and implementation. The Strategic Framework is not a static, traditional "plan," but rather a living and growing structure for change, and a guide to decision making. Continuing the civic conversation and revisiting the Strategic Framework's ideas and assumptions will be critical to maintaining the integrity and quality of its vision. This will mean continuous, transparent information traveling in both directions between the implementers and the civic community of Detroit. This exchange will track what kinds of implementation initiatives are happening; how the Consortium is progressing; the setbacks, challenges, and opportunities that are emerging; how money is being spent; what in the landscape is shifting; what milestones are being achieved; and frequent updates to share what kinds of change people can see and feel in the air (through stories and evaluation). The types of communications should remain as broad and multi-platformed as it was during the initial development of the civic engagement effort and the Strategic Framework. People from all parts of Detroit and all sectors that support Detroit should be asked for their energy, feedback, input, and resources as actions unfold and take root.

Because the realities are daunting, and the challenges will not go away tomorrow, they require that we fearlessly continue to engage in deep consideration and difficult—though sometimes inspirational and uplifting—conversations about what to do and what to make in Detroit. We cannot rest at a pat solution that would suit a different city. There won't be an easy "Getting to Yes" for Detroit this time tomorrow. How could there be, for a city as complex, as resilient, and as rich in both opportunities and challenges, as Detroit is today? Instead, we must proceed with open eyes and be willing to flex muscles and minds—not simply to "Get to Yes," but to "Get to Next."

This word cloud summarizes themes from participant feedback about the planning process. The size of the word corresponds to the frequency a participant's comment addressed that word or phrase—the larger the word or phrase, the more frequently it was mentioned.

Open & Improved Communication

Positive feedback about tactics

Be Inclusive (more & diverse participation) Transparency Keep people informed

No Expectations Expectations not met

Suggestions for future engagement

Positive feedback about engagement

Negative feedback about tactics Involvement & Participation

Use of Feedback Purpose of DWP

Short-term versus Long-term Met expectations Positive feeling about plan/future

Decision-making Process Implementation

Most face-to-face DWPLTP Civic Engagement activities included the opportunity to evaluate the DWPLTP process. Between November 2011 and September 2012, 1,725 participants responded to questions concerning their awareness of, feeling towards, and understanding of DWPLTP as well as if their feeling towards the process changed as a result of the engagement. The bar chart below shows responses to the "Awareness," "Feeling," and "Understanding" evaluation questions during each month of DWPLTP Civic Engagement through September 2012, as well as the number of responses received during the different engagement techniques used.

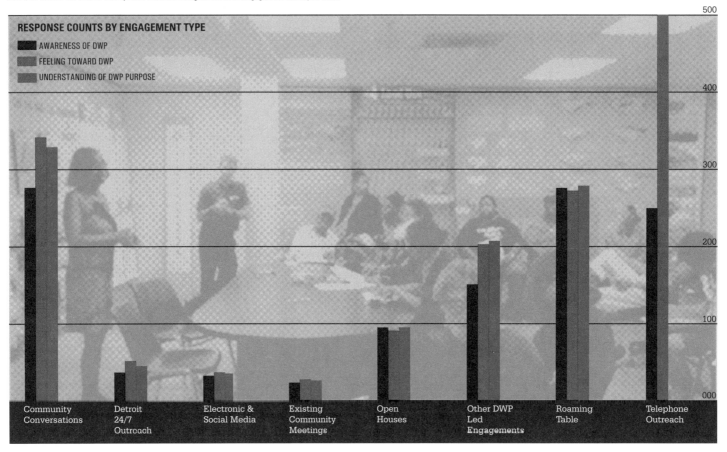

RESPONSE COUNTS BY ENGAGEMENT TYPE

- AWARENESS OF DWP
- FEELING TOWARD DWP
- UNDERSTANDING OF DWP PURPOSE

Community Conversations · Detroit 24/7 Outreach · Electronic & Social Media · Existing Community Meetings · Open Houses · Other DWP Led Engagements · Roaming Table · Telephone Outreach

NUMBER OF RESPONSES

THREE ENGAGEMENT STRATEGIES FOR THE FUTURE
BUILDING AN IMPROVED AND SUSTAINABLE CIVIC CULTURE

1 EXPAND CAPACITY FOR THE LONG TERM:
BUILDING ON STRENGTHS TO EXTEND RANGE.

To carry the idea of a "civic infrastructure" forward, a good infrastructure is coordinated, resilient, and adaptive to changing conditions. It is designed to move—be it electricity or information—from without and within, to conduct flows across boundaries and throughout the system. It also must be designed for the long term and to have "overflow capacity" that permits it to withstand urgent needs without breaking down. At the same time, it must function efficiently and primarily for daily needs, not just critical "hot spots." The remainder of this section begins to address the existing assets of Detroit's civic infrastructure, identify capacity needs, and draw on the possibilities revealed by the Strategic Framework Civic Engagement process for building and renewing that civic capacity.

Civic engagement capacity (or infrastructure) should have four components, like legs of a stool: (1) city government; (2) philanthropy; (3) Detroit institutions (including the nonprofit and business sectors; and (4) Detroit residents. Each of the four needs to be activated and involved at different times and for various issues, but there also should be strong connections and relationships across them. Within each of these four components, there is already a wide range of interest, experience and capacity around civic engagement in Detroit. Strengthening engagement capacity for each of these components has no "one size fits all", but there are general areas of engagement capacity for potential development and investment. These include:

1) City Government: Oftentimes, government agencies have an obligation or responsibility to inform, involve, and solicit input from constituents on various matters. Generally, these kinds of public involvement processes are already done well. To take engagement capacity to the next level, government may benefit from better understanding how civic engagement can help them better connect with and build constituents, beyond simply informing and asking for feedback. The government sector may also benefit from engagement training and technical assistance, especially on new and emerging engagement tools and practices (such as those highlighted within "A Mosaic of Tactics for a Mosaic of People"). In addition, government agencies may find it effective to initiate a public sector table in order to meet regularly and build relationships in service of increasing alignment and collaboration between agencies and/or between levels of government (city, state, and national). Financial resources and partnership resources from Detroit institutions and philanthropy, along with informed and engaged residents, would help city government develop these engagement capacities.

2) Philanthropy: Foundations that invest in Detroit also have a strong base of interest, experience, and investments in engagement that they can build upon. The philanthropic sector, like government, could also benefit from having its own tables to share engagement learning and initiate joint investments with colleagues. Indeed, some of this work is already happening. In addition, developing open communication and direct relationships with nonprofits helps strengthen their engagement roles and relationships in community. Finally, foundations can continue to bridge, connect, and convene organizations and other partners around emerging tools and issues related to engagement.

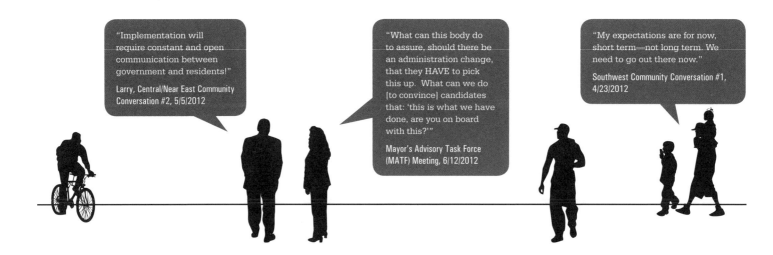

"Implementation will require constant and open communication between government and residents!"

Larry, Central/Near East Community Conversation #2, 5/5/2012

"What can this body do to assure, should there be an administration change, that they HAVE to pick this up. What can we do [to convince] candidates that: 'this is what we have done, are you on board with this?'"

Mayor's Advisory Task Force (MATF) Meeting, 6/12/2012

"My expectations are for now, short term—not long term. We need to go out there now."

Southwest Community Conversation #1, 4/23/2012

3) **Detroit institutions:** This component includes both the nonprofit sector and the private sector because the engagement capacities are very similar. Beyond the collaborative mechanisms and vehicles already referenced (such as tables, networks, and coalitions), Detroit institutions may benefit from leveraging new or deeper partnerships across other sectors. Organizations and institutions that are less familiar with civic engagement could become more effective through training, technical assistance, and partnering with organizations that are more adept at engagement. In addition, the work of Detroit nonprofits in particular may be enhanced by building the skills and capacity of staff to plan and execute engagement tactics effectively.

4) **Detroit residents:** Increasing engagement capacity for Detroit residents has two prongs. First, there must be acknowledgement, valuing, and support of where people already engage and gather, such as barber shops and block parties, churches and sports games. Resident-led efforts, meetings, and events should be celebrated and resourced. The second prong, then, is to encourage and equip residents to become involved with institutional engagement efforts. We must provide residents with meaningful ways to make change in their community and the city at large. People do not just decide to engage; they must have a connection with the issue at hand or with a person who is already involved. Residents will invite their neighbors and friends because social connectedness leads to a connection with organizations. Consequently, supporting individual residents to become involved requires dedicated investment. It requires leadership development, embracing resident involvement and sense of identity and place as a celebrated and critical ingredient to Detroit's future prosperity, and helping create entry points for people to connect with institutions and become involved through citizen advisory groups, listening sessions, issue summits, and a host of other opportunities.

Perhaps the most critical facets of civic engagement capacity are the connections, communications, and collaboration among sectors and networks. Supporting these connections requires dedicated investments. Detroiters have called on civic actors to move from unilateral actions ("silos") to multifaceted networks, forums, tables, and collaborations based in shared issues and common self-interests. Many effective collaborations are opportunistic in nature; they simply identify what the various stakeholders have in common. What are the shared interests? What are the shared motivations for taking action? What can we achieve together, even if all of our priorities and theories of change do not align? Collaboration happens on a spectrum from deciding to mutually work on or contribute to a specific, time-sensitive project to having an ongoing, consensus-driven alliance. Longer term relationships and efforts often travel along this spectrum from initial shared interests or relatively short-term outcomes to ongoing and expanded dialogue for systemic change.

"It's really been [impressive] to know that we can all come together and work on projects, even if you're not from my community. Because a lot of people that are from the team...they come from different areas, and everybody brings their own expertise to the table."

DWPLTP Civic Engagement Audit 2012

2 INFORMED, INCLUSIVE DECISIONS: DEVELOPING AND SHARING KNOWLEDGE AND INFORMATION.

Since transparency, accountability, and trust are critical to any civic engagement endeavor, the way that information is collected, analyzed, and shared matters a great deal. **But it is not only about input and exchange—it is also about valuing and demonstrating that value when initiating a process.** Through the Detroit Works process, the Strategic Framework teams learned that authentic and routine information gathering, sharing, and processing yield an authentic and credible process with more widespread interest and support. In other words, when people feel informed and can see their "fingerprints" (their voice and perspective) in a plan or initiative, they are more apt to believe in it, actively support it, and tell others about it. They feel like they were asked, they were heard, and that what they said matters.

Specific engagement strategies that relate to knowledge and information include:

1) Support the development of robust and reliable data. Good data helps pinpoint problems, see root causes, and identify the costs and viability of potential solutions. The work of Detroit organizations and institutions must be supported and built upon to gather, synthesize, and analyze high quality and illustrative information that helps aid informed decision making.

2) Facilitate open and transparent access to information. Information should be shared and "open-sourced" as much as possible with all concerned stakeholders of an effort through an established engagement feedback loop. Visual formats, engagement through the arts, games and simulations, experiential learning, and other ways to translate complex ideas into palatable, fun, energetic, and interactive formats are key to this strategy.

The impacts of increasing access are extending reach and building credibility. Open access enables the grassroots to move from "push" to power: instead of always having to act on the defensive, residents and smaller civic nonprofits would have access to information and be able to reflect back with the evidence of their own experiences in ways that can frame and shape official actions over the long and short term. Beyond the individual, better sharing of information helps at institutional levels. It helps government and businesses stay in better communication and coordination within each sector or with each other, and enables them to build trust, make better decisions, and collaborate better.

3) Integrate engagement with communications efforts. Those who are experts at communications strategies take the lead on crafting messages, while those who are engagement practitioners or trusted messengers in various communities or sectors can engage people on those messages. Together, they can determine multiple avenues for disseminating and sharing information, including diverse media such as print and radio, phones and SMS text, Internet and social media, and community-level communication such as sharing through faith institutions or community radio stations—places where people already get their information.

4) Incubate and support efforts for blending community expertise with technical expertise. Creating engagement opportunities that provide mutual exchange of knowledge and learning is key. This principle is true for many kinds of civic engagement endeavors, be they issue advocacy, election cycles, creative place making, planning or others. For a planning effort in particular, we must find ways that neighborhood-level plans and concerns can feed up to the citywide level and vice versa, and how community input and feedback will be used. We can build on the efforts of Detroit nonprofit organizations to synthesize community expertise into integrated data sets in both formal and informal ways.

Better information and data sharing can build transparency and trust, because people can see themselves reflected in a process. They can also lead to more informed decision making. This strategy, as with the others, requires dedicated support. In this case, it takes the form of both technical and human resources to facilitate information development, information sharing, and information blending.

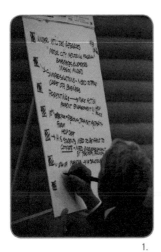    

1.   2.   3.   4.   5.

3 A MOSAIC OF TACTICS FOR A MOSAIC OF PEOPLE: DIVERSE PLATFORM OF OPPORTUNITIES TO ENGAGE.

Traditional engagement methods often ask for people to give their comments, reaction, or input to a proposal or plan. But more recently, much has been written and discussed about the rapid changes in our society in terms of how, when, and why communities choose to engage. The next frontier of civic engagement is responding to changing social realities, especially in the way people engage face to face and online. These social dynamics shape and complement people's expectations that they will have access to the process and to decision makers, that their time and opinions will be valued, that they may have fun through engagement, and that they can rely on trusted messengers and neighbor-to-neighbor recruitment and involvement, as well as organizations, institutions, and sectors in engagement efforts.

Events and meetings are a time-tested way for community to gather, share concerns, gain knowledge, and build relationships. Civic engagement, however, is not limited to an event. Meetings and forums are not the only mechanism for developing relationships, seeking input and expertise, making decisions, and creating joint plans for action. Civic engagement efforts tend to reach much greater depth and/or breadth of reach—and thus a greater potential for success—if a range of engagement methods and tactics are designed in order to attract different audiences and networks. This includes both inviting community in—through meetings, work sessions, events and other gatherings—as well as going to where communities already gather. Many new, creative, and innovative ways to engage people and institutions are being piloted and shared across the country.

Examples of such models, many of which were part of the Detroit Strategic Framework engagement process, include:

- Experiential learning, bike tours, or bus tours;

- Roundtables and one-on-ones;

- Virtual town hall events;

- Canvassing and door knocking;

- Trained speakers' bureaus or ambassador programs;

- Storytelling, community listening sessions, and oral histories;

- Presenting or participating in existing meetings of a professional association, a place of worship, or other scheduled gathering;

- Joint neighborhood councils, school councils, and other citizen spaces that have been made more participatory and inclusive;

- Proven processes for recruitment, issue framing, and facilitation of small-group discussions and large-group forums;

- New cross-sector models that approach an issue from the lens of collective impact (e.g. "cradle to career"), such as a broad-based consortium, task force, funders' collaborative, or a strategic commercial/business network;

- Online tools for network-building, idea generation, crowd-sourcing or crowd-funding, dissemination of public data, and serious games;

- Youth leadership efforts;

- Using the arts for dialogue, consensus building, or creative place making;

- Buildings that can be physical hubs for engagement;

- Participatory budgeting and other approaches to making public meetings more efficient, inclusive, and collaborative;

- Action research and other methods that involve citizens in data-gathering, evaluation, and accountability; and

- Food, music, and other social and cultural elements that make engagement more enjoyable and fun.

Image Sources: 1,2) Marvin Shaouni; 3-7) DWPLTP Civic Engagement Team—Flickr; 8) Marvin Shaouni; 9) DWPLTP Civic Engagement Team—Flickr; 10) Marvin Shaouni

6.　　　　　　　　7.　　　　　　　　8.　　　　　　　　9.　　　　　　　　10.

Successful civic engagement ultimately goes beyond a laundry list of tactics; it embraces a strategic and targeted plan in which a combination of tactics are woven together. A complete set of engagement tactics complement each other, because each is tailored to a specific group, such as an age group, an ethnic or cultural community, a specific neighborhood, a professional field (such as small business entrepreneurs or community developers), and so forth. Engagement can accomplish different goals at different times. Sometimes, as in much of the Detroit Works civic engagement, it's about listening and getting input and feedback to shape something. Other times, as in the next phase for Detroit as it builds a permanent, sustainable civic capacity to sustain and grow beyond the Strategic Framework time frame, it's about engaging people and groups to actually implement something together—to take action. It's both a process and an outcome.

"Maintaining a real degree of integrity and meaningfulness in what you communicate to the public...I think it's one area that we need to continue to improve on."

DWPLTP Civic Engagement Audit 2012

"We can continue to use the tools that Detroit Works incorporated, and on a smaller scale in our neighborhood, continue the same process."

DWPLTP Civic Engagement Audit 2012

PILOT PROJECTS

1   STAKEHOLDER COLLABORATION TOOLS

Establish Stakeholder Collaboration tools, which encourage cross-sector partnerships and include digital and non-digital methods.

2   LEADERSHIP TRAINING AND DEVELOPMENT TOOLS

Establish leadership training and development tools in various sectors of community, including residents, institutions, business, and government.

3   DETROIT STORIES CONTINUED

Support and expand the Detroit Stories oral histories project that was initiated by the DWPLTP Civic Engagement Team.

4   WEB TOOLS FOR CONTINUED CIVIC ENGAGEMENT

Coordinate existing and establish new web-based tools to facilitate engagement and capacity building.

5   WORK WITH EXISTING PLANNING PROCESSES THAT ARE ALREADY UNDERWAY TO ALIGN WITH DWPLTP FRAMEWORK

Support existing planning processes and facilitate aligning their work with the Strategic Framework recommendations.

6   DISTRICT PLANNING PROCESS UTILIZING DWPLTP FRAMEWORK

Encourage, support and facilitate detailed planning processes that work across neighborhoods at the district scale.

7   DISTRICT HOMEBASES

Establish physical HomeBases in each of the City Council Districts. These would function like the central HomeBase at the neighborhood scale.

CONCLUSION
DEDICATING OURSELVES TO OUR FUTURE

Throughout this Strategic Framework, we've talked in different ways about building a strong infrastructure and paving the way for prosperity. In an important sense, we have also been talking about love. For when all else is said and done, often it is love—love of a place, love of a neighborhood, love of a team or a landscape or family or just a moment in time that is bound up in the experience of Detroit—that can prompt this city of 714,000 to stand its ground and face its bitter truths, willing to work and hope for the days of change.

To be sure, not everyone in Detroit is yet standing on their own two feet. To be sure, many—individuals and institutions alike—will need a great deal of support in order to not only survive but flourish again. Such support will need to be focused and very strategic, stretching limited resources and time to fit all the urgent, sometimes competing needs of this great but still-hurting city.

For civic engagement, that means helping people see their stake in change, reminding them what they love in Detroit, in each other, and in themselves. Detroit can leverage the strengths of its rich civic history to create numerous ways for people to come together, support each other, face the hard work ahead and celebrate the possibilities for the city's future. What Detroit needs now are strong leaders who love what it stands for and what it can become, residents who have a voice in their neighborhoods and can imagine the possibilities for the entire city, and the best possible knowledge that comes from hard facts and deeply felt personal experiences—and yes, from an enduring love and understanding of Detroit. Such engagement can only be possible if it is supported by active institutions whose aim is to nourish a vibrant, multi-tiered civic culture to propel Detroit towards a prosperous future. At its core, this renewed way to talk and work together is an act of faith, an act of extraordinary yet grounded and realistic optimism. In short, a commitment to the city of Detroit.

ACKNOWLEDGEMENTS

STEERING COMMITTEE

George W. Jackson, Jr.
President and CEO, Detroit Economic Growth Corporation
Steering Committee Chair

Bishop Charles Ellis
Greater Grace Temple

Lydia Gutierrez
President, Hacienda Mexican Products

Heaster Wheeler
Assistant CEO, Wayne County

Alice Thompson
CEO, Black Family Development

Phillip Cooley
Owner, Slows Bar BQ

Don Chen
Senior Program Officer, Ford Foundation

Tyrone Davenport
CEO, Charles H. Wright Museum of African American History

Linda Jo Doctor
Program Officer, W.K. Kellogg Foundation

Rod Rickman
President and CEO, Rickman Enterprises

Dr. George Swan III, Ed.D.
Vice Chancellor, Wayne County Community College District

City Council Representative
Marcell Todd
Director, Detroit City Planning Commission

Laura Trudeau
Senior Program Director, Kresge Foundation

Mayor's Office Representative
Marja Winters
Deputy Director, Detroit Planning & Development Department

MAYOR'S OFFICE

Mayor Dave Bing
Deputy Mayor Kirk Lewis

CITY COUNCIL

Council President Charles Pugh
Council President Pro Tem Gary Brown
Councilman Kenneth V. Cockrel Jr.
Councilwoman Saunteel Jenkins
Councilwoman Brenda Jones
Councilman Kwame Kenyatta
Councilman Andre Spivey
Councilman James Tate
Councilwoman JoAnn Watson

PROJECT MANAGEMENT

Malik Goodwin
Vice President, Project Management, Detroit Economic Growth Corporation

Wendy Jackson
Senior Program Officer, Community Development, Kresge Foundation

Olga Savic-Stella
Vice President, Business Development, Detroit Economic Growth Corporation

PROJECT FUNDERS

Kresge Foundation
Ford Foundation
W.K. Kellogg Foundation
John S. and James L. Knight Foundation
Hudson Webber Foundation
Erb Family Foundation
Community Foundation for Southeast Michigan

PLANNING TEAM

Toni L. Griffin
Project Director

Hamilton Anderson Associates
Project Management, Land Use and Neighborhoods

Stoss Landscape Urbanism
Landscape, Ecology and Environment

Initiative for a Competitive Inner City
Economic Growth

Mass Economics
Economic Growth

Interface Studio
Economic Growth

Happold Consulting
City Systems

Center for Community Progress
Land and Buildings Assets

Carlisle Wortman
Zoning

AECOM
Landscape, Ecology and Environment Audit

Skidmore Owings and Merrill, LLP
Urban Design Audit

HR&A Advisors
Public Land Audit

CIVIC ENGAGEMENT TEAM

Detroit Collaborative Design Center
Co-Director

Michigan Community Resources
Co-Director

Grassroots Solutions
Advisor

ADDITIONAL CONTRIBUTORS

Brophy & Reilly, LLC
Cloudburst
Community Building Institute
Community Legal Resources
Data Driven Detroit

Detroit Collaborative Design Center
Justice & Sustainability, LLC
Lisa Schamess
McKinsey & Company
Southeast Michigan Council of Governments
The Reinvestment Fund
Wayne State University, Urban Studies and Planning

NATIONAL PEER ADVISORS

Lavea Brachman
Executive Director, Greater Ohio Policy Center

Paul Brophy
Principal, Brophy & Reilly, LLC

Garrick Davis
Legislative Director of Economic and Financial Policy, National Urban League Policy Institute

William A. Gilchrist
Director, Place-Based Planning, City of New Orleans

Bo Kemp
Managing Partner, Gari & Associates LLC

Tiffany Manuel
FrameWorks Institute/Enterprise Community Partners

William Rees Morrish
Professor of Urban Ecologies, Parsons, The New School of Design

Hunter Morrison
Director, Northeast Ohio Sustainable Communities Consortium

Carey Shea
Executive Director, Project Home Again

Mark Wyckoff
Senior Associate Director, Michigan State University Land Policy Institute

COMMUNICATIONS TEAM

Canning Communications
Media Relations and Communications Strategy

Lovio George
Communications Strategy and Branding

Applied Storytelling
Project Narrative, Messaging, and Communications Planning

MAYOR'S ADVISORY TASK FORCE

Bishop Charles Ellis, Co-Chair
Greater Grace Temple

Alice Thompson, Co-Chair
Black Family Development, Inc.

Heaster Wheeler, Co-Chair
Wayne County

Lydia Guiterriez, Co-Chair
Hacienda Mexican Products

Phillip Cooley, Co-Chair
Slow's BarBQ

Troy Adam
Henniges Automotive

Larry Alexander
Detroit Metro Convention & Visitors Bureau

Birdies Anderson
After School Connect & Promote Your Business

Erick Barnes
University of Detroit Mercy

Rufus Bartell
Simply Casual Clothing Store

Russ Bellant
Helco Block Club

Delores Bennett
Northend Improvement Council

Fay Beydoun
American Arab Chamber of Commerce

Austin Black
City Living Detroit

Robert Bland
Councilwoman JoAnne Watson

David Blaszkiewicz
Downtown Detroit Partnership

Paul Bridgewater
Detroit Area Agency on Aging

Edward Egnatios
Skillman Foundation

Tom Goddeeris
Grandmont Rosedale Development Corporation

Anika Goss Foster
Local Initiatives Support Corporation, National

Ponsella Hardaway
Metropolitan Organizing Strategy Enabling Strength

Charity Hicks
East Michigan Environmental Action Council

Adam Hollier
Formerly: State Representative Bert Johnson

Michelle Jackson
Green Explosion

Andre Johnson
Detroit Recovery Project

William Jones
Focus : HOPE

Christine Kageff
JP Morgan Chase Foundation

Luther Keith
ARISE Detroit

Renee Kent
PNC Bank Community Development

Ann Lang
Formerly: Downtown Detroit Partnership

Sharon Madison
Madison International

Conrad Mallet
DMC- Sinai Grace Hospital

Martin Manna
Chaldean American Chamber of Commerce

Scott Mason
Youth Representative

Patricia McCants
You Can International

Kwamena Mensah
Detroit Black Community Food Security Network

Faye Nelson
Detroit Riverfront Conservancy

Steve Ogden
Formerly: Next Detroit Neighborhood Initiative

Dan Ringo
Formerly: International Union of Engineers, Local 324

Shenay Shumake
Solid Rock Assembly of God

Christianne Sims
Urbanize (D)

Shirley Stancato
New Detroit, Inc.

Kim Tandy
Sherwood Forest Neighborhood Association

Tim Thorland
Community Development Advocates of Detroit

James Thrower
JAMJOMAR

Kevin Tolbert
United Auto Workers

Khary Turner
Black Bottom Collective

Jerome Warfield
Brightmoor Alliance Inc

Kathleen Wendler
Southwest Detroit Business Ass.

Alan Scott White
WISE Commercial Real Estate

Donele Wilkins
Formerly: Detroiters Working for Environmental Justice

Charles Williams
Historic King Solomon Baptist Church

Thomas Woiwode
Community Foundation for Southeast Michigan

INTER AGENCY WORKING GROUP

Detroit Assessment Division
Detroit Buildings Safety Engineering and Environmental Department
Detroit Building Authority
Detroit Department of Administrative Hearings
Detroit Department of Health and Wellness Promotion
Detroit Department of Human Services
Detroit Department of Public Works
Detroit Department of Transportation
Detroit Finance Department
Detroit Fire Department
Detroit General Services Department
Detroit Housing Commission
Detroit Land Bank Authority
Detroit Mayors Office
Detroit Municipal Parking Department
Detroit Planning and Development Department
Detroit Planning and Facilities
Detroit Police Department
Detroit Public Schools
Detroit Recreation Department
Detroit Workforce Development Department
Detroit Water and Sewerage Department
Greater Detroit Resource Recovery Authority
Michigan Land Bank
Michigan State Housing Development Authority
Southeast Michigan Council of Governments

PROCESS LEADERS

Norm Bent
Consortium of Hispanic Agencies

Phillip Cooley
Slows Bar BQ

Scott Alan Davis
Vanguard Community Development Corporation

Lydia Gutierrez
Hacienda Mexican Foods

Ponsella Hardaway
Metropolitan Organizing Strategy Enabling Strength

Judith Jackson
Youthville Detroit

Luther Keith
ARISE Detroit

Angela Reyes
Detroit Hispanic Development Corporation

James Ribbron
City of Detroit Board of Zoning Appeals

Rebecca Salminen Witt
Greening of Detroit

Christianne Sims
Urbanize (D)

Alice Thompson
Black Family Development, Inc.

Steve Tobocman
Global Detroit

Sandra Turner Handy
Michigan Environmental Council

Diane Van Buren
Zachary and Associates

Dan Varner
Excellent Schools Detroit

Heaster Wheeler
Wayne County

Guy Williams
Detroiters Working for Environmental Justice

PUBLIC LAND WORKING GROUP

Detroit City Planning Commission
Detroit Economic Growth Corporation
Detroit General Services Department
Detroit Housing Commission
Detroit Land Bank Authority
Detroit Public Schools
Detroit Planning and Development Department
Detroit Water and Sewerage Department
Katherine Beebe & Associates
Michigan Land Bank
Southeastern Michigan Council of Governments
University of Michigan
Wayne County Land Bank
Wayne County Treasurer

PARTICIPATING ORGANIZATIONS

12th Precinct Neighborhood Coalition
Adult Well-Being Services
Alliance of Rouge Communities
Allied Media Projects (AMP)
Alter Ego Management
American Association of Retired Persons
American Institute of Architects, Detroit
Archdiocese of Detroit
ARISE Detroit
AT&T
Bank of America
Benteler
BING Institute
Black Family Development, Inc.
Blight Busters
Boggs Center
Bridgewater
Bridging Communities

Brightmoor Alliance
Brown Environmental Construction
CB Richard Ellis
Centric Design Studio
Chadsey Condon Community Organization
City Council
City Living Detroit
City Mission
City of Detroit Department of Environmental Affairs
City of Detroit General Services Department
City of Detroit Mayor's Office
City of Detroit Planning and Development Department
City of Detroit Planning and Facilities
City of Detroit Public Lighting Department
City of Detroit Water and Sewage Department
City of Detroit Water and Sewerage Department
City Planning Commission
Clark Construction
College for Creative Studies
Comerica
Community Development Advocates of Detroit
Community Foundation for Southeast Michigan
Community Investment
Compuware
Conner Creek Greenway
Core City Neighborhoods
Corktown Housing LLC
Corktown Residents' Council
DANA Automotive
Data Driven Detroit
Deloitte Touche
Department of Housing and Urban Development
Department of Public Works
Detroit Area Agency on Aging
Detroit Association of Realtors
Detroit Black Community Food Security Network
Detroit Catholic Pastoral Alliance
Detroit City Airport
Detroit Creative Corridor Initiative
Detroit Department of Transportation
Detroit Economic Growth Corporation
Detroit Food Policy Council
Detroit Hispanic Development Corporation
Detroit Housing Commission
Detroit Land Bank Authority
Detroit Lives
Detroit Neighborhood Forum
Detroit Parent Network
Detroit Public Schools
Detroit Regional Chamber
Detroit Riverfront Conservancy
Detroit Summer
Detroit/Wayne County Port Authority
Detroiters Working for Environmental Justice
DMC Group
DTE Energy
East English Village Neighborhood Association
Eastern Market
Erb Family Foundation
First Independence Bank
Focus: HOPE
Ford Foundation
Ford Motor Company
Franklin Wright Settlements
Fringe City Development
Fulcrum EDGE

GalaxE.Solutions
GE Corporate IT
Genesis HOPE
Global Detroit
GM Ventures
Grandmont Rosedale Development Corporation
Great Lakes Bioneers
Greater Corktown Development Corporation
Greektown Casino
Green City Growers
Greening of Detroit
Greenways Coalition
Hantz Farm
Harriet Tubman Center
Heidelberg Project
Henry Ford Health System Innovation Institute
Henry Ford Medical Group
Heritage Realty Services
Highstone Associates
Hinshon Environmental Consulting
Hispanic IT Executive Council
Hudson-Webber Foundation
Invest Detroit
Jackson Lewis
James Group
JE Electric
Jefferson East Business Association
John S. and James L. Knight Foundation
Karmanos Cancer Institute
Katherine Beebe & Associates
Kresge Foundation
Larson Realty Group
Lawrence Technological Detroit Studio
Lawrence Technological University
Leamington Produce
Lee & Associates
Lewis & Munday
Liberty Bank
Local Initiative Support Corporation
Lower East Side Action Plan
Marygrove College
Masco Corporation Foundation
Mastronardi Produce
Matrix Human Services
McDougall Hunt CDC
McIntosh Poris Associates, AIA Detroit
MGM Detroit
MichAuto
Michigan Association of Planning
Michigan Department of Transportation
Michigan Economic Development Corporation
Michigan Environmental Council
Michigan Land Bank
Michigan Manufacturing Technology Center
Michigan State Housing Development Authority
Michigan State University
Midnight Golf
Midtown Detroit Inc
MOCAD
National Association of Minority Contractors, Detroit
National Heritage Academies
National Organization of Minority Architects, Detroit
Neighborhood Services Organization
Neighbors Building Brightmoor
New Detroit
New Economy Initiative

New Solutions Group
Newmark Knight Frank
Next Detroit Neighborhood Initiative
Next Energy
Northwest Detroit Neighborhood Development
Oakland Stamping
Original United Citizens of Southwest Detroit, 48217
Pablo Davis Elder Living Center
People's Community Services of Metropolitan Detroit
PNC Bank
Project for Public Spaces
Puzzle Piece Theater
Pyramid Farms
QuickenLoans
Recycle Here
RNF LLC
Robert Prud'homme Design
Rock Ventures
Roxbury Group
Sacred Heart/St. Elizabeth CDC
SER-Metro
SHAR Foundation
Sierra Club
Skillman Foundation
Southeastern Michigan Community College Consortium
Southeastern Michigan Council of Governments
Southwest Detroit Business Association
Southwest Detroit Development Collaborative
Southwest Detroit Environmental Vision
Southwest Housing Solutions
Southwest Solutions
Steel Market Development Institute
Strategic Staffing Solutions
Strength Capital
Suburban Mobility Authority for Regional Transportation
TechTown
The Brennan Group
The Green Door Initiative
The Reinvestment Fund
The Villages CDC
Transit Riders United
TransLinked
U3 Ventures
University Commons Organization
University of Detroit Mercy
University of Michigan
Urban Land Institute
Urban Neighborhood Initiatives
U-SNAP-BAC
Vanguard CDC
VITECH
W.K. Kellogg Foundation
WARM Training
Warren Connor Development Corporation
Wayne County Community College
Wayne County EDGE
Wayne County Land Bank
Wayne County Treasurer
Wayne State University
Windham Realty
WISE Commercial Real Estate
Workforce Intelligence Network
Young Detroit Builders
Youthville
Zero Waste Detroit

INDEX